Scientific Advances in
Positive Psychology

Scientific Advances in Positive Psychology

Meg A. Warren and Stewart I. Donaldson, Editors

 PRAEGER™

An Imprint of ABC-CLIO, LLC
Santa Barbara, California • Denver, Colorado

Library of Congress Cataloging in Publication Control Number: 2016058837

ISBN: 978-1-4408-3480-6
EISBN: 978-1-4408-3481-3

21 20 19 18 17   1 2 3 4 5

This book is also available as an eBook.

Praeger
An Imprint of ABC-CLIO, LLC

ABC-CLIO, LLC
130 Cremona Drive, P.O. Box 1911
Santa Barbara, California 93116-1911
www.abc-clio.com

This book is printed on acid-free paper ∞

Manufactured in the United States of America

This book is dedicated to
Michael Warren and the Donaldson family
for being living examples of virtue, love, and joy.
They bring out the best in us, so we may thrive.

Contents

Preface

The science undergirding positive psychology theories and principles has matured over the past two decades. Hundreds of empirical studies across a wide range of topics associated with positive psychology have been conducted using rigorous scientific methods commonly found across the discipline of psychology. In 2015, a review of this extensive peer-reviewed literature titled "Happiness, Excellence, and Optimal Functioning Revisited: Examining the Peer-Reviewed Literature Linked to Positive Psychology," was published in the *Journal of Positive Psychology*. The purpose of this volume is to understand those important scientific findings in much more detail. To accomplish this goal we invited leading researchers in positive psychology to evaluate the research in their subarea and to describe the most important scientific advances. It is our hope that thought leaders, researchers, and students will be inspired by this snapshot in 2017 of the scientific foundations, challenges, and opportunities that lie ahead for using the science of positive psychology to promote social betterment and justice across the globe.

Much of the support for this project was provided by the Claremont Evaluation Center at Claremont Graduate University. We are deeply grateful for the many contributions made by members of the Positive Organizational Psychology Research Lab in the Claremont Evaluation Center—Scott Donaldson, Vitoria De Valentim Meira, Joo Young Lee, and Lei Zhou for feedback and proofreading; Kathryn Doiron for project management; and undergraduate summer interns Russell Donaldson and Justin Shegerian for their support on various tasks. We are especially indebted to the authors of the chapters in this volume for providing thoughtful cutting-edge contributions in a timely manner. Special thanks to Debbie Carvalko and the entire editorial team at Praeger for believing in us and providing outstanding support throughout this entire project.

Stewart I. Donaldson
Meg A. Warren

CHAPTER ONE

Evaluating Scientific Progress in Positive Psychology

Meg A. Warren, Scott I. Donaldson, and Stewart I. Donaldson

The positive psychology literature has grown by leaps and bounds over the past two decades. A Google Scholar search of "positive psychology" from 1999 to 2016 produces over 36,000 results. It has influenced research across most subareas of psychology, including clinical, social, personality, cognitive, developmental, health, organizational, neuroscience, environmental, forensic, consumer, community, cross-cultural, gender, sports, gerontology, and psychosomatic medicine. This research has appeared in top-tier psychology journals such as *Frontiers in Psychology*, *Behavioral and Brain Sciences*, *Psychological Science*, *Psychological Inquiry*, and *Psychological Bulletin*; influential disciplinary journals such as *Journal of Personality and Social Psychology*, *Journal of Applied Psychology*, and *Administrative Science Quarterly*; and journals that showcase positive psychology, happiness, and quality of life research, such as the flagship *Journal of Positive Psychology*, *Journal of Happiness Studies*, and *Social Indicators Research*.

The positive psychology orientation has also extended far beyond psychology and is now witnessed in fields as disparate as education, sociology, philosophy, political science, economics, technology, engineering, law, public policy, criminology, military, medicine, oncology, psychiatry, pharmacology, epidemiology, biology, animal welfare, hospitality, religion, music, linguistics, anthropology, fine art, design, and social work. Furthermore, research and scholarship linked to positive psychology have been published in a wide range of high-impact, prestigious scientific journals, including *Nature*, *Science*, and *Journal of the American Medical Association*.

As the field of positive psychology has grown and developed, particularly across the breadth of subareas within psychology, we found that the range of new theories, research, applications, and explorations were not reflected in the existing literature in the field. Therefore, we invited prolific senior leaders who are actively shaping what positive psychology looks like and the next generation of scholarship in their areas to provide a commentary on the history and progression of their subarea, to carefully examine and report the latest scientific advances, and to share their vision for the future.

Positive Psychology in a Nutshell

So what is positive psychology? Positive psychology has been described as the scientific, rigorous, and organized inquiry on the positive aspects of human behavior (Gable & Haidt, 2005). The premise of this body of literature is that positive attributes of life and what gives meaning to it are just as worthy of scholarly attention as human dysfunction (Peterson, 2006). The early efforts of the founders of positive psychology strongly influenced the research trajectories and its interactions with specific subareas of psychology, such as social, clinical, cognitive, and organizational psychology. In broad terms, Seligman (2011) defined positive psychology as the scientific pursuit of well-being. Seligman and Csikszentmihalyi (2000) further conceptualized positive psychology as research organized around three main pillars: positive experiences and states of being, positive traits of individuals, and positive enabling institutions. Similarly, positive psychology has been described as a science that uses a unique interpretive lens to find out "what works, what is right, and what is improving" (Sheldon & King, 2001, p. 216). In contrast, the theory and research that emerged in response to these early calls took on a range of subdisciplinary flavors, offering new interpretations of "the positive," innovative theories, subdiscipline-preferred research methods, and applications in context. Positive psychology scholarship as it stands today has far outgrown the early visions of the first generation of positive psychology scholars. We refer to this expanded, inclusive perspective that encompasses a wide range of topics and interests, and is increasingly attentive to social issues, adversity, cultural nuances, and context as the next wave of positive psychology. The purpose of the current volume is to offer insight into some of the historical developments of positive psychology scholarship within specific subareas, the meanings it has come to take on, the cutting-edge scientific research that characterizes this next wave of positive psychology, and directions for future research and application.

Evaluating Positive Psychology Contributions

Since its inception in 1999–2000, a wealth of scientific research and scholarship has accumulated on topics associated with positive psychology. In order to assess the extent of the positive psychology contributions, we (first[1] and third authors[2]) examined the large and growing body of research of over 1,300 peer-reviewed articles that explicitly identified with positive psychology from 1999–2013 (Donaldson, Dollwet, & Rao, 2015). Since then, scholarship in positive psychology has continued to grow exponentially. This volume samples from some of the most generative areas revealed through our review and takes an in-depth look at recent scientific advances that are shaping the future of the field.

In our review (Donaldson et al., 2015), we found that well-being was the most studied topic, alongside character strengths and gratitude. Therefore, for the current volume we invited senior leaders in the field to provide an in-depth review and analysis of these topics. It also includes the examination of positive affect, which is studied in the context of happiness and other positive emotions, and is what we found to be a popular subject of intervention studies. Further, Donaldson et al. (2015) in combination with another ongoing review of the empirical literature (Ackerman, Warren, & Donaldson, 2017) indicated that the domains with the most measurement and application were positive youth development, positive educational contexts, and positive organizational psychology. Therefore, this volume features in-depth reviews from prominent scholars and their visions for exciting future directions in these areas of application.

Although positive psychology has made important contributions to the study of happiness and flourishing, it has been criticized as being dominated by Western perspectives. In reviews that examined positive psychology in nonhegemonic cultural contexts (e.g., Kim, Doiron, Warren, & Donaldson, 2016; Rao, Donaldson, & Doiron, 2015), we found that positive psychology was often interpreted to include positive ways of coping and being triumphant in the face of adversity. In an effort to showcase an important topic of relevance in this pursuit, this volume includes a review of recent advances in posttraumatic growth.

Another criticism leveled against the field has been a lack of attention to issues relevant to gender, race, and ethnicity. In our review (Rao & Donaldson, 2015), we assessed the extent to which this was an accurate reflection of the literature in positive psychology and found inadequate discussion of how the strengths and assets of marginalized groups could be harnessed to overcome adversity and how their positive qualities could be nurtured and preserved. Therefore, in this volume experts in cultural contexts and positive psychology share their most promising contributions in these areas and directions for future research.

Overview of Contributions

The foundational concepts in positive psychology are well-being and happiness. In Chapter 2, Shin and Lyubomirsky note that the positive psychology literature on happiness and well-being has been dominated by Western perspectives. They extend the prevailing literature and provide a refreshing take on subjective well-being from an Eastern perspective. The chapter begins by summarizing the historical roots of subjective well-being, dating back to Buddhist philosophies, and then compares interdependent versus independent cultures' (Eastern versus Western) constructions of happiness, well-being, and social support. They review the current research on self-administered interdependent positive activity interventions to increase happiness and well-being and provide future directions in this area. Shin and Lyubomirsky observe that in today's globalized world, the study of how positive activity interventions affect subjective well-being is incomplete until scholars include the development and testing of culturally relevant interventions appropriate for local contexts. They call for future investigations that go beyond Western ideas and values and fully incorporate socially oriented cultures in empirical research on well-being and happiness. This chapter sets the stage for the following chapter on positive emotions and foreshadows insights from the concluding chapter on cultural contexts.

Positive emotions, particularly, the broaden-and-build theory (Fredrickson, 2001), has been a bedrock of positive psychology scholarship on positive subjective experiences and, as such, the research on positive emotions is what many might consider the crux of positive psychology. In Chapter 3, Shiota, Yee, O'Neil, and Danvers trace the theoretical and empirical advances in positive emotion research over the past 20 years. They suggest that although research on emotion has traditionally focused on the survival value of negative emotions, the 21st century has seen a substantial increase in research on positive emotions and how they play adaptive functions for the human species. The authors discuss three areas for applying positive emotions research in important real-world interventions: promoting health behavior change, supporting close relationships, and helping troubled intergroup relations. Finally, they discuss recommendations for future research—examining when "positive" emotions are undesirable, measuring positive emotions, and investigating their downstream effects. Shiota and colleagues offer a bold vision for the future of positive emotion research and open the door for scholars to explore many new opportunities in this area.

In Chapter 4, Park, Barton, and Pillay delve into the topic of character strengths, another key pillar of positive psychology. The authors describe why character is important and how positive psychology and character strengths inform each other. They offer a comprehensive review of the scholarship on *Values in Action* (VIA) and offer deep insights on how character strengths function. Further, they share honest reflections on the shortcomings of the VIA and areas for clarification and growth in terms of measurement and applicability across contexts and cultures. The authors also discuss implications for practice, including how to cultivate character strengths and implement strengths-based approaches. They conclude by suggesting that future character strengths research should extend outward to hard outcome measures (e.g., health, work productivity, and educational achievement) and cultural differences. They recommend that positive psychology should take bold yet cautious steps in cultivating and sustaining a morally good life.

Gratitude is one of the prominent topics in positive psychology that has developed a considerable empirical evidence base. In Chapter 5, Watkins and Bell review the current research in the context of key theories of gratitude. They evaluate theories on the nature of gratitude (e.g., as an emotion and as a trait), the cognitive causes of gratitude, and how gratitude enhances well-being. A key contribution of this chapter is the development of a theory of appreciation. They discuss how gratitude must involve the psychological processes of appreciation and offer directions for future examination. The authors conclude with their candid perspective on the state of gratitude research. On one hand, they feel that some have an overly optimistic view of gratitude, particularly the popular press. On the other hand, the authors note that there has been an overwhelmingly pessimistic reception of gratitude by scholars who point out that gratitude is not always appropriate. They encourage a more balanced perspective with the hope that gratitude research can enhance happiness.

In Chapter 6, Tedeschi, Blevins, and Riffle review the history and development of posttraumatic growth (PTG) research. They outline the foundation of the PTG process (i.e., the assumptive world theory) and its role in how PTG is operationalized. They offer an overview of the most important measures of PTG and the empirical advances that have helped construct a strong evidence base on the PTG process. The chapter provides empirically derived insights about the PTG process, such as challenging core beliefs, self-disclosure, event centrality, and cross-cultural and individual differences. They discuss some of the conceptual challenges of PTG and discuss future directions for PTG research, including the application of PTG interventions to trauma survivors. The authors argue that trauma is ubiquitous to the human experience and that research on PTG interventions can make impactful contributions to society. The chapter concludes with future directions of conceptual and empirical advancement of PTG with children and adolescents, as well as in relationships, groups and larger systems. Finally, they offer recommendations for future directions in longitudinal and intervention research.

The next three chapters focus on positive psychology in applied settings. In Chapter 7, Larson, Orson, and Bowers offer an overview of intrinsic motivation (IM) and socioemotional (SE) learning as the next major contributions of positive youth development scholarship. They draw from roughly 50 years of research on IM and present five conditions that facilitate its experience. They propose that IM is a crucial component to youth's socioemotional learning because when youth are motivated their learning processes are amplified. Further, they point to youth programs as rich contexts for developing IM while noting that IM is missing in many adolescents' school experiences. The authors describe two large longitudinal qualitative studies of afterschool and out-of-school youth programs and outline the SE learning processes among high school–aged youth. They share key insights from the case examples to demonstrate how IM amplifies learning processes. The chapter concludes with their perspective on synergies between IM and positive youth development for the 21st century and suggests directions for future research. The authors forecast that for adolescents coming of age in a complex society, opportunity for development of nuanced socioemotional learning skills and access to conditions for the development of IM will be key to providing youth with the skills they need to flourish.

Employees are among the most studied populations from the positive psychology perspective (Ackerman et al., 2017). In Chapter 8, Warren, Donaldson, and Luthans explore the history of the positive psychological orientation in work and organizations. The authors trace the history of positively oriented inquiry in the area of work and organizations and discuss three streams of scholarship: (a) positive organizational psychology, (b) positive organizational behavior, and (c) positive organizational scholarship. The authors present the five most generative scholarly contributions that have expanded theory and research on employee attributes and organizational processes, including happiness and well-being at work, positive leadership, positive work relationships, psychological capital, and organizational virtuousness. Although these are important contributions to the field, the authors highlight the need for cross-pollination of research across the three streams and beyond. To reach this aim they propose a broad umbrella term for the positive orientation they call "positive work and organizations," to encourage discussion among scholars who approach the workplace from a positive perspective. Lastly, the authors suggest that the future of positive work and organizational literature lies in attention to issues of diversity and relevance to marginalized groups. They call for more research in this area, and offer directions for future research that can support and strengthen marginalized groups.

Positive education has become one of the key vehicles for applying positive psychology principles. In Chapter 9, Waters addresses this alliance between positive psychology and education, also known as positive education. She offers a macro perspective of the area, leading into three arguments for expanding the field: (a) well-being is crucial to global policy, (b) positive education enhances student well-being, and (c) student well-being is related to academic outcomes. She suggests that positive education interventions are a promising approach for enhancing the well-being of not only students, but the entire population. She acknowledges the limitations of existing and past positive education programs and offers a new framework, Visible Well-Being (VWB), to overcome them. The key thesis of the VWB framework is to imbue positive education into teacher practice and make positive outcomes for students visible and measurable. This also opens the door for new cross-disciplinary research. Waters concludes with the argument that positive education is critical in the creation of a collective upward spiral that can make global well-being a reality.

The final chapter sets the stage for a more inclusive positive psychology of the future. In Chapter 10, Pedrotti and Edwards provide a snapshot of the multifaceted nature of culture in positive psychology. Social identity facets such as race, ethnicity, gender, sexual orientation, disability, and social class are highlighted and measurement issues (i.e., conceptual, functional, metric, and linguistic equivalence across groups) are discussed. The authors highlight that culture is complex, and intersectionality (i.e., coexistence of multiple cultural facets in the same person) of these various social identity facets can shape culture in a number of ways. They provide an overview of the extant contributions of positive psychology on issues of race, gender, social class, disability, and sexual orientation. Pedrotti and Edwards call for future research to move away from a barriers-focused framing in multicultural populations and toward inclusion of both unique and shared experiences of individuals within these various social identity facets. They offer therapeutic applications of a culturally sensitive positive psychology and recommend that future research integrate genetic underpinnings and cultural context to address societal concerns. They also suggest future research address researchers' self-awareness of their own biases to further understand how certain individuals have been included and excluded in the extant psychological literature. Pedrotti and Edwards assert that there is a promising future, and a great need, for culture-sensitive positive psychological research.

Final Thoughts

The contributions in this volume have surpassed expectations. One of the most exciting revelations from this volume is that there is growing interest in scholarship that is more inclusive, rich, and contextualized. For instance, we see from the progression in the study of happiness and well-being that scholars are beginning to engage with non-Western populations and cross-cultural comparisons of happiness interventions. Across chapters, we witnessed the growth of what we think is the next wave of positive psychology—a science that is culturally responsive, sensitive to adversity, and where inclusion and engagement with questions of diversity are encouraged as part of the mainstream dialogue, rather than a "special interest." Positive psychology promises to offer a fresh, complementary perspective that enriches scholarly thinking about these issues. We invite students, faculty, scholars, practitioners, and curious-at-heart people from around the world to enjoy the chapters of this volume. For those seeking a handy introduction to the cutting edge of positive psychology, we hope you will benefit by mentally digesting these new approaches, learnings, and insights to human flourishing.

Notes

1. Rao, in all citations in this chapter, refers to the first author, Warren, who was previously Rao.
2. Donaldson, in all citations in this chapter, refers to the third author, Stewart I. Donaldson.

References

Ackerman, C. E., Warren, M. A., & Donaldson, S. I. (2017). Scaling the heights of positive psychology: A review of trends and opportunities in measurement scales. Manuscript under review.

Donaldson, S. I., Dollwet, M., & Rao, M. A. (2015). Happiness, excellence, and optimal functioning revisited: Examining the peer-reviewed literature linked to positive psychology. *Journal of Positive Psychology, 10*(3), 185–195.

Fredrickson, B. L. (2001). The role of positive emotions in positive psychology: The broaden-and-build theory of positive emotions. *American Psychologist, 56*, 218–226.

Gable, S. L., & Haidt, J. (2005). What (and why) is positive psychology? *Review of General Psychology, 9*, 103–110.

Kim, H., Doiron, K. M., Warren, M. A., & Donaldson, S. I. (2016). *The emerging science of positive psychology across the world: An overview of 17 years of research.* Manuscript under review.

Peterson, C. (2006). *A primer in positive psychology.* New York: Oxford University Press.

Rao, M. A., & Donaldson, S. I. (2015). Expanding opportunities for diversity in positive psychology: An examination of gender, race and ethnicity. *Canadian Psychology/Psychologie Canadienne, 56*(3), 271–282. doi: 10.1037/cap0000036

Rao, M. A., Donaldson, S. I., & Doiron, K. M. (2015). Positive psychology research in the Middle East and North Africa. *Middle East Journal of Positive Psychology, 1*(1), 60–76.

Seligman, M. P. (2011). *Flourish: A visionary new understanding of happiness and well-being.* New York: Free Press.

Seligman, M. E. P., & Csikszentmihalyi, M. (2000). Positive psychology: An introduction. *American Psychologist, 55*, 5–14.

Sheldon, K. M., & King, L. K. (2001). Why positive psychology is necessary. *American Psychologist, 56*, 216–217.

CHAPTER TWO

Increasing Well-Being in Independent and Interdependent Cultures

Lilian J. Shin and Sonja Lyubomirsky

"Happiness depends upon ourselves."
> —Aristotle (BCE 384–BCE 322), Greek philosopher

"Thousands of candles can be lighted from a single candle, and the life of the candle will not be shortened. Happiness never decreases by being shared."
> —Buddha (BCE 563–BCE 483), founder of Buddhism

What is happiness, and how can it be achieved? Billions of people throughout history have sought the answer to these questions, from philosophers and religious teachers to commoners and ordinary citizens. The quotations by Aristotle, an ancient Greek philosopher, and Buddha, the founder of a major world religion, endeavor to fathom the meaning of happiness. Their conceptions diverge considerably from one another, with Aristotle maintaining that happiness is within an individual's power and faculties to achieve, and Buddha contending that happiness is best experienced, and even multiplied, in relation to other people.

Western notions of happiness and well-being have dominated mainstream psychology, with subjective well-being (also known as happiness)
defined as the experience of frequent positive emotions, infrequent negative emotions, and satisfaction with life (Diener, 1984; Diener, Suh, Lucas,
& Smith, 1999). However, because Asians comprise 60 percent of the
world's population (Population Reference Bureau, 2014), a consideration
of Eastern notions of happiness is critical to a more complete understanding of the phenomenon. Thus, this chapter strives to 1) tease apart how
happiness concepts in Eastern cultures differ from those in Western cultures and 2) introduce the latest developments in positive activity interventions aiming to enhance happiness in Eastern cultures. We conclude
with suggestions for future directions in this area of research, as well as
their practical applications.

Cross-Cultural Differences in Subjective Well-Being

Although it is clear that people across the world strive to be happy (Diener, 2000), research has revealed national differences in the life domains
that people are satisfied with, how happy nations are relative to others,
and the antecedents leading to happiness for individuals within different
cultures. First, it is clear that nations differ in their overall levels of subjective well-being. In one study of 43 nations, 15 percent of the variance
in life satisfaction, 12 percent of the variance in financial satisfaction, and
12 percent of the variance in satisfaction with health was due to between-
nation differences (Inglehart, Basanez, & Moreno, 1998). In another study
of 39 nations, 12 percent of the variance in life satisfaction, 18 percent of
the variance in positive emotions, and 11 percent of the variance in negative emotions were due to between-nation differences (Suh, Diener, Oishi,
& Triandis, 1998). Shedding light on the nature of these differences, Asian
American, Korean, and Japanese participants were found to derive more
daily satisfaction from positive events than did European American participants (Oishi, Diener, Choi, Kim-Prieto, & Choi, 2007).

More importantly, studies have shown that these cross-cultural differences in subjective well-being emerge even after considering alternative
explanations. For example, in an investigation on happiness and life satisfaction in Japan, South Korea, China, and the United States, East Asian
participants scored lower than Americans on general happiness and life
satisfaction, not only in absolute terms, but also when income was controlled (Diener, Suh, Smith, & Shao, 1995). To account for these differences
in subjective well-being, artifactual explanations such as humility, fear of
fate, not wanting to stand out, or unimportance of subjective well-being

were ruled out (Diener et al., 1995). On the other hand, more substantive explanations, such as normative desirability of negative emotions, displeasure with specific life aspects, and pressure for achievement, were supported (Diener et al., 1995).

Other studies have found that national differences in levels of subjective well-being appear to be due to cultural factors such as differences in wealth, human rights and social equality, self-enhancement and self-critical tendencies, relative approach versus avoidance orientations of societies, and norms prescribing the extent to which subjective well-being is important (Diener, 2000; Diener, Diener, & Diener, 1995; Diener, Oishi, & Lucas, 2003; Heine, Takata, & Lehman, 2000; Lee, Aaker, & Gardner, 2000; Oishi, 2001). Culture can also moderate which emotion variables most influence subjective well-being—such as satisfaction with the self, satisfaction with one's level of personal freedom, financial satisfaction, and self-reported experiences of positive emotion (Diener & Diener, 1995; Diener et al., 2003; Oishi, Diener, Lucas, & Suh, 1999; Suh et al., 1998). Overall, the evidence demonstrates that there are indeed cross-cultural differences in subjective well-being.

Historical Roots of Subjective Well-Being

In the majority of both Eastern and Western cultures across time, happiness has been defined as "good luck" and as involving favorable external conditions (Kesebir & Diener, 2008; McMahon, 2006). In some Western cultures such as the United States, however, this definition has been replaced by one focused on internal feeling states (Oishi, Graham, Kesebir, & Galinha, 2013). To understand the reasons for this difference, we must delve into the historical roots and philosophical backgrounds of Eastern versus Western cultures.

Western notions of happiness include the pursuit of hedonia and eudaimonia, epitomized by Epicurus and Aristotle, respectively. Among hedonic-oriented psychologists, well-being is considered identical to subjective well-being, which is characterized by a predominance of positive over negative affect, as well as a global satisfaction with life (Diener, 1984). This definition is rooted in the arguments of utilitarian thinkers like Jeremy Bentham, who define a good life as consisting of the presence of pleasure and the absence of pain. By contrast, the eudaimonic traditions hold that humans can only live a good life when they actualize their potential and live in accordance with virtue, or moral excellence. Accordingly, there is an emphasis on valued traits such as self-esteem, meaning in life, optimism, personal expression, and autonomy (Ryan & Deci, 2001; Ryff, 1989).

This individualism and cherishing of personal rights further stem from the Judeo-Christian assertion that every person is created equal under God (Hwang, 2001); thus, every person is deserving and has rights and freedoms. The North American ethos, in particular, has been depicted as a "rugged" individualism in its pursuit of individual interests and rewarding of personal successes (Hsu, 1971).

In contrast, Eastern ideas of happiness derive their roots from Confucian, Taoist, and Buddhist philosophies. Confucius preached that a wise ruler must rule with "virtue" and render people equal by ritual. He taught that the dominant virtues of benevolence, righteousness (or justice), and propriety should regulate interpersonal relationships. Happiness does not lie in personal salvation or material accumulation, but in self-cultivation, maintaining a harmonious family, ruling a country wisely, and keeping peace in the world. For the ordinary citizen, Confucian philosophy presupposes that each individual is a continuation of his or her ancestors and, therefore, one should strive to promote the prosperity of one's family. Happiness is achieving this life goal through hard work and frugality to accumulate material resources, through intellectual labor and passing exams to obtain respectable social status, through suppression of selfish and earthly desires to lead a virtuous life, and ultimately through fulfillment of one's social duties.

Taoists assert that everything in the universe must follow *Tao*, the great natural force that commences everything. In the "two-poles" principle, the world is believed to exist through the operation of two opposite poles, *yin* and *yang*, and that peace is cultivated through accepting both good and bad, happiness and misery, and success and failure. Taoism contends that perfect happiness is liberation from all human desires, by following the natural force, not attempting to change circumstances, accepting fate calmly, and facing life with a peaceful mind. The ultimate goal is to become anonymous—to vanish into, transcend, and merge with nature.

Happiness in Buddhism can only be found in "nirvana," which promises eternal bliss beyond the everyday misery of this world (Chiang, 1996). Renunciation of illegitimate desires (e.g., material gains, bodily pleasures) is thought to bring freedom and peace.

Ordinary East Asian individuals may apply teachings from all of these traditions in different contexts; for example, they may act in accordance with Confucianism when interacting with other people, with Taoism when faced with nature, and with Buddhism when they are confronted with themselves (Lu, 2001). Taken together, Eastern traditions emphasize conceptualizations of happiness as harmonious, interdependent, accepting the bad with the good, and unifying oneself with the group and with nature. This stands in stark contrast to the Western schools of thought that emphasize personal autonomy and meaning, self-actualization and self-expression, and simply, more net positive affect than negative. In light of these philosophies, the Eastern view of happiness is quite distinct from Western views and may need to be conceptualized separately in order to reflect indigenous thoughts (Joshanloo, 2013).

Independent vs. Interdependent Conceptions of Happiness

Self-Construals

Given the distinct historical roots and doctrines characterizing East Asian cultures, subjective well-being for these cultures must be conceptualized independently of Western assumptions and schemas. However, the majority of studies aiming to increase subjective well-being have presumed Western or independent self-construals, emphasizing personal agency and self-improvement. Markus and Kitayama (1991) defined an independent self-construal as a view of the self in which individuals see themselves as separate entities who are bounded, unique, and autonomous. In such a self-view, individuals assert and protect their own rights, act on the basis of their own attitudes and judgments, and separate and distinguish themselves from the context. (See Figure 2.1A for a conceptual representation of the Western, independent view of the self.) In contrast, Eastern (i.e., Asian) cultures' interdependent self-construals are defined as a view of oneself as connected, relational, and a part of a larger social unit. In this type of self-construal, individuals maintain a social orientation in which roles, statuses, and in-group memberships are carefully considered (Markus & Kitayama, 1991). (See Figure 2.1B for a conceptual representation of the Eastern, interdependent view of the self.) East Asian cultures are a prominent example of highly interdependent cultures and have received the most attention in the literature; therefore, we will focus on East Asians for the remainder of this chapter. Similarly, we will focus on European American culture as the countervailing Western, independent culture.

Socially Engaging and Disengaging Emotions

These two distinct self-views have been found to be associated with two types of behavior: socially engaging versus socially disengaging. Socially engaging behavior involves taking one's proper place, perfecting one's own roles, empathizing with others and acting on the bases of these others' expectations and needs, and blurring the distinction between self and

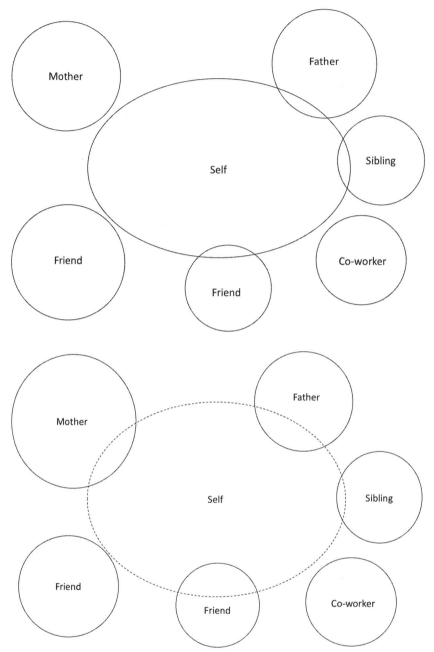

Figure 2.1 Conceptual representations of the self. (A: Independent construal. B: Interdependent construal.) (Adapted with permission from "Culture and the self: Implications for cognition, emotion, and motivation" by Markus, H. R. & Kitayama, S. (1991). *Psychological Review.*)

others in the social context. This type of behavior is associated with interdependence and interpersonal engagement of the self in East Asian cultures (Kitayama, Markus, & Kurokawa, 2000). Socially disengaging behavior, such as asserting and protecting one's own rights, acting on the basis of one's own attitudes or judgments, and separating or distinguishing the self from the context, is associated with independence and interpersonal disengagement of the self in the United States (Kitayama et al., 2000).

Studies have shown that Americans report more frequent positive emotions (e.g., happiness, elation) than negative emotions (e.g., sadness, anxiety), but Japanese report more frequent engaging emotions (e.g., respect, guilt) than disengaging emotions (e.g., pride, anger) (Kitayama et al., 2000). Across a range of situations, Japanese also report experiencing engaging emotions more strongly than disengaging emotions, but Americans report the reversed tendency (Kitayama, Mesquita, & Karasawa, 2006). Furthermore, researchers have found that the frequency of general positive emotions is positively related to the frequency of interpersonally engaging positive emotions in Japan, but with the frequency of interpersonally disengaging positive emotions in the United States (Kitayama et al., 2000), suggesting that positive emotions are associated with differences in interpersonal engagement across cultures.

The links between Western culture and interpersonally disengaging emotion, as well as between Eastern culture and engaging emotions, affect each culture's conceptualization of subjective well-being. Indeed, European American subjective well-being is better predicted by the experience of disengaging positive emotions than by that of engaging emotions (Kitayama et al., 2006). European American subjective well-being, with its cultural emphasis on free will, personal accountability, and individual reason, is characterized by an explicit pursuit of happiness (Lu & Gilmour, 2004). With an infrastructure built on democracy and equality, a constitution that upholds personal rights, and social customs that encourage personal striving, in the United States, explicitly seeking happiness by mastering the environment and achieving goals is compatible with living out an independent personhood (Lu & Gilmour, 2004). This European American pursuit of happiness has been conceptualized as "individually-oriented subjective well-being" (Yamaguchi & Kim, 2015).

In contrast, Japanese subjective well-being is better predicted by the experience of engaging positive emotions than by that of disengaging emotions (Kitayama et al., 2006). Asian subjective well-being, with its cultural emphasis on connectedness and social relationships, is distinctly characterized by role obligation. In "socially oriented subjective well-being," individuals strive for socially prescribed achievement, fulfillment of role obligations in close relationships, maintenance of interpersonal harmony, and welfare of the collective, such as family (Lu & Gilmour, 2004; Yamaguchi & Kim, 2015). Such a view of subjective well-being is consistent with a Confucian obligation-based moral discourse, in contrast with a Western discourse based on rights. Indeed, studies have shown that the connection between relationship harmony and self-esteem is stronger in Asian countries than in the United States (Kwan, Bond, & Singelis, 1997).

Measurement

Other researchers have conceptualized interdependent happiness as the global, subjective assessment of whether one is interpersonally harmonized with other people, quiescent, ordinary, and connected to the collective way of well-being (Hitokoto & Uchida, 2015). To measure such a happiness that is contingent upon significant others' happiness and approval, items such as "I believe that I and those around me are happy" and "I feel that I am being positively evaluated by those around me" may need to be used in place of classic happiness scales (e.g., the Subjective Happiness Scale; SHS) that distinguish an individual and her or his happiness from her or his context (e.g., the item "In general, I consider myself [1 = *not a very happy person*; 7 = *a very happy person*];" Lyubomirsky & Lepper, 1999). (Even the SHS item, "Compared with most of my peers, I consider myself (1 = *less happy*; 7 = *more happy*)," although addressing a person's context, does not presume that an individual's happiness is directly contingent upon others' happiness.) The nine-item Interdependent Happiness Scale (IHS) has been validated in East Asian samples, better explaining the subjective well-being of such individuals than traditional measures of subjective well-being (Hitokoto & Uchida, 2015).

Ideal Affect

Due to the ancient *yin-yang* philosophy, another characteristic of socially oriented subjective well-being is an observance of dialectical balance, in which a more solemn and reserved attitude is taken toward pursuing happiness (Lu & Gilmour, 2004). Affect valuation theory states that "ideal affect" (what people want to feel) differs from "actual affect" (what people actually feel) and that cultural factors shape ideal affect more than actual affect (Tsai, Knutson, & Fung, 2006; Tsai & Park, 2014). Such cultural factors might include interacting with parents, peers, or teachers; exposure to popular media; and engaging in religious practices. According to affect valuation theory, affect covaries along two dimensions—valence and arousal. Tsai and colleagues (2006) contend that residents of Western cultures aim to influence, change, and improve their environments, and thus initiate action in general more frequently. As a result, European and Asian Americans have been found to value high-arousal positive states (e.g., excited, energetic) more than do Asians.

In contrast, due to the East Asian cultural emphasis on fitting in and adjusting one's needs to fit the environment, people with interdependent concepts first assess the demands of the environment by allowing others to act first and observing situations. Because East Asians tend to observe before acting, the researchers predicted and found that Asians and Asian Americans value low-arousal positive states (e.g., calm, relaxed) more than European Americans do (Tsai et al., 2006). Additionally, the researchers found that the discrepancy between ideal and actual affect correlates with depression, especially for low-arousal positive emotions for Asians and Asian Americans and for high-arousal positive emotions for European as well as Asian Americans (Tsai et al., 2006; Tsai & Park, 2014).

Furthermore, the actual experience of positive and negative affect appears to be less mutually exclusive (i.e., more dialectical)—that is, they may co-occur—in East Asian contexts compared to Western contexts. Studies have shown that Beijing and Hong Kong Chinese show a weaker inverse relationship between actual positive and negative affect than European American and Chinese American groups (Sims, Tsai, Wang, Fung, & Zhang, 2012). Moreover, dialectical affective experience was mediated by ideal affect: the more individuals were experimentally induced to value positive states and devalue negative states, the more they reported both actual positive and negative affect.

In sum, these lines of research provide strong theoretical and empirical support for two distinctive types of subjective well-being. The European American (individual) conceptualization of subjective well-being is characterized by autonomy, explicit pursuit, high-arousal positive states, and low social engagement; this is the conceptualization employed in the majority of research and literature on subjective well-being. However, (social) subjective well-being in East Asian cultures functions in distinctive and often contrasting ways, specifically as a more relational, collectivistic, interdependent construct characterized by low-arousal positive states and high social engagement.

Independent vs. Interdependent Well-Being and Social Support

These two types of subjective well-being, socially and individually oriented, affect the use of social support in counterintuitive ways based on what is known about the nature of interdependent relationships. At first glance, social support may be expected to be highly beneficial for interdependent cultures due to their greater emphases on social relationships; however, some studies have found that Asians and Asian Americans rely *less* on social support for coping with stress than European Americans do, and these cultural differences are stronger for emotional support than for instrumental support (Taylor et al., 2004). Asians and Asian Americans are less likely to seek social support because they are concerned about the possible social ramifications of doing so, such as disturbing the harmony of the group, losing face, receiving criticism, or making the situation worse (Taylor et al., 2004). Other studies have found that Asian Americans are less likely to seek both instrumental and emotional support than European Americans (Kim, Sherman, Ko, & Taylor, 2006). Furthermore, European Americans reported that family and friends' support was more helpful in dealing with stressors than did Asian Americans (Kim et al., 2006). Additionally, while Asian Americans and European Americans do not differ in how successfully stressors are resolved in general, among Asian Americans who do seek emotional support, the support is less helpful for resolving the stressor (Kim et al., 2006). Asian Americans, who consider their fates to be more yoked with those of close others, are also less likely to seek social support when they are primed to think about close others. If an Asian American's identity is intertwined with that of a close other, the relationship implications for asking for help (e.g., imposing on the other) may be more chronically accessible, thereby deterring them from asking the close other for help. In contrast, European Americans' willingness to seek support was unaffected by relationship priming (Kim et al., 2006). Thus, these studies show that individuals from interdependent cultures may rely less on actual social support for coping with stressors due to their social implications.

On the other hand, some studies have shown that among Asians, *perceived* emotional support positively predicts subjective well-being, even after self-esteem is controlled (Uchida, Kitayama, Mesquita, Reyes, & Morling, 2008). For European Americans, the positive effect of perceived emotional support on subjective well-being is weak and disappears entirely after self-esteem is controlled.

Notably, two pathways to subjective well-being are self-related and other-related. In a recent study, Americans reported higher levels of subjective well-being, emotional expression, and social support provision than their Japanese counterparts, but both groups showed similar influences of self- (in this case, via the personal expression of emotions) and other-related pathways (via giving social support to others) on subjective well-being (Novin, Tso, & Konrath, 2014). In both groups, independent self-construal was found to have a direct positive effect on subjective well-being and to indirectly predict subjective well-being via increased emotional expression and giving support to others (Novin et al., 2014). Interdependent self-construal also had a positive direct relationship to subjective well-being; however, it also affected subjective well-being indirectly via giving more support to others and via showing less emotional expression. These findings were nearly identical across cultures, except that Americans showed a stronger positive relationship between independent self-construal and emotional expression, and Japanese showed a stronger positive relationship between independence and giving social support. Thus, in this study, both independent and interdependent self-construals had positive effects on subjective well-being by the provision of social support to others in both Eastern and Western cultures. In conclusion, the research reveals a complex relationship between social support and subjective well-being in interdependent and independent cultures and highlights that further research is needed to disentangle the effects of *actual* versus *perceived* support and *giving* versus *receiving* social support in both cultures.

Culture Influences Positive Activity Interventions

Thus far, we have discussed differences between independent and interdependent conceptualizations of happiness and well-being. For the remainder of the chapter, we describe implications of these different conceptualizations on happiness-increasing interventions in both contexts, as well as offer several practical applications. One such practical application involves the treatment of major depression. Major depression is a psychiatric disorder characterized by sadness, decreased pleasure, feelings of worthlessness, and physiological symptoms (e.g., sleep, appetite, cognitive changes) (American Psychiatric Association, 2013). Depression is currently the third-leading cause of disease burden globally, will be the second-leading cause by 2020, and will be the leading cause by 2030 (Murray & Lopez, 1996; World Health Organization, 2008). For clinical patients who have not responded to conventional care, positive activity interventions hold promise for augmenting traditional drug therapy and psychotherapy treatment (Layous, Chancellor, Lyubomirsky, Wang, & Doraiswamy, 2011; Shin & Lyubomirsky, 2016). If administered optimally, positive activity interventions can build positive psychological resources, such as social connections and meaning in life, and ameliorate existing maladaptive symptoms such as anxiety and rumination (Sin, Della Porta, & Lyubomirsky, 2011; Sin & Lyubomirsky, 2009). Positive activity interventions involve simple, self-administered cognitive and behavioral strategies (i.e., "positive activities") that can increase subjective well-being by promoting positive feelings, thoughts, and behaviors (Layous & Lyubomirsky, 2014). Positive activities such as counting one's blessings (Chancellor, Layous, & Lyubomirsky, 2015; Emmons & McCullough, 2003; Froh, Sefick, & Emmons, 2008; Lyubomirsky, Sheldon, & Schkade, 2005; Seligman, Steen, Park, & Peterson, 2005), writing letters of gratitude (Boehm, Lyubomirsky, & Sheldon, 2011; Layous, Lee, Choi, & Lyubomirsky, 2013; Lyubomirsky, Dickerhoof, Boehm, & Sheldon, 2011; Seligman et al., 2005), and performing acts of kindness (Dunn, Aknin, & Norton, 2008; Layous et al., 2013; Layous, Nelson, Oberle, Schonert-Reichl, & Lyubomirsky, 2012; Nelson et al., 2015; Nelson, Layous, Cole, & Lyubomirsky, in press; Sheldon, Boehm, & Lyubomirsky, 2012) have been shown to reliably boost well-being in European American and other independent cultures.

As mentioned previously, because Asians comprise 60 percent of the world's population (Population Reference Bureau, 2014) and Asian Americans are the fastest-growing minority group in the United States, there is a critical need to address this population's mental health needs (U.S. Census, 2010). For Asians in Asia, the 12-month prevalence rate for mental disorders is approximately 4–9 percent; however, it is unknown whether this relatively low rate is due to measurement artifacts (see later discussion of psychosomatic symptoms), underreporting, or actual differences (The WHO World Mental Health Survey Consortium, 2004). Although mental illness prevalence rates are the same for Asian Americans as those of the general U.S. population (approximately 26 percent for 12 months), Asian Americans use psychological services at lower rates than European Americans (The WHO World Mental Health Survey Consortium, 2004; U.S. Department of Health and Human Services, 2001). Furthermore, among the Asian Americans who do use services, their condition severity is high, indicating that they delay seeing a mental health professional until problems are very serious. Stigma and shame have been identified as major deterrents to the utilization of mental health services both in Asia and for Asians Americans in the United States (Lauber & Rössler, 2007; U.S. Department of Health and Human Services, 2001).

Self-administered positive activities may be especially valuable for Asians and Asian Americans because they are less stigmatizing, economical, and carry no side effects. A variety of different positive activity interventions, including recounting kindness, performing acts of kindness, and practicing gratitude, have worked successfully in interdependent populations. In Japan, people increased their subjective well-being and became kinder and more grateful after counting their own acts of kindnesses over one week (Otake, Shimai, Tanaka-Matsumi, Otsui, & Fredrickson, 2006).

The authors suggested that gratitude may promote happiness by enhancing one's experience of positive events and one's social network. In another study, relative to controls, Japanese participants who recounted three positive events at work reported greater happiness over time, were less sedentary, engaged in less socializing (perhaps indicating higher productivity), and left the office earlier (Chancellor et al., 2015). Furthermore, those who put more effort into the positive activity showed greater changes. In South Korea, performing kind acts while receiving autonomy support led to greater improvements in subjective well-being than performing kind acts without autonomy support or engaging in comparison activities (Nelson et al., 2015). These well-being improvements were mediated by feelings of autonomy, competence, and relatedness. In Hong Kong, researchers implemented gratitude, hope, and open-mindedness interventions (Zhou et al., 2016). The interventions—particularly, open-mindedness—were effective in increasing attitude and intention to perform behaviors, frequency of targeted behaviors, and family health and happiness. The authors surmised that the open-mindedness intervention improved family communication, which plays a critical role in family relationships. As a whole, these studies exemplify how conventional positive activity interventions can also work in interdependent cultural contexts and that similar underlying mechanisms (e.g., the role of connections with others) are shared by both independent and interdependent cultures.

Despite the evidence that positive activity interventions do increase subjective well-being in interdependent cultures, emerging research shows that culture may affect the interpretation and meaning of conventional positive activities, the features of the positive activities that must be altered for optimal efficacy, and the types of subjective well-being (i.e., hedonic vs. eudaimonic) that are bolstered. In one cross-cultural study conducted in South Korea and the United States, U.S. participants experienced increased subjective well-being from practicing both gratitude and kindness, but South Korean participants benefitted only from performing kind acts (Layous et al., 2013). The researchers posited that South Koreans did not derive as much benefit from practicing gratitude because they felt indebted and guilty about being the recipient of others' kind acts. This interpretation aligns well with the idea that socially oriented, interdependent subjective well-being is concerned with the maintenance of interpersonal harmony, the welfare of the collective group, and the fulfillment of role obligations in close relationships. This interpretation is also consistent with the findings that social support (a typical catalyst for gratitude) is less sought out—but not less offered—in interdependent cultures. Taken together, these findings suggest that when psychologists prescribe positive activities to practice for persons from interdependent cultures, they must consider the social ramifications of the target positive activity, such as its effects on group harmony, losing or saving face, or receiving criticism from others. Notably, the activity of performing acts of kindness takes these social ramifications into consideration, whereas writing gratitude letters does not.

In another study, expressing optimism about their personal futures and writing letters of gratitude to family and friends increased life satisfaction more in European Americans compared to predominantly foreign-born Asian Americans (Boehm et al., 2011). Further, Asian Americans benefitted marginally more from conveying gratitude to people in their lives compared to expressing optimism about their personal futures. These results are consistent with individualist cultures' value on self-improvement and personal agency (leading to a direct pursuit of happiness) and interdependent cultures' valuation of harmonious relationships (resulting in reluctance to experience intense positive states) and role obligations (prompting familial duty to help each other). That is—gratitude is, by its nature, an interpersonal activity, whereas optimism primarily applies to the individual. Positive activity interventions for interdependent cultures must be designed in accordance with cultural values and norms for happiness. For example, the intervention might have more effectively increased well-being in Asian and Asian American populations if an act of gratitude were performed with a material item (i.e., a gift) and done by a collective group (such as a family) toward another collective group (such as a business).

Finally, a recent study showed that affirming their most significant values (e.g., relationships, career, honesty) increased both hedonic and eudaimonic well-being for U.S. participants, but only eudaimonic well-being for South Koreans (Nelson, Fuller, Choi, & Lyubomirsky, 2014). Researchers deduced that based on Eastern cultures' emotional dialecticism, the South Koreans derived both positive and negative meanings when affirming their values. By contrast, U.S. participants likely focused on the positive aspects of their values, given their preference for high-arousal positive emotions, and thereby experienced hedonic well-being when considering their core values. As discussed earlier, subjective well-being may need to be defined distinctly for interdependent and independent cultures—what is considered the ideal for independent cultures (more positive emotions) may be different from what is considered the ideal for interdependent cultures (a balance of positive and negative emotions). Overall, positive activity interventions do seem to be effective at increasing subjective well-being in interdependent cultures, but their careful design, implementation, and interpretation of their findings appear to be critically relevant to their success.

Current Research on Interdependent Positive Activity Interventions

Studies have already shown that due to their positive focus on others, both remembering and enacting prosocial behavior are positive activities that have the potential to be successful in Eastern interdependent cultures (Chancellor et al., 2015; Nelson et al., 2015; Otake et al., 2006). Additional studies in our laboratory are currently underway to test the mechanisms (i.e., *who* to help, *how* to help, and *why* to help) underlying the success of positive activities in interdependent cultures.

In one study, to determine *who* is the optimal target to help, Hong Kong (Asian) and U.S. (European American) participants are writing about either kindnesses they have done for close others, strangers, or themselves (active control) or about their daily activities (neutral control) (Shin, Yue, Sheldon, & Lyubomirsky, 2016). Specifying and assigning who participants write about is expected to help determine how Asians' emphasis on interpersonal harmony, the welfare of the collective group, and role obligations affects the benefits derived from practicing prosocial behavior. Due to their interdependent orientation, Asian participants who recall times they helped close others are hypothesized to experience greater subjective well-being via feelings of greater connectedness and relationship closeness relative to controls. Asian participants who recall times they helped strangers are hypothesized to experience decreased or no change in subjective well-being due to the discomfort associated with interacting with individuals outside of their collective group and the lack of role obligation to such individuals. In contrast, European Americans, due to their independent orientation, will likely experience greater subjective well-being from recalling times they helped both strangers and close others, and this effect is expected to be mediated by greater personal autonomy and competence.

In another ongoing study, to determine optimal ways of *how* to help, Hong Kong (Asian) and U.S. (European American) participants are asked to give *solicited* support (i.e., to meet practical needs that a close other explicitly asks of them), to give *unsolicited* support (i.e., to anticipate and then meet a close other's practical needs), or to organize household items (control) (Shin et al., 2016). By distinguishing unsolicited social support from solicited social support in practicing prosocial behavior, our study aims to confirm the significance of empathizing with others, acting on the bases of their expectations and needs, and blurring the distinction between the helper and the helped in increasing subjective well-being within interdependent Asian cultures. Relative to controls, we expect Asian participants who give unsolicited support to experience greater subjective well-being because of their comfort and proficiency with anticipating others' needs due to their interdependent orientation. In contrast, Asian participants who give solicited support are expected to experience decreased or no change in subjective well-being due to the discomfort and awkwardness of being unable to anticipate others' needs and thereby disrupt relational harmony. European Americans, on account of their independent orientation, are hypothesized to experience greater subjective well-being from giving solicited support, mediated by greater personal autonomy and competence, due to their fluency with distinguishing themselves from the one they are helping.

Finally, to test the effect of the reasons (the *why*) for valuing kind acts on the effort put forth toward them, South Korean (Asian) and U.S. (European American) participants are asked to read a news article that frames acts of kindness as good for oneself versus good for others and then to perform acts of kindness throughout the week (Layous, Shin, Choi, & Lyubomirsky, 2016). Experimentally manipulating whether individuals value kindness as good for themselves versus good for others will help determine the effect of cultural values (such as acting on the bases of others' needs) on effort put forth toward a kindness intervention. Due to their interdependent orientation, Asian participants who value kindness as good for others are expected to experience greater subjective well-being owing to increased motivation to make close others happier. Asian participants who value kindness as good for themselves are hypothesized to experience decreased or no change in subjective well-being due to the discomfort of having to consider their own personal preferences. Due to their independent orientation, European Americans are hypothesized to experience greater subjective well-being from valuing kindness as good for themselves by virtue of the stock they put into their personal wants and propensity to strive for happiness. Preliminary results are showing that the European Americans did experience greater subjective well-being from valuing kindness as good for themselves, but the South Korean participants did not experience greater well-being from valuing kindness as good for others. Future research with alternative manipulations and additional cross-cultural samples is needed to further understand and replicate these findings.

In determining whom, how, and why to help others in interdependent cultures, this new ongoing research aims to test and confirm the unique effects of interdependent self-construals in increasing subjective well-being.

Future Questions and Directions for Positive Activity Interventions

Despite the advances in theory and empirical research on positive activity interventions across cultures, the field is still in its infancy, with substantial theoretical gaps to be filled and empirical questions to be answered. Studies have shown that subjective well-being measures with the highest cross-cultural validity are those that account for cultural differences—for example, by including indigenous emotion words or considering their factor structure and reliability cross-culturally (Diener et al., 2003). Because emotions in interdependent cultures are expressed indirectly so as not to disturb relational harmony (e.g., asking "Are you eating proper meals?" may be more appropriate than asking "How are you doing?" because in an interdependent culture, you shouldn't have to ask how the other person is doing; you should already know), subjective well-being questionnaires for such cultures may need to be adapted to inquire about well-being more indirectly. To measure well-being, a physical health questionnaire inquiring about psychosomatic symptoms (e.g., the Kim Depression Scale for Korean Americans; Kim, 2002) could be used as a proxy for measuring emotional health. Asking about insomnia or heart palpitations is more socially appropriate and relevant for interdependent cultures than asking directly about one's happiness, which is more appropriate in independent cultures. (For more information on somatization in Asian cultures see Hong, Lee, & Lorenzo, 1995; Kleinman, 1982; Park & Bernstein, 2008; Parker, Cheah, & Roy, 2001; Zhou et al., 2015.)

The designs of positive activity interventions also need to be sensitive to the distinct self-concepts of individuals from interdependent and independent cultures. As mentioned earlier, when developing positive activity interventions for interdependent cultures, social ramifications of the positive activity intervention, such as its effects on group harmony, saving face, or receiving criticism from others, must be taken into consideration. Writing gratitude letters, for example, may not only have different mechanisms of operation in interdependent cultures, but may even backfire if not implemented properly (Layous et al., 2013). Gratitude is a type of emotional (rather than instrumental) support that has been shown to be a less effective form of social support for interdependent cultures (Kim et al., 2006). Thus, rather than writing a letter, treating a friend to a meal or giving a thoughtful gift may more aptly and effectively express gratitude. Furthermore, positive activity interventions may not have the same effect even among members of ostensibly similar Western independent cultures. For example, preliminary data suggest that workers in France who practice gratitude feel more guilt and embarrassment relative to U.S. workers (Armenta, 2014).

Likewise, more research is necessary for developing potentially new positive activity interventions in both interdependent and independent cultures. For example, due to the Confucian values of roles and propriety, positive activity interventions for East Asian cultures may be most effective when they are role specific and context specific. Positive activities for Asians and Asian Americans might best be conceptualized as those for a teacher, a student, a son/daughter, a parent, a boss, and an employee, for example, rather than for "individuals" in general. For Western cultures or other cultures with independent self-concepts, positive activity interventions may be most effective when they are goal oriented or self-asserting. For example, a kindness intervention for Europeans and European Americans might prompt individuals to focus on the autonomous choices they can make to be kind or the benefits they personally glean from performing a kind act.

In contrast to members of independent cultures, members of interdependent cultures may find the pursuit of their own personal happiness selfish and non-normative and might rather aspire to maintain the welfare of the collective whole. To be more efficacious in interdependent cultures, positive activity interventions may need to be targeted to the level of the "collective unit" rather than to individuals within those units—for example, positive activity interventions could target whole families, businesses, and classrooms and be framed as enhancing those units rather than the self.

Furthermore, due to emotional dialecticism and the emerging research on affect valuation theory, positive activity interventions need to be designed with a different set of emotional outcomes for interdependent cultures than they are for independent cultures. Although the overarching goal is the same, to increase overall well-being, positive activities for interdependent cultures may be more effective if they generate calmness, serenity, and an acceptance of both good and bad rather than intense positive emotions only. Instead of practicing optimism or counting one's blessings (solely), members of interdependent cultures may derive more benefit from a more balanced view of the past and future through an acceptance of the bad along with the good and expected failures as well as successes.

Finally, although the research reviewed in this chapter has focused primarily on East Asian interdependent cultures, members of Southeast Asian, South Asian, Latino, and African cultures may also embody interdependent mind-sets. In order to account for idiosyncratic features of these cultures as compared to East Asian cultures, well-being and positive activity intervention research should be expanded to include such cultures. Researchers should also note that most independent cultures also include some elements of interdependent self-concepts. Accordingly, conceptualizing self-concepts on a continuum may be more appropriate for the design of positive activity interventions.

Practical Applications of Interdependent Positive Activity Interventions

As the world of the 21st century becomes increasingly globalized and Asian populations—in both Asia and in countries like the United States—continue to grow, interdependent considerations will be critically relevant to efforts to bolster well-being in these populations. The advancements in culturally relevant definitions of subjective well-being and the developments and future improvements in culturally specific positive activity interventions have a myriad of potential real-world applications.

With the increasing prevalence of mental disorders, positive activity interventions have the potential to augment traditional forms of treatment (Layous et al., 2011; Shin & Lyubomirsky, 2016). Underutilization of mental health services by Asians and Asian Americans due to stigma and shame indicate that novel methods of treatment are needed. Researchers can better tailor positive activity interventions to Asians and Asian Americans as they become increasingly knowledgeable about the harmonious relationships and dialectical emotional styles characteristic of interdependent cultures, rendering such interventions more effective in increasing well-being. Importantly, culturally tailored positive activity interventions may also serve as protective factors to prevent future mental health conditions for Asians and Asian Americans (e.g., Layous, Chancellor, & Lyubomirsky, 2014).

A wealth of evidence also suggests that positive activity interventions can strengthen pre-existing social relationships such as those with family and friends (for example, see Layous et al., 2012; Lyubomirsky & Sin, 2009). Ongoing and future research on characteristics of interdependent cultures, such as harmonious relationships, prioritizing the welfare of the collective group, and fulfillment of role obligations in close relationships, will inform the tailoring of positive activity interventions for Asians and Asian Americans. Furthermore, positive activity interventions tuned in to such social ramifications will help augment social connections within Asian American immigrant communities, whose members often feel disconnected from their home countries as well as isolated from mainstream U.S. society.

Advances in increasing flourishing and well-being in interdependent cultures will also be relevant to general self-help applications for Asians throughout the world, as well as for members of ethnic minorities in the United States. Strategies for increasing happiness among people of interdependent cultures may be disseminated to media such as books, Web sites, and apps, along with mental health professionals such as counselors, coaches, and even primary care physicians, who are often the first to catch mental health conditions such as depression or anxiety.

The future is bright and promising for the field of subjective well-being and positive activity interventions. As the world population becomes increasingly internationalized, happiness-enhancing programs and guidelines can no longer be dominated by Western values and ideas. Instead, researchers, policy makers, and clinicians alike must acknowledge the growing importance of advancing well-being in socially oriented, interdependent cultures.

References

American Psychiatric Association. (2013). *Diagnostic and statistical manual of mental disorders* (5th ed.). Arlington, VA: American Psychiatric Publishing.

Armenta, C. (2014). *The mixed emotional effects of expressing gratitude in the workplace.* Master's thesis, Department of Psychology, University of California, Riverside.

Boehm, J. K., Lyubomirsky, S., & Sheldon, K. M. (2011). A longitudinal experimental study comparing the effectiveness of happiness-enhancing strategies in Anglo Americans and Asian Americans. *Cognition and Emotion, 25*(7), 1263–1272. doi:10.1080/02699931.2010.541227

Chancellor, J., Layous, K., & Lyubomirsky, S. (2015). Recalling positive events at work makes employees feel happier, move more, but interact less: A 6-week randomized controlled intervention at a Japanese workplace. *Journal of Happiness Studies, 16,* 871–887. doi:10.1007/s10902-014-9538-z

Chiang, S. M. (1996). *The philosophy of happiness: A history of Chinese life philosophy.* Taipei, Taiwan: Hong Yei Publication.

Diener, E. (1984). Subjective well-being. *Psychological Bulletin, 95*(3), 542–575. doi:10.1037/0033-2909.95.3.542

Diener, E. (2000). Subjective well-being: The science of happiness and a proposal for a national index. *American Psychologist, 55,* 34–43.

Diener, E., & Diener, M. (1995). Cross-cultural correlates of life satisfaction and self-esteem. *Journal of Personality and Social Psychology, 68*(4), 653–663. doi:10.1037/0022-3514.68.4.653

Diener, E., Diener, M., & Diener, C. (1995). Factors predicting the subjective well-being of nations. *Journal of Personality and Social Psychology, 69*(5), 851–864. doi:10.1037/0022-3514.69.5.851

Diener, E., Oishi, S., & Lucas, R. E. (2003). Personality, culture, and subjective well-being: Emotional and cognitive evaluations of life. *Annual Review of Psychology, 54,* 403–425. doi:10.1146/annurev.psych.54.101601.145056

Diener, E., Suh, E. M., Lucas, R. E., & Smith, H. L. (1999). Subjective well-being: Three decades of progress. *Psychological Bulletin, 125*(2), 276–302. doi:10.1037/0033-2909.125.2.276

Diener, E., Suh, E. M., Smith, H., & Shao, L. (1995). National differences in reported subjective well-being: Why do they occur? *Social Indicators Research, 34*(1), 7–32. doi:10.1007/BF01078966

Dunn, E. W., Aknin, L. B., & Norton, M. I. (2008). Spending money on others promotes happiness. *Science, 319*, 1687–1688. doi:10.1126/science. 1150952

Emmons, R. A., & McCullough, M. E. (2003). Counting blessings versus burdens: An experimental investigation of gratitude and subjective well-being in daily life. *Journal of Personality and Social Psychology, 84*, 377–389. doi:10 .1037/0022-3514.84.2.377

Froh, J. J., Sefick, W. J., & Emmons, R. A. (2008). Counting blessings in early adolescents: An experimental study of gratitude and subjective well-being. *Journal of School Psychology, 46*(2), 213–233. doi:10.1016/j.jsp.2007 .03.005

Heine, S. J., Takata, T., & Lehman, D. R. (2000). Beyond self-presentation: Evidence for self-criticism among Japanese. *Personality and Social Psychology Bulletin, 26*(1), 71–78. doi:10.1177/0146167200261007

Hitokoto, H., & Uchida, Y. (2015). Interdependent happiness: Theoretical importance and measurement validity. *Journal of Happiness Studies, 16*, 211–239. doi:10.1007/s1090201495058

Hong, G. K., Lee, B. S., & Lorenzo, M. K. (1995). Somatization in Chinese American clients: Implications for psychotherapeutic services. *Journal of Contemporary Psychotherapy, 25*(2), 105–118. doi:10.1007/BF02306684

Hsu, F. L. (1971). Psychosocial homeostasis and jen: Conceptual tools for advancing psychological anthropology. *American Anthropologist, 73*(1), 23–44.

Hwang, K. K. (2001). Morality (East and West): Cultural concerns. In N. J. Smelser & P. B. Baltes (Eds.), *International encyclopedia of the social and behavioral science* (pp. 10039–10043). Oxford, England: Pergamon.

Inglehart, R., Basanez, M., & Moreno, A. (1998). *Human values and beliefs: A cross-cultural source book.* Ann Arbor, MI: University of Michigan.

Joshanloo, M. (2013). Eastern conceptualizations of happiness: Fundamental differences with Western views. *Journal of Happiness Studies, 15*(2), 475–493. doi:10.1007/s10902-013-9431-1

Kesebir, P., & Diener, E. (2008). In pursuit of happiness: Empirical answers to philosophical questions. *Perspectives on Psychological Science, 3*(2), 117–125. doi:10.1111/j.1745-6916.2008.00069.x

Kim, H. S., Sherman, D. K., Ko, D., & Taylor, S. E. (2006). Pursuit of comfort and pursuit of harmony: Culture, relationships, and social support seeking. *Personality and Social Psychology Bulletin, 32*(12), 1595–1607. doi:10 .1177/0146167206291991

Kim, M. T. (2002). Measuring depression in Korean Americans: Development of the Kim Depression Scale for Korean Americans. *Journal of Transcultural Nursing, 13*(2), 109–117. doi:10.1177/104365960201300203

Kitayama, S., Markus, H. R., & Kurokawa, M. (2000). Culture, emotion, and well-being: Good feelings in Japan and the United States. *Cognition and Emotion, 14*(1), 93–124. doi:10.1080/026999300379003

Kitayama, S., Mesquita, B., & Karasawa, M. (2006). Cultural affordances and emotional experience: Socially engaging and disengaging emotions in Japan and the United States. *Journal of Personality and Social Psychology, 91*(5), 890–903. doi:10.1037/0022-3514.91.5.890

Kleinman, A. (1982). Neurasthenia and depression: A study of somatization and culture in China. *Culture, Medicine and Psychiatry, 6*(2), 117–190. doi:10.1007/BF00051427

Kwan, V. S. Y., Bond, M. H., & Singelis, T. M. (1997). Pancultural explanations for life satisfaction: Adding relationship harmony to self-esteem. *Journal of Personality and Social Psychology, 73*(5), 1038–1051. doi:10.1037/0022-3514.73.5.1038

Lauber, C., & Rössler, W. (2007). Stigma towards people with mental illness in developing countries in Asia. *International Review of Psychiatry, 19*(2), 157–178. doi:10.1080/09540260701278903

Layous, K., Chancellor, J., & Lyubomirsky, S. (2014). Positive activities as protective factors against mental health conditions. *Journal of Abnormal Psychology, 123*(1), 3–12. doi:10.1037/a0034709

Layous, K., Chancellor, J., Lyubomirsky, S., Wang, L., & Doraiswamy, P. M. (2011). Delivering happiness: Translating positive psychology intervention research for treating major and minor depressive disorders. *The Journal of Alternative and Complementary Medicine, 17*(8), 675–683. doi:10.1089/acm.2011.0139

Layous, K., Lee, H., Choi, I., & Lyubomirsky, S. (2013). Culture matters when designing a successful happiness-increasing activity: A comparison of the United States and South Korea. *Journal of Cross-Cultural Psychology, 44*(8), 1294–1303. doi:10.1177/0022022113487591

Layous, K., & Lyubomirsky, S. (2014). The how, why, what, when, and who of happiness: Mechanisms underlying the success of positive interventions. In J. Gruber & J. T. Moscowitz (Eds.), *Positive emotion: Integrating the light sides and dark sides* (pp. 473–495). New York: Oxford University Press.

Layous, K., Nelson, S. K., Oberle, E., Schonert-Reichl, K. A., & Lyubomirsky, S. (2012). Kindness counts: Prompting prosocial behavior in preadolescents boosts peer acceptance and well-being. *PLoS ONE, 7*(12), e51380. doi:10.1371/journal.pone.0051380

Layous, K., Shin, L., Choi, I., & Lyubomirsky, S. (2016). *Framing kindness as good for self versus good for others.* Manuscript in preparation, Department of Psychology, University of California, Riverside, Riverside, CA.

Lee, A. Y., Aaker, J. L., & Gardner, W. L. (2000). The pleasures and pains of distinct self-construals: The role of interdependence in regulatory focus. *Journal of Personality and Social Psychology, 78*(6), 1122–1134. doi:10.1037/0022-3514.78.6.1122

Lu, L. (2001). Understanding happiness: A look into the Chinese folk psychology. *Journal of Happiness Studies, 2*, 407–432.

Lu, L., & Gilmore, R. (2004). Culture and conceptions of happiness: Individual oriented and social oriented SWB. *Journal of Happiness Studies, 5*, 269–291.

Lyubomirsky, S., Dickerhoof, R., Boehm, J. K., & Sheldon, K. M. (2011). Becoming happier takes both a will and a proper way: An experimental longitudinal intervention to boost well-being. *Emotion, 11,* 391–402. doi:10.1037/a0022575

Lyubomirsky, S., & Lepper, H. S. (1999). A measure of subjective happiness: Preliminary reliability and construct validation. *Social Indicators Research, 46*(2), 137–155.

Lyubomirsky, S., Sheldon, K. M., & Schkade, D. (2005). Pursuing happiness: The architecture of sustainable change. *Review of General Psychology, 9,* 111–131. doi:10.1037/1089-2680.9.2.111

Lyubomirsky, S., & Sin, N. L. (2009). Positive affectivity and interpersonal relationships. In H. Reis & S. Sprecher (Eds.), *Encyclopedia of human relationships* (pp. 1264–1266). New York: Sage.

Markus, H. R., & Kitayama, S. (1991). Culture and the self: Implications for cognition, emotion, and motivation. *Psychological Review, 98*(2), 224–253. doi:10.1037/0033-295X.98.2.224

McMahon, D. M. (2006). *Happiness: A history.* New York: Atlantic Monthly Press.

Murray, C. J. L., & Lopez, A. D. (1996). *The global burden of disease: A comprehensive assessment of mortality and disability from diseases, injuries and risk factors in 1990 and projected to 2020.* Cambridge, MA: Harvard University Press.

Nelson, S. K., Della Porta, M. D., Jacobs Bao, K., Lee, H. C., Choi, I., & Lyubomirsky, S. (2015). "It's up to you": Experimentally manipulated autonomy support for prosocial behavior improves well-being in two cultures over six weeks. *The Journal of Positive Psychology, 10,* 463–476. doi:10.1080/17439760.2014.983959

Nelson, S. K., Fuller, J. A. K., Choi, I., & Lyubomirsky, S. (2014). Beyond self-protection: Self-affirmation benefits hedonic and eudaimonic well-being. *Personality and Social Psychology Bulletin, 40*(8), 998–1011. doi:10.1177/0146167214533389

Nelson, S. K., Layous, K., Cole, S., & Lyubomirsky, S. (in press). Do unto others or treat yourself?: The effects of prosocial and self-focused behavior on psychological flourishing. *Emotion.*

Novin, S., Tso, I. F., & Konrath, S. H. (2014). Self-related and other-related pathways to subjective well-being in Japan and the United States. *Journal of Happiness Studies, 15,* 995–1014. doi:10.1007/s1090201394609

Oishi, S. (2001). Culture and memory for emotional experiences: On-line vs. retrospective judgments of subjective well-being. *Dissertation Abstracts International, 61*(10-B), 5625.

Oishi, S., Diener, E. F., Choi, D.-W., Kim-Prieto, C., & Choi, I. (2007). The dynamics of daily events and well-being across cultures: When less is more. *Journal of Personality and Social Psychology, 93*(4), 685–698. doi:10.1037/00223514934685

Oishi, S., Diener, E. F., Lucas, R. E., & Suh, E. M. (1999). Cross-cultural variations in predictors of life satisfaction: Perspectives from needs and values.

Personality and Social Psychology Bulletin, 25(8), 980–990. doi:10.1177/01461672992511006

Oishi, S., Graham, J., Kesebir, S., & Galinha, I. C. (2013). Concepts of happiness across time and cultures. *Personality and Social Psychology Bulletin 39*(5), 559–577. doi:10.1177/0146167213480042

Otake, K., Shimai, S., Tanaka-Matsumi, J., Otsui, K., & Fredrickson, B. L. (2006). Happy people become happier through kindness: A counting kindnesses intervention. *Journal of Happiness Studies, 7*(3), 361–375. doi:10.1007/s10902-005-3650-z

Park, S.-Y., & Bernstein, K. S. (2008). Depression and Korean American immigrants. *Archives of Psychiatric Nursing, 22*(1), 12–19. doi:10.1016/j.apnu.2007.06.011

Parker, G., Cheah, Y.-C., & Roy, K. (2001). Do the Chinese somatize depression? A cross-cultural study. *Social Psychiatry and Psychiatric Epidemiology, 36*(6), 287–293. doi:10.1007/s001270170046

Population Reference Bureau. (2014). *2014 world population data sheet.* Retrieved from http://www.prb.org/pdf14/2014-world-population-data-sheet_eng.pdf

Ryan, R. M., & Deci, E. L. (2001). On happiness and human potentials: A review of research on hedonic and eudaimonic well-being. *Annual Review of Psychology, 52,* 141–166.

Ryff, C. D. (1989). Happiness is everything, or is it? Explorations on the meaning of psychological wellbeing. *Journal of Personality and Social Psychology, 57,* 1069–1081.

Seligman, M. E. P., Steen, T. A., Park, N., & Peterson, C. (2005). Positive psychology progress: Empirical validation of interventions. *American Psychologist, 6,* 410–421. doi:10.1037/0003-066X.60.5.410

Sheldon, K. M., Boehm, J. K., & Lyubomirsky, S. (2012). Variety is the spice of happiness: The hedonic adaptation prevention (HAP) model. In I. Boniwell & S. David (Eds.), *Oxford handbook of happiness* (pp. 901–914). Oxford, England: Oxford University Press.

Shin, L. J., & Lyubomirsky, S. (2016). Positive activity interventions for mental health conditions: Basic research and clinical applications. In J. Johnson & A. Wood (Eds.), *The handbook of positive clinical psychology* (pp. 349–363). New York: Wiley.

Shin, L., Yue, X., Sheldon, K., & Lyubomirsky, S. (2016). *Prosocial behaviors in interdependent cultures.* Manuscript in preparation, Department of Psychology, University of California, Riverside, Riverside, CA.

Sims, T., Tsai, J. L., Jiang, D., Wang, Y., Fung, H. H., & Zhang, X. (2015). Wanting to maximize the positive and minimize the negative: Implications for mixed affective experience in American and Chinese contexts. *Journal of Personality and Social Psychology, 109*(2), 292–315. doi:10.1037/a0039276

Sin, N. L., Della Porta, M. D., & Lyubomirsky, S. (2011). Tailoring positive psychology interventions to treat depressed individuals. In S. I. Donaldson,

M. Csikszentmihalyi, & J. Nakamura (Eds.), *Applied positive psychology: Improving everyday life, health, schools, work, and society* (pp. 79–96). New York: Routledge.

Sin, N. L., & Lyubomirsky, S. (2009). Enhancing well-being and alleviating depressive symptoms with positive psychology interventions: A practice-friendly meta-analysis. *Journal of Clinical Psychology, 65*(5), 467–487. doi:10.1002/jclp.20593

Suh, E., Diener, E., Oishi, S., & Triandis, H. C. (1998). The shifting basis of life satisfaction judgments across cultures: Emotions versus norms. *Journal of Personality and Social Psychology, 74*(2), 482–493. doi:10.1037/0022-3514.74.2.482

Taylor, S. E., Sherman, D. K., Kim, H. S., Jarcho, J., Takagi, K., & Dunagan, M. S. (2004). Culture and social support: Who seeks it and why? *Journal of Personality and Social Psychology, 87*(3), 354–362. doi:10.1037/0022-3514.87.3.354

Tsai, J. L., Knutson, B., & Fung, H. H. (2006). Cultural variation in affect valuation. *Journal of Personality and Social Psychology, 90*(2), 288–307. doi:10.1037/0022-3514.90.2.288

Tsai, J., & Park, B. (2014). The cultural shaping of happiness: The role of ideal affect. In J. Gruber & J. T. Moscowitz (Eds.), *Positive emotion: Integrating the light sides and dark sides* (pp. 345–362). New York: Oxford University Press.

Uchida, Y., Kitayama, S., Mesquita, B., Reyes, J. A. S., & Morling, B. (2008). Is perceived emotional support beneficial? Well-being and health in independent and interdependent cultures. *Personality and Social Psychology Bulletin, 34*(6), 741–754. doi:10.1177/0146167208315157

U.S. Census Bureau. (2010). *Overview of race and Hispanic origin: 2010.* Retrieved from http://www.census.gov/prod/cen2010/briefs/c2010br-02.pdf

U.S. Department of Health and Human Services. (2001). *Mental health: Culture, race, and ethnicity—A supplement to mental health: A report of the Surgeon General.* Retrieved from http://www.ncbi.nlm.nih.gov/books/NBK44243/

World Health Organization (2008). *The global burden of disease: 2004 update.* Retrieved from http://www.who.int/healthinfo/global_burden_disease/GBD_report_2004update_full.pdf

The WHO World Mental Health Survey Consortium. (2004). Prevalence, severity, and unmet need for treatment of mental disorders in the World Health Organization world mental health surveys. *The Journal of the American Medical Association, 291*(21), 2581–2590. doi:10.1001/jama.291.21.2581

Yamaguchi, A., & Kim, M.-S. (2015). Effects of self-construal and its relationship with subjective well-being across cultures. *Journal of Health Psychology, 20*(1), 13–26. doi:10.1177/1359105313496448

Zhou, Q., Chan, S. S., Stewart, S. M., Leung, C. S., Wan, A. & Lam, T. H. (2016). The effectiveness of positive psychology interventions in enhancing positive behaviors and family relationships in Hong Kong: A community-based participatory research project. *The Journal of Positive Psychology, 11*(1), 70–84. doi:10.1080/17439760.2015.1025421

Zhou, X., Min, S., Sun, J., Kim, S. J., Ahn, J., Peng, Y., . . . Ryder, A. G. (2015). Extending a structural model of somatization to South Koreans: Cultural values, somatization tendency, and the presentation of depressive symptoms. *Journal of Affective Disorders, 176*, 151–154. doi:10.1016/j.jad.2015 .01.040

CHAPTER THREE

Positive Emotions

Michelle N. Shiota, Claire I. Yee,
Makenzie J. O'Neil, and Alexander F. Danvers

The positive psychology movement began in response to a long-standing imbalance in empirical psychology, which had focused far more on human pathologies, foibles, and limitations than on our strengths (Seligman & Csikszentmihalyi, 2000). Clinical psychology had sought to explain and treat psychological disorders, as defined by the *Diagnostic and Statistical Manual* (DSM), rather than studying positive functioning and psychological well-being (Seligman & Csikszentmihalyi, 2000). After World War II, social psychology focused heavily on real-world problems such as prejudice and intergroup conflict, aggression, groupthink, biases in social cognition, and relationship conflict and divorce (Gable & Haidt, 2005; Ross, Lepper, & Ward, 2010). Within cognitive psychology, dominant topics included perceptual illusions (Coren & Girgus, 1978), errors in judgment and reasoning (Kahneman & Tversky, 1973), and failures of memory (Roediger, 1996). This work was both well intentioned and extremely informative. It aimed not only to alleviate suffering and dysfunction, but also to reveal underlying psychological mechanisms by documenting when and how they lead us astray. As a result, late 20th-century psychology had invested more in understanding the negative than the positive aspects of the human mind.

The psychological study of emotion has, traditionally, also placed far more emphasis on the negative than on the positive. Early theorists, such as Charles Darwin (1872/1965) and William James (1884), gave similar levels of attention to positive and negative emotions. However, emotion fell out of favor as a research topic in psychology during the behaviorist movement of the mid-20th century. Ekman's (1972) and Izard's (1971) groundbreaking cross-cultural studies of emotional facial expression recognition revitalized the field, but included only "happiness" or "joy" to represent positive emotion states, along with several negative emotions, and either "surprise" or "interest." Following this lead, subsequent major studies of expression, physiology, and appraisal also focused mostly or even exclusively on negative emotions such as fear, anger, sadness, and disgust (e.g., Ekman et al., 1987; LeDoux, 2003; Lerner & Keltner, 2000; Levenson, Ekman, Heider, & Friesen, 1992; Scherer, 1997; Smith & Lazarus, 1993; see Smith & Ellsworth, 1985 for an exception), and theorists' taxonomies of emotion were dominated by negative-valence states (e.g., Fehr & Russell, 1984; Oatley & Johnson-Laird, 1987; Roseman, Spindel, & Jose, 1990; Tomkins, 1984; although Lazarus, 1991 included several positive emotions). By the end of the 20th century, we had learned far more about negative than about positive emotions.

Why were positive emotions neglected for so long? One likely reason is that, although positive emotions are experienced far more frequently (Carstensen, Pasupathi, Mayr, & Nesselroade, 2000; Zelenski & Larsen, 2000), negative stimuli and emotions are generally more salient (Rozin & Royzman, 2001). Examples of a "negativity bias" in processing environmental stimuli abound in the psychological literature, from the strong pull that negative stimuli exert on our attention (e.g., Pratto & John, 1991) to the primacy of loss aversion (Tversky & Kahneman, 1991), the speed and intensity of conditioned taste aversion (Rozin & Kalat, 1971), and "contagion" effects in which even the idea of contact with a contaminant makes an otherwise desirable substance inedible (e.g., chocolate shaped like dog feces; Rozin, Millman, & Nemeroff, 1986). Although considerable evidence suggests that this bias diminishes with typical aging, even reversing to a positivity bias (Reed, Chan, & Mikels, 2014), this appears to reflect a controlled, motivated override of the default negativity bias, rather than its elimination (Knight et al., 2007). Given their links to important health problems such as mood and anxiety disorders, as well as societal problems such as violence and marital distress, negative emotions themselves command greater attention than positive ones as well (Fredrickson, 1998).

A greater emphasis on negative than on positive emotion states is also apparent in the vocabulary of a number of languages. For example, when Philip Shaver and colleagues (1987) asked undergraduates at a U.S. university to rate the extent to which 213 nouns from Averill's (1975) *A Semantic Atlas of Emotional Concepts* were good examples of "emotion," just over a third of the 135 terms rated as most emotional were characterized by positive valence. A follow-up study using hierarchical cluster analysis revealed a superordinate split between negative and positive terms, with "basic" level clusters for anger, fear, sadness, happiness, and love. Studies using these methods have produced similar results in the Indonesian (Shaver, Murdaya, & Fraley, 2001) and Basque (Alonso-Arbiol et al., 2006) languages; in Chinese, positive love terms were subsumed under the happiness cluster, and additional clusters were seen for shame and "sad love" (e.g., unrequited love; Shaver, Wu, & Schwartz, 1992). In each language, the emotion lexicon was clearly dominated by negative-valence terms.

However, theories of positive emotions' functions and significance were also weak for many years, creating a major impediment to research (Fredrickson, 2001). Theories emphasizing negative emotions' adaptive functions—especially those of specific emotions such as fear and disgust— had long provided a valuable foundation for empirical work and used to derive hypotheses about various aspects of emotional responding and to integrate research findings in conceptually coherent ways. According to most major theorists, negative emotions evolved to help our ancestors respond quickly, automatically, and adaptively to threats posed by the environment to survival and/or reproductive fitness (e.g., Cosmides & Tooby, 2000; Ekman, 1992; Frijda, 1986; Izard, 1977; Lazarus, 1991; Levenson, 1999; Plutchik, 2003). Prototypical eliciting situations (e.g., fear—threat of physical harm; disgust—threat of contamination; anger—insult/offense; sadness—irrevocable loss) and the corresponding "action tendencies" (e.g., fear—escape; disgust—rejection; anger—aggression and status assertion; sadness—support seeking, withdrawal) for specific emotions had been articulated, and rich programs of research have grown around these functional definitions (e.g., Keller & Nesse, 2006; Öhman, 1986; Rozin & Fallon, 1987; Schaller & Park, 2011; Tiedens, 2001; Van Kleef & De Dreu, 2010. In contrast, theoretical definitions of "happiness" and "joy" remained vague. Rather than identifying prototypical eliciting situations, theorists proposed that general appraisals of pleasantness and/or progress toward a goal led to positive emotion (e.g., Frijda, Kuipers, & ter Schure, 1989; Lazarus, 1991). Instead of specific action tendencies, positive emotions were thought to promote overall behavioral activation and approach motivation (e.g., Cacioppo, Gardner, & Berntson, 1999; Davidson, 1993; Frijda, 1986; Lazarus, 1991). Without a more detailed theory of what positive emotions should help us *do*, researchers had a limited basis for developing interesting hypotheses to test.

This situation has improved dramatically in the 21st century. Beginning with Fredrickson's (1998; 2001) broaden-and-build theory, which highlights the role positive emotions play in building fitness-relevant resources, positive emotion theory and research have developed rapidly over the last 20 years. In this chapter we summarize key theoretical advances emphasizing the functions of positive emotions and offer examples of empirical research guided by these perspectives. We then consider ways in which positive emotions might prove valuable in addressing three real-world problems that are traditionally framed in terms of negative emotion: promoting healthy behavior, supporting marriages and other intimate relationships, and easing troubled intergroup relations. We conclude by considering both the promise of and challenges facing the science of positive emotions.

What Is Positive Emotion?

When asked to generate examples of positive emotion, lay people as well as scientists can easily do so—happiness, love, pride, and contentment or serenity commonly come to mind. Despite this intuitive simplicity, the meaning of the term "emotion" has been the subject of extensive debate in affective science. As a result, the terms "positive emotion" and "positive affect" are used by different researchers to denote somewhat different constructs. Because various uses of these terms reflect distinct theoretical perspectives, leading to distinct bodies of empirical research, it is important to address their meanings.

One approach, typically referred to as the "basic" or "discrete" emotion perspective, defines emotions as multicomponent responses to specific kinds of threats and opportunities faced by human ancestors (e.g., Ekman 1992; Frijda, 1986; Levenson, 1999; Plutchik, 1980; Tooby & Cosmides, 2008). Researchers adopting this perspective consider the capacity for *specific* emotions such as fear, anger, and sadness to be part of human nature, though they may disagree about the exact number and taxonomy. The functional analyses summarized earlier, describing the prototypical elicitors and action tendencies of several negative emotions, reflect this perspective. Researchers' use of the term "positive emotion" typically indicates endorsement of this perspective.

The basic/discrete emotion perspective emphasizes the adaptive value of instinctive, complex behavioral responses to eliciting situations. Because such responses rely on the coordination of various physiological, sensory, cognitive, expressive, and motivational processes that otherwise operate independently, "emotions" are defined as psychological mechanisms producing this coordination automatically under the right circumstances (Levenson, 1999). For example, "fear" would be a mechanism for focusing attention on a nearby predator, increasing "fight-or-flight" physiological arousal, prioritizing the goal of self-protection over other goals, activating memory of escape strategies, and communicating one's danger and need for assistance to kin and other group members (Tooby & Cosmides, 2008). Research emerging from the basic/discrete perspective often compares multiple emotions against each other or examines one emotion at a time. From this perspective, "positive emotions" can be defined as fairly brief responses to opportunities in the environment, such as high-quality food, a desirable mate, affiliation partners, or new and useful information, that facilitate acquiring and building important resources (e.g., Fredrickson, 1998; Shiota et al., 2014; Shiota et al., in press).

Another conceptualization of emotion proposes that the true elements of emotion in human nature are not discrete categories such as fear and anger, but instead continuous dimensions, such as positive versus negative valence of feeling, degree of activation or arousal, and motivational direction of approach versus avoidance (e.g., Barrett, 2006; Cacioppo, Berntson, Norris, & Gollan, 2011; Harmon-Jones, 2003; Russell, 2003). Although different theorists emphasize different sets of dimensions, a common implication is that the categories emphasized by the basic/discrete emotions theory are social and psychological concepts, defined by a particular cultural worldview rather than by human nature (e.g., Barrett, 2006). Research emerging from this perspective typically asks whether various aspects of emotional responding, such as facial expression, neural activation, and cognitive processing, can be predicted by one of these dimensions. From this perspective, "positive emotion" is defined in terms of subjectively pleasant and desirable feelings (Harmon-Jones, Price, Gable, & Peterson, 2014). Because pleasant feelings need not be elicited by a specific event in the environment and may be lasting rather than brief, the terms "positive affect" and "positive mood" are often used instead of "positive emotion" in research emerging from this theoretical perspective.

We will not get embroiled here in the debate over which of these perspectives is "right." A growing number of researchers have proposed alternative theories allowing for both dimensionality and at least partial differentiation among cross-culturally "modal" regions of emotion space corresponding to emotions such as fear, anger, and so forth (e.g., Nesse, 2014; Scherer, 2009). For our purpose, the key point is that these different theoretical traditions have each led to valuable theoretical innovations and programs of research on positive affect and emotion, to which we now turn.

The Functions of Positive Emotions: Theoretical and Empirical Advances

We noted earlier that in order to serve as a strong foundation for empirical research, a theory of emotion must articulate the means by which some emotional response is functional, leading to useful or desirable outcomes that can be predicted and measured. In the majority of emotion research (though by no means all; for examples of approaches emphasizing primarily sociocultural functions of emotion see Frijda & Mesquita, 1994; Mesquita & Boiger, 2014; Tsai, 2007), the emphasis has been on *adaptive* function, or the ways in which emotional responses increased our ancestors' evolutionary fitness. It is easy to describe certain negative emotions in this way, articulating how fear helps individuals survive predator threat (Tooby & Cosmides, 2008) and how disgust helps individuals avoid contamination and disease (Oaten, Stevenson, & Case, 2009; Rozin & Fallon, 1987). Yet for decades, emotion researchers had difficulty articulating comparable, plausible theories of positive emotions. This difficulty was due to certain constraints in terms of the aspects of emotion that were considered functionally relevant. Breakthroughs in positive emotion theory took place when some of these constraints were challenged, recognizing a wider range of ways in which emotional responses can enhance fitness. In each case, the innovation has led to extensive and informative programs of research on positive emotion.

Increased Emphasis on Cognitive Processing

The first constraint to be challenged was the field's emphasis on immediate, overt behavior, or "action tendency," as the functional aspect of emotion (Fredrickson, 1998). Dozens of studies conducted during the 1990s had examined effects of positive as well as negative affect or mood on cognitive processing, with implications for judgment and decision-making (for reviews see Forgas, 1995; Lerner, Li, Valdesolo, & Kassam, 2015). For example, the positive versus negative valence of experimentally elicited mood was found to influence people's evaluation of a wide range of targets. Specifically, the "rose-colored glasses" effect, in which pleasant mood leads to more positive evaluation of some target unrelated to the cause of the mood, has been observed for targets ranging from political candidates (e.g., Isbell & Wyer, 1999) to consumer products (e.g., Gorn, Goldberg, & Basu, 1993) and advertisements (e.g., Murry & Dacin, 1996). Although the effect is observed when research participants are not thinking carefully, allowing current mood to serve as a heuristic for the judgment in question, it can sometimes be amplified when they are, subtly biasing the valence of information that is processed systematically, and thus "infusing" the initial positive (or negative) bias into a more deeply held and lasting positive (or negative) attitude (Forgas, 1995).

Another common theme that emerged was that positive mood promotes more heuristic, rule-of-thumb cognitive processing, at the expense of careful, systematic analysis (Schwartz & Bless, 1991). Experimentally elicited positive mood was found to increase stereotyping (e.g., Bodenhausen, Kramer, & Süsser, 1994; Park & Banaji, 2000); over-reliance on "event scripts" or mental schemas of similar types of situations in encoding details about the current, specific situation (e.g., Bless et al., 1996); reliance on superficial cues such as the number of arguments, rather than argument quality, in evaluating persuasive messages (e.g., Mackie & Worth, 1989); and commission of the fundamental attribution error, a bias in which others' behavior is automatically attributed to their personality rather than their situation (e.g., Forgas, 1998).

Taken together, these findings suggest that positive mood/affect might be useful in signaling that all is well, whatever we have been doing is working, and we should continue along the same path (Isbell, Lair, & Rovenpor, 2013; Russell, 2003). Key neurological structures mediating the response to positive, rewarding stimuli include a "go" pathway in the ventral striatum supporting motivated approach behavior (Floresco, 2015; Shiota et al., in press). Increasingly, evidence suggests that positive mood serves as a green light for cognition as well as behavior, prompting continued use of whatever information-processing approach is most readily accessible (Huntsinger, Isbell, & Clore, 2012, 2014). At least for people in individualistic, Western cultures, the heuristics described earlier are examples of default settings, used automatically in the absence of a reason to invest greater cognitive effort (Evans & Stanovich, 2013). Positive mood generally tends to increase use of these mental shortcuts; however, if an alternative cognitive strategy is primed (e.g., the participant is presented with multiple counter-stereotypical examples prior to a task measuring stereotyping), then positive mood tends to increase use of the *alternative* strategy instead (e.g., Huntsinger, Sinclair, Dunn, & Clore, 2010).

In the broaden-and-build model of positive emotion, Barbara Fredrickson (1998, 2001) proposed that positive emotions' functionality might be linked more closely to cognition than to immediate, overt action. According to this model, positive emotions are adaptive by virtue of distributing our attention more broadly across the environment, enhancing creative thinking, and thereby facilitating detection and acquisition of fitness-enhancing resources that will be beneficial in the long term. Supporting this proposal, early experiments showed that positive emotion manipulation shifted people's attention away from elemental details, or the "trees," and toward the big picture or "forest" (Fredrickson & Branigan, 2005). Research by Alice Isen and colleagues (1987) had previously demonstrated that positive affect/mood promotes creativity, facilitating innovative use of items to solve a mechanical puzzle (i.e., "candle-matchbox" test), and identification of a common concept linking three other words (i.e., Remote Associates Test). Both effects are thought to be mediated by an increased tendency toward loose, flexible conceptual association—another way in which attention can be "broadened"—and studies show that participants in a positive mood offer more unusual associations to priming words than those in a neutral or negative mood (Isen, Johnson, Mertz, & Robinson, 1985).

Broadened attention increases the chance that we will identify opportunities in the environment and acquire valuable information for future use (Fredrickson, 2001). Creativity increases the likelihood that we will succeed in taking advantage of opportunities, overcoming any barriers that might get in the way. Positive emotion also plays an important role in coping with negative experiences; those who are able to find positive meaning in challenging events and make time for positive emotion-eliciting activities during periods of stress tend to be more psychologically resilient (Tugade & Fredrickson, 2004). Crucially for the broaden-and-build model, evidence supports an "upward spiral" by which positive emotions lead to an increase in personal resources, which in turn facilitate the experience of more positive emotion, and so forth (Fredrickson, Cohn, Coffey, Pek, & Finkel, 2008). Some of these resources involve information, and others material goods. However, positive emotions are especially important for acquiring social resources, bringing us to a second innovation in positive emotion theory.

The Social Functions of Positive Emotions

The functions of negative emotions, as described by theorists in the late 20th century, tended to emphasize their implications for one's survival and ability to reproduce. Such functions are *intrapersonal*, fitness relevant through direct consequences for the organism experiencing the emotion (Levenson, 1999). For mammals, however, relationships with mates, offspring, kin, and other members of social groups have a powerful indirect impact on individual fitness (de Waal, 1996). Humans in particular are *ultrasocial*, performing crucial life tasks such as acquiring food, finding or building shelter, protecting against predators and other threats, and raising offspring in large groups, rather than individually (Campbell, 1983;

Lancaster, 1976). An important human adaptive strategy, group living also creates new challenges, as individual members must navigate and commit to various kinds of relationships in order to work well as a team (Krebs & Davies, 1993; Trivers, 1971).

In the 1990s, researchers began to propose that emotions play a valuable role in navigating these complex relationships; in this way, emotions can serve *interpersonal* or social functions, indirectly benefiting the individual fitness of group members by strengthening relationships within the group (Averill, 1992; Keltner & Haidt, 1999; Keltner, Haidt, & Shiota, 2006). While some negative emotions are thought to serve primarily interpersonal functions (e.g., embarrassment and shame help heal relationships after one commits a transgression; Keltner, 1995), it has been argued that positive emotions are especially important in this regard (Shiota, Campos, Keltner, & Hertenstein, 2004). Research now supports the proposal that positive emotions play important roles in the initial formation of affiliative relationships; in the maintenance of closer, more intimate relationships; and even in the coordination of larger cooperative groups.

Positive emotion has powerful and lasting implications. For example, people who smile—the prototypical display of positive emotion (Ekman et al., 1987)—are perceived as more extraverted, agreeable, conscientious, emotionally stable, likable, trustworthy, and more desirable as social partners (e.g., Harker & Keltner, 2001; Hess, Blairy, & Kleck, 2000; Naumann, Vazire, Rentfrow, & Gosling, 2009). Smiling is an "honest signal" in this regard, as people who smile spontaneously in photographs actually report higher levels of extraversion and agreeableness than those who do not (Naumann et al., 2009). In one study, women who showed stronger smiles in college yearbook photos up to 30 years earlier were more likely to have been married, reported higher levels of marital satisfaction, and reported higher personal well-being (including satisfaction with their relationships) in their early fifties (Harker & Keltner, 2001).

Other, more subtle nonverbal behaviors facilitated by positive emotion can promote affiliation as well. For example, experience of positive emotion (with the exception of pride) increases nonconscious mimicry (Dickens & DeSteno, 2014), which both communicates and elicits affiliative intent and liking (Chartrand & Bargh, 1999; Lakin & Chartrand, 2003). Exploratory research on the dynamics of mother–infant dyads finds that high-intensity positive states tend to be reciprocated in successful conversations, whereas expressions of interest tend to follow a turn-taking dynamic (Main, Paxton, & Dale, 2016). Those who express pride—particularly "authentic" pride in one's specific, effort-driven achievements rather than general arrogance or hubris—are presumed by observers to be relatively high status, prosocially motivated, and worthy of prestige (e.g., Cheng, Tracy, & Henrich, 2010; Martens, Tracy, & Shariff, 2012; Wubben, De Cremer, & van Dijk, 2012).

Beyond expressive displays, the experience of some positive emotions also promotes early-stage affiliation and bonding. For example, admiration leads people to want to emulate, and adoration leads people to want to affiliate with, the object of their emotion (Schindler, Paech, & Lowenbruck, 2015). Elevation, a feeling resulting from viewing moral exemplars, increases a desire to act prosocially toward others in general (Algoe & Haidt, 2009). In particular, theories of gratitude emphasize the role this emotion plays in motivating investment in individuals who are likely to be good long-term social partners (Algoe, 2012; Algoe & Haidt, 2009). On one hand, gratitude serves as a signal to the beneficiary of another's prosocial action that the benefactor is a valuable ally (McCullough, Kimeldorf, & Cohen, 2008). A beneficiary's expression of gratitude promotes increased commitment to the relationship by the benefactor as well (Williams & Bartlett, 2015. Felt gratitude for gifts given by a "big sister" in a sorority to her "little sister" predicted higher ratings of relationship quality by both sisters, as well as greater connection with the sorority, a month after gift giving (Algoe, Haidt, & Gable, 2008). Together, these findings suggest that gratitude is particularly important in promoting new affiliative bonds.

Aron and colleagues' self-expansion model of love suggests that as new relationships become increasingly close, positive emotional experience can also change one's conception of the self in relation to the partner (Aron, Aron, & Smollan, 1992; Aron, Aron, Tudor, & Nelson, 1991). In this model, closeness involves expansion of the self-concept to include the partner's traits and characteristics. High ratings of this "inclusion of other in the self" are strongly correlated with reports of positive emotions toward the partner (Aron et al., 1992). Falling in love has been linked longitudinally to expanded self-concept, as well as increased self-efficacy and self-esteem (Aron, Paris, & Aron, 1995). Self-expansion has been linked, in turn, to greater feelings of positive emotion (Graham, 2008; Mattingly, Lewandowski, & McIntyre, 2014). Experimentally induced positive emotion also tends to increase the complexity with which a social partner is viewed—less in terms of stable personality traits, and more in terms of how they are likely to respond to different situations (Waugh & Frederickson, 2006). This suggests that positive emotions facilitate development of a richer, more nuanced conceptualization of the partner.

Beyond the early relationship stage, positive emotions contribute to maintenance of long-term close relationships as well. In general, positive affect has been linked to desirable outcomes such as relationship quality

(Seiffge-Krenke, 2003), closeness (Rotkirch, Lyons, David-Barrett, & Jokela, 2014), and satisfaction (Lyubomirsky, Tkach, & DiMatteo, 2006; see Ramsey & Gentzler, 2015 for a review). In one study, couples asked to relive events in which they shared laughter and amusement reported higher relationship satisfaction, above and beyond effects of current mood that could reflect the "rose-colored glasses" effect described earlier (Bazzini, Stack, Martincin, & Davis, 2007). Love, in particular, is thought to promote commitment to close relationship partners. In a series of conversations by romantic couples, partners' self-reported experiences and expressive displays of love—but not sexual desire—predicted commitment-enhancing processes such as perceived trust and use of constructive attempts to resolve conflicts (Gonzaga, Keltner, Londahl, & Smith, 2001). In other studies, participants primed to feel love toward their current romantic partner showed less attention toward, and were more successful in suppressing thoughts about, attractive alternative partners (Gonzaga, Haselton, Smurda, Davies, & Poore, 2008; Maner, Rouby, & Gonzaga, 2008).

Gratitude, again, continues to play an important role in supporting close relationships, as well as newer ones. In one study, actively expressing gratitude to a close friend predicted stronger relationship bonds with that friend six weeks later (Lambert, Clark, Durtschi, Fincham, & Graham, 2010). In romantic relationships, individuals with higher levels of dispositional gratitude tend to report higher levels of intimacy (Murray & Hazelwood, 2011). As with early-stage relationships, gratitude affects the benefactor as well as the beneficiary. Participants assigned to hearing their romantic partner express gratitude have been found to report higher relationship satisfaction than those in a control condition the next day (Algoe, Gable, & Maisel, 2010), six weeks later (Lambert et al., 2010), and even six months later (Algoe, Fredrickson, & Gable, 2013; Algoe & Zhaoyang, 2016).

Consistent with predictions of the broaden-and-build model (Fredrickson, 2001), positive emotions and relational closeness appear to interact dynamically in a positive feedback loop. Pleasant exchanges within the relationship produce positive emotions, which lead in turn to stronger ties between partners (Lawler, 2001). These processes extend from pleasant contexts to implications for more challenging situations within the relationship. For example, newlywed couples who display more positive affect during daily interactions also express more affection during arguments (Driver & Gottman, 2004). Couples who show more positive affect during their arguments are more likely to be happily married years later (Gottman, Coan, Carrere, & Swanson, 1998). Looking at overall relationship trajectory, newlywed couples who express and report experiencing high levels of love and affection in the first two years of marriage are more likely to remain married, and report being more satisfied with the relationship, than couples showing less of these emotions (Huston, Caughlin, Houts, Smith, & George, 2001).

Beyond close relationships, positive emotions support investment in larger groups and members of those groups. A growing body of research demonstrates that expressions of positive emotion (i.e., Duchenne smiles) serve as a reliable signal of intent to cooperate (Brown, Palameta, & Moore, 2003; Mehu, Grammer, & Dunbar, 2007; Mehu, Little, & Dunbar, 2007; Schug, Matsumto, Horita, Yamagishi, & Bonnet, 2010). Positive affect and prosocial behavior have a bidirectional relationship, such that prosocial acts increase both benefactors' and beneficiaries' positive affect, and in turn, positive affect increases one's tendency to behave prosocially (Bartlett & DeSteno, 2006; Isen, Clark, & Schwartz, 1976; Lennon & Eisenberg, 1987). When people experience negative affect, they are motivated to help others in hopes of improving their mood or building positive relationships though prosociality (Baumeister, Stillwell, & Heatherton, 1994; Clark & Isen, 1982; Isen & Levin, 1972; Rosenhan, Karylowski, Salovey & Hargis, 1981). In contrast, those in a positive mood behave prosocially in order to *prolong* this mood, particularly when helping does not threaten to diminish it through empathic distress (Carlson, Charlin, & Miller, 1988; Clark & Isen, 1982; Isen & Levin, 1972). Again, this effect is not limited to close others; compassion, hope, companionate love, and even pride have all been found to promote prosocial behavior toward close others, but companionate love also increases altruistic giving toward *distant* others (Cavanaugh, Bettman, & Luce et al., 2015). Thus, when in an emotional state of loving care for others, individuals extend prosocial tendencies to a much wider set of recipients.

Diversity of Functions and Positive Emotion Differentiation

As the field of positive emotion has grown, researchers have increasingly recognized the diversity of functions positive emotions may serve. As a result, many are moving beyond general theories of positive emotion or positive mood/affect to posit theories of particular varieties of positive emotion. For example, Gable and Harmon-Jones (2010a) have called attention to positive emotions' variability in intensity of approach motivation— the instinct to move toward the eliciting stimulus. Across several studies, they have found that the attention-broadening effect predicted by broaden-and-build theory best characterizes low-approach positive emotion (e.g., elicited by images of cats in amusing situations), whereas high-approach positive emotion (e.g., elicited by images of desserts) tends to focus attention on local details (Gable & Harmon-Jones, 2008; Harmon-Jones & Gable, 2009) and on the center rather than the periphery of the visual field (Gable & Harmon-Jones, 2010b)—an effect opposite to that suggested by broaden and build theory.

While acknowledging the general principle of broaden-and-build theory—that positive emotions support acquiring and building fitness-relevant resources—researchers are increasingly differentiating among distinct kinds of resources, the adaptive challenges they present, and the potentially "discrete" positive emotions that may have evolved to address those challenges (Shiota et al., in press). Programs of research on individual positive emotions are now thriving. For example, pride has been defined theoretically as an emotion experienced when one takes credit for a valued achievement, earning the right to increased social status (e.g., Lazarus, 1991; Tracy & Robins, 2007). Empirical research documenting a cross-culturally recognized postural pride display that closely resembles the primate power display, as well as the effect of pride in motivating increased perseverance at a difficult task, is grounded in and consistent with this definition (Tracy & Robins, 2007; Tracy, Shariff, Zhao, & Henrich, 2013; Williams & DeSteno, 2008). Similar programs of research are growing for gratitude (Algoe, 2012; Bartlett, Condon, Cruz, Baumann, & DeSteno, 2012; Bartlett & DeSteno, 2006), love and sexual desire (Diamond, 2003; Gonzaga, Turner, Keltner, Campos, & Altemus, 2006; Muise, Impett, & Desmarais, 2013), and awe (Danvers & Shiota, in press; Piff, Dietze, Feinberg, Stancato, & Keltner, 2015; Shiota, Keltner, & Mossman, 2007), among others.

In addition, more studies are comparing multiple positive emotions against each other in a methodological tradition long applied in the research on negative emotions. This work has uncovered important differences among positive emotions in terms of facial, postural, and vocal expression (e.g., Campos, Shiota, Keltner, Gonzaga, & Goetz, 2013; Mortillaro, Mehu, & Scherer, 2011; Sauter & Scott, 2007; Simon-Thomas, Keltner, Sauter, Sinicropi-Yao, & Abramson, 2009); bodily effects such as changes in heart rate, blood pressure, and sweat gland activity (e.g., Shiota, Neufeld, Yeung, Moser, & Perea, 2011); the cognitive "appraisals," or interpretations of a situation's meaning, that are thought to produce emotional responses (Roseman, 1996); effects on cognitive processing and consumer product evaluation (e.g., Danvers & Shiota, in press; Griskevicius, Shiota, & Neufeld, 2010; Griskevicius, Shiota, & Nowlis, 2010); and correlations with personality traits (e.g., Güsewell & Ruch, 2012; Shiota, Keltner, & John, 2006). With this explosion of theory and associated programs of research, work on positive emotions is finally beginning to catch up to research on their negative counterparts.

Applying Positive Emotion Science to Real-World Problems

We have emphasized the role that theoretical constraints played in limiting attention to positive emotion and the impact new theoretical developments have had on the field. However, a number of real-world applied issues have also been framed primarily in terms of negative emotion. On one hand, we applaud the recognition that emotions—including negative emotions—are deeply embedded in social problems such as unhealthy lifestyles, marital distress and dissolution, and troubled intergroup relations (e.g., Cottrell & Neuberg, 2005; Gottman & Levenson, 1992; Williams & Evans, 2014). On the other hand, we propose that framing these and other issues in terms of positive emotions may lead to new, valuable insights with strong implications for intervention.

Promoting Health Behavior Change

Emotions play powerful roles in health-related behaviors, motivating both current behavior and efforts to change future behavior, altering the way we process health-related information and shaping health-related judgments and decisions (Williams & Evans, 2014). After many years in which theoretical models of health behavior—and intervention efforts based on these models—emphasized knowledge, beliefs, attitudes, and self-efficacy (e.g., Ajzen, 1985; Rosenstock, 1990), emotions are increasingly recognized as playing a crucial role. However, attempts to add an emotional component to behavior change interventions have focused almost exclusively on fear. Public service announcements (PSAs) promoting behavior change (e.g., smoking cessation, healthy diet) routinely present frightening facts and images in an effort to scare the viewer into adopting a healthier lifestyle. Although fear appeals are highly memorable (Biener, Wakefield, Shiner, & Siegel, 2008), they are effective in promoting behavior change only if they also boost self-efficacy so viewers believe they are able to do whatever is needed to avoid the dangerous outcome; otherwise, they simply tune out the message (Hastings, Stead, & Webb, 2004; Peters, Ruiter, & Kok, 2013). Because a typical viewer has already tried several times to make the change in question and failed, this is a substantial challenge.

Positive emotions may offer an opportunity to approach behavior change in another way, and health psychologists are beginning to advocate for their use in interventions (e.g., Cameron & Chan, 2008; Peters et al., 2013). Many positive emotions are rooted in mechanisms for behavioral activation, moving toward valuable resources and rewards (Shiota et al., in press). These emotions could be useful in supporting adoption of new behaviors, such as physical exercise. Positive emotions involving high motivation to approach rewards are less suitable for efforts to *inhibit* behaviors, such as smoking or unhealthy snacking, as they involve activation of neural "go" systems (Floresco, 2015). However, positive emotions that involve lower levels of approach motivation, such as contentment and awe, may serve as more effective "brakes." Evidence from research on promoting environmentally sustainable behavior (e.g., recycling, reduced use of fossil fuels) suggests that pride can serve as both motivation and reward for behaviors that are socially valued, earning the actor an increase in status (Griskevicius, Tybur, & Van den Bergh, 2010); this principle could be applied to health behavior change as well. Appeals highlighting love for friends and family and the benefits *they* would accrue from one's behavior change may also motivate new efforts (Griskevicius, Cantú, & van Vugt, 2012).

Bringing a positive emotion perspective to behavior change efforts means framing them in terms of benefits, opportunities, resources, and rewards rather than risks, losses, and threats. Especially for individuals with a dispositional tendency toward promotion regulatory focus (which emphasizes achieving desired goals) rather than prevention focus (which emphasizes avoiding unwanted outcomes), this approach may be quite useful for encouraging adoption of healthy lifestyles (Spiegel, Grant-Pillow, & Higgins, 2004).

Supporting Marriages and Other Close Relationships

Although divorce rates have declined from their peak in the 1970s–1980s, analyses suggest that 30–40% of marriages in the United States still end in divorce (Stevenson & Wolfers, 2007). Acknowledging that a wide range of family structures can be healthy and satisfying for their members, evidence is strong that stable, harmonious family environments are generally associated with higher parenting quality and child well-being (e.g., Fomby & Cherlin, 2007; Osborne & McLanahan, 2007), and people who marry at all presumably do so in the hope of achieving a lasting partnership. Healthy marriages have been linked to better physical and mental health, whereas unhappy marriages may negatively affect health (e.g., Holt-Lunstad, Birmingham, & Jones, 2008; Kiecolt-Glaser & Newton, 2001; Robles & Kiecolt-Glaser, 2003). Thus, there is a clear social and public health interest in supporting marriages and other committed partnerships.

The important role of emotion in marital satisfaction and stability is supported by extensive research evidence (e.g., Bradbury & Karney, 2004; Gottman et al., 1998; Levenson & Gottman, 1985; Sullivan, Pasch, Johnson, & Bradbury, 2010). The greatest attention has been paid to the toxic effects of negative emotional expression and external stressors affecting relationships (Bradbury, Fincham, & Beach, 2000; Levenson & Gottman, 1985). Increasingly, however, research is revealing the importance of positive emotion in strengthening close relationships (Bradbury & Karney, 2004). Whereas negative affect expressed during conflict has often been found to predict divorce, especially in the first several years, at least one study has found that low positive affect during conflict, as well as "events of the day" conversations, predicts divorce later in the marriage (Gottman & Levenson, 2000). The expression of positive affect (especially affection and shared humor) during conflict has been found to help down-regulate spouses' arousal levels, helping couples cool off during an argument (Yuan, McCarthy, Holley, & Levenson, 2010). Partners also provide each other with valuable social support during periods of stress external to the relationship (Cohen & Wills, 1985; Uchino, Cacioppo, & Kiecolt-Glaser, 1996).

Another program of research highlights the relationship-enhancing benefits of positive emotion during good times, as well as during conflict and stress. An early study found that sharing or celebrating a positive event with another person enhanced positive affect above and beyond that resulting directly from the event (Langston, 1994). In this process relationship partners who "capitalize" on a positive event can extract more emotional benefits by discussing the event together (Gable & Reis, 2010). For example, romantic partners who share positive events with each other report higher life satisfaction and positive affect during the day (Gable, Gosnell, Maisel, & Strachman, 2012). Preliminary evidence suggests that capitalization is an important way to maintain close relationships, as well as enhancing positive affect. In one study, sharing positive events with one's romantic partner led to greater feelings of intimacy and feelings of closeness, as well as higher relationship satisfaction (Gable, Reis, Impett, & Asher, 2004). In another study, more active and constructive responses to a partner describing a positive event predicted higher relationship quality eight weeks later (Gable, Gonzaga, & Strachman, 2006).

These studies raise intriguing questions for future research. One future direction involves examining dyad-level processes and outcomes as well as individual-level ones. Much of the research on capitalization has focused on benefits experienced by the disclosing individual—the one describing his or her positive event. Future studies might examine how the disclosing individual's *partner*, and the relationship itself, might also benefit from capitalizing on the discloser's good fortune. In another direction, research is needed on the implications of individual differences, such as attachment style, for capitalization and other processes involving positive emotions. Individuals with insecure attachment styles tend to minimize positive experiences and may be less likely to orient toward positive, rewarding stimuli in their environment (e.g., Gentzler, Kerns, & Keener, 2010; Yee & Shiota, 2015). For these individuals, partner support for the experience of positive emotions may prove especially valuable. Finally, future research might address the roles positive emotions play in supporting other close relationships, such as those with family and intimate friends, as well as marriages and romantic relationships. Much work is needed to fully understand the dynamics of how positive emotions support our close relationships, and vice versa.

Healing Troubled Intergroup Relations

Decades' worth of research shows that people express stronger preference for, cooperate better with, and give more resources to ingroup versus outgroup members, as well as underestimate outgroup success while inflating ingroup success (Balliet, Wu, & De Dreu, 2014; Brewer, 1979; Turner, Brown, & Tajfel, 1979). Although the power of implicit stereotypes and attitudes has received increasing recognition (Greenwald et al., 2002), the problems of prejudice and discrimination have often been framed in terms of negative emotion. Indeed, prejudice is defined largely in terms of the experience of negative affect toward members of an outgroup (Allport, 1954), and recent analyses have mapped prejudice against particular outgroups to the experience of specific negative emotions in theory-driven, sophisticated ways (e.g., Cottrell & Neuberg, 2005). Analyses of intergroup conflict highlight the role of negative emotions as well (e.g., Iyer & Leach, 2008; Mackie, Smith, & Ray, 2008).

In an increasingly multicultural and globalized society, it is crucial to identify mechanisms by which intergroup relations can be facilitated in a positive way. Previous research demonstrates that increased contact between groups can improve intergroup relations, provided that the contact is pleasant and presumes equal status (Allport, 1954; Cook, 1985; Pettigrew, 1998; Tausch & Hewstone, 2010). Not only can positive interaction between individuals from conflicting groups improve their attitudes of one another, but *vicarious* positive intergroup contact can reduce intergroup conflict as well (Wright, Aron, McLaughlin-Volpe, & Ropp, 1997). Emphasizing shared identity and goals plays an important role in improving intergroup relations, and contact-focused interventions commonly involve a task that requires intergroup cooperation (Aronson & Bridgeman, 1979; Mackie et al., 2008; Page-Gould, Mendoza-Denton, & Tropp, 2008; Sherif, Harvey, White, Hood, & Sherif, 1954). Such tasks may elicit a sense of collective pride—an emotion that facilitates identification and further cooperation with the larger group (Tyler & Blader, 2001). Moreover, experimentally elicited positive emotion has been found to reduce the cognitive bias in which faces of people of one's own race are more easily differentiated and remembered than those of other races, suggesting expansion of the ingroup in terms of psychological process (Johnson & Fredrickson, 2005).

As noted earlier, people are motivated to help and cooperate with ingroup members preferentially because the opportunity for building a long-term interdependent relationship is perceived as being greater than with outgroup members (Kiyonari & Yamagishi, 2004; Yamagishi, Jim, & Kiyonari, 1999). When giving crosses group boundaries, however, processes associated with gratitude might lead to improved intergroup dynamics beyond the individuals involved. Gratitude not only motivates people to reciprocate prosocial action toward the benefactor (DeSteno et al., 2010; Tsang, 2006), but also promotes helping third-party bystanders (Bartlett & DeSteno, 2006). Research is needed to address whether this "pay-it-forward" effect would continue to cross group boundaries after an initial prosocial act between groups. If so, one instance of outgroup prosociality could spark a ripple effect that facilitates additional prosocial and cooperative intergroup action on a broader scale.

Conclusions and Future Directions

The science of positive emotion has come a long way in a short time. After almost complete neglect during the 1980s and 1990s, positive emotions are now a primary focus in dozens of research laboratories, producing an explosion of new knowledge. A Google Scholar search for "positive emotion" produces over 50,000 results in 2016, only a few thousand of which were published prior to 2000. New theories abound, not only of positive emotion or affect in general, but also of specific positive emotions. Positive emotions have been linked to an array of desirable life outcomes, from marital and relationship satisfaction to workplace success, higher income, and better physical as well as mental health (e.g., Cohen & Pressman, 2006; Danner, Snowdon, & Friesen, 2001; Fredrickson & Joiner, 2002; Harker & Keltner, 2001; Lyubomirsky, King, & Diener, 2005; Richman et al., 2005). As a result, there is growing interest in the use of positive emotions in interventions targeting these and other benefits.

Still, much about positive emotion remains minimally explored. For example, although there is growing interest in the use of positive emotions to promote academic achievement, few studies have addressed this relationship or mechanisms that might account for such an effect (Valiente, Swanson, & Eisenberg, 2012). Surprisingly little research has addressed the effects of positive emotions on the body (e.g., heart rate, blood pressure, sweat gland activity), despite the wealth of research on this aspect of negative emotions (Kreibig, 2010). Although many programs of research have addressed the characteristics of individual positive emotions, it is still rare for studies to explicitly compare different positive emotions against each other; the tendency to treat "positive emotion" as a single uniform category remains (Shiota et al., in press). Particular positive emotions are still neglected as well; although we have learned much about pride (Tracy, Weidman, Cheng, & Martens, 2014), gratitude (Algoe, 2012), and hope (Snyder, 2002), we know far less about contentment, love, amusement/humor, and awe.

Although we strongly encourage new research in these and other areas, some suggestions are in order for future research. The first is a recommendation to avoid the potential pitfall of assuming that all effects of positive emotion are desirable, regardless of context. Like negative emotions, positive emotions presumably evolved as responses to particular kinds of situations, with profiles of effects tailored to those situational contexts. Outside those contexts, the same response might prove irrelevant or even detrimental. For example, constantly elevated positive emotion not responsive to one's current situation is a risk factor for bipolar disorder (Gruber, 2011). Although positive emotion expression generally predicts positive social outcomes, participants in one study who smiled and laughed while describing experiences of childhood abuse showed worse social adjustment than those who displayed less positive emotion, presumably because such expressions violate strong social norms and expectations for the context (Bonanno et al., 2007).

Our second recommendation is to supplement measures of subjective experience with objective measures of cognitive processing, physiology, and/or overt behavior whenever possible. A great majority of research on positive emotion still relies exclusively on self-reports of emotional feelings, motivations, perceptions, attitudes, beliefs, and to some extent, behavior. Self-reports are the only valid method of assessing many important variables, but they have profound limitations as well, vulnerable to self-presentation and social desirability biases, an "acquiescence bias" in which respondents are more likely to agree than disagree with any statement offered, preference for extreme versus middle response options, and reliance on subjective reference groups, each of which are subject to individual differences as well as population-typical biases (Paulhus & Vazire, 2007). Especially where the aim of a study is to ask whether positive emotions produce some kind of valuable outcome (beyond psychological well-being, an inherently subjective construct), objective measures of that outcome will be far more compelling than self-reports alone.

The third recommendation, closely linked to the first and second, is to develop detailed, a priori theories about the mechanisms producing desired downstream effects and ensure that these are measured in study designs. For example, although it is clear that high dispositional positive emotionality predicts better physical health (Cohen & Pressman, 2006; Richman et al., 2005), the physiological mechanisms behind this outcome are still under investigation (Ong, 2010). It is especially important to obtain objective measures of mediating variables, such as changes in implicit/unconscious cognitive processing, physiological response, and/or observable social behavior. Documenting proximal effects of emotion manipulations that account for desired outcomes not only enhances theoretical knowledge, but also facilitates greater precision and stronger effect sizes in future interventions and helps ensure that positive emotion interventions will not backfire when transferred from one context or population to another.

These recommendations are intended to be guideposts for much-needed future science. Fortunately, the field of positive emotion now offers both a strong foundation in prior theory and research and many opportunities to break new ground. We look forward to seeing the directions it takes in the decades to come.

References

Ajzen, I. (1985). From intentions to actions: A theory of planned behavior. In J. Kuhl & J. Beckmann (Eds.), *Action control* (pp. 11–39). Berlin: Springer Berlin Heidelberg.

Algoe, S. B. (2012). Find, remind, and bind: The functions of gratitude in everyday relationships. *Social and Personality Psychology Compass, 6*(6), 455–469.

Algoe, S. B., Fredrickson, B. L., & Gable, S. L. (2013). The social functions of the emotion of gratitude via expression. *Emotion, 13*(4), 605.

Algoe, S. B., Gable, S. L., & Maisel, N. C. (2010). It's the little things: Everyday gratitude as a booster shot for romantic relationships. *Personal Relationships, 17*(2), 217–233. doi:10.1111/j.1475-6811.2010.01273.x

Algoe, S. B., & Haidt, J. (2009). Witnessing excellence in action: The 'other-praising' emotions of elevation, gratitude, and admiration. *The Journal of Positive Psychology, 4*, 105–127.

Algoe, S. B., Haidt, J., & Gable, S. L. (2008). Beyond reciprocity: gratitude and relationships in everyday life. *Emotion, 8*(3), 425–429.

Algoe, S. B., & Zhaoyang, R. (2016). Positive psychology in context: Effects of expressing gratitude in ongoing relationships depend on perceptions of enactor responsiveness. *The Journal of Positive Psychology, 11*(4), 399–415.

Allport, G. W. (1954). *The nature of prejudice.* Cambridge, MA: Addison-Wesley.

Alonso-Arbiol, I., Shaver, P. R., Fraley, R. C., Oronoz, B., Unzurrunzaga, E., & Urizar, R. (2006). Structure of the Basque emotion lexicon. *Cognition & Emotion, 20*(6), 836–865.

Aron, A., Aron, E. N., & Smollan, D. (1992). Inclusion of other in the self scale and the structure of interpersonal closeness. *Journal of Personality and Social Psychology, 63*(4), 596–612.

Aron, A., Aron, E. N., Tudor, M., & Nelson, G. (1991). Close relationships as including other in the self. *Journal of Personality and Social Psychology, 60*(2), 241–253.

Aron, A., Paris, M., & Aron, E. N. (1995). Falling in love: Prospective studies of self-concept change. *Journal of Personality and Social Psychology, 69*(6), 1102–1112.

Aronson, E. & Bridgeman, D. (1979). Jigsaw groups and the desegregated classroom: In pursuit of common goals. *Personality and Social Psychology Bulletin, 5,* 438–446.

Averill, J. R. (1975). A semantic atlas of emotional concepts. *JSAS Catalog of Selected Documents in Psychology, 5*(330), Ms. No. 421.

Averill, J. R. (1992). The structural bases of emotional behavior: A metatheoretical analysis. In M. S. Clark (Ed.), *Review of Personality and Social Psychology, No. 13* (pp. 1–24). Thousand Oaks, CA: Sage Publications, Inc.

Balliet, D., Wu J., & De Dreu, C. K. W., (2014). Ingroup favoritism in cooperation: A meta-analysis. *Psychological Bulletin, 140,* 1556–1581.

Barrett, L. F. (2006). Solving the emotion paradox: Categorization and the experience of emotion. *Personality and Social Psychology Review, 10*(1), 20–46.

Bartlett, M. Y., Condon, P., Cruz, J., Baumann, J., & Desteno, D. (2012). Gratitude: Prompting behaviours that build relationships. *Cognition and Emotion, 26*(1), 2–13.

Bartlett, M. Y., & DeSteno, D. (2006). Gratitude and prosocial behavior: Helping when it costs you. *Psychological Science, 17,* 319–325.

Baumeister, R. F., Stillwell, A. M., & Heatherton, T. F. (1994). Guilt: An interpersonal approach. *Psychological Bulletin, 115,* 243–267.

Bazzini, D. G., Stack, E. R., Martincin, P. D., & Davis, C. P. (2007). The effect of reminiscing about laughter on relationship satisfaction. *Motivation and Emotion, 31*(1), 25–34.

Biener, L., Wakefield, M., Shiner, C. M., & Siegel, M. (2008). How broadcast volume and emotional content affect youth recall of anti-tobacco advertising. *American Journal of Preventive Medicine, 35*(1), 14–19.

Bless, H., Clore, G. L., Schwarz, N., Golisano, V., Rabe, C., & Wölk, M. (1996). Mood and the use of scripts: Does a happy mood really lead to mindlessness?. *Journal of Personality and Social Psychology, 71*(4), 665–679.

Bodenhausen, G. V., Kramer, G. P., & Süsser, K. (1994). Happiness and stereotypic thinking in social judgment. *Journal of Personality and Social Psychology, 66*, 621–632.

Bonanno, G. A., Colak, D. M., Keltner, D., Shiota, M. N., Papa, A., Noll, J. G., . . . & Trickett, P. K. (2007). Context matters: The benefits and costs of expressing positive emotion among survivors of childhood sexual abuse. *Emotion, 7*(4), 824–837.

Bradbury, T. N., Fincham, F. D., & Beach, S. R. (2000). Research on the nature and determinants of marital satisfaction: A decade in review. *Journal of Marriage and Family, 62*(4), 964–980.

Bradbury, T. N., & Karney, B. R. (2004). Understanding and altering the longitudinal course of marriage. *Journal of Marriage and Family, 66*(4), 862–879.

Brewer, M. B. (1979). Ingroup bias in the minimal intergroup situation: A cognitive-motivational analysis. *Psychological Bulletin, 86*, 307–324.

Brown, W. M., Palameta, B., & Moore, C. (2003). Are there non-verbal cues to commitment? An exploratory study using the zero-acquaintance video presentation paradigm. *Evolutionary Psychology, 1*, 42–69.

Cacioppo, J. T., Berntson, G. G., Norris, C. J., & Gollan, J. K. (2011). The evaluative space model. In P. A. M. Van Lange, A. W. Kruglanski, & E. T. Higgins (Eds.), *Handbook of theories of social psychology: volume one*, pp. 50–72. Thousand Oaks, CA: Sage.

Cacioppo, J. T., Gardner, W. L., & Berntson, G. G. (1999). The affect system has parallel and integrative processing components: Form follows function. *Journal of Personality and Social Psychology, 76*(5), 839–855.

Cameron, L. D., & Chan, C. K. (2008). Designing health communications: Harnessing the power of affect, imagery, and self-regulation. *Social and Personality Psychology Compass, 2*(1), 262–282.

Campbell, D. T. (1983). The two distinct routes beyond kin selection to ultrasociality: Implications for the humanities and social sciences. In D. Bridgeman (Ed.), *The nature of prosocial development: Theories and strategies* (pp. 11–39). New York: Academic Press.

Campos, B., Shiota, M. N., Keltner, D., Gonzaga, G. C., & Goetz, J. (2013). What is shared, what is different?: Core relational themes and expressive displays of eight positive emotions. *Cognition and Emotion, 27*(1), 37–52.

Carlson, M., Charlin, V., & Miller, N. (1988). Positive mood and helping behavior: A test of six hypotheses. *Journal of Personality and Social Psychology, 55*, 211–229.

Carstensen, L. L., Pasupathi, M., Mayr, U., & Nesselroade, J. R. (2000). Emotional experience in everyday life across the adult life span. *Journal of Personality and Social Psychology, 79*(4), 644–655.

Cavanaugh, L. A., Bettman, J. R., & Luce, M. F. (2015). Feeling love and doing more for distant others: Specific positive emotions differentially affect prosocial consumption. *Journal of Marketing Research, 52*(5), 657–673.

Chartrand, T. L., & Bargh, J. A. (1999). The chameleon effect: The perception–behavior link and social interaction. *Journal of Personality and Social Psychology, 76*(6), 893–910.

Cheng, J. T., Tracy, J. L., & Henrich, J. (2010). Pride, personality, and the evolutionary foundations of human social status. *Evolution and Human Behavior, 31*(5), 334–347.

Clark, M. S., & Isen, A. M. (1982). Toward understanding the relationship between feeling states and social behavior. In A. Hastorf & A. M. Isen (Eds.), *Cognitive social psychology* (pp. 73–108). New York: Elsevier.

Cohen, S., & Pressman, S. D. (2006). Positive affect and health. *Current Directions in Psychological Science, 15*(3), 122–125.

Cohen, S., & Wills, T. A. (1985). Stress, social support, and the buffering hypothesis. *Psychological Bulletin, 98*(2), 310–357.

Cook, S. W. (1985). Experimenting on social issues: The case of school desegregation. *American Psychologist, 40*, 452–460.

Coren, S., & Girgus, J. S. (1978). *Seeing is deceiving: The psychology of visual illusions*. Oxford, England: Lawrence Erlbaum.

Cosmides, L., & Tooby, J. (2000). Evolutionary psychology and the emotions. In M. Lewis & J. M. Haviland-Jones (Eds.), *Handbook of emotions, 2nd Edition* (pp. 91–115). New York: Guilford.

Cottrell, C. A., & Neuberg, S. L. (2005). Different emotional reactions to different groups: a sociofunctional threat-based approach to "prejudice." *Journal of Personality and Social Psychology, 88*(5), 770–789.

Danner, D. D., Snowdon, D. A., & Friesen, W. V. (2001). Positive emotions in early life and longevity: Findings from the nun study. *Journal of Personality and Social Psychology, 80*(5), 804–813.

Danvers, A. F., & Shiota, M. N. (2016). Going off script: Effects of awe on memory for script-typical and -irrelevant narrative detail. Manuscript accepted for publication in *Emotion*.

Darwin, C. (1872/1965). *The expression of the emotions in man and animals*. Chicago: University of Chicago Press.

Davidson, R. J. (1993). Cerebral asymmetry and emotion: Conceptual and methodological conundrums. *Cognition and Emotion, 7*(1), 115–138.

DeSteno, D., Bartlett, M. Y., Baumann, J., Williams, L. A., & Dickens, L. (2010). Gratitude as moral sentiment: Emotion-guided cooperation in economic exchange. *Emotion, 10*, 289–293.

de Waal, F. B. (1996). *Good natured*. Cambridge, MA: Harvard University Press.

Diamond, L. M. (2003). What does sexual orientation orient? A biobehavioral model distinguishing romantic love and sexual desire. *Psychological Review, 110*(1), 173–192.

Dickens, L., & DeSteno, D. (2014). Pride attenuates nonconscious mimicry. *Emotion, 14*(1), 7–11.

Driver, J. L., & Gottman, J. M. (2004). Daily marital interactions and positive affect during marital conflict among newlywed couples. *Family Process, 43*(3), 301–314.

Ekman, P. (1972). Universals and cultural differences in facial expressions of emotion. In J. Cole (Ed.), *Nebraska symposium on motivation, 1971,* vol. 19 (pp. 207–283). Lincoln, NE: University of Nebraska Press.

Ekman, P. (1992). An argument for basic emotions. *Cognition and Emotion, 6,* 169–200.

Ekman, P., Friesen, W. V., O'Sullivan, M., Chan, A., Diacoyanni-Tarlatzis, I., Heider, K., et al. (1987). Universals and cultural differences in the judgments of facial expressions of emotion. *Journal of Personality and Social Psychology, 51,* 712–717.

Ellsworth, P. C., & Smith, C. A. (1988). Shades of joy: Patterns of appraisal differentiating pleasant emotions. *Cognition and Emotion, 2*(4), 301–331.

Evans, J. S. B., & Stanovich, K. E. (2013). Dual-process theories of higher cognition advancing the debate. *Perspectives on Psychological Science, 8*(3), 223–241.

Fehr, B., & Russell, J. A. (1984). Concept of emotion viewed from a prototype perspective. *Journal of Experimental Psychology: General, 113*(3), 464–486.

Floresco, S. B. (2015). The nucleus accumbens: an interface between cognition, emotion, and action. *Annual Review of Psychology, 66,* 25–52.

Fomby, P., & Cherlin, A. J. (2007). Family instability and child well-being. *American Sociological Review, 72*(2), 181–204.

Forgas, J. P. (1995). Mood and judgment: the affect infusion model (AIM). *Psychological Bulletin, 117*(1), 39–66.

Forgas, J. P. (1998). On being happy and mistaken: mood effects on the fundamental attribution error. *Journal of Personality and Social Psychology, 75*(2), 318–331.

Fredrickson, B. L. (1998). What good are positive emotions? *Review of General Psychology, 2,* 300–319.

Fredrickson, B. L. (2001). The role of positive emotions in positive psychology: The broaden-and-build theory of positive emotions. *American Psychologist, 56,* 218–226.

Fredrickson, B. L., & Branigan, C. (2005). Positive emotions broaden the scope of attention and build thought-action repertoires. *Cognition and Emotion, 19,* 313–332.

Fredrickson, B. L., Cohn, M. A., Coffey, K. A., Pek, J., & Finkel, S. M. (2008). Open hearts build lives: positive emotions, induced through loving-kindness meditation, build consequential personal resources. *Journal of Personality and Social Psychology, 95*(5), 1045–1062.

Fredrickson, B. L., & Joiner, T. (2002). Positive emotions trigger upward spirals toward emotional well-being. *Psychological Science, 13*(2), 172–175.

Frijda, N. H. (1986). *The emotions.* Cambridge, England: Cambridge University Press.

Frijda, N. H., Kuipers, P., & Ter Schure, E. (1989). Relations among emotion, appraisal, and emotional action readiness. *Journal of Personality and Social Psychology, 57*(2), 212–228.

Frijda, N. H., & Mesquita, B. (1994). The social roles and functions of emotions. In S. Kitayama & H. R. Markus (Eds.), *Emotion and culture: Empirical studies of mutual influence* (pp. 51–87). Washington, DC: American Psychological Association.

Gable, P. A., & Harmon-Jones, E. (2008). Approach-motivated positive affect reduces breadth of attention. *Psychological Science, 19*(5), 476–482.

Gable, P., & Harmon-Jones, E. (2010a). The motivational dimensional model of affect: Implications for breadth of attention, memory, and cognitive categorisation. *Cognition and Emotion, 24*(2), 322–337.

Gable, P., & Harmon-Jones, E. (2010b). The blues broaden, but the nasty narrows: Attentional consequences of negative affects low and high in motivational intensity. *Psychological Science, 21*(2), 211–215.

Gable, S. L., Gonzaga, C. E., & Strachman, A. (2006). Will you be there for me when things go right?: Supportive responses to positive event disclosures. *Journal of Personality and Social Psychology, 91*(5), 904–917.

Gable, S. L., Gosnell, C. L., Maisel, N. C., & Strachman, A. (2012). Safely testing the alarm: Close others' responses to personal positive events. *Journal of Personality and Social Psychology, 103*(6), 963.

Gable, S. L., & Haidt, J. (2005). What (and why) is positive psychology?. *Review of General Psychology, 9*(2), 103–110.

Gable, S. L., & Reis, H. T. (2010). Good news! Capitalizing on positive events in an interpersonal context. *Advances in Experimental Social Psychology, 42,* 195–257.

Gable, S. L., Reis, H. T., Impett, E. A., & Asher, E. R. (2004). What do you do when things go right?: The intrapersonal and interpersonal benefits of sharing positive events. *Journal of Personality and Social Psychology, 87*(2), 228–245.

Gentzler, A. L., Kerns, K. A., & Keener, E. (2010). Emotional reactions and regulatory responses to negative and positive events: Associations with attachment and gender. *Motivation and Emotion, 34*(1), 78–92.

Gonzaga, G. C., Haselton, M. G., Smurda, J., Davies, M. S., & Poore, J. C. (2008). Love, desire, and the suppression of thoughts of romantic alternatives. *Evolution and Human Behavior, 29,* 119–126.

Gonzaga, G. C., Keltner, D., Londahl, E. A., & Smith, M. D. (2001). Love and the commitment problem in romantic relationships and friendship. *Journal of Personality and Social Psychology, 81,* 247–262.

Gonzaga, G. C., Turner, R. A., Keltner, D., Campos, B., & Altemus, M. (2006). Romantic love and sexual desire in close relationships. *Emotion, 6,* 163–179.

Gorn, G., Goldberg, M., & Basu, K., (1993), Mood, awareness and product evaluation, *Journal of Consumer Psychology, 2*, 237–256.

Gottman, J., Coan, J., Carrere, S., & Swanson, C. (1998). Predicting marital happiness and stability from newlywed interactions. *Journal of Marriage and Family, 60*(1), 5–22.

Gottman, J. M., & Levenson, R. W. (1992). Marital processes predictive of later dissolution: Behavior, physiology, and health. *Journal of Personality and Social Psychology, 63*(2), 221–233.

Gottman, J. M., & Levenson, R. W. (2000). The timing of divorce: predicting when a couple will divorce over a 14-year period. *Journal of Marriage and Family, 62*(3), 737–745.

Graham, J. M. (2008). Self-expansion and flow in couples' momentary experiences: An experience sampling study. *Journal of Personality and Social Psychology, 95*(3), 679–694.

Greenwald, A. G., Banaji, M. R., Rudman, L. A., Farnham, S. D., Nosek, B. A., & Mellott, D. S. (2002). A unified theory of implicit attitudes, stereotypes, self-esteem, and self-concept. *Psychological Review, 109*(1), 3–25.

Griskevicius, V., Cantú, S. M., & Vugt, M. V. (2012). The evolutionary bases for sustainable behavior: Implications for marketing, policy, and social entrepreneurship. *Journal of Public Policy & Marketing, 31*(1), 115–128.

Griskevicius, V., Shiota, M. N., & Neufeld, S. L. (2010). Influence of different positive emotions on persuasion processing: A functional evolutionary approach. *Emotion, 10*, 190–206.

Griskevicius, V., Shiota, M. N., & Nowlis, S. M. (2010). The many shades of rose-colored glasses: Discrete positive emotions and product perception. *Journal of Consumer Research, 37*(2), 238–250.

Griskevicius, V., Tybur, J. M., & Van den Bergh, B. (2010). Going green to be seen: Status, reputation, and conspicuous conservation. *Journal of Personality and Social Psychology, 98*(3), 392–404.

Gruber, J. (2011). Can feeling too good be bad? Positive emotion persistence (PEP) in bipolar disorder. *Current Directions in Psychological Science, 20*(4), 217–221.

Güsewell, A., & Ruch, W. (2012). Are only emotional strengths emotional? Character strengths and disposition to positive emotions. *Applied Psychology: Health and Well-Being, 4*(2), 218–239.

Harker, L. A., & Keltner, D. (2001). Expressions of positive emotion in women's college yearbook pictures and their relationship to personality and life outcomes across adulthood. *Journal of Personality and Social Psychology, 80*, 112–124.

Harmon-Jones, E. (2003). Clarifying the emotive functions of asymmetrical frontal cortical activity. *Psychophysiology, 40*(6), 838–848.

Harmon-Jones, E., & Gable, P. A. (2009). Neural activity underlying the effect of approach-motivated positive affect on narrowed attention. *Psychological Science, 20*(4), 406–409.

Harmon-Jones, E., Price, T. F., Gable, P. A., & Peterson, C. K. (2014). Approach motivation and its relationship to positive and negative emotions. In M. M. Tugade, M. N. Shiota, & L. D. Kirby (Eds.), *Handbook of positive emotions* (pp. 103–118). New York: Guilford.

Hastings, G., Stead, M., & Webb, J. (2004). Fear appeals in social marketing: Strategic and ethical reasons for concern. *Psychology & Marketing, 21*(11), 961–986.

Hess, U., Blairy, S., & Kleck, R. E. (2000). The influence of facial emotion displays, gender, and ethnicity on judgments of dominance and affiliation. *Journal of Nonverbal Behavior, 24*(4), 265–283.

Holt-Lunstad, J., Birmingham, W., & Jones, B. Q. (2008). Is there something unique about marriage? The relative impact of marital status, relationship quality, and network social support on ambulatory blood pressure and mental health. *Annals of Behavioral Medicine, 35*(2), 239–244.

Huntsinger, J. R., Isbell, L. M., & Clore, G. L. (2014). The affective control of thought: Malleable, not fixed. *Psychological Review, 121*(4), 600–618.

Huntsinger, J. R., Sinclair, S., Dunn, E., & Clore, G. L. (2010). Affective regulation of stereotype activation: It's the (accessible) thought that counts. *Personality and Social Psychology Bulletin, 36*(4), 564–577.

Huntsinger, M., Isbell, L. M., & Clore, G. L. (2012). Sometimes happy people focus on the trees and sad people focus on the forest: Context-dependent effects of mood in impression formation. *Personality and Social Psychology Bulletin, 38*(2), 220–232.

Huston, T. L., Caughlin, J. P., Houts, R. M., Smith, S. E., & George, L. J. (2001). The connubial crucible: Newlywed years as predictors of marital delight, distress, and divorce. *Journal of Personality and Social Psychology, 80*(2), 237–252.

Isbell, L. M., Lair, E. C., & Rovenpor, D. R. (2013). Affect-as-information about processing styles: A cognitive malleability approach. *Social and Personality Psychology Compass, 7*(2), 93–114.

Isbell, L. M., & Wyer, R. S. (1999). Correcting for mood-induced bias in the evaluation of political candidates: The roles of intrinsic and extrinsic motivation. *Personality and Social Psychology Bulletin, 25*(2), 237–249.

Isen, A. M., Clark, M., & Schwartz, M. F. (1976). Duration of the effect of good mood on helping: "Footprints in the sands of time." *Journal of Personality and Social Psychology, 34*, 385–393.

Isen, A. M., Daubman, K. A., & Nowicki, G. P. (1987). Positive affect facilitates creative problem solving. *Journal of Personality and Social Psychology, 52*, 1122–1131.

Isen, A. M., Johnson, M. M., Mertz, E., & Robinson, G. F. (1985). The influence of positive affect on the unusualness of word associations. *Journal of Personality and Social Psychology, 48*(6), 1413–1426.

Isen, A. M., & Levin, P. F. (1972). Effects of feeling good on helping: Cookies and kindness. *Journal of Personality and Social Psychology, 21*, 384–388.

Iyer, A., & Leach, C. W. (2008). Emotion in inter-group relations. *European Review of Social Psychology, 19*, 86–125.

Izard, C. E. (1971). *The face of emotion.* New York: Appleton-Century-Crofts.

Izard, C. E. (1977). *Human emotions.* New York: Plenum Press.

James, W. (1884). What is an emotion? *Mind, 9*, 188–205.

Johnson, K. J., & Fredrickson, B. L. (2005). "We all look the same to me": Positive emotions eliminate the own-race bias in face recognition. *Psychological Science, 16*(11), 875–881.

Kahneman, D., & Tversky, A. (1973). On the psychology of prediction. *Psychological Review, 80*(4), 237–251.

Keller, M. C., & Nesse, R. M. (2006). The evolutionary significance of depressive symptoms: Different adverse situations lead to different depressive symptom patterns. *Journal of Personality and Social Psychology, 91*(2), 316–330.

Keltner, D. (1995). Signs of appeasement: Evidence for the distinct displays of embarrassment, amusement, and shame. *Journal of Personality and Social Psychology, 68*(3), 441–454.

Keltner, D., & Haidt, J. (1999). Social functions of emotions at four levels of analysis. *Cognition and Emotion, 13*(5), 505–521.

Keltner, D., Haidt, J., & Shiota, M. N. (2006). Social functionalism and the evolution of emotions. In M. Schaller, J. A. Simpson, & D. T. Kenrick (Eds.), *Evolution and social psychology* (pp. 115–142). New York: Psychology Press.

Kiecolt-Glaser, J. K., & Newton, T. L. (2001). Marriage and health: His and hers. *Psychological Bulletin, 127*(4), 472–503.

Kiyonari, T., & Yamagishi, T. (2004). In-group cooperation and the social exchange heuristic. In R. Suleiman, D. V. Budescu, I. Fischer, & D. M. Messick (Eds.), *Contemporary psychological research on social dilemmas* (pp. 269–286). New York: Cambridge University Press.

Knight, M., Seymour, T. L., Gaunt, J. T., Baker, C., Nesmith, K., & Mather, M. (2007). Aging and goal-directed emotional attention: Distraction reverses emotional biases. *Emotion, 7*(4), 705–714.

Krebs, J. R., & Davies, N. B. (1993). Parental care and mating systems. In N. B. Davis, J. R. Krebs, & S. A. West (Eds.), *An introduction to behavioural ecology* (pp. 208–243). London: Blackwell.

Kreibig, S. D. (2010). Autonomic nervous system activity in emotion: A review. *Biological Psychology, 84*(3), 394–421.

Lakin, J. L., & Chartrand, T. L. (2003). Using nonconscious behavioral mimicry to create affiliation and rapport. *Psychological Science, 14*(4), 334–339.

Lambert, N. M., Clark, M. S., Durtschi, J., Fincham, F. D., & Graham, S. M. (2010). Benefits of expressing gratitude: Expressing gratitude to a partner changes one's views of the relationship. *Psychological Science, 21*, 574–580.

Lancaster, J. B. (1976). *Primate behavior and the emergence of human culture.* New York: Holt.

Langston, C. A. (1994). Capitalizing on and coping with daily-life events: Expressive responses to positive events. *Journal of Personality and Social Psychology, 67*, 1112–1125.

Lawler, E. J. (2001). An affect theory of social exchange. *The American Journal of Sociology, 107*, 321–352.

Lazarus, R. S. (1991). *Emotion and adaptation*. New York: Oxford University Press.

LeDoux, J. (2003). The emotional brain, fear, and the amygdala. *Cellular and Molecular Neurobiology, 23*(4–5), 727–738.

Lennon, R., & Eisenberg, N. (1987). Emotional displays associated with preschoolers' prosocial behavior. *Child Development, 58*, 992–1000.

Lerner, J. S., & Keltner, D. (2000). Beyond valence: Toward a model of emotion-specific influences on judgement and choice. *Cognition and Emotion, 14*(4), 473–493.

Lerner, J. S., Li, Y., Valdesolo, P., & Kassam, K. S. (2015). Emotion and decision making. *Annual Review of Psychology, 66*, 799–823.

Levenson, R. W. (1999). The intrapersonal functions of emotion. *Cognition and Emotion, 13*, 481–504.

Levenson, R. W., Ekman, P., Heider, K., & Friesen, W. V. (1992). Emotion and autonomic nervous system activity in the Minangkabau of West Sumatra. *Journal of Personality and Social Psychology, 62*, 972–988.

Levenson, R. W., & Gottman, J. M. (1985). Physiological and affective predictors of change in relationship satisfaction. *Journal of Personality and Social Psychology, 49*(1), 85–94.

Lyubomirsky, S., King, L., & Diener, E. (2005). The benefits of frequent positive affect: Does happiness lead to success?. *Psychological Bulletin, 131*(6), 803–855.

Lyubomirsky, S., Tkach, C., & DiMatteo, M. R. (2006). What are the differences between happiness and self-esteem?. *Social Indicators Research, 78*(3), 363–404.

Mackie, D. M., Smith, E. R., & Ray, D. G. (2008). Intergroup emotions and intergroup relations. *Social and Personality Psychology Compass, 2*, 1866–1880.

Mackie, D. M., & Worth, L. T. (1989). Processing deficits and the mediation of positive affect in persuasion. *Journal of Personality and Social Psychology, 57*, 27–40.

Main, A., Paxton, A., & Dale, R. (2016). An exploratory analysis of emotion dynamics between mothers and adolescents during conflict discussions. *Emotion, 16*(6), 913–928.

Maner, J. K., Rouby, D. A., & Gonzaga, C. E. (2008). Automatic inattention to attractive alternatives: The evolved psychology of relationship maintenance. *Evolution and Human Behavior, 29*(5), 343–349.

Martens, J. P., Tracy, J. L., & Shariff, A. F. (2012). Status signals: Adaptive benefits of displaying and observing the nonverbal expressions of pride and shame. *Cognition and Emotion, 26*(3), 390–406.

Mattingly, B. A., Lewandowski, G. W., & McIntyre, K. P. (2014). "You make me a better/worse person": A two-dimensional model of relationship self-change. *Personal Relationships, 21*(1), 176–190.

McCullough, M. E., Kimeldorf, M. B., & Cohen, A. D. (2008). An adaptation for altruism: The social causes, social effects, and social evolution of gratitude. *Current Directions in Psychological Science, 17*(4), 281–285.

Mehu, M., Grammer, K., & Dunbar, R. I. (2007). Smiles when sharing. *Evolution and Human Behavior, 28*, 415–422.

Mehu, M., Little, A. C., & Dunbar, R. I. M. (2007). Duchenne smiles and the perception of generosity and sociability in faces. *Journal of Evolutionary Psychology, 5*, 133–146.

Mesquita, B., & Boiger, M. (2014). Emotions in context: A sociodynamic model of emotions. *Emotion Review, 6*(4), 298–302.

Mortillaro, M., Mehu, M., & Scherer, K. R. (2011). Subtly different positive emotions can be distinguished by their facial expressions. *Social Psychological and Personality Science, 2*(3), 262–271.

Muise, A., Impett, E. A., & Desmarais, S. (2013). Getting it on versus getting it over with: Sexual motivation, desire, and satisfaction in intimate bonds. *Personality and Social Psychology Bulletin, 39*(10), 1320–1332.

Murray, A. J., & Hazelwood, Z. J. (2011). Being grateful: Does it bring us closer? Gratitude, attachment and intimacy in romantic relationships. *Journal of Relationships Research, 2*(1), 17–25.

Murry, J. P., & Dacin, P. A. (1996). Cognitive Moderators of Negative Emotion Effects: Implications for understanding media-context. *Journal of Consumer Research, 22*, 439–447.

Naumann, L. P., Vazire, S., Rentfrow, P. J., & Gosling, S. D. (2009). Personality judgments based on physical appearance. *Personality & Social Psychology Bulletin, 35*(12), 1661–1671.

Nesse, R. M. (2014). Comment: A general "theory of emotion" is neither necessary nor possible. *Emotion Review, 6*(4), 320–322.

Oaten, M., Stevenson, R. J., & Case, T. I. (2009). Disgust as a disease-avoidance mechanism. *Psychological Bulletin, 135*(2), 303–321.

Oatley, K., & Johnson-Laird, P. N. (1987). Towards a cognitive theory of emotions. *Cognition and Emotion, 1*, 29–50.

Öhman, A. (1986). Face the beast and fear the face: Animal and social fears as prototypes for evolutionary analyses of emotion. *Psychophysiology, 23*(2), 123–145.

Ong, A. D. (2010). Pathways linking positive emotion and health in later life. *Current Directions in Psychological Science, 19*(6), 358–362.

Osborne, C., & McLanahan, S. (2007). Partnership instability and child well-being. *Journal of Marriage and Family, 69*(4), 1065–1083.

Page-Gould, E., Mendoza-Denton, R., & Tropp, L. R. (2008). With a little help from my cross-group friend: reducing anxiety in intergroup contexts through cross-group friendship. *Journal of Personality and Social Psychology, 95*(5), 1080–1094.

Park, J., & Banaji, M. R. (2000). Mood and heuristics: The influence of happy and sad states on sensitivity and bias in stereotyping. *Journal of Personality and Social Psychology, 78*(6), 1005–1023.

Paulhus, D. L., & Vazire, S. (2007). The self-report method. In R. W. Robins, R. C. Fraley, & R. F. Krueger (Eds.), *Handbook of research methods in personality psychology* (pp. 224–239). New York: Guilford.

Peters, G. J. Y., Ruiter, R. A., & Kok, G. (2013). Threatening communication: A critical re-analysis and a revised meta-analytic test of fear appeal theory. *Health Psychology Review, 7*(Supp 1), S8–S31.

Pettigrew, T. F. (1998). Intergroup contact theory. *Annual Review of Psychology, 49*, 65–85.

Piff, P. K., Dietze, P., Feinberg, M., Stancato, D. M., & Keltner, D. (2015). Awe, the small self, and prosocial behavior. *Journal of Personality and Social Psychology, 108*(6), 883–899.

Plutchik, R. (1980). A general psychoevolutionary theory of emotion. In R. Plutchik & H. Kellerman (Eds.), *Theories of emotion* (pp. 3–31). New York: Academic Press.

Plutchik, R. (2003). *Emotions and life: Perspectives from psychology, biology, and evolution.* Washington, DC: American Psychological Association.

Pratto, F., & John, O. P. (1991). Automatic vigilance: The attention-grabbing power of negative social information. *Journal of Personality & Social Psychology, 61*, 380–391.

Ramsey, M. A., & Gentzler, A. L. (2015). An upward spiral: Bidirectional associations between positive affect and positive aspects of close relationships across the life span. *Developmental Review, 36*, 58–104.

Reed, A. E., Chan, L., & Mikels, J. A. (2014). Meta-analysis of the age-related positivity effect: Age differences in preferences for positive over negative information. *Psychology and Aging, 29*(1), 1–15.

Richman, L. S., Kubzansky, L., Maselko, J., Kawachi, I., Choo, P., & Bauer, M. (2005). Positive emotion and health: Going beyond the negative. *Health Psychology, 24*(4), 422–429.

Robles, T. F., & Kiecolt-Glaser, J. K. (2003). The physiology of marriage: Pathways to health. *Physiology and Behavior, 79*(3), 409–416.

Roediger III, H. L. (1996). Memory illusions. *Journal of Memory and Language, 35*(2), 76–100.

Roseman, I. J. (1996). Appraisal determinants of emotions: Constructing a more accurate and comprehensive theory. *Cognition and Emotion, 10*(3), 241–278.

Roseman, I. J., Spindel, M. S., & Jose, P. E. (1990). Appraisals of emotion-eliciting events: Testing a theory of discrete emotions. *Journal of Personality and Social Psychology, 59*(5), 899–915.

Rosenhan, D. L., Karylowski, J., Salovey, P., & Hargis, K. (1981). Emotion and altruism. In J. P. Rushton & R. M. Sorrentino (Eds.), *Altruism and helping behavior* (pp. 233–248). Hillsdale, NJ: Lawrence Erlbaum Associates.

Rosenstock, I. M. (1990). The health belief model: Explaining health behavior through expectancies. In K. Galnz, F. M. Lewis, & B. K Rimer (Eds.), *Health behavior and health education: Theory, research, and practice* (pp. 39–62). San Francisco: Jossey-Bass.

Ross, L., Lepper, M., & Ward, A. (2010). History of social psychology: Insights, challenges, and contributions to theory and application. In D. T. Gilbert, S. T. Fiske, & G. Lindzey (Eds.), *The handbook of social psychology, 5th edition* (pp. 3–50). Hoboken, NJ: John Wiley & Sons, Inc.

Rotkirch, A., Lyons, M., David-Barrett, T., & Jokela, M. (2014). Gratitude for help among adult friends and siblings. *Evolutionary Psychology, 12*(4), 673–686.

Rozin, P., & Fallon, A. E. (1987). A perspective on disgust. *Psychological Review, 94*(1), 23–41.

Rozin, P., & Kalat, J. W. (1971). Specific hungers and poison avoidance as adaptive specializations of learning. *Psychological Review, 78*(6), 459–486.

Rozin, P., Millman, L., & Nemeroff, C. (1986). Operation of the laws of sympathetic magic in disgust and other domains. *Journal of Personality and Social Psychology, 50*(4), 703–712.

Rozin, P., & Royzman, E. B. (2001). Negativity bias, negativity dominance, and contagion. *Personality and Social Psychology Review, 5*(4), 296–320.

Russell, J. A. (2003). Core affect and the psychological construction of emotion. *Psychological Review, 110*, 145–172.

Sauter, D. A., & Scott, S. K. (2007). More than one kind of happiness: Can we recognize vocal expressions of different positive states? *Motivation and Emotion, 31*, 192–199.

Schaller, M., & Park, J. H. (2011). The behavioral immune system (and why it matters). *Current Directions in Psychological Science, 20*(2), 99–103.

Scherer, K. R. (1997). The role of culture in emotion-antecedent appraisal. *Journal of Personality and Social Psychology, 73*(5), 902–922.

Scherer, K. R. (2009). The dynamic architecture of emotion: Evidence for the component process model. *Cognition and Emotion, 23*(7), 1307–1351.

Schindler, I., Paech, J., & Löwenbrück, F. (2015). Linking admiration and adoration to self-expansion: Different ways to enhance one's potential. *Cognition and Emotion, 29*(2), 292–310.

Schug, J., Matsumoto, D., Horita, Y., Yamagishi, T. & Bonnet, K. (2010). Emotional expressivity as a signal of cooperation. *Evolution and Human Behavior, 31*, 87–94.

Schwartz, N., & Bless, H. (1991). Happy and mindless, but sad and smart? The impact of affective states on analytic reasoning. In J. P. Forgas (Ed.), *Emotion and social judgments* (pp. 55–71). Oxford, England: Pergamon.

Seiffge-Krenke, I. (2003). Testing theories of romantic development from adolescence to young adulthood: Evidence of a developmental sequence. *International Journal of Behavioral Development, 27*(6), 519–531.

Seligman, M. E., & Csikszentmihalyi, M. (2000). Positive psychology: An introduction. *American Psychologist, 55*(1), 5–14.

Shaver, P. R., Murdaya, U., & Fraley, R. C. (2001). Structure of the Indonesian emotion lexicon. *Asian Journal of Social Psychology, 4*(3), 201–224.

Shaver, P., Schwartz, J., Kirson, D., & O'Connor, C. (1987). Emotion knowledge: Further exploration of a prototype approach. *Journal of Personality and Social Psychology, 52*(6), 1061–1086.

Shaver, P. R., Wu, S., & Schwartz, J. C. (1992). Cross-cultural similarities and differences in emotion and its representation. In M. S. Clark (Ed.), *Review of personality and social psychology, no. 13* (pp. 175–212). Thousand Oaks, CA: Sage.

Sherif, M. H., Harvey, O. J., White, B. J., Hood, W. R., & Sherif, C. 1954. *Experimental study of positive and negative intergroup attitudes between experimentally produced groups: Robbers Cave experiment.* Norman, OK: University of Oklahoma.

Shiota, M. N., Campos, B., Keltner, D., & Hertenstein, M. J. (2004). Positive emotion and the regulation of interpersonal relationships. In P. Philippot & R. S. Feldman (Eds.), *The regulation of emotion* (pp. 127–155). Mahwah, NJ: Lawrence Erlbaum.

Shiota, M. N., Campos, B., Oveis, C., Hertenstein, M., Simon-Thomas, E., & Keltner, D. (in press). Beyond happiness: Toward a science of discrete positive emotions. Manuscript accepted for publication in *American Psychologist.*

Shiota, M. N., Keltner, D., & John, O. P. (2006). Positive emotion dispositions differentially associated with Big Five personality and attachment style. *Journal of Positive Psychology, 1*(2), 61–71.

Shiota, M. N., Keltner, D., & Mossman, A. (2007). The nature of awe: Elicitors, appraisals, and effects on self-concept. *Cognition and Emotion, 21*(5), 944–963.

Shiota, M. N., Neufeld, S. L., Danvers, A. F., Osborne, E. A., Sng, O., & Yee, C. I. (2014). Positive emotion differentiation: A functional approach. *Social and Personality Psychology Compass, 8*(3), 104–117.

Shiota, M. N., Neufeld, S. L., Yeung, W. H., Moser, S. E., & Perea, E. F. (2011). Feeling good: Autonomic nervous system responding in five positive emotions. *Emotion, 11*(6), 1368–1378.

Simon-Thomas, E. R., Keltner, D. J., Sauter, D., Sinicropi-Yao, L., & Abramson, A. (2009). The voice conveys specific emotions: Evidence from vocal burst displays. *Emotion, 9*(6), 838–846.

Smith, C. A., & Ellsworth, P. C. (1985). Patterns of cognitive appraisal in emotion. *Journal of Personality and Social Psychology, 48*(4), 813–838.

Smith, C. A., & Lazarus, R. S. (1993). Appraisal components, core relational themes, and the emotions. *Cognition and Emotion, 7*(3–4), 233–269.

Snyder, C. R. (2002). Hope theory: Rainbows in the mind. *Psychological Inquiry, 13*(4), 249–275.

Spiegel, S., Grant-Pillow, H., & Higgins, E. T. (2004). How regulatory fit enhances motivational strength during goal pursuit. *European Journal of Social Psychology, 34*(1), 39–54.

Stevenson, B., & Wolfers, J. (2007). Marriage and divorce: Changes and their driving forces. *The Journal of Economic Perspectives, 21*(2), 27–52.

Sullivan, K. T., Pasch, L. A., Johnson, M. D., & Bradbury, T. N. (2010). Social support, problem solving, and the longitudinal course of newlywed marriage. *Journal of Personality and Social Psychology, 98*(4), 631–644.

Tausch, N., & Hewstone, N. (2010). Intergroup contact. In J. F. Dovidio, M. Hewstone, P. Glick, & V. M. Esses (Eds.), *Handbook of prejudice, stereotyping, and discrimination* (pp. 544–560). London: Sage.

Tiedens, L. Z. (2001). Anger and advancement versus sadness and subjugation: The effect of negative emotion expressions on social status conferral. *Journal of Personality and Social Psychology, 80*(1), 86–94.

Tomkins, S. S. (1984). Affect theory. In K. R. Scherer & P. Ekman (Eds.), *Approaches to Emotion* (pp. 163–195). Hillsdale, NJ: Erlbaum.

Tooby, J., & Cosmides, L. (2008). The evolutionary psychology of the emotions and their relationship to internal regulatory variables. In M. Lewis, J. M. Haviland-Jones, & L. F. Barrett (Eds.), *Handbook of emotions (3rd ed.)* (pp. 114–137). New York: Guilford Press.

Tracy, J. L., & Robins, R. W. (2007). Emerging insights into the nature and function of pride. *Current Directions in Psychological Science, 16*(3), 147–150.

Tracy, J. L., Shariff, A. F., Zhao, W., & Henrich, J. (2013). Cross-cultural evidence that the nonverbal expression of pride is an automatic status signal. *Journal of Experimental Psychology: General, 142*(1), 163–180.

Tracy, J. L., Weidman, A. C., Cheng, J. T., & Martens, J. P. (2014). The fundamental emotion of success, power, and status. In M. M. Tugade, M. N. Shiota, & L. D. Kirby, (Eds.), *Handbook of positive emotions* (pp. 294–310). New York: Guilford.

Trivers, R. L. (1971). The evolution of reciprocal altruism. *Quarterly Review of Biology, 46*(1), 35–57.

Tsai, J. L. (2007). Ideal affect: Cultural causes and behavioral consequences. *Perspectives on Psychological Science, 2*(3), 242–259.

Tsang, J. (2006). Gratitude and prosocial behaviour: An experimental test of gratitude. *Cognition and Emotion, 20,* 138–148.

Tugade, M. M., & Fredrickson, B. L. (2004). Resilient individuals use positive emotions to bounce back from negative emotional experiences. *Journal of Personality and Social Psychology, 86*(2), 320–333.

Turner, J. C., Brown R. J., & Tajfel, H. (1979). Social comparison and group interest in ingroup favouritism. *European Journal of Social Psychology, 9,* 187–204.

Tversky, A., & Kahneman, D. (1991). Loss aversion in riskless choice: A reference-dependent model. *The Quarterly Journal of Economics, 106*(4), 1039–1061.

Tyler, T. R., & Blader, S. L. (2001). Identity and cooperative behavior in groups. *Group Processes & Intergroup Relations, 4*(3), 207–226.

Uchino, B. N., Cacioppo, J. T., & Kiecolt-Glaser, J. K. (1996). The relationship between social support and physiological processes: A review with emphasis on underlying mechanisms and implications for health. *Psychological Bulletin, 119*(3), 488–531.

Valiente, C., Swanson, J., & Eisenberg, N. (2012). Linking students' emotions and academic achievement: When and why emotions matter. *Child Development Perspectives, 6*(2), 129–135.

Van Kleef, G. A., & De Dreu, C. K. (2010). Longer-term consequences of anger expression in negotiation: Retaliation or spillover?. *Journal of Experimental Social Psychology, 46*(5), 753–760.

Waugh, C. E., & Fredrickson, B. L. (2006). Nice to know you: Positive emotions, self–other overlap, and complex understanding in the formation of a new relationship. *The Journal of Positive Psychology, 1*(2), 93–106.

Williams, L. A., & Bartlett, M. Y. (2015). Warm thanks: Gratitude expression facilitates social affiliation in new relationships via perceived warmth. *Emotion, 15*(1), 1–5.

Williams, L. A., & DeSteno, D. (2008). Pride and perseverance: The motivational role of pride. *Journal of Personality and Social Psychology, 94*(6), 1007–1017.

Williams, D. M., & Evans, D. R. (2014). Current emotion research in health behavior science. *Emotion Review, 6*(3), 277–287.

Wright, S. C., Aron, A., McLaughlin-Volpe, T., & Ropp, S. A. (1997). The extended contact effect: Knowledge of cross-group friendships and prejudice. *Journal of Personality and Social Psychology, 73*, 73–90.

Wubben, M. J., De Cremer, D., & van Dijk, E. (2012). Is pride a prosocial emotion? Interpersonal effects of authentic and hubristic pride. *Cognition and Emotion, 26*(6), 1084–1097.

Yamagishi, T., Jin, N., & Kiyonari, T. (1999). Bounded generalized reciprocity: Ingroup boasting and ingroup favoritism. In E. J. Lawler (Series Ed.) & S. R. Thye, E. J. Lawler, M. W. Macy, & H. A. Walker (Vol. Eds.), *Advances in group processes* (pp. 161–197). Bingley, England: Emerald.

Yee, C. I., & Shiota, M. N. (2015). An insecure base: Attachment style and orienting response to positive stimuli. *Psychophysiology, 52*(7), 905–909.

Yuan, J. W., McCarthy, M., Holley, S. R., & Levenson, R. W. (2010). Physiological down-regulation and positive emotion in marital interaction. *Emotion, 10*(4), 467–474.

Zelenski, J. M., & Larsen, R. J. (2000). The distribution of basic emotions in everyday life: A state and trait perspective from experience sampling data. *Journal of Research in Personality, 34*(2), 178–197.

CHAPTER FOUR

Strengths of Character and Virtues: What We Know and What We Still Want to Learn

Nansook Park, Michael Barton, and Jace Pillay

In the movie *The American President*, President Andrew Shepherd (played by Michael Douglas) responds to attacks from a political opponent by saying,

> [He] . . . has suggested that being president of this country [is] . . . to a certain extent about character . . . I've been here three years and three days, and I can tell you without hesitation that being president of this country is *entirely* about character.

Good character matters, we can all agree. Good character is important in the daily lives of individuals and families, in the workplace, in school, and in the larger community. Good character is what citizens look for in their leaders, what we seek in a spouse, what friends and colleagues look for in each other, and what parents wish for and try to encourage in their children. Strengths of character are foundation of optimal lifelong human development and thriving (Baumrind, 1998).

Centuries ago, the Athenian philosophers—Socrates, Plato, and especially Aristotle—framed morality in terms of good character and in particular virtues, traits of character that make someone a good person (Rachels, 1999). This tradition is also found in Eastern cultures in the writings of Confucius (1992), who similarly enumerated virtues that made people morally praiseworthy and allowed them to contribute to the good society (Smart, 1999). He discussed such virtues as *jen* (benevolence), *yi* (duty), *li* (etiquette), *zhi* (wisdom), and *xin* (sincerity). Although specific definitions of good character may vary across different times and cultures, emphasis on the importance of character and virtues for personal and societal well-being has been a constant.

Despite the importance of good character, psychology neglected the topic throughout much of the 20th century. At one time character was a popular topic within psychology. There was even a professional journal titled *Character and Temperament*, which boldly, if inexactly, divided the ways that people differ into character—which could be changed—and temperament—which could not be changed. But Gordon Allport (1921), the premier personality theorist in the United States, banished the term character from scientific scrutiny, and many followed his lead (Nicholson, 1998). Allport believed that character was too value laden to be amenable to empirical study and suggested instead that psychology study traits, which he defined "scientifically" as neuropsychic entities. Interestingly, the journal *Character and Temperament* is alive and today, known as the *Journal of Personality*.

However, people's interests in character did not go away. It has figured in public discourse throughout human history and remains a major societal concern today (Aristotle, 2000; Hunter, 2000). During every election cycle, there has been no shortage of discussion on character. We often hear stories in the media about highly successful people—in sports, politics, business, journalism, and so on—who fell from grace due to misconduct associated with lack of character.

Positive Psychology and Character

The new field of positive psychology has refocused scientific attention on character, unabashedly calling it one of the pillars of this new field and central to the understanding of the psychological good life (Seligman & Csikszentmihalyi, 2000). Among the pillars of positive psychology, character may occupy the most central role. In their introduction to positive psychology, Seligman and Csikszentmihalyi (2000) described the study of positive traits (e.g., character) as a central pillar of this new field, and Park and Peterson (2003) proposed that character links together the other central topics of positive psychology: positive experiences, positive social relationships, and positive institutions. Thus, positive experiences like pleasure and flow (Csikszentmihalyi, 1990) and close relationships with others are enabled by good character. Positive institutions like families, schools, and communities make it easier or harder for individuals to have and display good character, but these institutions are only positive in the first place when composed of people with good character.

What is good character, and how can we measure it? There has been a deliberate effort to answer these questions scientifically (e.g., Park & Peterson, 2006a, 2006b; Peterson & Seligman, 2004; Peterson, Park, & Seligman, 2005). Since 2000, a group of researchers led by Christopher Peterson have worked from the positive psychology perspective on a project that first identifies important components of good character and then devises ways to measure individual differences in these components. This research program is sometimes identified as the *Values in Action (VIA) Project.*

Character refers to those aspects of personality that are morally valued. Here, character strengths are defined as a family of widely valued positive traits that are reflected in thoughts, feelings, and behaviors. They exist in degrees and can be measured as individual differences. They are malleable across the life span and subject to influences of numerous contextual factors. It has been speculated that they are grounded in biology through an evolutionary process that selected for these predispositions toward moral excellence as means of solving the important tasks necessary for survival of the species (cf. Bok, 1995; Schwartz, 1994).

The resulting project—the *VIA Classification of Strengths*—focuses on what is right about people and specifically about the character strengths that make the good life possible (Peterson & Seligman, 2004). The VIA Classification includes 24 character strengths organized in terms of the six core virtues (see Table 4.1).

Virtues are the core characteristics valued by moral philosophers and religious thinkers: wisdom, courage, humanity, justice, temperance, and transcendence (see details in Peterson & Seligman, 2004). These six broad categories of virtue appear consistently from historical surveys (Dahlsgaard, Peterson, & Seligman, 2005). *Character strengths* are the psychological ingredients—processes or mechanisms—that define the virtues. They are distinguishable routes to displaying one or another of the virtues.

Our measurement work has been deliberately broad to study character strengths comprehensively (Park & Peterson, 2006b; Peterson, Park, & Seligman, 2005; Peterson & Seligman, 2004). The *VIA Inventory of Strengths for Youth (VIA-Youth)* is a self-report survey that allows for a comprehensive assessment of the 24 character strengths among youth ages 10 to 17. Those who are aged 18 or older can use the *VIA Inventory of Strengths*

Table 4.1 VIA Classification of Strengths

1. Wisdom and knowledge: cognitive strengths entailing the acquisition and use of knowledge
   - creativity: thinking of novel and productive ways to do things
   - curiosity: taking an interest in all of ongoing experience
   - open-mindedness: thinking things through and examining them from all sides
   - love of learning: mastering new skills, topics, and bodies of knowledge
   - perspective: being able to provide wise counsel to others

2. Courage: emotional strengths involving the exercise of will to accomplish goals in the face of opposition, external or internal
   - honesty: speaking the truth and presenting oneself in a genuine way
   - bravery: not shrinking from threat, challenge, difficulty, or pain
   - persistence: finishing what one starts
   - zest: approaching life with excitement and energy

3. Humanity: interpersonal strengths that involve "tending and befriending" others
   - kindness: doing favors and good deeds for others
   - love: valuing close relations with others
   - social intelligence: being aware of the motives and feelings of self and others

4. Justice: civic strengths underlying healthy community life
   - fairness: treating all people the same according to notions of fairness and justice
   - leadership: organizing group activities and seeing that they happen
   - teamwork: working well as a member of a group or team

5. Temperance: strengths protecting against excess
   - forgiveness: forgiving those who have done wrong
   - modesty: letting one's accomplishments speak for themselves
   - prudence: being careful about one's choices; not saying or doing things that might later be regretted
   - self-regulation: regulating what one feels and does

6. Transcendence: strengths that forge connections to the larger universe and provide meaning
   - appreciation of beauty and excellence: noticing and appreciating beauty, excellence, and/or skilled performance in all domains of life
   - gratitude: being aware of and thankful for the good things that happen
   - hope: expecting the best and working to achieve it
   - humor: liking to laugh and joke; bringing smiles to other people
   - religiousness: having coherent beliefs about the higher purpose and meaning of life

Source: VIA Classification of Strengths from *The Oxford Handbook of Positive Psychology* (2nd ed.), edited by Shane J. Lopez and C. R. Snyder (2009). Reprinted by permission of Oxford University Press, USA.

(VIA-IS). These surveys are available online at no cost. Once individuals complete the strengths survey, feedback is given about one's top strengths: "signature strengths." To date, more than 2 million people from around the world have completed these surveys.

One of many unique aspects of the VIA strengths measure is that this is a systematic approach to studying character in multidimensional terms. Most existing research on character has focused on one aspect of character at a time, leaving unanswered questions about the underlying structure of character within an individual. Some individuals may be wise and have integrity but may be neither courageous nor kind, or vice versa (Park, 2004). Furthermore, measuring the full family of positive traits may even reduce concerns about socially desirable responding by allowing most research participants to say something good about themselves. There is the possibility that some people may lack all of the strengths in the classification when compared to others; however, the data show that virtually everyone has some notable character strengths within themselves. These are called *signature strengths*, and they are akin to what Allport (1961) identified decades ago as personal traits. Signature strengths are positive traits that a person owns, celebrates, and frequently exercises. A study suggested that identifying their signature strengths and using them in their everyday lives may lead to a psychologically fulfilling life (Seligman, Steen, Park, & Peterson, 2005).

The VIA measure is also unique in that it not only allows the comparison of character strengths across individuals, but also can be scored ipsatively—identifying an individual's "signature strengths" relative to his or her other strengths (Park, 2004). For each respondent, we rank his or her character strength scores from 1 (top) to 24 (bottom). Ipsative scoring also reduces concerns about response biases, including social desirability and undue modesty. External correlates of ipsatively scored strengths, such as subjective well-being, are much the same as the correlates of the strength scores per se, implying that our surveys tap into something more than artifact.

In addition to self-report questionnaires, several different methods have been devised and evaluated (Park & Peterson, 2006b, 2006c; Peterson & Seligman, 2004): (a) *focus groups* to flesh out the everyday meanings of character strengths among different groups; (b) *structured interviews* to identify what we call signature strengths; (c) *informant reports* (e.g., by parents, teachers, or peers) of how target individuals rise to the occasion (or not) with appropriate strengths of character (e.g., open-mindedness when confronting difficult decisions or hope when encountering setbacks); (d) *case studies* of nominated paragons of specific strengths; and (e) a *content analysis* procedure for assessing character strengths from unstructured descriptions of self and others. Each of these methods allows researchers to study a broader range of people in different ages and situations, which complements limitations of the popular survey method. For instance, in order to study character strengths of young children three to nine years old, we used the content analyses method of parental description of their children (Park & Peterson, 2006a).

What We Know about Strengths of Character

Evidence concerning the correlates, consequences, development, and cultivation of the VIA strengths is accumulating. Here is a summary of some of what we have learned to date.

First, *character strengths are structured and there are tradeoffs*. The classification of character strengths under core virtues is a conceptual scheme and not an empirical claim. The question remains of how the strengths in the VIA Classification are related to one another. One answer comes from an exploratory factor analysis of data from an adult sample, in which we first standardized subscale scores within individual respondents, thereby removing response sets like extremity. Oblique factor analysis (which allows factors to be correlated) revealed a clear two-factor solution (for details see Peterson, 2006, p. 158). The two factors were interpreted as heart versus head and self-oriented versus other-oriented. Strengths of the "head" are intellectual (e.g., creativity, curiosity, judgment, love of learning), and strengths of the "heart" are emotional and interpersonal (e.g., forgiveness, gratitude, love, kindness, teamwork). This is a circumplex model, meaning that strengths close together are more likely to co-occur, whereas those more distant are less likely. This model implies that tradeoffs do occur and that people make them in characteristic ways. All things being equal, some of us will tend to be kind, and others of us will tend to be honest. The structure of these tradeoffs might reveal something about how the real world allows good character to present itself.

It seems that no one can have all of the character strengths. There are always soft tradeoffs, although there are exceptions. It means that certain character strengths tend not to co-occur. A study found that some people have notable strengths of the "head," and these are usually not the same people who have notable strengths of the "heart" (Peterson & Park, 2009). Additional analyses suggest that respondents with a high school degree tend to score higher than those with college degrees on many of the "focus on others" strengths, and those with a college degree tend to score higher than those with a high school degree on many of the "focus on self" strengths (cf. Snibbe & Markus, 2005). The mechanism for this finding is unclear. Note that the "focus on self" label does not imply selfishness, but, rather, seeing the self as the agent of change and valuing independence. Meanwhile, the "focus on others" label implies valuing and pursuing community or a group-oriented life.

Second, *character strengths have a developmental trajectory*. The components of character are moderately stable over time but not set in stone. Character strengths can and do change in response to specific events or as the result of maturation. Character strengths among youth and among adults are relatively stable across time, in keeping with our view of them as trait-like. Character strengths show an interpretable developmental trajectory. Similar to adults, among youth, interpersonal, humanity strengths (e.g., kindness, fairness, gratitude, love) are more frequently developed and displayed than are the temperance strengths (e.g., prudence, modesty, self-regulation). Although there is a degree of convergence when comparing the relative prevalence of strengths among youth and adults, there are also interesting differences. The most common strengths among youth are gratitude, humor, and love. The least common strengths among young children and adolescents are those that require cognitive maturation: for example, appreciation of beauty and excellence, authenticity, forgiveness, modesty, and open-mindedness (Park & Peterson, 2006a, 2006c; Peterson, 2006).

Third, *character strengths are distributed sensibly across sociodemographics*. A study with 111,676 adults from 54 countries and all 50 U.S. states found an interesting convergence in the relative prevalence of the 24 VIA strengths (Park, Peterson, & Seligman, 2006). Across almost all countries, the most commonly reported strengths were kindness, fairness, honesty, gratitude, and open-mindedness, and the least endorsed strengths included prudence, modesty, and self-regulation. Religiousness was the only character strength that showed differences within the U.S. sample as a function of state or geographical region. These results may suggest universal human nature and/or the minimum character requirements for a viable society (Bok, 1995). According to Bok (1995), kindness, love, and gratitude reflect what she identified as *positive duties* of mutual care and reciprocity; the strength of authenticity enables what she called *negative injunctions* against deceit and betrayal; and the strengths of open-mindedness and fairness underlie *norms for fairness and procedural justice* in cases of conflict regarding positive duties and/or negative injunctions.

We also examined demographic correlates of the VIA strengths among the U.S. sample (Peterson & Park, 2009). There were some modest and sensible differences. Females showed higher levels of the interpersonal strengths of gratitude, kindness, and love than males. Older adults scored higher than younger adults on strengths of temperance. Education level was associated with higher score on the strength of love of learning. Married respondents were more forgiving than those who were unmarried. African Americans and Asian Americans reported higher score on religiousness than European Americans.

Fourth, *character strengths differ across cities*. Although few differences in character strengths were found across larger geographical units such as countries, U.S. regions, or U.S. states, meaningful differences across cities were observed (Park & Peterson, 2010). We looked at character strengths among residents in the 50 largest U.S. cities and related these aggregated measures to city-level features like entrepreneurship and voting patterns. Differences in character strengths that were found to exist across cities were robustly related to important city-level outcomes such as entrepreneurship and presidential election voting and were associated in theoretically predicted ways with city-level features. Cities whose residents had higher levels of "head" strengths were those rated as creative and innovative. Differences in city residents' character strengths were also associated in theoretically predicted ways with city-level features. Residents in cities with greater strengths of the heart reported more positive affect, a greater orientation to positive emotions, and more meaning in life.

Fifth, *character strengths have important consequences that vary depending on the strength*. Certain character strengths are linked to flourishing and their absence to problems.

Strengths that are robustly related to life satisfaction and happiness for adults are love, gratitude, hope, curiosity, and zest (Park, Peterson, & Seligman, 2004a). Similarly, love, gratitude, hope, and zest are also robust predictors of life satisfaction for youth (Park & Peterson, 2006c; Park, Peterson, & Seligman, 2004b). In a study with children between three and nine years of age, parents were asked to describe their young children. Interestingly, parents who described their children as showing love, zest, and hope also described their child as happy (Park & Peterson, 2006a). Thus, there are common character strengths that are consistently associated with life satisfaction for people across all ages. They are love, hope, and zest. Gratitude, however, is related to life satisfaction for people seven years of age and older. Perhaps strengths such as gratitude may require cognitive maturation. These data imply that although the character strengths that contribute to an individual's well-being at younger ages continue to be significant, new character strengths also enter the picture as one ages.

Important aspects of healthy and flourishing life are also related to the character strengths (Peterson & Park, 2009). For example, students' academic achievement at the end of the school year was predicted by strengths of perseverance, love, and gratitude, among others, at the beginning of school year above and beyond their IQ scores; in a one-year longitudinal study, the strongest predictor for leadership performance among West Point cadets, rated by their commanding officers and peers, was a strength of love; popular students were more likely to score highly on civic strengths such as leadership and fairness and temperance strengths such as self-regulation, prudence, and forgiveness; the strengths of hope, zest, and leadership were significantly related to fewer internalizing problems such as depression and anxiety disorders, whereas the strengths of persistence, honesty, prudence, and love were substantially related to fewer externalizing problems such as aggression; although the self-regulation of a parent was not strongly related to the parent's own life satisfaction, it was related to their children's life satisfaction; perception of one's job as a calling and high job satisfaction were both related to higher levels of zest.

Furthermore, the consequences of character in which we are most interested are often associated with several character strengths, implying considerable complexity. For example, good leaders possess not only social intelligence but also the capacity to form close emotional relationships with others. Medal of Honor winners are not only brave but also capable of exceptional self-regulation (Park, 2005). In many cases, character strengths of perseverance, self-regulation, teamwork, and leadership are evident as well. There is additional evidence that Medal of Honor recipients exhibit humility (Collier, 2003).

Sixth, *character strengths are influenced by genetics, but also by family, friends, and teachers.* Although we know little about the origins of character strengths, it seems that a variety of influences contribute to the development of good character—genetics, family, schools, peers, and communities. As expected, the character strengths of parents and children converge, in particular, between fathers and sons and between mothers and daughters. A twin study showed that strengths are moderately heritable (Steger, Hicks, Kashdan, Krueger, & Bouchard, 2007). This result is consistent with many individual differences. The study also showed that some of the strengths, such as love of learning, are influenced by a shared family environment. This is a rather unusual finding because, once genetics are controlled for, any influence of growing up in a given family is rarely observed (Dunn & Plomin, 1992). For positive characteristics, family influence may be more relevant than it is for negative characteristics, which are often the focus of twin studies. For all VIA strengths, the most important influence was found to be the nonshared family environment such as peers and teachers.

Seven, *character strengths are changed and/or revealed by challenge.* Dramatic life events can increase certain character strengths. For instance, in a longitudinal study the character strengths of religiousness, hope, and love were elevated among U.S. respondents in the six months after the 9/11 attacks. However, this change was not observed among European respondents (Peterson & Seligman, 2003). People who recovered successfully from psychological disorders showed modest increases in the strengths of appreciation of beauty and love of learning, whereas those who recovered successfully from physical illnesses showed modest increases in the strengths of bravery, kindness, and humor (Peterson, Park, & Seligman, 2006). Individuals who experienced a variety of adverse life events reported higher levels of the character strengths of religiousness, gratitude, kindness, hope, and bravery. These are the components of post-traumatic growth (Peterson, Park, Pole, D'Andrea, & Seligman, 2008). Higher levels of these strengths are associated with greater life satisfaction. Based on these results, it is conceivable that in the face of challenging life events, certain character strengths may function as a buffer and help sustain or even promote well-being (Park, 2012).

What We Still Want to Learn About Strengths of Character

The field of character strengths has made significant scientific progress over the last decade, as was described in the previous section. However, further work, both conceptual and empirical, needs to be done to continue to advance our understanding of the structure and nature of character strengths and refine our research and applied efforts. Additionally, advancements in measurement and statistical techniques could help further the study of character strengths. In this section, we would like to discuss several important considerations that require careful attention from the scientific community in light of conceptual and methodological issues in studies of character.

Issue of Conceptualization of Character Strengths as Positive Traits

Theodore Roosevelt said, "A vote is like a rifle; its usefulness depends upon the character of the user." We have had a nagging question about studying character strengths as positive traits. Does having positive traits such as love of learning, curiosity, creativity, humor, zest, and leadership make someone a necessarily morally good person? Although character strengths are generally defined as morally valued traits, several character strengths in the VIA Classification are positive traits but not moral traits. If we have to qualify a positive trait by saying its moral value depends on the character of the person displaying it, that positive trait, in and of itself, is not a character strength. We dubbed this the *Hitler problem*. That is, leadership is one of the positive traits on which we have focused, but leadership per se is not a character strength. This is because the moral worth of being a leader depends on how one behaves as a leader. There are leaders who do morally praiseworthy things, like Lincoln, Gandhi, and Mandela, but there are also leaders who do reprehensible things, like Pol Pot, Gaddafi, and, of course, Hitler. But the evil leaders are still leaders, and whatever else we may think about Hitler, most of us would agree that he was an effective leader, morality aside.

So maybe leadership should not be considered a character strength, at least not without appropriate and heroic qualifications. The same point can also be made about some of the other positive traits included among our ostensible character strengths, those which can be morally good or bad depending on how they are manifested. Consider humor, which can bring people together or drive them apart. Other positive traits included among our ostensible character strengths like zest and creativity are best described as morally neutral.

In general, people assume that having positive traits makes someone a better person. For example, a positive trait such as emotional intelligence has been popularized in the media as a requirement for moral conduct (Goleman, 1995). Some studies have supported these assumptions. Emotional intelligence has been linked to more prosocial behavior (Penner, Dovidio, Piliavin, & Schroeder, 2005), being less critical to others (Brackett, Rivers, Shiffman, Lerner, & Salovey, 2006), being less aggressive toward others (Brackett & Mayer, 2003), and helping others more (Lopes, Salovey, Côté, & Beers, 2005). However, there have also been studies that reported the opposite findings. Contrary to our assumption, a study found that school bullies were good at understanding others' emotions (Sutton, Smith, & Swettenham, 1999). More recently, interesting research by Côté, DeCelles, McCarthy, Van Kleer, and Hideg (2011) found that the trait of emotional intelligence, akin to what we describe as social intelligence, is not only associated with prosocial behavior, but also with antisocial behavior. It all depends on the personality trait, which means that social intelligence, certainly a desirable trait in the abstract, is not necessarily a character strength. In the first study, they found that people with a higher moral identity were kinder to others and they were even more so if they also had a higher emotional intelligence. In the second study, people who were found to be more Machiavellian tended to treat their coworkers badly; furthermore, having a higher emotional intelligence made them behave even worse.

Our point here is not the same as the argument that there can be too much of a good thing (Grant & Schwartz, 2011), although it is related. Aristotle's *doctrine of the mean* proposes that all virtues reside between two extremes, each of which can be considered a vice. So, too much humor (or wit as Aristotle termed it) is buffoonery, and too little humor is dourness (Peterson, 2006). Our point is a more general one: other things being equal, not all positive traits (meaning dispositions that are desirable) are necessarily character strengths.

This does not mean that the empirical research people have done on positive traits is invalidated. The research results remain important. By all means, we should continue to study positive traits, not just those on which our research team has focused, but others as well. Positive traits are those which are admired in the abstract and typically lead to desirable outcomes. However, we would like to suggest that researchers and practitioners need to be conceptually careful. We should reserve the term character strengths for positive traits that are morally praiseworthy, without obvious qualifications.

We believe that some of the 24 strengths are cut from a different moral cloth than the others. Strengths like humor and zest are not morally valued in their own right but become morally valued when coupled with other strengths in the classification. So a humorous person is simply funny, but a humorous person who is kind is very special and morally praiseworthy. We call these value-added strengths and intend to study them further.

Issue of Tonic versus Phasic Character Strengths

Not all strengths of character show their characteristics equally across settings. Certain character strengths such as bravery can be observed on rare occasions. If researchers are interested in various character strengths, they cannot always study typical behavior. Some character strengths are observed at the high points of a person's life. These are the psychological equivalents of the personal bests tracked by athletes at all levels of ability. Muscle physiology distinguishes between *tonic activity* (the baseline electrical activity when muscles are idle) and *phasic activity* (the burst of electrical activity that occurs when muscles are challenged and contract)

(Park & Peterson, 2006b; Peterson & Seligman, 2004). Most of psychology is about tonic activity—typical thoughts, feelings, and actions. For example, introversion, intelligence, and hope are all measured in the absence of any real-world challenge, with the assumption that these summary measures will predict what a person actually does when challenged. At best, tonic measures are moderate predictors of phasic action, $r = .30$ upper limit (the so-called personality coefficient). Although for many purposes, moderate correlations are useful, they may miss what is most exceptional about people. Therefore, different strategies of assessment should be considered for *tonic* (e.g., kindness) vs. *phasic* character strengths (e.g., bravery).

The imperfect prediction of optimal action from tonic characteristics has been called the *Harry Truman effect* (Peterson & Seligman, 2001). After a largely undistinguished life, Harry Truman rose to the occasion after the death of President Franklin D. Roosevelt during the final months of World War II to become one of the most accomplished presidents of the United States. What made it possible for him to do so? Psychology has not yet provided clear answers to this question. Besides work on resilience (Luthar, Cicchetti, & Becker, 2000; Masten, 2001), psychology has few accounts of rising to the occasion, even though evolution has no doubt shaped people to respond well to challenges. We may all possess strengths that we do not display until we are truly challenged. Crises do not forge character, but they reveal it. If we are interested in studying people at their best when they display certain character strengths, it is necessarily a phasic psychology.

Therefore, we must be cautious about relying solely on summary measures. We must be interested not only in variation across people but also within people. No one wins multiple Congressional Medals of Honor. Researchers must consider that character strengths vary along the tonic-phasic continuum. The study of the more phasic character strengths requires different research strategies than the investigation of the more tonic character strengths.

Issue of Universal versus Culture-Bound Character Strengths

The VIA Classification is not an exhaustive classification of character strengths. There are many more than those on which past studies have focused. The VIA Classification includes positive traits that seem to be universally recognized and acclaimed, an assumption we are systematically confirming in studies around the world. Our original focus was on understanding what is common across respondents from different groups and not what is unique, and we believe that the commonalities we have discovered are both striking and real. In addition to using our Internet surveys, we have sought to establish the cross-cultural generality (or lack thereof) of our constructs by deliberately surveying people from different nations and cultures about their recognition and valuing of different strengths of character, using focus groups for nonliterate samples and written surveys for literate samples (Biswas-Diener, 2006; Peterson, Boniwell, Park, & Seligman, 2003). Furthermore, our colleagues around the world have translated our inventories into Chinese, French, German, Hindi, Italian, Japanese, Portuguese, Spanish, and Urdu. Preliminary data are consistent with the premise of universality. However, these projects are in progress.

In a culturally diverse society like the contemporary United States, there is good reason for researchers interested in character and its components to focus on widely valued positive traits and not those that some people have dubbed culture bound (Peterson & Seligman, 2004). Culture-bound strengths of character are positive traits valued in some places but not others, such as ambition, achievement, and autonomy in the contemporary United States and solemnity, filial piety, and interdependence in East Asian countries. Measuring character in a way that privileges culture-bound traits to the exclusion of more universally valued traits is likely to lack generality and, thus, validity. However, depending on the interests and purposes of a researcher or practitioner, attention to these culture-bound strengths may be important.

In some cases, what is meant by the good life will prove to be thoroughly situated in time and place, but in other cases, generalization will be possible. Consider investigations like those by Bok (1995) or Schwartz (1994) into the universality of values. Depending on the level of abstraction, given values can be described either as culture bound or as universal.

The ubiquity of positive psychology constructs is partly an empirical issue, and positive psychologists should use the research strategies of cross-cultural psychology to map out their boundaries. Samples of research participants from different cultures should be studied, the equivalence of measures should be demonstrated, and constructs of concern should not just be exported (from Western cultures to elsewhere) but imported (from elsewhere to Western cultures). Our own research on character strengths has emphasized cross-cultural commonalities. From conceptual and methodological perspectives, it was a more sensible decision to take the universal-commonality approach in the study of character at the initial stage of the project. However, as we learn more about this topic, it is time to expand our efforts to include culture-bound positive traits. The investigation of what is culturally unique is just as important and needs serious attention.

Issue of Longitudinal and Multivariate Research Designs

The development and consequences of character strengths unfold over time, and researchers must, therefore, undertake longitudinal studies. We need more research that will elucidate development, correlates, consequences, and mechanisms of good character within a comprehensive framework that emphasizes its dynamics and interactions across cultures, social contexts, outcomes, and stages of life span development.

Most character research thus far has been cross-sectional correlational studies or short-term longitudinal studies. These studies can provide important insights into the topics of concern by providing snapshots of phenomena, but it must eventually be placed in larger perspective. We need ambitious longitudinal studies that start with young people and follow them over time to reveal the processes that promote flourishing.

We currently know something about the cross-sectional correlates and short-term consequences of character; however, we know relatively little about the origins of positive traits, their development, and long-term consequences. Our research that compared the relative frequencies of character strengths among youth and adults (Park et al., 2004b, Figure 4.1) indicated that there were developmental differences in character strengths described earlier in this chapter. Some strengths, such as authenticity, open-mindedness, and appreciation of beauty, were less common among youths than adults. These strengths may require cognitive and emotional maturation in order to appear. However, we do not know how these transitions occur during the developmental process.

Another study on parental descriptions of character strengths among very young children revealed that even very young children possess various character strengths (Park & Peterson, 2006a). However, there is still much that is not yet known, including the early manifestation of each character strength, the precursors of certain character strengths in different developmental stages, and how strengths change and are maintained throughout life. Some character strengths may be rooted in temperament differences like sociability and may take on moral meaning very early in life. For example, the infant-mother relationship may set the stage for the character component we identify as love (Ainsworth, Blehar, Waters, & Wall, 1978), and early sibling relationships may be the crucible for the character strength of kindness (Dunn & Munn, 1986). Other components of good character—like open-mindedness and fairness—require a degree of cognitive maturation, as developmental psychologists have long documented (cf. Kohlberg, 1981, 1984; Piaget, 1932). These are empirical questions that need to be answered.

Future studies on the natural history of good character might profitably be patterned on the Terman (1925) study of adolescent geniuses, and the Grant Study of the best and brightest of Harvard University undergraduates (Vaillant, 1977) in the sense that they be large scale—large samples, longitudinal designs, and multiwave assessments—not because they start with the most fortunate or the most privileged in our society. Studies of individuals in difficult circumstances—so-called "at-risk" samples—might be especially interesting if the focus were on how they rise to the occasion and flourish despite adversity. Strengths of character do not belong just to the "haves" of the world. They are also found among the "have-nots."

Because of its complex nature with a multidimensional structure, this is quite a challenging task with traditional statistical techniques. However, with advances in the field such as *latent growth modeling* technique (Curran & Muthén, 1999), longitudinal studies will help shed light on the normative developmental process of character strengths, the predictors and correlates of individual differences in growth pattern and growth rates of different components of character strengths, and the short-term and long-term psychosocial and behavioral consequences of different character strengths. Hopefully, this method will help us identify people with outstanding specific character strengths and give us insight into how the development of their strength is different from or similar to that of others. This will also give us valuable information for developing youth intervention and prevention programs.

Furthermore, we know nothing about the dynamic processes of character strengths in a healthy and thriving life and the potential neurobiological, emotional, behavioral, social, environmental, and cultural mediators and moderators of those processes. With the progress of studies of character, research attention should turn to understanding the mechanisms and processes that underlie positive phenomena and go beyond mere description. In addition, there are multiple routes to building and sustaining good character. We speculate that there is no single right way to good character, but rather there exist various routes to good character. We do not back off from endorsing good character as a goal for all, but we must recognize that character strengths can develop in different ways and show themselves in different forms. Good character is not only plural but diverse. Multivariate studies are therefore demanded in studying character strengths.

Issue of Measurements of Character Strengths

With a few exceptions, most studies of character to date have heavily depended on self-report online survey methods with a more educated adult sample. We need to utilize more diverse samples and research methods to generalize findings. But more importantly, character strengths are not found only in what people say and how it is said, although they are good places to start. If we truly want to understand anyone's strengths of character, we also really need to look at what a person actually does.

Most philosophers emphasize that moral activity involves choosing virtue in light of a justifiable life plan (Yearley, 1990). This characterization means that people can reflect on their own strengths of character and talk about them to others. Self-report surveys are, therefore, one reasonable way to assess the components of character. However, there are also legitimate concerns about the pitfalls of self-report and the validity threat (Crowne & Marlowe, 1964). There is the possibility that some strengths of character lend themselves less readily to self-report than do others. For example, strengths like authenticity, humility, and bravery are not the sorts of traits usually attributed to oneself. But this consideration does not preclude the use of self-report to assess other strengths of character. In order to improve the validity of assessment, additional or alternative strategies are needed, such as reports from knowledgeable informants (family members, friends, and teachers), in vivo observations, and scenario methods. Different strategies of assessment should converge.

In addition to self-report, researchers must turn to knowledgeable informants as well as more objective indices of thriving. There is a temptation to treat multiple sources of information as idiosyncratically fallible but substantively interchangeable (Campbell & Fiske, 1959). Certainly, different research strategies provide checks on one another, and we would not expect different sources of information to be routinely orthogonal in what they convey. But it is also important to appreciate that each source of information can provide a unique vantage on a topic. Therefore, we like the metaphor of 360-degree methodology, meaning that different sources of information are not automatically combined into a single composite; rather, they are used to create a picture with breadth and depth (Hedge, Borman, & Birkeland, 2001). For example, in our studies of character strengths, we have found that observers (friends, parents, teachers) usually agree with research participants about the presence or absence of traits like kindness and humor that are displayed interpersonally— that is, publicly—but not necessarily about more private strengths like spirituality.

Although we anticipate that these different methods will converge in the strengths they identify within given individuals, each method will also provide unique information about good character.

In addition, the good character is one that has significance to the person who owns it. Positive psychologists must tackle meaning head on in their research, which means it cannot be modeled on natural science approaches that study phenomena solely from the outside. Beside quantitative methods, researchers must take seriously stories, narratives, and accounts, the typical starting points for qualitative research. Case histories of exceptional individuals should be encouraged, historical archives and cultural products should be consulted, and the sociocultural context should always be kept in mind.

Issue of VIA Classification as a Work in Progress

The VIA Classification is a work in progress. At the beginning of the VIA project, it was not wedded to a given theory. An impetus for the project was the need to know more about good character, and no consensual theory had emerged within psychology or elsewhere up to that point. The classification was best described as aspirational, meaning that it attempted to specify mutually exclusive and exhaustive categories of moral traits without claiming finality or a deep theory (Bailey, 1994).

The hierarchical organization of the VIA Classification—strengths under virtues—is a conceptual scheme and not a hypothesis to be tested with data. Indeed, several empirical investigations of the structuring of character strengths (Gillham et al., 2011; McGrath, 2014; Park & Peterson, 2005a; Park & Peterson, 2009a) yield a coherent picture but not exactly the one implied in Table 4.1. Future studies could help us establish a conceptually driven but empirically validated VIA classification system and character strengths measure.

The classification should not be a locked system, but iteratively changed as empirical data accumulate. Some existing strengths may be dropped, others may be combined, and still other strengths may be added. Exiting criteria provide the guidelines for changing the VIA Classification (Park & Peterson, 2005b; Peterson & Seligman, 2004). Studies to date have demonstrated that strengths of character can be specified and measured as a multidimensional construct. Given this success, challenging but exciting tasks are ahead of us. With the help of state-of-the-art quantitative as well as qualitative research methods, we will know more about strengths of character and how to cultivate them. The new studies of character strengths require new perspectives on both conceptualization and mea-sures. As much as traditional approaches can contribute to the study of character, methodological issues and new approaches must be considered when the subject matter of research entails good character (Park & Peterson, 2003).

Implications for Practice

Cultivation of Character Strengths

Given the important and desirable consequences of character strengths, questions, of course, arise about how they might be cultivated and strengthened. It is not known exactly how each of the strengths of character are created, changed, and sustained, because the VIA Classification is deliberately descriptive and not based on a single theory. However, we have some ideas about how they might develop.

Character strengths are like habits that are reflected in our thoughts, feelings, and actions (cf. Aristotle, BCE 350/2000). When character strengths are described as trait-like, it means that they are relatively stable across time and relatively general across situations. Although character strengths are moderately heritable, as we have measured them, this does not mean that they are unchangeable (Peterson, 2006). According to Aristotle, virtues—a reflection of the individual's character—can be taught and acquired only by practicing them. He argued that a virtue is a habit that a person can develop by choosing the good and consistently acting in accordance with it. Other scholars have similarly emphasized that character must be developed by action and not merely by thinking or talking about it (e.g., Maudsley, 1898). These approaches suggest that character can be cultivated by appropriate parenting, schooling, and socialization and that it becomes manifested through habitual action.

Role Models

Positive role models are important for character development (Bandura, 1977; Sprafkin, Liebert, & Poulos 1975). Important adults in young people's lives may play roles as character mentors. If adults value and want to teach young people good character, they should start by showing them how to do so through their own actions. James A. Baldwin famously said, "Children have never been very good at listening to their elders, but they have never failed to imitate them." The power of modeling over preaching in cultivating character strengths has been well documented. In a classic experimental study (Rushton, 1975), 140 children ages seven to eleven played a game to win tokens, where they were given the option to either keep all of them for themselves or donate some to a child in poverty. First, they observed an adult playing the game either selfishly or generously, and then they were preached to about the value of taking, giving, or neither. The results showed that actions spoke louder than words. When children watched the adult behave generously, the children acted the same way, regardless of whether the adult verbally advocated selfishness or generosity. When the children watched the adult act generously, they donated 85 percent more than the norm whether generosity was preached or not. Even if the adult preached selfishness, after watching the adult act generously, children still donated 49 percent more than the norm. This experiment had lasting effects even two months later.

We assume that the situation matters not only in the acquisition of character strengths but also in their use. It is easier to display certain character strengths in some settings than in others. In the community where sharing and helping behaviors are valued and recognized, these prosocial behaviors can become a natural part of everyday life. In contrast, in a setting where genuine attention and gestures of aid are seen with suspicion, it discourages people to engage in such behaviors. It is important to create a society where it is easy for individuals to be and do good.

Strengths Vocabulary

Change does not occur in a vacuum, and the first step in cultivating character strengths is to legitimize a strengths vocabulary in whatever settings people happen to be. Here the VIA Project can be extremely helpful by providing the words with which we can describe our own strengths and those of others, strengths that already exist, and strengths that we want to build. With a strengths vocabulary in place, one needs to start using these words often enough so they become a natural part of everyday language.

Good character is not simply the absence of deficits, problems, and pathology, but rather a well-developed family of positive traits. Schools and programs should start to measure young people's assets, such as character strengths, as much as deficits. Measures of problems, deficits, and weaknesses have a long lineage within education and mental health, whereas measures of positive assets such as character strengths are neither as numerous nor as well developed (Park, 2009; Park & Peterson, 2005). Good character is not singular, but plural, and must be measured in ways that do justice to its breadth. Good character can only be captured by a set of components that vary across people. The VIA Classification provides a vocabulary for people to talk about character strengths in an appropriately sophisticated way (Park, 2004; Park & Peterson, 2008). Simply saying that someone has good character (or not) does not lead anywhere useful. In contrast, using the VIA Classification, people can describe the *profile* of character strengths that characterize each individual. The VIA measures not only allow the comparison of character strengths across individuals but also within individuals (e.g., rank ordered for the individual)— to identify one's signature strengths relative to his or her other strengths. We believe that everybody has strengths regardless of where they stand compared to others.

It has been said that one measures what one values and that one values what one measures (Park & Peterson, 2009b). If society really values good character, especially, among young people, we should start assessing character strengths and paying attention to how they develop. All educators, parents, and policy makers are busy measuring young people's academic abilities and monitoring their progress of learning. We hope that someday schools will assess the character strengths of students and record the progress of their development in addition to academic achievement. We hope more families, schools, workplaces, and communities will recognize, reward, and celebrate good character among its members.

Strength-Based Approach

Problem-focused approaches can be useful only in reducing and treating the specific targeted problems, but they do not necessarily prepare people to have healthy, fulfilling, and productive lives (Seligman & Csikszentmihalyi, 2000). In contrast, strengths-based approaches may pay much greater dividends, not only in preventing or reducing immediate problems, but also in the long run, in building moral, healthy, and happy people who can overcome challenges and enjoy a good and fulfilling life (Cowen, 1998; Park & Peterson, 2008). We have hypothesized that the exercise of signature strengths is particularly fulfilling. Consider a study with adults who completed a VIA survey, identified their top strengths, and were then asked to use these strengths in novel ways (Seligman, Steen, Park, & Peterson, 2005). Relative to a comparison group without this instruction, these individuals showed significant increases in happiness as well as decreases in depression at a six-month follow-up. Not surprisingly, these changes were evident only if research participants continued to use their strengths in new ways. Finding *novel* ways to use strengths every day is therefore critical and reflects the importance of ongoing personal effort in producing a flourishing life.

A strengths-based approach can be used with people at any level. Because signature strengths are the ones people already possess, it is often easier and more enjoyable to work with them and on them. Once people build their confidence by using their signature strengths, they can be taught how to use these strengths to work on less developed strengths. It is frustrating and difficult to work solely on weaknesses and problems because often people give up or become defensive about their problems. However, if discussions and interventions start with the strengths of individuals— things at which they are already proficient—rapport can be built and motivation increased.

This strengths-based approach may be particularly useful for working with people with a history of disability, poor achievement, and other troubles (e.g., Resnick & Rosenheck, 2006). When we compare these individuals against the norm, as often we do, it may be difficult to find anything at which they are good. However, if we compare the 24 VIA strengths *within* an individual, we can identify those strengths that are stronger than others for that person, enabling educators, parents, and professionals to help people use these strengths in their lives, in relationships, at play, and in school.

Most people want to do well and to live in happy and fulfilling ways. These goals are fundamental human desires and rights. But more often than not, people do not know how to find happiness and meaning in the right place and in the right way. Perhaps identifying character strengths is where we can start. Everyone has strengths. They need to be recognized, celebrated, strengthened, and used.

Conclusion and Future Directions

What is the good in a person? How can we cultivate good character in individuals and in a society? Although these are age-old questions that have captured attention from philosophers, theologians, and educators from the East to the West over centuries, scientific answers to these questions lie at the heart of contemporary positive psychology (Peterson, 2006). Positive psychologists have reclaimed good character and virtue as an important topic of study central to the understanding of what makes life worth living. Research has shown that character strengths have important consequences in the lives of individuals, families, and communities. Strengths of character buffer against negative outcomes, as well as enable positive outcomes in life (e.g., Park & Peterson, 2009; Peterson et al., 2008).

Two centuries ago, Thomas Jefferson wrote that "happiness is the aim of life, [but] virtue is the foundation of happiness." In his 2009 inaugural address, U.S. President Barack Obama eloquently stated that

> Our challenges may be new. The instruments with which we meet them may be new, but those values upon which our success depends—honesty and hard work, courage and fair play, tolerance and curiosity, loyalty and patriotism—these things are old. These things are true. They have been the quiet force of progress throughout our history.

He reminded us that virtues can help us survive and, indeed, thrive. He reminded us that cultivating character should be an important goal for all individuals and societies. He reminded everyone that virtue is, and always will remain, the foundation of a flourishing nation. Indeed, character matters—then and now.

The field is hugely indebted to Christopher Peterson for his pioneering work and dedication to the study of character (Peterson & Seligman, 2004).[1] Largely due to his leadership and scholarship, significant progress has been made in the study of character strengths regarding their definition, classification, measurements, correlates, and consequences. However, the study of character strengths is far from complete. A lot more work is needed to address gaps in the field and make meaningful strides in research and practice. Research on character is increasingly spreading outward to several areas, including how character relates to hard outcome measures (such as health, work productivity, and educational achievement), cultural differences and similarities of character, character development, character-based interventions, and the biological processes by which strengths of character give rise to actual behavior. Future studies will continue to refine measures and use empirical findings to understand the structure of character, its development, its long-term consequences, effective interventions, and the processes by which strengths of character give rise to healthy outcomes.

Five decades ago, Abraham Maslow, a humanistic psychologist (who actually used the phrase "positive psychology" to describe his own approach), made a distinction between "safety science" and "growth science" (Maslow, 1966). He viewed "safety science" like a "security system"—an approach that is ordering, stabilizing, cautious, and timid. This is in contrast with "growth science"—an approach that is more bold, courageous, discovering, and innovative. "Safety science" would be more attractive to the like-minded, on guard against critics and defensive, whereas "growth science" is open to opposing ideas and criticism, open to questioning its own work, and willing to be wrong. Maslow cautioned against science becoming too much of a "safety science." He suggested that a good scientist should be able to be both daring and cautious and to know when each is called for.

Researchers and practitioners need to learn from history and continue their efforts in finding answers to important questions of the discipline, all the while being informed by good science. Inspired by Maslow's "growth science" to discover truth about the good life, we need to constantly challenge ourselves, ask big questions, and take bold approaches. If it is worth doing, it is worth doing right. If we can muster the courage to take this "growth-based approach," we will be well on our way to achieving one of the most important goals we all share—cultivating and sustaining a happy, healthy, and morally good life, which is to say, the life most worth living.

Note

1. Christopher Peterson (1950–2012) was a professor of psychology at the University of Michigan who helped to found the field of positive psychology. He guided this discipline through the first decade of the 21st century until he passed away in 2012. When asked for a concise definition of positive psychology, Peterson coined the phrase "other people matter." One of his most influential works was the creation of a coherent classification of character strengths and virtues with reliable and valid strategies for assessing them—the Values in Action (VIA) Project. Subsequently, he extensively studied the conceptualization, correlates, and consequences of character strengths and virtues in a variety of populations and settings. His seminal works became a foundation of the field of character and virtues, and he paved the way for scholars to study these topics utilizing a more scientific approach.

References

Ainsworth, M. D. S., Blehar, M. C., Waters, E., & Wall, S. (1978). *Patterns of attachment: A psychological study of the strange situation.* Hillsdale, NJ: Erlbaum.

Allport, G. W. (1921). Personality and character. *Psychological Bulletin, 18,* 441–455.

Allport, G. W. (1961). *Pattern and growth in personality.* New York: Holt, Rinehart, & Winston.

Aristotle. (2000). *Nicomachean ethics* (R. Crisp, Trans.). Cambridge, England: Cambridge University Press [originally written ~BCE 350].

Bailey, K. D. (1994). *Typologies and taxonomies: An introduction to classification techniques.* Thousand Oaks, CA: Sage Publications.

Bandura, A. (1977). *Social learning theory*. Englewood Cliffs, NJ: Prentice Hall.

Baumrind, D. (1998). Reflections on character and competence. In A. Colby, J. James, & D. Hart. (Eds.), *Competence and character through life* (pp. 1–28). Chicago: The University of Chicago Press.

Biswas-Diener, R. (2006). From the equator to the North Pole: A study of character strengths. *Journal of Happiness Studies, 7*, 293–310.

Bok, S. (1995). *Common values*. Columbia, MO: University of Missouri Press.

Brackett, M. A., & Mayer, J. D. (2003). Convergent, discriminant, and incremental validity of competing measures of emotional intelligence. *Personality and Social Psychology Bulletin, 29*, 1147–1158.

Brackett, M. A., Rivers, S., Shiffman, S., Lerner, N., & Salovey, P. (2006). Relating emotional abilities to social functioning: A comparison of self-report and performance measures of emotional intelligence. *Journal of Personality and Social Psychology, 91*, 780–795.

Campbell, D. T., & Fiske, D. W. (1959). Convergent and discriminant validation by the multitrait-multimethod matrix. *Psychological Bulletin, 56*, 81–105.

Collier, P. (2003). *Medal of Honor: Portraits of valor beyond the call of duty*. New York: Workman.

Confucius (1992). *Analects* (D. Hinton, Trans.). Washington, DC: Counterpoint.

Côté, S., DeCelles, K. A., McCarthy, J. M., Van Kleer, G. A., & Higeg, I. (2011). The Jekyll and Hyde of emotional intelligence: Emotion-regulation knowledge facilitates both prosocial and interpersonally deviant behavior. *Psychological Science, 22*,1073–1080.

Cowen, E. L. (1998). Changing concepts of prevention in mental health. *Journal of Mental Health, 7*, 451–461.

Crowne, D. P., & Marlowe, D. (1964). *The approval motive: Studies in evaluative dependence*. New York: Wiley.

Csikszentmihalyi, M. (1990). *Flow: The psychology of optimal experience*. New York: Harper and Row.

Curran, P. J., & Muthén, B. O. (1999). The application of latent curve analysis to testing developmental theories in intervention research. *American Journal of Community Psychology, 2*, 567–595.

Dahlsgaard, K., Peterson, C., & Seligman, M. E. P. (2005). Shared virtue: The convergence of valued human strengths across culture and history. *Review of General Psychology, 9*, 209–213.

Dunn, J., & Munn, P. (1986). Siblings and the development of prosocial behaviour. *Journal of Behavioral Development, 93*, 265–284.

Dunn, J., & Plomin, R. (1992). *Separate lives: Why siblings are so different*. New York: Basic Books.

Gillham, J., Adams-Deutsch, Z., Werner, J., Reivich, K., Coulter-Heindl, V., Linkins, M., . . . Seligman, M. E. P. (2011). Character strengths predict subjective well-being during adolescence. *The Journal of Positive Psychology, 6*, 31–44.

Goleman, D. (1995). *Emotional intelligence*. New York: Bantam.

Grant, A. M., & Schwartz, B. (2011). Too much of a good thing: The challenge and opportunity of the inverted U. *Perspectives on Psychological Science, 6,* 61–76.

Hedge, J. W., Borman, W. C., & Birkeland, S. A. (2001). History and development of multisource feedback as a methodology. In D. W. Bracken, C. W. Timmreck, & A. H. Church (Eds.), *The handbook of multisource feedback* (pp. 15–32). San Francisco: Jossey-Bass.

Hunter, J. D. (2000). *The death of character: Moral education in an age without good or evil.* New York: Basic Books.

Kohlberg, L. (1981). *Essays on moral development* (Vol. 1). *The philosophy of moral development.* New York: Harper & Row.

Kohlberg, L. (1984). *Essays on moral development* (Vol. 2). *The nature and validity of moral stages.* San Francisco: Harper & Row.

Lopes, P. N., Salovey, P., Côté, S., & Beers, M. (2005). Emotion regulation abilities and the quality of social interaction. *Emotion, 5,* 113–118.

Luthar, S. S., Cicchetti, D., & Becker, B. (2000). The construct of resilience: A critical evaluation and guidelines for future work. *Child Development, 71,* 543–562.

Maslow, A. (1966). *The psychology of science: A reconnaissance.* New York: Harper & Row.

Masten, A. S. (2001). Ordinary magic: Resilience processes in development. *American Psychologist, 56,* 227–238.

Maudsley, H. (1898). *Responsibility in mental disease.* New York: Appleton and Company.

McGrath, R. E. (2014). Scale- and item-level factor analysis of the VIA Inventory of Strengths. *Assessment, 21,* 4–14.

Nicholson, I. A. M. (1998). Gordon Allport, character, and the "culture of personality": 1897–1937. *History of Psychology, 1,* 52–68.

Park, N. (2004). Character strengths and positive youth development. *The Annals of the American Academy of Political and Social Science, 591,* 40–54.

Park, N. (2005, August 21). *Congressional Medal of Honor recipients: A positive psychology perspective.* Paper presented at the 113th Annual Meeting of the Conference of the American Psychological Association, Washington, DC.

Park, N. (2009). Building strengths of character: Keys to positive youth development. *Reclaiming Children and Youth, 18,* 42–47.

Park, N. (2012). Adversity, resilience, and thriving: A positive psychology perspective on research and practices. In R.A. McMackin, T. M. Keane, E. Newman, & J. M. Fogler (Eds.), *Toward an integrated approach to trauma focused therapy: Placing evidence-based interventions in an expanded psychological context* (pp.120–141). Washington, DC: American Psychological Association.

Park, N., & Peterson, C. (2003). Virtues and organizations. In K. S. Cameron, J. E. Dutton, & R. E. Quinn (Eds.), *Positive organizational scholarship: Foundations of a new discipline* (pp. 33–47). San Francisco: Berrett-Koehler.

Park, N., & Peterson, C. (2005a). Character strengths among youth. *Adolescent and Family Health, 4*, 35–40.

Park, N., & Peterson, C. (2005b). The Values in Action Inventory of Character Strengths for Youth. In K. A. Moore & L. H. Lippman (Eds.), *What do children need to flourish? Conceptualizing and measuring indicators of positive development* (pp. 13–23). New York: Springer.

Park, N., & Peterson, C. (2006a). Character strengths and happiness among young children: Content analysis of parental descriptions. *Journal of Happiness Studies, 7*, 323–341.

Park, N., & Peterson, C. (2006b). Methodological issues in positive psychology and the assessment of character strengths. In A. D. Ong & M. van Dulmen (Eds.), *Handbook of methods in positive psychology* (pp. 292–305). New York: Oxford University Press.

Park, N., & Peterson, C. (2006c). Moral competence and character strengths among adolescents: The development and validation of the Values in Action Inventory of Strengths for Youth. *Journal of Adolescence, 29*, 891–905.

Park, N., & Peterson, C. (2008). Positive psychology and character strengths: Application to strengths-based school counseling. *Professional School Counseling, 12*, 85–92.

Park, N., & Peterson, C. (2009a). Strengths of character in schools. In R. Gilman, E. S. Huebner, & M. J. Furlong (Eds.), *Handbook of positive psychology in the schools: Promoting wellness in children and youth* (pp. 65–76). Mahwah, NJ: Erlbaum.

Park, N., & Peterson, C. (2009b). Character strengths: Research and practice. *Journal of College and Character, 10*(4), 1–10.

Park, N., & Peterson, C., (2010). Does it matter where we live? Toward an urban psychology of character strengths. *American Psychologist, 65*, 535–547.

Park, N., Peterson, C., & Seligman, M. E. P. (2004a). Strengths of character and well-being. *Journal of Social and Clinical Psychology, 23*, 603–619.

Park, N., Peterson, C., & Seligman, M. E. P. (2004b). *Strengths of character and well-being among youth.* Unpublished manuscript, University of Rhode Island.

Park, N., Peterson, C., & Seligman, M. E. P. (2006). Character strengths in fifty-four nations and the fifty U.S. states. *Journal of Positive Psychology, 1*, 118–129.

Penner, L. A., Dovidio, J. F., Piliavin, J. A., & Schroeder, D. A. (2005). Prosocial behavior: Multilevel perspectives. *Annual Review of Psychology, 56*, 365–392.

Peterson, C. (2006). *A primer in positive psychology.* New York: Oxford University Press.

Peterson, C., Boniwell, I., Park, N., & Seligman, M. E. P. (2003). *Cross-national survey of character strengths.* Unpublished data, University of Michigan.

Peterson, C., & Park, N. (2003). Positive psychology as the evenhanded positive psychologist views it. *Psychological Inquiry, 14*, 141–146.

Peterson, C., & Park, N. (2009). Classifying and measuring strengths of character. In S. J. Lopez & C. R. Snyder (Eds.), *Oxford handbook of positive psychology* (2nd ed., pp. 25–33). New York: Oxford University Press.

Peterson, C., Park, N., Pole, N., D'Andrea, W., & Seligman, M. E. P. (2008). Strengths of character and posttraumatic growth. *Journal of Traumatic Stress, 21*, 214–217.

Peterson, C., Park, N., & Seligman, M. E. P. (2005). Assessment of character strengths. In G. P. Koocher, J. C. Norcross, & S. S. Hill, III (Eds.), *Psychologists' desk reference* (2nd ed., pp. 93–98). New York: Oxford University Press.

Peterson, C., Park, N., & Seligman, M. E. P. (2006). Greater strengths of character and recovery from illness. *Journal of Positive Psychology, 1*, 17–26.

Peterson, C., & Seligman, M. E. P. (2001). How can we allow character to matter? *University of Michigan Business School Leading in Trying Times Webpage.* Retrieved from http://www.bus.umich.edu/leading/index.html

Peterson, C., & Seligman, M. E. P. (2003). Character strengths before and after September 11. *Psychological Science, 14*, 381–384.

Peterson, C., & Seligman, M. E. P. (2004). *Character strengths and virtues: A handbook and classification.* New York: Oxford University Press/Washington, DC: American Psychological Association.

Piaget, J. (1932). *Moral judgment of the child.* New York: Harcourt, Brace.

Rachels, J. (1999). *The elements of moral philosophy* (3rd ed.). New York: McGraw-Hill.

Resnick, S. G., & Rosenheck, R. A. (2006). Recovery and positive psychology: Parallel themes and potential synergies. *Psychiatric Services, 57*, 120–122.

Rushton, J. P. (1975). Generosity in children: Immediate and long-term effects of modeling, preaching, and moral judgment. *Journal of Personality and Social Psychology, 31*, 459–466.

Schwartz, S. H. (1994). Are there universal aspects in the structure and content of human values? *Journal of Social Issues, 50*(4), 19–45.

Seligman, M. E. P., & Csikszentmihalyi, M. (2000). Positive psychology: An introduction. *American Psychologist, 55*, 5–14.

Seligman, M. E. P., Steen, T. A., Park, N., & Peterson, C. (2005). Positive psychology progress: Empirical validation of interventions. *American Psychologist, 60*, 410–421.

Smart, N. (1999). *World philosophies.* New York: Routledge.

Snibbe, A. C., & Markus, H. R. (2005). You can't always get what you want: Educational attainment, agency, and choice. *Journal of Personality and Social Psychology, 88*, 703–720.

Sprafkin, J. H., Liebert, R. M., & Poulos, R. W. (1975). Effects of a prosocial televised example on children's helping. *Journal of Experimental Child Psychology, 20*, 119–126.

Steger, M. F., Hicks, B., Kashdan, T. B., Krueger, R. F., & Bouchard, T. J., Jr. (2007). Genetic and environmental influences on the positive traits of the Values in Action classification, and biometric covariance with normal personality. *Journal of Research in Personality, 41*, 524–539.

Sutton, J., Smith, P. K., & Swettenham, J. (1999). Social cognition and bullying: Social inadequacy or skilled manipulation? *British Journal of Developmental Psychology, 17*, 435–450.

Terman, L. M. (1925). *Genetic studies of genius* (Vol. 1) *Mental and physical traits of a thousand gifted children.* Stanford, CA: Stanford University Press.

Vaillant, G. E. (1977). *Adaptation to life.* Boston: Little, Brown.

Yearley, L. H. (1990). *Mencius and Aquinas: Theories of virtue and conceptions of courage.* Albany, NY: State University of New York Press.

CHAPTER FIVE

Current Theories and Research in the Psychology of Gratitude

Philip C. Watkins and Joshua Bell

How much has psychology been interested in the topic of gratitude? In the century before the year 2000, a PsycInfo keyword search shows only 44 citations dealing with gratitude (.44 per year), whereas from 2000 to 2015, fully 583 publications dealt with gratitude (36.44 per year). Although this upsurge must be interpreted against the backdrop of the general increase in psychology publications over this duration, this 82-fold increase demonstrates how gratitude has captured the interest of researchers recently.[1] Why the huge increase of interest in gratitude? If our experience is any indication, it might be because in study after study, gratitude shows positive results, and naturally researchers pursue those topics that bear fruit. Indeed, research has shown that gratitude is one of the foremost strengths predicting subjective well-being (SWB), and treatment outcome studies have consistently shown that gratitude interventions have enhanced happiness (Watkins, 2014). Although a few reviews have cast doubt as to how effective these treatments actually are (Davis et al., 2016; Wood, Froh, & Geraghty, 2010), there is now adequate evidence to suggest that it is not just that grateful people tend to be happy people; gratitude actually *causes* increases in SWB (for reviews, see Watkins, 2014; Watkins & McCurrach, in press).

In this chapter we will review current research in the context of important theories of gratitude. Although an exhaustive review is beyond the scope of this chapter, our somewhat selective review will highlight the strengths and weaknesses of these theories. We have divided gratitude theories into three major categories: theories of the nature of gratitude, theories about what causes gratitude, and theories about how gratitude enhances well-being. Following our discussion of these theories, we will conclude the chapter by presenting a theory on appreciation—a construct we believe is crucial for the science of gratitude to progress. With this approach we hope that readers will gain a good understanding of the current state of the science of gratitude.

Theory and Research on the Nature of Gratitude

What is gratitude and what is it like? This is obviously a fundamental question for a science of gratitude to progress. Before delving into this question, however, it is important that we are clear as to the level of analysis that we seek to explain gratitude, and here we follow Rosenberg's (1998) approach. She argued that emotion can be studied at any of three different levels of analysis: affective trait (one's general disposition toward a certain emotion), mood (a more background level of a particular emotion that lasts longer than emotions but is not about anything in particular), and emotional state (the immediate—usually brief—psychophysiological response to an appraisal of a particular circumstance). Because little work has investigated gratitude as a mood (but see McCullough, Tsang, & Emmons, 2004), we will focus on the nature of gratitude as an emotion and an affective trait.

First, we discuss the nature of grateful emotion. Following Emmons' approach (2004), we have defined grateful emotion as the emotion people experience "when they affirm that something good has happened to them, and they recognize that someone else is largely responsible for this benefit" (Watkins & McCurrach, in press). Although this definition has several controversial aspects, virtually all gratitude scholars agree that gratitude is an emotion that results when a benefit is appraised as being caused by outside forces. But what is the *nature* of grateful emotion? Here, we find that McCullough, Kilpatrick, Emmons, and Larson's (2001) moral affect theory is still a useful model for understanding gratitude.

Perhaps the paper that launched the recent wave of gratitude research was McCullough and colleagues' (2001) review of gratitude research, which proposed that gratitude was a moral emotion. Up to that point, there were no research programs that targeted gratitude, but a number of studies had included gratitude as a variable. McCullough et al. (2001) argued that gratitude was a moral emotion in that it served as a moral barometer (the feeling of gratitude was an indicator of how good others had been to oneself), a moral reinforcer (the expression of gratitude was an effective reinforcer of benevolent acts), and a moral motivator (gratitude motivates good behavior toward others). At the time this article was published there was considerable evidence for the first two aspects of this theory but not much evidence supporting the third. Now, however, there is strong evidence that when one feels grateful, they are more likely to be helpful and kind to others, and we will review some of this evidence later in the chapter (DeSteno, 2009). Some have criticized this approach because "prosocial" could be effectively substituted for "moral" in their theory, and others have complained that the theory is "outdated," but we struggle to see how new data have in any way falsified this theory, and thus we maintain that McCullough and colleagues' moral affect theory effectively summarizes the nature of grateful affect.

We now turn to the nature of trait gratitude. Very simply, people high in the affective trait of gratitude should have a low threshold for gratitude; they should experience gratitude frequently across a wide variety of situations and benefits. McCullough, Emmons, and Tsang (2002) were the first to attempt to describe what the disposition for gratitude would look like, and they developed a measure that effectively measured trait gratitude (the GQ-6). These authors argued that people high in the disposition of gratitude should possess four co-occurring facets: intensity, frequency, span, and density. First, a grateful person should experience more *intensity* of gratitude in response to a favor or benefit. Second, people high in trait gratitude should experience gratitude more *frequently* than those low in gratitude. This implies that grateful people respond with gratitude to a wider variety of experiences than those lower in gratitude. Third, if asked what they are grateful for at a given point in time, grateful people should be more likely to cite a larger variety of experiences and life domains than less grateful people. This facet is what McCullough and colleagues referred to as *span*. Finally, these authors proposed that people high in dispositional gratitude should have the facet of *density*, which means that the grateful person will feel grateful toward a greater number of people for a particular benefit. For example, when a grateful person is awarded a grant, they should be more likely to attribute this benefit to a greater number of benefactors—the university grants department, colleagues, family members—in addition to themselves. The GQ-6 was developed based on this formulation of trait gratitude, and it has been the most utilized and successful of all the gratitude measures to date.

In our development of the Gratitude Resentment and Appreciation Test (GRAT) we took a somewhat different approach to the measurement of trait gratitude (Watkins, Woodward, Stone, & Kolts, 2003). In general, we felt that people with a grateful disposition would appreciate the giftedness of life; they would be able to see all of life as a gift. We reasoned that those high in the disposition toward gratitude should possess three related but distinct lower-order traits. First, we argued that grateful people should be high in the *sense of abundance*, or conversely, low in a sense of deprivation. In other words, grateful people should feel that the benefits they have received in life have been more than enough, whereas people low in trait gratitude should feel that they deserve and are entitled to much more good than they have received. Second, grateful people should be high in the *appreciation of simple pleasures*. Grateful people are not waiting for a trip to Maui to be grateful; they take joy in the simple mundane pleasures that they encounter every day. Our reasoning here was that simple pleasures are, by definition, more frequent than spectacular pleasures, and in order to experience gratitude frequently one must be able to appreciate the everyday benefits that cross one's path. Note how this lower-order trait of gratitude is related to the frequency facet in the conception of McCullough and colleagues (2002). Finally, we proposed that grateful people have an *appreciation for others*. Those with a low threshold for experiencing gratitude should appreciate the contributions of others in their life. This aspect of gratitude is likely related to McCullough and colleagues' facet of density. Although this may seem unsurprising, it is worth pointing out that it is quite possible for people to be aware of benefits without appreciating how others have contributed to those positive outcomes. We have now developed a shorter version of the GRAT, and this measure has also shown good validity (Thomas & Watkins, 2003; Diessner & Lewis, 2007; Froh, Fan, Emmons, Bono, Huebner, & Watkins, 2011). This scale has 16 items and contains items that loaded highest on each of the three lower-order traits.

As we close our discussion of dispositional gratitude, we would like to highlight a cognitive component that runs through all three of these lower-order traits of gratitude: *appreciation*. A sense of abundance demands that one appreciate the many benefits of life. Almost by definition, appreciation of simple pleasures implies that grateful people will not only notice the everyday benefits that come their way—they will go on to appreciate them. Finally, a grateful person does not merely acknowledge that others have contributed to their well-being—they go on to appreciate these contributions. Clearly, appreciation is a fundamental characteristic of gratitude, and research supports the conclusion that appreciation runs through all definitions and instruments that attempt to assess trait gratitude (Wood,

Maltby, Stewart, & Joseph, 2008). If appreciation is indeed the critical component of gratitude, then this is an important construct to explore. Surprisingly, with very few exceptions, researchers have not attempted to clarify the cognitive components of appreciation, and this is a theme we will return to throughout this chapter.

Theory and Research on the Causes of Gratitude

If gratitude is important to well-being, then it is important to understand the factors that lead to gratitude. Following our earlier format, we first discuss factors that are known to enhance the emotion of gratitude, followed by a discussion of the causes of trait gratitude.

Causes of Grateful Emotion

Gratitude is a cognitively imbued emotion in that much of a person's gratitude response depends on how they are thinking about a particular situation. There is considerable research on the cognitive appraisals that tend to create gratitude (see McCullough et al., 2001; Watkins, 2014 for reviews), and we have organized this research into what we have called the *four recognitions of gratitude* (Watkins, 2014). In other words, there are four cognitive processes that make a gratitude response more likely. First, in order for gratitude to ensue, one must *recognize the gift*. Stated differently, one must recognize that a benefit has occurred before one can feel grateful for the benefit. Although this is almost too obvious, it is important to highlight because individuals tend to become adapted to consistent benefits and then fail to take notice of them, which prevents grateful responses to these blessings. Indeed, as we shall argue later, a critical cognitive component of trait gratitude is that one notices and even looks for the benefits in their life.

Second, when people *recognize the goodness of the gift*, a grateful response is more likely. The more people psychologically value a gift, the more grateful they will be for that gift (McCullough et al., 2001). Here again, appreciation becomes important, and this recognition of gratitude highlights the importance of elucidating the psychological components of appreciation. In short, the more people see the value of a benefit to them, the more likely they will experience gratitude.

Third, research shows that gratitude is more likely when one *recognizes the goodness of the giver* (aka the altruism gratitude appraisal, e.g., Tesser, Gatewood, & Driver, 1968; Watkins, Wood, & Shields, 2016; Wood, Maltby, Stewart, Linley, & Joseph, 2008). In other words, when one believes that a favor was motivated in the giver by a genuine concern for their well-being, gratitude is more likely to ensue. On the other hand, if one believes that a benefit was provided for ulterior motives—for example, the giver would like to get some future favor from the beneficiary—gratitude is less likely to be experienced (Watkins, Scheer, Ovnicek, & Kolts, 2006). One aspect of the "goodness of the giver" is that the more one sees the cost of a benefit to the giver, the more gratitude results. Although the appraisal of cost has long been held to be an important facet of the appraisals important to gratitude (e.g., McCullough et al., 2001; Tesser et al., 1968; Wood et al., 2008), recent findings have cast some doubt as to the importance of this appraisal to gratitude (Scheibe, Watkins, McCurrach, & Mathews, 2016; Watkins, Sparrow, Pereira, & Suominen, 2013; Watkins et al., 2016). Clearly, more research needs to investigate the boundary conditions of the cost gratitude appraisal, but in general we may say that when one recognizes the goodness of the giver in the context of a benefit, gratitude is more likely to result.

Finally, when one recognizes the gratuitousness of the gift, one is more likely to experience gratitude. In other words, when a favor or benefit exceeds the receiver's expectations of the giver, the receiver is more likely to feel grateful. For example, oftentimes gratitude is more likely when gifts are received on dates other than one's birthday, because whereas one expects gifts on their birthday, one may not expect gifts on other days of the year. Clearly, individual differences likely bear on this recognition of gratitude because individuals differ widely in their expectations of others. For example, individuals high in narcissism probably expect much in terms of favors and benefits from others and because of these high expectations are less likely to experience gratitude, and indeed research shows that narcissists tend to be less grateful (e.g., Solom, Watkins, McCurrach, & Scheibe, 2016). In short, four recognitions characterize the cognitive predictors of the emotion of gratitude—when one recognizes the gift, recognizes the goodness of the gift, recognizes the goodness of the giver, and recognizes the gratuitousness of the gift, grateful responses are more likely.

Causes of Trait Gratitude

We turn now to the causes of dispositional gratitude. What causes a *person* to be grateful? What contributes to the development of gratitude as a trait? Although there is much research on the causes of grateful emotion, we should be quick to point out that the research on the development of dispositional gratitude is actually quite scant. Nonetheless, we believe that this is a very important question for the science of gratitude.

A very simple and straightforward theory takes the approach that those high in trait gratitude should habitually engage the four recognitions of gratitude discussed earlier. Thus, grateful people should easily recognize gifts, they should have a tendency to value and appreciate the gifts that come their way, they should be quick to recognize the goodness of the giver, and they should be less likely to feel as though they are entitled to benefits from others. Clearly, factors that enhance these cognitive tendencies should promote the development of dispositional gratitude. There is suggestive evidence that "counting blessings"—an exercise we shall later describe as *grateful recounting*—enhances one's ability to look for and notice the good in one's life (Emmons & McCullough, 2003; Watkins & McCurrach, 2016; Watkins, McCurrach, & Timbrook, 2016; Watkins, Uhder, & Pichinevskiy, 2015), but to date there is almost no evidence suggesting that gratitude treatments modify the interpretation biases that would be involved with the remaining recognitions of gratitude (Watkins et al., 2016). To be fair, only a handful of studies have attempted to investigate these mechanisms, and we will describe this issue in more depth when discussing how gratitude enhances well-being.

We are aware of only one study where the researchers actually attempted to teach the cognitive processes that are likely to be fundamental to trait gratitude. Because traits are difficult to change, it follows that dispositional gratitude should be difficult to enhance, but Froh and colleagues (2014) showed some success in changing trait gratitude. They developed and tested an educational program for youth designed to train cognitive appraisals that are important to gratitude (see also Froh & Bono, 2013). Specifically, this program trained students about the importance of the contribution of others in their life, and thus, was training them in "recognizing the goodness of the gift." Second, this treatment package trained their students to recognize the intentionality and cost of benefits from others, and in this way trained their participants to "recognize the goodness of the giver." Indeed, Froh and colleagues found that this educational program changed grateful appraisals as expected and resulted in increased well-being and expressions of gratitude compared to an attention-control group. We believe that this paper provides researchers with an important way forward for understanding how dispositional gratitude can be enhanced, and this treatment approach could be easily adapted for adults.

Nonetheless, this evidence for understanding the causes of trait gratitude is somewhat indirect because although they measured habitual appraisals that should be important to trait gratitude (through self-report), they did not measure trait gratitude directly. Furthermore, we propose that the program could be more effective by adding training procedures that encourage the "recognition of the gift" (noticing benefits in one's day-to-day experience) and "recognizing the gratuitousness of the gift." As we will describe in more detail later, we believe that grateful recounting exercises may indeed train individuals to notice and look for the good in their lives, but research has yet to confirm this hypothesis.

Perhaps an even more difficult question relates to how one can be trained to recognize the gratuitousness of the gift. Much research has shown that we easily adapt to consistent blessings in our lives and thus, we easily take for granted benefactors such as one's spouse or one's parents. We have suggested that one way to combat this process of adaptation is by simply identifying the implicit expectations one has of others (Watkins, 2014), although more theory and empirical research is needed. In sum, Froh and collaborators (2014) showed some success in modifying cognitive processes important to dispositional gratitude. More research should investigate how one might train the cognitive processes important to grateful responding.

We suggest that the *cognitive bias modification* paradigm may be uniquely adapted for such a purpose (Hertel & Mathews, 2011; Watkins & McCurrach, 2016). Research has shown that cognitive biases are associated with emotional disorders (for reviews, see Mathews & MacLeod, 1994; Williams, Watts, MacLeod, & Mathews, 1988). For example, anxiety is associated with negative interpretations of ambiguous situations (Eysenck, Mogg, May, Richards, & Mathews, 1991) and an attention bias to threat (e.g., Macleod, Mathews, & Tata, 1986). Depression is also associated with negative interpretation biases and negative memory bias (e.g., Watkins, Martin, & Stern, 2000; Watkins, Vache, Verney, Muller, & Mathews, 1996; for a review, see Watkins, 2002). Following the logic that these biases are actually important in causing anxiety and depression, researchers in the cognitive bias modification paradigm have developed computerized techniques that modify these biases. For example, using multiple training trials, individuals are encouraged to resolve ambiguous scenarios in a non-negative manner, and this training has been shown to change habitual interpretation tendencies and lower anxiety and depression (e.g., Mackintosh, Mathews, Eckstein, & Hoppitt, 2013; Mathews & Mackintosh, 2000; for a review, see Hertel & Mathews, 2011).

Might these cognitive training techniques be used to enhance habitual interpretation biases that might be associated with gratitude? Almost all benefit situations involve some ambiguity, and it follows that grateful people should be more likely to resolve this ambiguity in a positive manner. For example, if a colleague provides you with an article in your area of scholarship, you could interpret this as a benevolent act, or you could see this "gift" as an attempt to demonstrate your lack of knowledge. The interpretation of benefits is crucial to grateful responses. Recently we have found that trait gratitude is associated with positive interpretation biases of benefits (Scheibe, et al., 2016), and this leads to the hope that procedures from the cognitive bias modification approach may be used to train attention and interpretation biases that are important to gratitude.

The studies conducted by Froh et al. (2014) were based on the social-cognitive theory of gratitude developed by Wood and colleagues (2008). One unique aspect of this theory is that it combines aspects of the causes of trait and state gratitude. Briefly, they proposed that proximal benefit appraisals of value, cost to the benefactor, and altruism of the benefactor cause grateful emotions. Trait gratitude then is essentially defined as individuals who habitually make these appraisals in the context of benefits. Thus, according to this model, both situations and trait gratitude independently contribute to how one appraises a benefit. For example, a person who is high in trait gratitude should be more likely to appraise a Christmas bonus as valuable, as more costly to their employer, and as motivated by the good will of their employer, thus resulting in more gratitude for the bonus. On the other hand, a person who is low in trait gratitude would be likely to see the same bonus as less valuable, they might ignore the cost of the bonus to their employer, and might see the bonus as only an attempt by their workplace to get them to work harder. This pattern of appraisals would obviously result in a lower level of gratitude. Note, however, that the bonus itself is still critical in determining gratitude responses—one is not likely to engage in these appraisals at all unless they are aware of a benefit. In sum, what causes grateful emotion? Wood and colleagues (2008) proposed that a composite of appraisals determines gratitude responses, but these appraisals are independently determined by one's level of dispositional gratitude and by the benefit situation itself. Across three studies Wood et al. (2008) showed strong support for this theory, and we believe that this is an important model for understanding past research and for guiding future research on the causes of state and trait gratitude.

But why do individuals habitually make these gratitude-enhancing appraisals? Wood and colleagues (2008) argued that this composite of appraisals results from the activation of a *gratitude cognitive schema*. When a schema is activated from memory, it guides attention, encoding, and the interpretation of events. Whereas all individuals probably have a gratitude schema, these schemas should be more easily and chronically activated in grateful individuals (individuals high in trait gratitude). Moreover, these schemas are likely to be more organized and are associated with more positive memories, whereas the gratitude schemas of people low in trait gratitude should be less easily activated, less organized, and may even be associated with negative autobiographical memories. We believe that this theory has heuristic value and should be further explored by gratitude researchers, but it begs the question: How do grateful schemas develop? Why do some individuals have well-developed and easily activated gratitude schemas, but others do not? We turn now to this important question in the science of gratitude.

The Development of Dispositional Gratitude

How does the disposition of gratitude develop in a person? Stated even more simply, why are some people grateful but others are not? We believe that this is one of the most important questions facing the science of gratitude, but very few studies have investigated this issue. In theories about the development of gratitude the usual suspects are proposed, and parenting styles are often implicated as important for the development of gratitude. Although parental modeling and the encouragement of gratitude are likely to be important to the development of the grateful person, because almost no data speak to these causes, we limit our discussion of these theories (but see Froh & Bono, 2013).

It is not surprising that secure attachment has been proposed as fundamental to the development of gratitude (Watkins, 2014). In order for one to respond with gratitude to a benefactor, they must be able to trust them (i.e., recognize the goodness of the giver), and thus, being securely attached to one's caregivers is likely to influence the development of gratitude (Bowlby, 1988). Indeed, some evidence supports this theory. Correlational studies show that individuals high in trait gratitude are more likely to be securely attached (Lystad, Watkins, & Sizemore, 2005; Mikulincer, Shaver, & Slav, 2006), and in an experimental study we found that priming secure attachment enhances gratitude responses (Konkler, Nienhuis, Hutchinson, Vance, & Watkins, 2015). However, these studies were all conducted with adults, and longitudinal studies are clearly needed.

Although theorists have focused on the variables that might help create a grateful person, research supports the notion that most people are fairly grateful (McCullough et al., 2002; Watkins et al., 2003), and thus, the development of gratitude might be the default mode rather than an unusual circumstance. Similarly, Peterson (2006) argued that secure attachment should be the default mode of development (and research supports this idea, Colin, 1991), and thus we should focus more on what inhibits secure attachment rather than what promotes it. Similarly, it could be argued that just as secure attachment is the default mode of development, so is the trait of gratitude. Thus, it may be more beneficial to look for the factors that inhibit gratitude. Research again is scant on this issue, but recently we conducted a 2-month prospective study to investigate four putative inhibitors of gratitude: narcissism, cynicism, materialism/envy, and trait indebtedness (Solom et al., 2016). We found that narcissism, cynicism, and materialism predicted declines in gratitude over time, although the evidence for indebtedness was mixed. Narcissism and cynicism were the strongest of the "thieves of thankfulness," and it appeared that these two traits also acted in a vicious cycle: narcissism promoted cynicism and cynicism promoted narcissism over time. To our knowledge this is the first prospective study investigating inhibitors of gratitude, but we must conclude this section by highlighting the fact that we still know very little about the causes of dispositional gratitude.

Theory and Research on How Gratitude Enhances Well-Being

We turn now to a discussion of the link between gratitude and well-being and the mechanisms underlying this relationship. In other words, does gratitude enhance well-being? And how? Almost from the beginning of the recent wave of gratitude research, scholars have argued that gratitude is important to the good life; being grateful increases well-being. Although there have been some very strong statements made recently about gratitude causing happiness,[2] several recent reviews of experimental treatment outcome studies have cast some doubt as to the effectiveness of gratitude interventions for improving subjective well-being (Davis et al., 2016; Wood et al., 2010). Indeed in their meta-analysis, Davis et al. suggested that the effect size of gratitude interventions may be due to placebo effects. Although this was a needed review of the literature, in our view there were several problems with this meta-analysis, such as including studies with no evidence of treatment integrity. Also, effect sizes were apparently assessed only at post-treatment, and there is now evidence that the largest effect sizes for grateful recounting are often found in follow-up assessments (Seligman, Steen, Park, & Peterson, 2005; Watkins et al., 2015). To be fair to Davis and colleagues, most studies investigating gratitude treatments did not administer follow-up assessments of subjective well-being, and because there were a relatively small number of studies for their meta-analysis, they had to rely on post-treatment assessments. But we believe this is an important issue, and future research should also assess well-being using at least one follow-up assessment.

So do gratitude treatments merely encourage a placebo effect? The two most relevant studies that speak to this issue are Seligman et al. (2005) and Watkins et al. (2015). Both of these studies compared their grateful recounting treatment with a placebo treatment, and both studies showed that their placebo treatment had a significant effect on subjective well-being. But in both of these studies the grateful recounting treatment significantly outperformed the placebo treatment in improving well-being, and thus, we believe this speaks against the notion that gratitude treatments merely exhibit a placebo effect. Therefore, we submit that when considering the well-constructed studies that have evaluated the effectiveness of gratitude treatments, we can safely conclude that gratitude enhances subjective well-being (for reviews, see Watkins, 2014; Watkins & McCurrach, in press).

But *how* does gratitude enhance well-being? What are the mechanisms that can help us understand how gratitude increases happiness? We now turn to the theories and research that speak to this issue. Perhaps one of the most influential theories of positive psychology is Fredrickson's *broaden-and-build theory of positive emotions* (1998; 2001), which she has also applied to understanding gratitude (2004). She has argued that whereas negative emotions function to narrow attention and action tendencies so as to promote short-term survival, positive emotions broaden attention, cognition, and action tendencies that function to promote living well in the long-term. So whereas fear promotes a flight response to escape from immediate danger, gratitude may broaden thought action tendencies to promote well-being in the future. According to Fredrickson (2004), when one feels grateful this promotes creative cognition that results in a wide array of possible prosocial responses toward one's benefactor. For example, if one feels merely indebted to another for the gift of a meal, their response is likely to be a simple tit-for-tat response: they will return the favor with another meal. If, however, an individual feels grateful for a meal provided by someone, they will likely reflect on a number of ways in which they could express their gratitude, and providing a meal to their benefactor would be only one of many different responses they might consider. Although more research could be conducted to test the broaden hypothesis as it applies to gratitude, in a scenario study, we found that gratitude resulted in a broader array of action tendencies than indebtedness (Watkins et al., 2006). Moreover, we have argued that gratitude should also broaden one's scope of those who might be the recipients of one's prosocial grateful response (Watkins, 2014). In other words, although one's benefactor should be the primary focus of grateful responses, individuals who feel grateful will engage in prosocial responses to people in addition to their benefactors. In fact, some evidence supports this idea (e.g., Bartlett & DeSteno, 2006). We find the broaden hypothesis of gratitude to be intriguing, and yet very little research has directly tested this idea; thus we recommend more research be directed to the broadening effects of gratitude.

How do the broadening effects of gratitude build personal resources for the future? Fredrickson (2004) argues that gratitude builds personal resources in several ways. In general, she argues that gratitude may have transformative effects in that gratitude triggers *upward spirals*—or what we have called *cycles of virtue* (Watkins, 2004; 2014)—that promote well-being. Fredrickson argues that gratitude fosters self-sustaining systems that provide for continued growth. For example, gratitude exercises may help train individuals to attend to and appreciate benefits in their life, which should enhance future well-being. Two studies that investigated grateful recounting provide some support for this hypothesis, in that the subjective well-being of those in the gratitude treatments continued to climb after the intervention stage, in contrast to those in the placebo condition (Seligman et al., 2005; Watkins et al., 2015).

How do these upward spirals support long-term well-being? First, Fredrickson makes an interesting proposal that gratitude should strengthen spiritual bonds. Just as gratitude binds human relationships—an issue we will discuss further—gratitude should also strengthen one's relationship with the divine. Grateful people have been shown to be more religious and spiritual than those less grateful (e.g., McCullough et al., 2002; Watkins et al., 2003), and research into gratitude toward God lends additional support to this notion (Uhder, Webber, & Watkins, 2010; Watkins, Uhder, Webber, Pichinevenskiy, & Sparrow, 2011). To be sure though, this seems to be an important idea that deserves more research.

Second, Fredrickson (2004) argues that gratitude builds personal resources by creating more civil communities and organizations. Adam Smith (1790/1976) argued that gratitude was the glue that held free societies together, and we look forward to more studies that actually investigate this idea. Finally, Fredrickson asserts that gratitude should build social resources by building and strengthening social bonds. Because perceived social support is important to subjective well-being (Lakey, 2013), gratitude may build social resources that enhance happiness, and we now explore this idea in more detail in the context of Algoe's (2012) *find, remind, and bind theory of gratitude*.

Extending Fredrickson's broaden and build theory of gratitude, Algoe (2012) specifically attempts to explain how gratitude builds social resources through her find, remind, and bind theory. She argues that gratitude is important to the well-lived life because it helps us *find* new dyadic relationships that enhance our well-being, it helps *remind* us of existing relationships that support subjective well-being, and it assists in *binding* social bonds. Research shows that people like and value grateful people (e.g., Watkins, Martin, & Faulkner, 2003), when people feel grateful they tend to act in a prosocial manner (Bartlett & DeSteno, 2006; Watkins et al.,

2006; for a review, see DeSteno, 2009), expressed gratitude between roman-tic partners enhances their relationship (Algoe, Gable, & Maisel, 2010), and gratitude enhances social bonds (Algoe, Haidt, & Gable, 2008; Bartlett, Condon, Cruz, Baumann, & DeSteno, 2012). Thus, considerable evidence supports Algoe's theory, and one of the primary ways that gratitude might support subjective well-being is through building social resources.

We have proposed a more encompassing theory that we believe helps explain the gratitude and well-being relationship: *the amplification theory of gratitude* (Watkins, 2008; 2011; 2014). We propose that gratitude sup-ports subjective well-being in that it *amplifies* the good in one's life. Just as an amplifier increases the volume of sound going into a microphone, so gratitude psychologically amplifies the good it is focused on. Just as a mag-nifying glass enlarges the text it is focused on, so gratitude psychologi-cally magnifies the benefits it is focused on. We propose that gratitude enhances the signal strength of blessings in one's life. In short, this theory proposes that gratitude enhances the signal strength of who and what is good in one's life. When one is keenly aware of what is good in their life, they will spend more of their resources pursuing these things, which should enhance well-being. Moreover, when one is more conscious of the good in their life, this will enhance their sense of bounty, which should enhance life satisfaction. Gratitude—both as state and trait—should amplify the good one experiences in the present, it should amplify the good of one's past, and it should amplify the good in one's relationships.

How does gratitude amplify the good in life? First, we propose that grat-itude amplifies the good in our present experience. In other words, when we experience benefits with gratitude, positive affect is enhanced. It is somewhat surprising that little research has pursued this notion, but we did find that "gifts are better than goods" in that people said they would experience a benefit more positively if it were a gift rather than a mere good, and this effect was completely mediated by gratitude (Watkins et al., 2013). Second, gratitude may amplify the good in one's past, and thereby increase life satisfaction. In other words, gratitude may amplify the good in memory. In several studies we have found that grateful people have a more positive autobiographical memory bias than less grateful people, and in general their memories from the past have a more positive emotional impact when they recall them (Scheibe et al., 2016; Watkins, Grimm, & Kolts, 2004). Of course, autobiographical memory tasks such as these may be more reflective of past events than memory biases, but at minimum we can conclude that positive events from the past come to mind more easily for grateful than less grateful individuals. Moreover, when these events are recalled, they have a more positive emotional impact on grateful people.

Similarly, two recent experiments lend more support to the idea that processing memories with gratitude amplifies the good in those memories (Watkins et al., 2015; Watkins et al., 2016). Both of these studies tested the effects of a daily grateful recounting exercise on subjective well-being. In this version of grateful recounting, participants recalled "three good things" from the past 48 hours (similar to Seligman et al., 2005), and then they wrote about how each thing made them feel more grateful. In both of these studies, after the end of treatment participants in the grateful recounting condition recalled more positive events from the past week than those in the control conditions. Moreover, in our first study (Watkins et al., 2015), we found that those in the grateful recounting condition recalled more positive events than those in a "pride three-blessings" treatment. In the pride treatment individuals also daily recalled "three good things," but instead of writing about how each made them feel more grateful, they wrote about how these good things "make you feel better than others or better than average." Because participants from both three-blessings treatments were recalling an equivalent number of good things, it cannot be argued that the increase in positive recollection was simply because they were recalling positive events in their exercises. Because the gratitude three-blessings treatment enhanced recent memory bias more than the pride three-blessings treatment, it must have been the grateful processing that enhanced the memory bias.

Not only might gratitude amplify the good in positive events, some evidence suggests that gratitude also amplifies the good in bad events from one's past. First, we have found that grateful individuals are much more likely to use positive reappraisal in writing about troubling memories from their past (Hutchison, 2015). Second, a study of unpleasant open memories suggested that gratitude helps amplify the good in the bad. Briefly, an open memory is one that is an "open book" and has some unfinished psychological business associated with it. For example, memories of unsuccessful romantic relationships are often open memories for college students because the student doesn't quite understand why the relationship ended. We found that encouraging grateful reappraisal of a troubling "open" memory increased closure of the memory, decreased the memory's negative emotional impact, and decreased intrusiveness of the memory compared to a control condition or an emotional disclosure condition where participants wrote about their thoughts and emotions about the memory (Watkins, Cruz, Holben, & Kolts, 2008). Text analysis supported the idea that healing of the memory was enhanced because people in the grateful reappraisal condition wrote with a combination of positivity and insight about the troubling event (Uhder, Kononchuk, Sparrow, & Watkins, 2010). Thus, some research exists to support the notion that gratitude enhances well-being by amplifying the good in one's past.

Third, it is likely that gratitude also amplifies the good in one's social world, thereby supporting their well-being. For example, gratitude should amplify our awareness of how good others have been to us. In this way, regularly experiencing and expressing gratitude may help shape a more positive worldview. As reviewed previously, gratitude may also amplify our desire to do good to others. We have seen that gratitude is a strongly pro-social emotion, and we propose this is largely because it amplifies our desire to benefit others. We believe that the amplification theory effectively explains the research of how gratitude contributes to SWB, but the psychological processes of amplification need to be delineated. What are the psychological mechanisms of amplification? For example, we have argued that the amplification theory implies that processing positive memories with gratitude should enhance the accessibility of these memories (i.e., it should amplify them in our consciousness), it should enhance the positive emotional impact of these memories (it should amplify positive affect), and it should amplify the meaning and importance of these memories. Although we believe this theory explains the extant data well, we urge scholars to test this in future research. In sum, gratitude may enhance well-being because it amplifies the good in our experience of the present, it amplifies the good in our experience of the past, and it amplifies the good in our social world. In short, gratitude enhances the signal strength of what is good in one's life, and this may be why gratitude is so important to the good life.

Conclusions and Future Directions: Toward a Theory of Appreciation

Summary

In this chapter we have reviewed recent research in the psychology of gratitude through the lens of relevant gratitude theories. First, we presented theories of the nature of gratitude and found that McCullough and colleagues' (2001) moral affect theory was a helpful model for understanding grateful emotion. We also discussed theories related to the trait of gratitude. What helps us understand the disposition of gratitude? Grateful individuals are those who have a low threshold for gratitude, and we argued that this is because these individuals appreciate all of life as a gift. Three lower-order traits may contribute to this appreciation for life: appreciation for the bounty of life, appreciation for simple pleasures, and appreciation of others. We then presented the four recognitions of gratitude in an attempt to explain the cognitive causes of gratitude. Grateful emotion is more likely when one recognizes the gift, the goodness of the gift, the goodness of the giver, and the gratuitousness of the gift. We also explored how the trait of gratitude develops, with the admission that there is very little research on the development of the disposition of gratitude. Three characteristics probably inhibit this development, however: narcissism, cynicism, and materialism.

After reviewing studies that support the theory that gratitude enhances well-being, we then explored theories that help us understand this relationship. Gratitude may broaden our momentary thought action tendencies in a way that builds personal resources for our future well-being (Fredrickson, 1998; 2001; 2004). In particular, gratitude may build our social resources, and in this sense, Algoe's (2012) find, remind, and bind theory of gratitude is a useful model for understanding how gratitude enhances social well-being. Finally, we explained our amplification theory of gratitude (Watkins 2014), which attempts to explain how gratitude enhances well-being from a more global perspective. We argued that gratitude enhances well-being by amplifying the good in one's life. Although we believe that our amplification theory has heuristic value for explaining the gratitude and well-being relationship, it remains for us to delineate the psychological processes of amplification.

Future Research on Appreciation

It strikes us that much of what we have discussed thus far involves the psychological processes of *appreciation*. As we have tried to emphasize in this chapter, appreciation seems to run through many of the theories of gratitude we have discussed. For example, the four recognitions of gratitude must involve the psychological processes of appreciation. Moreover, the components of trait gratitude all seem to involve appreciation. Finally, it could be argued that the effectiveness of grateful recounting can be explained in that these exercises essentially train an individual in the cognitive processes of appreciation (Watkins & McCurrach, 2016; Watkins et al., 2016). But from a psychological perspective, what is appreciation? It is somewhat surprising to us that this topic has been relatively unexplored in psychology. Although the word "appreciation" is used in the psychological literature (e.g., in the aesthetic appreciation paradigm), rarely have researchers attempted to define this construct. This may be due in part to researchers feeling that appreciation is essentially a synonym for gratitude, and indeed "appreciative" is one of the three adjectives used in the Gratitude Adjectives Scale (McCullough et al., 2002), the most frequently used measure of grateful affect. Following Fagley (2016), however, we believe that although appreciation is closely related to gratitude, the two constructs should not be considered equivalent. Although the psychological processes of appreciation are crucial to grateful responses, they are neither sufficient to cause gratitude, nor does appreciation necessarily result in gratitude. Thus, we propose that an understanding of appreciation is crucial to progress in the science of gratitude. This is because appreciation involves cognitive processes foundational to gratitude, but appreciation may also result in other positive emotions distinct from gratitude (e.g., awe, elevation, etc.).

How can we best understand the psychological processes of appreciation? First, we will define appreciation in terms of cognitive processes. Although emotional processes undoubtedly become involved and may even influence cognitive processing as appreciation unfolds, we feel it is most helpful to understand appreciation as primarily a cognitive process. In our review of the literature, we believe that Janoff-Bulman and Berger have provided the most helpful definition of appreciation (2000; see also Janoff-Bulman, & Frantz, 1997. According to Janoff-Bulman and Berger (2000), when we appreciate something, there is an "[a]ppraisal of increased value or worth . . . We increase its perceived value in our eyes" (p. 32). When our home appreciates, its monetary value increases. When we appreciate something, the psychological value of the object increases.

Since we theorize that cognitive processes of appreciation are foundational to gratitude, the crucial question for future gratitude research is this: What cognitive processes lead to appreciation? As Janoff-Bulman and Berger (2000) rightly note, to appreciate something you must first notice it. "Attending and noticing" are necessary, but not sufficient, for appreciation to take place. Why don't we notice things that we might appreciate? Janoff-Bulman and Berger emphasize that often automatic processes prevent us from noticing things because, as we explained earlier, many benefits in one's life "fly under the radar," so to speak, because they are so regular and we adapt to them. Indeed, according to Janoff-Bulman and Berger this is one of the positive sides of trauma in one's life: often a trauma releases us from the automatic and we begin to notice simple blessings that were formerly taken for granted. For example, many individuals who go through trauma report an increased appreciation for life itself. Indeed, gratitude increased after the trauma of the events of 9/11 (Peterson & Seligman, 2003), and we believe this was probably because these disturbing events disrupted automatic processes such that people noticed benefits that they formerly took for granted. Can one be "released from the automatic" without going through trauma? We believe that one reason grateful recounting is effective is that it encourages and perhaps even trains individuals to notice benefits in life that they formerly took for granted (Watkins & McCurrach, 2016; Watkins et al., 2016). Perhaps positive attention bias training[3] might also assist individuals in taking notice of the positive in life (e.g., MacLeod & Clarke, 2015). In short, attending and noticing is the obvious first step to appreciation, and future research that investigates how individuals might enhance their awareness of the positive in life would be valuable.

Once something comes into our awareness, what cognitive processes underlie increasing its value? In general, processes that enhance the "specialness" of a benefit—where the ordinary is made extraordinary—should enhance appreciation (Janoff-Bulman & Berger, 2000, p. 32). How is this "specialness" created? First, Janoff-Bulman and Berger argue that we view things as more special when we acknowledge their potential unavailability, in their words, "that which we may lose is suddenly perceived as valuable" (p. 35). Thus, the *scarcity principle* helps explain how benefits become more special to us and thus enhances appreciation for a benefit. Some evidence supports this notion. Koo, Algoe, Wilson, and Gilbert (2008) found that people felt better about benefits when they thought about their potential absence than when they thought about their presence (the so-called "George Bailey effect"[4]). Similarly, we found that students felt more grateful when they vividly imagined their own death (Frias, Watkins, Webber, & Froh, 2011). Presumably this was because they became more aware of the possibility of death, which enhances the "specialness" of life. In the words of Chesterton, "Until we realize that things might not be, we cannot realize that things are" (1905/1986, p. 69). Janoff-Bulman and Berger also note that the more unique a benefit is, the more we will view it as special, thus enhancing appreciation. This begs the question, psychologically, what makes something unique? Cognitive psychology has a rich research tradition with regard to this question, and their findings should inform our understanding. Scarcity and uniqueness should contribute to the specialness of a benefit, but surely there are other cognitive processes that we have neglected, and thus we encourage further theory development here. What makes the ordinary extraordinary? We believe that this is an important question for future gratitude research.

Another important aspect of the appraisal of increased value is what Janoff-Bulman and Berger (2000) term "reciprocal valuing"—we value those who value us (p. 36). When benefits from others communicate to us that they value us, this enhances the "specialness" of the benefit and of those who value us, thus enhancing appreciation for both the benefit and the benefactor. Indeed, some evidence supports this notion. Algoe and colleagues (2010) studied how the anonymous gifts of older sorority sisters affected new sorority members' gratitude and their later relationship. One important finding of this study was that the more a gift communicated to the younger sister that the older sister was concerned for her unique needs, the more grateful she was, and this in turn positively affected their relationship formation later. In essence, gifts that communicated to the younger sister that she was valued resulted in greater gratitude. Similarly, Janoff-Bulman and Berger suggest that a perception of increased effort on the part of the benefactor should contribute to the benefit's perceived value and thus appreciation.

Janoff-Bulman and Berger (2000) also suggest that increased effortful understanding of the benefit should enhance its perceived value. Thus, the more time and effort one spends on understanding a benefit, the more she or he will tend to value it. This suggests that the more we engage with a benefit, the more we will tend to value it. We should be quick to note that not all additional information about a benefit will enhance appreciation. For example, if one finds out that a particular individual compliments everyone (i.e., the additional information makes the extraordinary ordinary), or if additional information about the favor suggests that it was motivated by selfish concerns (see Watkins et al., 2006), then appreciation should decrease rather than increase. But in general, we propose that increased engagement and absorption in a positive object should enhance appreciation. Our understanding of appreciation in this regard would clearly benefit from knowing what kind of information enhances appreciation, and it would seem as though the aesthetic appreciation literature may have something to offer us here (see, for example, Carlson, 2011). For us, this aspect of appreciation provokes another question for future research: How does absorption in the object enhance gratitude? Once again, in this regard the aesthetic appreciation literature is likely to provide a good guide for future research (Leder & Nadal, 2014), as well as the flow research tradition initiated by Csikszentmihalyi (e.g., 2000).

In sum, Janoff-Bulman and Berger (2000) propose that appreciation is essentially increased perception of value. Very simply, the "specialness" of a benefit should enhance perception of value and appreciation. Thus, they propose that there are three basic psychological processes underlying appreciation: perceptions of scarcity and potential unavailability, reciprocal valuing, and effort-based discovery of special qualities of the object of appreciation. Although the psychological processes of appreciation need not result in gratitude, we believe that these processes are foundational for gratitude, and thus, research that investigates these psychological processes should significantly enhance our understanding of gratitude.

Final Thoughts

As we conclude this chapter we would like to highlight two equal and opposite errors that we have seen in response to gratitude research. First, some have taken what we believe to be an overly optimistic view of gratitude. In particular, the popular press—but even gratitude scholars such as ourselves—has overstated the potential of gratitude. We have sometimes implied that gratitude is *the* key to happiness; that it is the "elixir for all that ails you." Although gratitude is surely one of the success stories of the positive psychology movement, not all who start counting their blessings will experience a transformation in happiness. Indeed, in one of our recent studies we found that those who were high in trait gratitude did not gain as much from grateful recounting as those low in trait gratitude (Watkins et al., 2015). This only seems to make sense: those who need gratitude most are those most likely to gain from gratitude exercises. Some individuals may already habitually engage in the processes of appreciation and thus, don't have as much to gain from gratitude exercises. But the point is clear: it is probably inappropriate to recommend gratitude exercises as a guaranteed path to increased well-being for everyone. Indeed, there may even be a "dark side" to gratitude. For example, philosophers have often pointed out the inappropriate gratitude that is sometimes seen in kidnapping victims. These victims are sometimes grateful to their oppressors for letting them engage in basic living behaviors like going to the bathroom. In short, as gratitude scholars, we should be careful not to overstate the potential of gratitude (see Wood et al., 2016).

Just as it is easy to be too optimistic about gratitude, so it has also been easy for some to be overly pessimistic about the potential of gratitude for well-being. In some ways, it is our task as scholars to be critical of new findings, but it is easy for this criticism to morph into cynicism. As shown in the example earlier, philosophers are often quick to point out examples of inappropriate gratitude. But to be fair, these are extremely rare and unusual circumstances (how many of us have been kidnapped?), and for most of us, we need to express more—not less—gratitude. It's not that we are experiencing and expressing gratitude for things that aren't really benefits; rather, many blessings pass by us without gratitude. Studies overwhelmingly find that gratitude is strongly related to well-being, and over 30 experimental studies have shown that gratitude exercises enhance well-being (Watkins & McCurrach, in press). We should not let our criticism of gratitude overwhelm the encouraging potential of gratitude that research has so clearly demonstrated. And so we would like to conclude by encouraging a more balanced perspective on gratitude. Although gratitude is not likely to radically transform the well-being of everyone, the research to date suggests that it is successful in enhancing happiness and appears to be one of the most important facets of living well.

Notes

1. For a more thorough review of the increase in the interest in positive psychology and gratitude that presents data that control for the general increase in publications in psychology, see Watkins, 2014, chapter 1.

2. We use "happiness" as a synonym for subjective well-being throughout this chapter. Subjective well-being is usually understood to be a combination of a high frequency of positive affect, low frequency of negative affect, and high satisfaction with life.

3. Positive attention bias training is one procedure from the Cognitive Bias Modification paradigm. In this technique individuals are trained to attend to positive over negative information.

4. George Bailey was the primary character in Frank Capra's Christmas classic *It's a Wonderful Life.*

References

Algoe, S. B. (2012). Find, remind, and bind: The functions of gratitude in everyday relationships. *Social and Personality Psychology Compass, 6*, 455–469.

Algoe, S. B., Gable, S. L., & Maisel, N. C. (2010). It's the little things: Everyday gratitude as a booster shot for romantic relationships. *Personal Relationships, 17*, 217–233.

Algoe, S. B., Haidt, J., & Gable, S. L. (2008). Beyond reciprocity: Gratitude and relationships in everyday life. *Emotion, 8*, 425–429.

Bartlett, M. Y., Condon, P., Cruz, J., Baumann, J., & DeSteno, D. (2012). Gratitude: Prompting behaviours that build relationships. *Cognition and Emotion, 26*, 2–13.

Bartlett, M. Y., & DeSteno, D. (2006). Gratitude and prosocial behavior: Helping when it costs you. *Psychological Science, 17*, 319–325.

Bowlby, J. (1988). *A secure base: Parent-child attachment and healthy human development.* London: Routledge.

Carlson, A. (2011). Aesthetic appreciation of nature and environmentalism. *Royal Institute of Philosophy Supplement, 69*, 137–155.

Chesterton, G. K. (1986). Heretics. In G. K. Chesterton, *Collected works* (Vol. I). San Francisco: Ignatius Press. Original work published in 1905.

Colin, V. (1991, June 21). *Infant attachment: What we know now.* Retrieved from http://aspe.hhs.gov/daltcp/reports/inatrpt.htm

Csikszentmihalyi, M. (2000). Happiness, flow, and economic equality. *American Psychologist, 55*, 1163–1164.

Davis, D. E., Choe, E., Meyers, J., Wade, N., Varjas, K., Gifford, A., & . . . Worthington, E. J. (2016). Thankful for the little things: A meta-analysis of gratitude interventions. *Journal of Counseling Psychology, 63*, 20–31.

DeSteno, D. (2009). Social emotions and intertemporal choice: "Hot" mechanisms for building social and economic capital. *Current Directions in Psychological Science, 18*, 280–284.

Diessner, R., & Lewis, G. (2007). Further validation of the Gratitude, Resentment, and Appreciation Test (GRAT). *The Journal of Social Psychology, 147*, 445–447.

Emmons, R. A. (2004, July). Gratitude is the best approach to life. In L. Sundarajan (Chair), *Quest for the good life: Problems/promises of positive psychology.* Symposium presented at the Annual Convention of the American Psychological Association, Honolulu, HI.

Emmons, R. A., & McCullough, M. E. (2003). Counting blessings versus burdens: An experimental investigation of gratitude and subjective well-being in daily life. *Journal of Personality and Social Psychology, 84*, 377–389.

Eysenck, M. W., Mogg, K., May, J., Richards, A., & Mathews, A. (1991). Bias in interpretation of ambiguous sentences related to threat in anxiety. *Journal of Abnormal Psychology, 100*, 144–150.

Fagley, N. S. (2016). The construct of appreciation: It is so much more than gratitude. In D. Carr (Ed.), *Perspectives on gratitude: An interdisciplinary approach* (pp. 70–84). Oxford, England: Taylor & Francis.

Fredrickson, B. L. (1998). What good are the positive emotions? *Review of General Psychology, 2*, 300–319.

Fredrickson, B. L. (2001). The role of positive emotions in positive psychology: The broaden-and-build theory of positive emotions. *American Psychologist, 56*, 218–226.

Fredrickson, B. L. (2004). Gratitude, like other positive emotions, broadens and builds. In R. A. Emmons & M. E. McCullough (Eds.), *The psychology of gratitude* (145–166). New York: Oxford Press.

Frias, A., Watkins, P. C., Webber, A., & Froh, J. (2011). Death and gratitude: Death reflection enhances gratitude. *Journal of Positive Psychology, 6*, 154–162.

Froh, J. J., & Bono, G. (2013). *Making grateful kids: A scientific approach to helping youth thrive.* West Conshohocken, PA: Templeton Press.

Froh, J. J., Bono, G., Fan, J., Emmons, R. A., Henderson, K., Harris, C., & . . . Wood, A. M. (2014). Nice thinking! An educational intervention that teaches children to think gratefully. *School Psychology Review, 43*, 132–152.

Froh, J. J., Fan, J., Emmons, R. A., Bono, G., Huebner, E. S., & Watkins, P. (2011). Measuring gratitude in youth: Assessing the psychometric properties of adult gratitude scales in children and adolescents. *Psychological Assessment, 23*, 311–324.

Hertel, P. T., & Mathews, A. (2011). Cognitive bias modification: Past perspectives, current findings, and future applications. *Perspectives on Psychological Science, 6*, 521–536.

Hutchison, D. E. (2015). How do grateful people cope? Exploring the mechanism of positive reappraisal. Unpublished master's thesis completed at Eastern Washington University. Retrieved from http://dc.ewu.edu/cgi/viewcontent .cgi?article=1292&context=theses

Janoff-Bulman, R., & Berger, A. R. (2000). The other side of trauma: Towards a psychology of appreciation. In J. H. Harvey & E. D. Miller (Eds.), *Loss and trauma: General and close relationship perspectives* (pp. 29–44). Philadelphia: Brunner-Routledge.

Janoff-Bulman, R., & Frantz, C. M. (1997). The impact of trauma on meaning: From meaningless world to meaningful life. In M. Power & C. Brewin (Eds.), *The transformation of meaning in psychological therapies*. London: Wiley.

Konkler, J. G., Nienhuis, A., Hutchinson, D. E., Vance, P., & Watkins, P. C. (2015, May). *Security and gratitude: Secure attachment priming enhances gratitude.* Poster presented to the Annual Convention of the Western Psychological Association, Las Vegas, NV.

Koo, M., Algoe, S. B., Wilson, T. D., & Gilbert, D. T. (2008). It's a wonderful life: Subtracting positive events improves people's affective states, contrary to their affective forecasts. *Journal of Personality and Social Psychology, 95,* 1217–1224.

Lakey, B. (2013). Perceived social support and happiness: The role of personality and relational processes. In S. A. David, I. Boniwell, & A. C. Aters (Eds.), *The Oxford handbook of happiness* (pp. 847–859). Oxford, England: Oxford University Press.

Leder, H., & Nadal, M. (2014). Ten years of a model of aesthetic appreciation and aesthetic judgments: The aesthetic episode—Developments and challenges in empirical aesthetics. *British Journal of Psychology, 105,* 443–464.

Lystad, A., Watkins, P., & Sizemore, L. (2005, April). *The importance of attachment processes to gratitude.* Presentation to the 85th Annual Convention of the Western Psychological Association, Portland, OR.

Mackintosh, B., Mathews, A., Eckstein, D., & Hoppitt, L. (2013). Specificity effects in the modification of interpretation bias and stress reactivity. *Journal of Experimental Psychopathology, 4,* 133–147.

MacLeod, C., & Clarke, P. F. (2015). The attentional bias modification approach to anxiety intervention. *Clinical Psychological Science, 3,* 58–78.

MacLeod, C., Mathews, A., & Tata, P. (1986). Attentional bias in emotional disorders. *Journal of Abnormal Psychology, 95,* 15–20.

Mathews, A., & Mackintosh, B. (2000). Induced emotional interpretation bias and anxiety. *Journal of Abnormal Psychology, 109,* 602–615.

Mathews, A., & MacLeod, C. (1994). Cognitive approaches to emotion and emotional disorders. *Annual Review of Psychology, 4,* 525–50.

McCullough, M. E., Emmons, R. A., & Tsang, J. (2002). The grateful disposition: A conceptual and empirical topography. *Journal of Personality and Social Psychology, 82,* 112–127.

McCullough, M. E., Kilpatrick, S. D., Emmons, R. A., & Larson, D. B. (2001). Is gratitude a moral affect? *Psychological Bulletin, 127*, 249–266.

McCullough, M. E., Tsang, J., & Emmons, R. A. (2004). Gratitude in intermediate affective terrain: Links of grateful moods to individual differences and daily emotional experience. *Journal of Personality and Social Psychology, 86*, 295–309.

Mikulincer, M., Shaver, P. R., & Slav, K. (2006). Attachment, mental representations of others, and gratitude and forgiveness in romantic relationships. In M. Mikulincer, G. S. Goodman, M. Mikulincer, & G. S. Goodman (Eds.), *Dynamics of romantic love: Attachment, caregiving, and sex* (pp. 190–215). New York: Guilford Press.

Peterson, C. (2006). *A primer in positive psychology.* New York: Oxford University Press.

Peterson, C., & Seligman, M. P. (2003). Character strengths before and after September 11. *Psychological Science, 14*, 381–384.

Rosenberg, E. (1998). Levels of analysis and the organization of affect. *Review of General Psychology, 2*, 247–270.

Scheibe, D., Watkins, P. C., McCurrach, D., & Mathews, A. (2016, May). *Cognitive characteristics of gratitude.* Poster presented to the Annual Convention of the Association for Psychological Science, Chicago, IL.

Seligman, M. E. P., Steen, T. A., Park, N., & Peterson, C. (2005). Positive psychology progress: Empirical validation of interventions. *American Psychologist, 60*, 410–421.

Smith, A. (1976). *The theory of moral sentiments* (6th ed.). Oxford, England: Clarendon Press. (Original work published 1790).

Solom, S., Watkins, P. C., McCurrach, D., & Scheibe, D. (2016). Thieves of thankfulness: Traits that inhibit gratitude. *Journal of Positive Psychology, 12*, 120–129.

Tesser, A., Gatewood, R., & Driver, M. (1968). Some determinants of gratitude. *Journal of Personality and Social Psychology, 9*, 233–236.

Thomas, M., & Watkins, P. (2003, May). *Measuring the grateful trait: Development of the revised GRAT.* Presentation to the 83rd Annual Convention of the Western Psychological Association, Vancouver, BC, Canada.

Uhder, J., Kononchuk, Y., Sparrow, A., & Watkins, P. C. (2010, May). *Language use in grateful processing of painful memories.* Poster presented at the Annual Convention of the Association for Psychological Science, Boston, MA.

Uhder, J., Webber, A., & Watkins, P. C. (2010, August). *Favors from heaven: Sources and benefits of gratitude toward God.* Poster presented at the Annual Convention of the American Psychological Association, San Diego, CA.

Watkins, P. C. (2002). Implicit memory bias in depression. *Cognition and Emotion, 16*, 381–402.

Watkins, P. C. (2004). Gratitude and subjective well-being. In R. A. Emmons & M. E. McCullough (Eds.), *The psychology of gratitude* (pp. 167–192). New York: Oxford University Press.

Watkins, P. C. (2008). Gratitude: The amplifier of blessing. In A. Przepiorka (Ed.), *Closer to emotions II* (pp. 49–62). Lublin, Poland: Publishing House of Catholic University of Lublin.

Watkins, P. C. (2011). Gratitude and well-being. In C. Martin-Kumm & C. Tarquinio (Eds.), *Traité de psychologie positive: Théories et implications pratiques* (pp. 519–537). Bruxelles, France: De Boeck Publishers.

Watkins, P. C. (2014). *Gratitude and the good life: Toward a psychology of appreciation.* Dordrecht, Netherlands: Springer.

Watkins, P. C., Cruz, L., Holben, H., & Kolts, R. L. (2008). Taking care of business? Grateful processing of unpleasant memories. *Journal of Positive Psychology, 3,* 87–99.

Watkins, P. C., Grimm, D. L., & Kolts, R. (2004). Counting your blessings: Positive memories among grateful persons. *Current Psychology, 23,* 52–67.

Watkins, P. C., Martin, B. D., & Faulkner, G. (2003, May). *Are grateful people happy people? Informant judgments of grateful acquaintances.* Presentation to the 83rd Annual Convention of the Western Psychological Association, Vancouver, BC, Canada.

Watkins, P. C., Martin, C. K., & Stern, L. D. (2000). Unconscious memory bias in depression: Perceptual and conceptual processes. *Journal of Abnormal Psychology, 109,* 282–289.

Watkins, P. C., & McCurrach, D. (2016). Exploring how gratitude trains cognitive processes important to subjective well-being. In D. Carr (Ed.), *Perspectives on gratitude: An interdisciplinary approach* (pp. 27–40). Oxford, England: Taylor & Francis.

Watkins, P. C., & McCurrach, D. (in press). Progress in the science of gratitude. In S. Lopez, L. Edwards, & S. Marques (Eds.), *The Oxford handbook of positive psychology* (3rd ed.). New York: Oxford.

Watkins, P. C., McCurrach, D., & Timbrook, T. (2016, May). *Grateful recounting impacts eudaimonic more than hedonic well-being.* Poster presented to the Annual Convention of the Association for Psychological Science, Chicago, IL.

Watkins, P. C., Scheer, J., Ovnicek, M., & Kolts, R. (2006). The debt of gratitude: Dissociating gratitude from indebtedness. *Cognition and Emotion, 20,* 217–241.

Watkins, P. C., Sparrow, A., Pereira, A., & Suominen, S. (2013, August). *Are gifts better than goods? Benefits are better when experienced with gratitude.* Poster presented to the Annual Convention of the American Psychological Association, Honolulu, HI.

Watkins, P. C., Uhder, J., & Pichinevskiy, S. (2015). Grateful recounting enhances subjective well-being: The importance of grateful processing. *Journal of Positive Psychology, 2,* 91–98.

Watkins, P. C., Uhder, J., Webber, A., Pichinevenskiy, S., & Sparrow, A. (2011, May). *Religious affections: The importance of gratitude toward God to spiritual well-being.* Poster presented at the Annual Convention of the Association for Psychological Science, Washington, DC.

Watkins, P. C., Vache, K., Verney, S. P., Muller, S., & Mathews, A. (1996). Unconscious mood-congruent memory bias in depression. *Journal of Abnormal Psychology, 105*, 34–41.

Watkins, P. C., Wood, A., & Shields, V. (2016, June). *Institutional gratitude: Understanding grateful responses to salary raises.* Poster presented to the 8th Annual European Convention for Positive Psychology, Angers, France.

Watkins, P. C., Woodward, K., Stone, T., & Kolts, R. D. (2003). Gratitude and happiness: The development of a measure of gratitude and its relationship with subjective well-being. *Social Behavior and Personality, 31*, 431–452.

Williams, J. G., Watts, F. N., MacLeod, C., & Mathews, A. (1988). *Cognitive psychology and emotional disorders.* Oxford, England: John Wiley & Sons.

Wood, A. M., Emmons, R. A., Algoe, S. B, Froh, J. J., Lambert, N. M., & Watkins, P. C. (2016). A dark side of gratitude? Distinguishing between beneficial gratitude and its harmful impostors for the positive clinical psychology of gratitude and well-being. In Wood, A. M. & Johnson, J. (Eds.), *The Wiley handbook of positive clinical psychology.* Chichester, England: Wiley.

Wood, A. M., Froh, J. J., & Geraghty, A. W. A, (2010). Gratitude and well-being: A review and theoretical integration. *Clinical Psychology Review, 30*, 890–905.

Wood, A. M., Maltby, J., Stewart, N., & Joseph, S. (2008). Conceptualizing gratitude and appreciation as a unitary personality trait. *Personality and Individual Differences, 44*, 621–632.

Wood, A. M., Maltby, J., Stewart, N., Linley, P. A., & Joseph, S. (2008). A social-cognitive model of trait and state levels of gratitude. *Emotion, 8*, 281–290.

CHAPTER SIX

Posttraumatic Growth: A Brief History and Evaluation

Richard G. Tedeschi, Cara L. Blevins,
and Olivia M. Riffle

Posttraumatic growth (PTG) as an area of research and practice, although often considered a construct within the positive psychology framework (e.g. Carr, 2011; Linley & Joseph, 2004), preceded the definition of positive psychology by Seligman and Csikszentmihalyi (2000). After garnering little attention initially, it has become increasingly influential in the psychology of trauma literature, as there are over 100 citations listed in the PsycINFO database for the period of 18 months prior to this writing, and over 600 in total. PTG has also been introduced to the general public through two recent trade publications (Haas, 2015; Rendon, 2015). In this chapter we will review the history of this concept, contributions of the research literature to the understanding of the PTG process, areas that need to be explored and developed to deepen our understanding, and applications of PTG to interventions for trauma survivors.

History and Development of the Concept of Posttraumatic Growth

PTG was introduced by Tedeschi and Calhoun (1995) in a book that reviewed its literary, philosophical, theological, and psychological roots and described an initial conceptual model for the psychological processes involved when traumatic events appear to transform how people live their lives. They had been developing the construct for several years (e.g., Calhoun & Tedeschi, 1989–1990), but had not coined the term until they introduced it when describing their quantitative measure, the Posttraumatic Growth Inventory (PTGI) in the 1995 book and in a journal article published almost simultaneously (Tedeschi & Calhoun, 1996). In that article, the definition of PTG was offered as "personal benefits, including changes in perceptions of self, relationships with others, and philosophy of life, accruing from their attempts to cope with trauma and its aftermath" (Tedeschi & Calhoun, 1996, p. 458). In a later book (Tedeschi, Park, & Calhoun, 1998) they defined PTG as "both a process and an outcome" (p.1), and later as "positive psychological change experienced as a result of the struggle with highly challenging life circumstances" (Tedeschi & Calhoun, 2004, p.1).

Pre-PTG Concepts

Besides the work of Tedeschi and Calhoun and their colleagues beginning in the 1980s, there were some other researchers who were developing ideas similar to PTG in the late 20th century. Scholars were interested in how people live healthy lives in the face of difficulty, and in order to explain this, new concepts were introduced, such as sense of coherence (Antonovsky, 1987), hardiness (Kobasa, 1979), and resilience (Garmezy, 1985; Rutter, 1987; Werner, 1984). However, these ideas focused on how people can stay well in the face of difficulty, rather than how people can respond to life events in a fashion that produces personal transformation. Transformative processes are clearer in the work of Gerald Caplan (1964), who described how times of personal crisis can also be opportunities for personal change. Another key figure in the discussion of post-traumatic growth is Victor Frankl (1963), who is well known for his descriptions of how people find meaning in adversity. Further, Stephen Joseph and colleagues described "changes in outlook" that can follow tragedy (Joseph, Williams, & Yule, 1993). Reviews of how PTG relates to these and other constructs can be found in several sources (Calhoun & Tedeschi, 2006; Tedeschi & Calhoun, 1995; Tedeschi, Park & Calhoun, 1998). O'Leary, Alday and Ickovics (1998) examined eight conceptual models of how people change positively and found that the following concepts tended to appear in at least two: self-efficacy, sense of coherence, meaning-making, locus of control, motivation, optimism, cognitive status, hardiness, past experiences, coping style, social support, community resources, and socioeconomic status. They also found many other concepts that were specific to individual models. In the past 20 years, most research on PTG has been based on Tedeschi and Calhoun's model development.

PTG Based on Assumptive World Theory

Besides the general concept that positive changes or personal transformations can follow traumatic events, an idea that has a long history in literature and religion, perhaps the most influential concept on which PTG has been built is the idea that trauma shatters the assumptive world. The assumptive world is a set of fundamental beliefs that are seldom questioned by a person, as they form the basis for understanding the world, the self, and the future. This idea is found in the work of Piaget (1954) and Kelly (1955) who described how information about our experience must either fit our understandings or these understandings must be revised. These understandings have been called schemas, personal constructs, and the assumptive world. Piaget's and Kelly's concepts were further developed in the literature on trauma and loss. Parkes and Weiss (1983) described how bereavement can "invalidate a large part of our assumptive worlds" (p.71). Seymour Epstein (1985, 1991) noted that the implicit theory of the self that we all construct operates to an extent unconsciously and when it is violated by events results in a profound emotional and cognitive reaction. Ronnie Janoff-Bulman (1985, 1992) described how the assumptive world can be "shattered" by traumatic events. This application of the assumptive world construct to trauma allows a new definition of traumatic events that does not rely on a list of events as found in the psychiatric diagnostic systems. Instead, we can more fully understand trauma as a shattering of the assumptive world, as Janoff-Bulman has suggested. Tedeschi and Calhoun build from this concept in the creation of their PTG model.

Measures of PTG

Measurement of PTG has usually been accomplished with the use of the PTGI, but some measures of similar constructs have been developed as well, including the Stress Related Growth Scale (Park, Cohen, & Murch, 1996), the Benefit-Finding Scale (Antoni et al., 2001), and the Changes in Outlook Questionnaire (Joseph, Williams & Yule, 1993). New versions of the PTGI have been developed, including a short form (Cann et al., 2010) and versions that can be used with children (Cryder, Kilmer, Calhoun, & Tedeschi, 2006; Kilmer et al., 2009). The concept of *posttraumatic depreciation* has also been developed, referring to the negative changes that can result for traumatic experiences within the same five domains of PTG. The

Posttraumatic Growth and Depreciation Inventory measures both positive and negative personal changes after trauma that can occur simultaneously on the same dimensions of change (Baker, Kelly, Calhoun, Cann, & Tedeschi, 2008; Cann, Calhoun, Tedeschi & Solomon, 2010). In addition, the PTGI has been translated and used in various nations and cultures, including China (Liu et al., 2015), Turkey (Senol-Durak & Ayvasik, 2010), and India (Thombre, Sherman, & Simonton, 2010). Weiss and Berger (2010) provide a source that summarizes some of this cross-cultural research using translated versions of the PTGI. Some of these translations are being published with associated validity studies (Garcia & Wlodarczyk, 2016; Lamela, Figueiredo, Bastos, & Martins, 2014; Liu et al., 2015).

The PTGI was developed from earlier qualitative research that yielded statements from participants who reported transformational changes after trauma. Their statements became the basis for the 21 items of the PTGI. In the original publication (Tedeschi & Calhoun, 1996) and in subsequent work (Taku, Cann, Tedeschi & Calhoun, 2008), factor analyses of the PTGI yielded five domains: Appreciation of Life, Relating to Others, Personal Strength, New Possibilities, and Spiritual Change. *Appreciation of Life* refers to the ability to perceive the value of simple aspects of living that are often taken for granted. *Relating to Others* refers to improvements in interpersonal relationships that may come about when people receive support from others, recognize they need help, and are able to be more empathic and compassionate now that they have encountered significant life difficulties. *Personal Strength* refers to the recognition that they have been able to endure their traumatic circumstances and have coping competencies. *New Possibilities* arise when these circumstances close off existing life paths or encourage the consideration of new ways of living. *Spiritual Change* involves the strengthening or revision of spiritual, religious, and perhaps existential understandings of life. Evidence of these domains of PTG have been supported by qualitative research (e.g., Hussain & Bhushan, 2013; Morris & Shakespeare-Finch, 2012), although some factor analyses from other cultures yield somewhat different solutions. Conceptually, these factors seem to cover the ways people experience PTG in the Western world, and this may be due to the fact that the original item pool was derived from qualitative work with trauma survivors in the United States.

It is important to keep in mind that although PTG is an outcome, it is also a process. The conceptual description of the PTG process has undergone change since the first version was offered by Tedeschi and Calhoun in 1995, with modifications published on several occasions. The most significant modifications were the models published over several years (Calhoun, Cann, and Tedeschi, 2010; Tedeschi & Calhoun, 2004). To generally summarize the PTG model, it is useful to recognize the main variables that are the focus of the PTG process. The model refers to the interaction of the person before the trauma, including various personality characteristics and cognitive and emotional capabilities, with a life event that is described as "seismic." The term seismic refers to the effect of the event on the person's core belief system or assumptive world. This set of core beliefs about the self, the world, and one's future can be either shattered by events or subjected to closer examination in persons not previously prone to considering what they believe about their lives. As this experience is emotionally as well as cognitively challenging, the trauma survivor brings to bear their coping resources in order to calm down the emotional reactions and intrusive rumination that are set off by the trauma. The Tedeschi and Calhoun model emphasizes rumination processes in the wake of trauma that start with intrusive thoughts and images of trauma, or brooding, giving way to more deliberate, reflective thought, as described in more recent models of rumination (Watkins, 2008). Assisting in this process may be people who provide the kind of support that leads to reconsideration and rebuilding of core beliefs so that a new perspective on life can emerge. These people have been described as *expert companions*, as they have the interpersonal skills that encourage exploration of personal change in trauma survivors (Tedeschi & Calhoun, 2010). When core beliefs or the assumptive world are reconstructed, the new system incorporates the experiences of trauma so that these experiences become more comprehensible and meaningful. In this process, the life narrative is elaborated so that the traumatic event can be incorporated into a meaningful story and, therefore, has value rather than be relegated to an event that is an anomaly or something to be avoided. The new life narrative is a further development of PTG for many people, and in this way corresponds to the concept of the "possible self" (Markus & Nurius, 1986). Trauma survivors are introduced to ways they can live that they had never considered before, perhaps because life had not made it necessary, because they were otherwise preoccupied, they did not understand the value of other ways of living, or the new ways have gained new meaning. For any or all of these reasons, trauma survivors may then find that life has taken a turn and they are living out a new narrative and a new life path. For these reasons, the final resolution of trauma for those who report PTG is a sense that they are wiser, that is, they know better how to live life well. Of course, this is known in the colloquial expression "sadder but wiser." This idea incorporates another aspect of PTG that needs to be understood. The experience of PTG comes after a *struggle*, and a good deal of distress is involved. Recall that the shattering of the assumptive world is an emotional experience as described by Epstein (1985) and Janoff-Bulman (1992), and this is not merely a cognitive realignment. Although the new understandings of life and the new pathways that are adopted bring some relief, they do not relieve all distress. Some people may report that in retrospect their traumatic event was the "best thing that ever happened" to them (Tedeschi & Calhoun, 1995, p.1), yet most still see the trauma as full of loss and distress that they are continuing to manage, even as they see the benefits of the experience (Tedeschi, Calhoun, & Cann, 2007).

In order to track this process of PTG, some new measures were developed. The two most important are measures of core belief change (Core Beliefs Inventory [CBI]; Cann et al., 2009) and rumination about the traumatic event (Event Related Rumination Inventory [ERRI]; Cann et al., 2011). The CBI is composed of nine items that ask trauma survivors to indicate the degree to which they seriously examined certain core beliefs as a result of experiencing the event. The core beliefs on this measure involve their understandings of other people, the course of their own life, what is meaningful, under control, etc. This measure of the disruption of the assumptive world is predictive of PTG (Triplett, Tedeschi, Cann, Calhoun, & Reeve, 2012). The ERRI is a measure of both intrusive, or brooding, rumination and deliberate, or reflective, rumination. Unlike other measures of rumination that are focused on the tendency toward rumination as a trait, this measure determines the degree to which the trauma survivor has been ruminating about the traumatic event and its aftermath. Furthermore, it incorporates both types of rumination, with the expectation that intrusive rumination must give way to deliberate rumination for PTG to occur. Deliberate rumination tends to be more highly predictive of PTG than intrusive rumination, as measured by the ERRI. Other measures of the PTG process that have been introduced but are not as highly developed are measures of disclosure tendencies (Lindstrom, Cann, Calhoun, & Tedeschi, 2013) and the degree to which the traumatic experience has been resolved (Triplett, et al., 2012). These concepts are contained in the PTG model and await further development of measurement instruments.

In recent years, PTG applications have been built on the PTG process model and the underlying assumption that expert companions are crucial in the facilitation of growth (Calhoun & Tedeschi, 1999, 2013). The descriptions of expert companions are rather general (Tedeschi & Calhoun, 2010), and there is currently no measure of expert companionship. However, expert companions are described as possessing relationship qualities that resemble Roger's (1957) concept of therapeutic relating, and individuals are not expected to be professionals in order to provide this type of companionship. Trauma survivors can be adept at describing the kind of relating that helped them most, and the "expertise" of expert companions has little to do with knowledge of trauma theory, and mostly involves good listening, patience, acceptance, and humility. PTG occurs "naturally" without professional intervention in most cases, and untrained individuals are routinely able to serve in the role of expert companions. Beyond expert companionship, clinicians find it helpful to be aware of how the PTG process works and how to facilitate it. Tedeschi and McNally (2011) first described the clinical application of the PTG process in a schematic designed for working with military veterans, and Calhoun and Tedeschi (2013) expanded it into a more general clinical approach. This approach includes phases of PTG processes that begin with psychoeducation about trauma and methods of managing emotional distress and intrusive rumination, encouragements to self-disclose, work on narrative development, and attention to elements of PTG that can lead to altruistic behavior.

Established Knowledge and Areas for Further Development

Much of the PTG process described earlier has been found to operate in trauma survivors who have encountered a variety of traumatic events. The availability of appropriate measures has allowed researchers to uncover these relationships. Next we will review measures that have been developed to examine crucial components of the PTG process.

Core Belief Challenge and Rumination

The more "seismic" an experience is, the more one is caused to question fundamental assumptions and schemas regarding safety, predictability, identity, and meaning. As a result, an individual may either revert back to previously held schemas and core beliefs or begin a process whereby new schemas and belief systems are created, presenting the opportunity for a new sense of meaning and enhanced ability to manage and cope with future shocks (Tedeschi & Calhoun, 2004; Cann et al., 2011). This process of shift in core beliefs, measured by the CBI, has been shown to be a catalyst for rumination and, ultimately, PTG (Taku, Cann, Tedeschi, & Calhoun, 2015; Triplett et al., 2012). The importance of rumination, measured by the ERRI, in predicting PTG is also being established (Zhou & Wu, 2016). Evidence suggests that intrusive ruminations relating to traumatic events are positively associated with distress and a failure to cope (Cann et al., 2011). For outcomes of PTG to occur, ruminative processes must shift from predominately intrusive and unintentional patterns to more deliberate and contemplative patterns. A moderate degree of insight, cognitive organization, and other factors, including personality characteristics, coping style, gender, self-disclosure, and the sociocultural context in which trauma and corresponding self-disclosure exist, can contribute to constructive processes of deliberate and reflective rumination (Tedeschi, 2011).

Self-Disclosure and Responsiveness

Constructive processes of self-disclosure support the shift from intrusive to deliberative reflection. Self-disclosure has been identified as an important component of cognitive processing and coping in the aftermath of trauma and has been associated with a variety of positive outcomes, including lower levels of distress, enhanced physical functioning, a resilient self-concept, and outcomes of PTG (Calhoun & Tedeschi, 2013; Pennebaker & Stone, 2003; Taku et al., 2009). As one reveals aspects of one's identity or experience to another through verbal or written modes of communication, there is an opportunity to reorganize and reconstruct the system of core beliefs and the life narrative (Taku et al., 2009). The frequency and complexity of disclosure are important and may occur within the context of psychotherapy, prayer, expressive writing or journaling, or conversations with trusted friends and skilled companions (Pennebaker & Stone, 2003; Taku et al., 2009). Recounting and disclosing traumatic experiences can be a difficult process for survivors to engage in and requires a great deal of courage and vulnerability (Calhoun & Tedeschi, 2013; Lindstrom et al., 2013; Taku et al., 2009).

Cross-Cultural and Individualistic Characteristics Associated with PTG

Survivors of a wide range of traumatic events from individualistic and collectivistic cultures have reported experiences of PTG. For example, PTG has been reported in first responders and emergency personnel in the United States and Australia (Chopko & Schwartz, 2009; Shakespeare-Finch, Gow, & Smith, 2005); military veterans and active duty service members (Bush, Skopp, McCann, & Luxton, 2011; Gallaway, Millikan, & Bell, 2011; Maguen, Vogt, King, King, & Litz, 2006; Tedeschi, 2011; Tsai, Mota, Southwick, & Pietrzak, 2016); Chinese and Japanese earthquake survivors (Taku, Cann, Tedeschi, & Calhoun, 2015; Wu, Xu, & Sui, 2016; Zhou & Wu, 2016), patients with severe/chronic illness in the United States, Australia, Japan, and Eastern and Western Europe (Castonguay, Crocker, Hadd, McDonough, & Sabaston, 2015; Coroiu, Körner, Burke,

Meterissian, & Sabiston, 2015; Danhauer et al., 2015; Matsui & Taku, 2016; Yi, Zebrack, Kim, & Cousino, 2015); Iraqi schoolchildren (Magruder, Kilic, & Koryurek, 2015); and a wide variety of other traumatic events (Calhoun & Tedeschi, 2013).

Although people in a wide variety of situations and contexts experience trauma, the extent of PTG may vary based on individual characteristics. For example, younger individuals tend to report greater levels of PTG than older individuals (Dekel & Nuttman-Shwartz, 2009; Levine, Laufer, Stein, Hamama-Raz, & Solomon, 2009; Pietrzak et al., 2010; Shakespeare-Finch & Lurie-Beck, 2014; Solomon & Dekel, 2007). Additionally, a 2010 meta-analysis revealed a trend in gender differences, such that women report higher PTG than men, regardless of trauma type (Vishnevsky, Cann, Calhoun, Tedeschi, & Demakis, 2010). Several psychological factors, including optimism, extraversion, sense of coherence, positive reappraisal, and problem-focused coping (Forstmeier, Kuwert, Spitzer, Freyberger, & Maercker, 2009; Helgeson, Reynolds, & Tomich, 2006; Levine et al., 2009; Linley & Joseph, 2004; McCaslin et al., 2009); cognitive factors including bravery, fortitude, and perseverance (Peterson, Park, Pole, D'Andrea, & Seligman, 2008); and social factors including increased perceptions of social support (Cadell, Regehr, & Hemsworth, 2003; Dirik & Karanci, 2008; Rosenbach & Renneberg, 2008; Schroevers, Helgeson, Sanderma, & Ranchor, 2010), and spirituality and religious coping (Calhoun, Cann, Tedeschi, & McMillan, 2000; Linley & Joseph, 2004) have been associated with PTG.

Event type may also have a unique influence on outcomes of PTG. A study by Shakespeare-Finch and Armstrong (2010) suggested that bereaved individuals and survivors of motor vehicle accidents report greater levels of PTG than survivors of sexual assault. Survivors of different types of cancer also report differing amounts of PTG, with breast cancer survivors having the highest PTG scores (Morris & Shakespeare-Finch, 2011b). In addition, there is some evidence to suggest that shared traumas that target a community in addition to the individual (i.e., natural disaster, terrorist attacks) may result in higher levels of growth than individually experienced trauma (Kilic, Magruder, & Koryurek, 2016).

Event Centrality, PTG, and PTD

Posttraumatic distress (PTD) and PTG are distinct, yet related, constructs. Although one may assume that PTG and PTD represent two sides of the same coin, evidence suggests the possibility of independent positive and negative trauma consequences (Cann et al., 2010; Linley, Joseph,

Cooper, Harris, & Meyer, 2003). For instance, posttraumatic distress has been associated with suicide and decreased life satisfaction in a wide variety of samples, whereas PTG has been associated with increased meaning in life and well-being (Bush et al., 2011; Gallaway et al., 2011). How central one views the traumatic event to the life narrative, identity, and attribution of new experiences may have meaningful implications for outcomes of PTD and PTG (Berntsen & Rubin, 2006; Blix, Birkeland, Hansen, & Heir, 2015; Groleau, Calhoun, Cann, & Tedeschi, 2013). For example, several studies have demonstrated associations between event centrality and symptoms of PTD, including agitation, guilt, anxiety, and sleep difficulties (Blix, Solberg, & Heir, 2014; Brown, Antonius, Kramer, Root, & Hiurst, 2010; Robinaugh & McNally, 2011). Studies have also demonstrated a link between PTG and event centrality, independent of PTD symptoms or diagnoses, suggesting that event centrality may contribute to both PTG and PTD independently (Barton, Boals, & Knowles, 2013; Blix et al., 2015; Groleau et al., 2013; Roland, Currier, Rojas-Flores, & Herrera, 2014).

Although some degree of distress is necessary to initiate the ruminative processes essential to the development of PTG, evidence suggests that an inverted curvilinear relationship exists between PTD and PTG (Colville & Cream, 2009; Dekel & Nuttman-Shwartz, 2009; Kleim & Ehlers, 2009; Levine, Laufer, Stein, Hamama-Raz, & Solomon, 2009; Shakespeare-Finch & Lurie-Beck, 2014; Solomon & Dekel, 2007; Taku, Tedeschi, & Cann, 2015). Specifically, these studies suggest that a certain degree of PTD is necessary for PTG to occur and that greater PTD leads to increases in PTG. However, this relationship is demonstrated only to a certain point, and once the severity of PTD symptoms reach a certain threshold, outcomes of PTG begin to decrease.

Research suggests that PTD and PTG often coexist and may have similar initial pathways. Both PTD and PTG occur in response to a highly stressful or traumatic event that elicits heightened levels of distress. This distress is typically characterized by unwanted and intrusive thoughts or a re-experiencing of the trauma, and several studies have found positive associations between PTD, PTG, and intrusion (Dekel, Ein-Dor, & Soloman, 2012; Salsman, Segerstrom, Brechting, Carlson, & Andrykowski, 2009; Shigemoto & Poyrazli; 2013). As described earlier, it is not uncommon for seismic and highly stressful experiences to prompt disruptive thoughts about the event and one's life; however, for PTG to occur this intrusive pattern of thought must eventually shift to a more deliberate pattern of cognitive processing (Calhoun & Tedeschi, 2013; Calhoun et al., 2010; Cann et al., 2011). When symptoms of both PTD and PTG are present, it is possible that PTG may protect or buffer against some of the more negative symptoms of post-traumatic stress disorder (PTSD). For example, PTG has been associated with reduced revictimization following sexual assault (Kunst, Winkel, & Bogaerts, 2010), increased social affiliation and reduced avoidant coping following a breast cancer diagnosis (Silva, Moreira, & Canavarro, 2012), higher psychological well-being and reduced distress following a diagnosis of cardiovascular disease (Bluvstein, Moravchick, Sheps, Schreiber, & Bloch, 2013), and better self-reported physical health in HIV/AIDS and cancer patients (Sawyer, Ayers, & Field, 2010). In addition, PTG has been associated with decreased suicide ideation in military personnel post-deployment (Bush et al., 2011) and with increased life satisfaction in a variety of samples (Triplett et al., 2012).

Conceptual Challenges

PTG has attracted considerable attention since its initial introduction into the psychological literature, and research seeking to explore and validate the construct has grown exponentially (Blackie, Jayawickreme, Helzer, Forgeard, & Roepke, 2015; Frazier et al., 2006; Jayawickreme & Blackie, 2014; Linley & Joseph, 2004). However, this attention has not been without controversy since researchers have challenged the definition of PTG and questioned the scientific validity of the construct (Coyne & Tennen, 2010; Hobfoll, Hall, Canetti-Nisim, Galea, Johnson, & Palmieri, 2007; Jayawickreme & Blackie, 2014; Tennen & Affleck, 2009; Zoellner & Maercker, 2006). Skepticism has arisen due to the cross-sectional and retrospective measurement design of many existing PTG studies (Jayawickreme & Blackie, 2014; Tennen & Affleck, 2009). Scholars have also posited that reports of PTG may represent a self-enhancing cognitive bias reflective of "positive illusions." Rather than reflecting actual positive psychological change, they have argued that PTG is instead motivated by a desire to restore self-esteem, optimism for the future, and a sense of control in threatening situations while attempting to cope and derive meaning from the experience (Hobfoll et al., 2007; Jayawickreme & Blackie, 2014; Park, 2010; Roepke, Jayawickreme, & Riffle, 2014; Sumalla, Ochoa, & Blanco, 2009; Taylor, Kemeny, Reed, Bower, & Gruenewald, 2000; Tennen & Affleck, 2009). Similarly, skeptics have suggested that only when individuals translate cognitive benefit-finding processes into behavioral action can we be sure PTG is real (Hall et al., 2008; Hobfoll et al., 2007).

Although we agree that a degree of caution is warranted whenever interpreting self-reported and retrospective information, existing evidence largely supports the theoretical model of PTG and confirms that outcomes of PTG are valid and representative of psychosocial change. Specifically, research has demonstrated that reports of PTG tend to be accurate (Blackie et al., 2015; Shakespeare-Finch & Barrington, 2012; Shakespeare-Finch & Enders, 2008). This has been supported by studies illustrating that outcomes of PTG can be observed, often in distinctive ways, by individuals in the social network who describe significant and beneficial changes in trauma survivors both behaviorally (Shakespeare-Finch & Barrington, 2012; Shakespeare-Finch & Enders, 2008) and psychologically (Blackie et al., 2015; Shand, Cowlishaw, Brooker, Burkey, & Ricciardelli, 2014). Additionally, recent prospective evidence has supported the assertion that PTG trajectories remain generally stable over time and are associated with better long-term adjustment following trauma (Wang, Chang, Chen, Chen, & Hsu, 2014; Danhauer et al., 2015). There is also recent evidence that event centrality may be a crucial distinction in understanding the effects of trauma on growth outcomes. Highly central events tend to produce the findings predicted by the Tedeschi and Calhoun model, whereas events low in centrality may not (Johnson & Boals, 2015).

This evidence helps to further validate the overall construct of PTG and is aligned with our notion that growth follows seismic events and represents lasting positive psychological change (Calhoun & Tedeschi, 2013); however, further longitudinal research and self-other corroboration is needed to continue to establish the reliability and validity of PTG theory and related outcomes. Employing methodologically rigorous analyses will help advance the existing research related to PTG and allow scientists to answer critical questions about the degree and extent of psychosocial change following experiences of seismic adversity.

Future Directions and Potential Applications

Tremendous progress has been made in furthering the science of PTG, but several areas that warrant further study remain. The frontiers of this research field hold promise for better understanding the variables underlying when, why, and how individuals undergo positive transformation in the wake of trauma. Furthermore, given the universality of trauma to the human experience, many can benefit from applications of PTG aimed at maximizing the positive outcomes survivors are able to elicit from their experiences. Here, we consider how future research might examine two populations in which the presentation and mechanisms of PTG are less understood and perhaps differ: (1) children and adolescents and (2) relationships, groups, and larger systems of people. We also discuss two approaches to PTG research, longitudinal studies and interventions, which may elucidate its mechanisms and applications to both clinical and general populations. This is not an exhaustive exploration of possibilities for the future of PTG, but rather a survey of a few promising directions.

PTG in Children and Adolescents

Although there remains a relatively small literature on PTG in younger individuals, researchers are increasingly attending to understanding this process in children and adolescents and how it might resemble or differ from that in adults (Alisic, van der Schoot, om, van Ginkel, & Kleber, 2008; Kilmer, 2006; Meyerson, Grant, Carter, & Kilmer, 2011). Several recent studies have investigated PTG in youth who experienced a range of traumatic events, including natural disasters (e.g., Hafstad, Gil-Rivas, Kilmer, & Raeder, 2010; Kilmer & Gil-Rivas, 2010), terrorism (e.g., Laufer, Solomon, & Levine, 2010; Levine et al., 2009), traffic accidents (e.g., Salter & Stallard, 2004), cancer (e.g., Turner-Sack, Menna, & Setchell, 2012), and parental bereavement (e.g., Wolchik, Coxe, Tein, Sandler, & Ayers, 2008). Researchers recognize that the means by which PTG unfolds may differ in children by virtue of ongoing emotional and cognitive development, but have found that children still possess, to some extent, the capability to reflect on how they and their situations have changed as a result of a traumatic event (Cryder, Kilmer, Tedeschi, & Calhoun, 2006; Kilmer et al., 2009). There is mixed evidence regarding specific variables, but a recent literature review of 25 studies indicated that many of the correlates of PTG in children and adolescents are fairly consistent with those in adults (Meyerson et al., 2011). For example, social support, intrusive and deliberate rumination, and certain coping strategies (e.g., religious coping) relate to PTG in a manner similar to existing evidence from adult samples.

However, there are ways PTG can be explored further in children. Future studies need to more clearly distinguish between reported growth that is trauma related and that which is simply due to normative development. Two studies thus far have suggested that in children, positive changes associated with trauma are distinct from those due to nontrauma-related maturational growth (Alisic et al., 2008; Taku, Calhoun, Kilmer, & Tedeschi, 2008); however, most studies lack nontrauma comparison groups and therefore they are limited in the ability to make this discernment (Meyerson et al., 2011). Researchers can attempt to replicate these few findings with prospective-longitudinal designs that control for normative growth. Furthermore, mixed results in a few studies make it difficult to conclude how PTG is unique in youth. There is some evidence that PTG may decay over time more quickly in children than in adults, that there may be an "optimal" age to experience a traumatic event in terms of potential growth, and that gender differences may not emerge until early adulthood (Meyerson et al., 2011). Replication will be key to address these possibilities. Finally, future research should address the extent to which culture and context, particularly the role of caregivers, influence children's PTG. For instance, one sample of children reported particularly large increases in religiosity and spirituality as compared to other domains of PTG (Kilmer et al., 2009), an effect that might have been a reflection of the especially religious community and families from which these children came. Parents could certainly promote certain types of coping strategies and explanations or interpretations of a traumatic event, a variable unique to children and adolescents and worth exploring.

PTG in Relationships, Groups, and Larger Systems

Traumatic events often affect several people at once (e.g., natural disasters, acts of terror, war conflict), and even those events that are seemingly individual (e.g., chronic illness, sexual assault) significantly affect one's loved ones and surrounding social network. Human systems of any size—romantic partners, families, communities, and even an entire nation's citizens—can come together in the wake of trauma to support and enhance one another's psychological growth (Calhoun & Tedeschi, 2006). Thus far, research on relationships in PTG has focused mostly on the role of social support in promoting a trauma survivor's PTG (Calhoun & Tedeschi, 2006), with a meta-analysis illustrating a moderate positive relationship (Prati & Pietrantoni, 2009). However, researchers are now seeking a more sophisticated and nuanced understanding of how PTG might function interpersonally, extending beyond the individual to affect close others, as well as how PTG manifests in larger groups and systems of people.

At the most proximal and intimate level, growth may occur between two individuals in a close relationship. One way in which this manifests is the "spreading" of PTG between partners. Several studies have demonstrated that when one partner in a close relationship reports PTG, the other reports a corresponding level of PTG (Shakespeare-Finch & Barrington, 2012; Shakespeare-Finch & Enders, 2008; Thornton & Perez, 2006). This effect is seen in bereaved parents (Büchi et al., 2009), cancer patients and their partners or caregivers (Moore et al., 2011; Weiss, 2004), and married couples who have endured a severe flood (Canevello, Michels, & Hilaire, in press-b). Canevello, Michels, and Hilaire (in press-a) found that this "contagious" effect was mediated by increased interpersonal responsiveness—when one person experiences PTG, they become more responsive to and understanding of their partner, which in turn leads to the partner's increased growth. Dyadic research in PTG has also turned to examining the consequences of one partner's PTG for the other. For instance, Canevello, et al. (in press-b) found that in close relationships, one partner's PTG was associated with downstream effects for the other partner, particularly increased relationship quality and decreased psychological distress. Another growth process that has been demonstrated between two people is that of *vicarious* or *secondary* PTG (Arnold, Calhoun, Tedeschi, & Cann, 2005; Shoji et al., 2014). Mental health professionals treating traumatized clients often experience growth and benefits from secondary exposure to a traumatic experience. These findings demonstrate that close others are sensitive to victims' PTG (Shakespeare-Finch & Barrington, 2012; Shakespeare-Finch & Enders, 2008; Thornton & Perez, 2006; Weiss, 2004) and extend them to examine the mechanisms by which this sensitivity occurs. Future research might examine how to use interventions to promote relationship-focused coping strategies (e.g., Bodenmann & Randall, 2012) in order to improve close others' psychological well-being, reduce distress, and potentially, foster their PTG.

The scope of possible growth after trauma can extend to encompass several people, from family systems to communities, organizations, entire cultural subgroups, or nations. Families have traditionally been considered as a context for supporting or hindering an individual's growth (Berger, 2015; Harvey, Barnett, & Rupe, 2006), but there has been some consideration of interpersonal and collective growth processes among family members (e.g., Figley, 1989), such as the family's shared changes in assumptive world beliefs and increased conviction that together, they can successfully brave future stressors (Antonovsky & Sourani, 1988). Future research might address suggestions for formally extending the PTG model to families (Berger & Weiss, 2009) and expand upon how trauma shapes individual members' experiences and collective processes (Berger, 2015).

On a larger scale, entire communities and cultural subgroups can share particular post-traumatic responses and consequent coping strategies in response to major world events (e.g., Abu-Raiya, Pargament, & Mahoney, 2011). Often, in the wake of trauma, communities develop a *collective narrative*, or a way for members to interpret and give meaning to the event—a process not unlike schema reconstruction that happens on an individual level (Calhoun & Tedeschi, 2006). Bloom (1998) and Tedeschi (1999) pointed out that larger groups and societies appear to respond to widespread or collective trauma with social change efforts. Perhaps this perspective is more sociological, but there are likely links between the transformations of cultures and the transformations of individuals. There may be a reciprocal relationship where individuals and larger social systems experience PTG by continually influencing each other through the exchange of narratives, reconsideration of social norms, and breaking apart of traditions.

Longitudinal Research

Most of the PTG literature has examined its many correlates, spanning environmental, social, psychological, and demographic factors through cross-sectional design (see Helgeson, Reynolds, & Tomich, 2006 and Prati & Pietrantoni, 2009 for meta-analyses). However, few studies have examined PTG over time, which remains a barrier to fully understanding causality in PTG: What precedes and succeeds personal transformation after trauma? Vazquez, Perez-Sales, and Ochoa (2015) claim that no standard causal model exists, leading to varied interpretations of how this transformation might be occurring, such as improved coping strategies (e.g., Zoellner & Maercker, 2006), distortions of reality (Frazier et al., 2009; Taylor & Armor, 1996; Tennen & Affleck, 2009), personality changes (e.g., Jayawickreme & Blackie, 2014), manifestation of a natural tendency to change and grow with time (Tennen & Affleck, 2002), or genuine changes in behavior and identity (Tedeschi, Addington, Cann, & Calhoun, 2014). To answer this question of mechanism(s), more longitudinal examination of PTG is necessary to better understand its predictors and consequences. For instance, in the months and years following a traumatic event, which individual and environmental factors differentially predict PTG, and does PTG predict changes in well-being and adjustment over time?

To date, only a handful of longitudinal studies have addressed these questions. One study of female breast cancer patients found that greater social support seeking and cognitive coping at the time of surgery were associated with greater PTG five months later (Silva, Crespo, & Canavarro, 2012). In a sample of patients undergoing treatment for acute leukemia, Danhauer et al. (2013) found that a longer period of time since diagnosis, younger age, greater deliberate rumination, and greater challenge to core beliefs all predicted greater increases in PTG in the weeks following diagnosis and initiation of chemotherapy. These researchers have also reported stability of PTG over time in breast cancer patients (Danhauer, et al., 2015). In contrast, Wang et al. (2014) reported stable high (27.4 percent), high decreasing (39.4 percent), low increasing (16.9 percent), and low decreasing (16.9 percent) trajectories of PTG over one year in breast cancer patients. Blix and colleagues (2015) reported stable levels of PTG over two years in trauma survivors of the Oslo bombing. Finally, Valdez and Lilly (2014) examined longitudinal changes in assumptive beliefs in women who were recent victims of intimate partner violence, finding that they experienced significant positive changes to their beliefs about themselves and the world one year later as compared to women who had not experienced this trauma. These changes in assumptive world beliefs accounted for 37 percent of the variance seen in PTG changes from baseline to follow-up. Thus, there seems to be evidence for PTG stability over time, but not in everyone. Predicting what will determine lasting PTG requires much more research consideration.

Although studies are beginning to point to individual characteristics that may differentially predict PTG, including demographic variables and nature of the traumatic event (e.g., Morris & Shakespeare-Finch, 2011a), many more psychosocial variables remain contenders for future study as predictors and/or consequences of PTG longitudinally. Possibilities include optimism (Prati & Pietrantoni, 2009; Zoellner, Rabe, Karl, & Maercker, 2008), self-efficacy (e.g., Cieslak et al., 2009), emotion regulation (e.g., Larsen & Berenbaum, 2015; Wild & Paivio, 2003), personality traits like openness to experience (e.g., Wilson & Boden, 2008; Zoellner et al., 2008), coping strategies (e.g., Prati & Pietrantoni, 2009), meaning in life (Triplett et al., 2012), social support (e.g., Prati & Pietrantoni, 2009), mindfulness (e.g., Chopko & Schwartz, 2009), gratitude (e.g., Vernon, 2012), empathy (Morris, Shakespeare-Finch, & Scott, 2011), and many others. Ultimately, studies that address changes in growth over time can elucidate possible causal consequences of PTG, which holds tremendous potential for developing and implementing interventions to garner growth and associated positive changes.

PTG Interventions

As we further clarify the processes underlying PTG, attention can turn to supporting and fostering growth through interventions. Several researchers have cited general guidelines for how PTG might be promoted, often applying elements of various psychotherapeutic approaches in order to alleviate pain and disruptions in functioning while fostering well-being and resolution (e.g., Berger, 2015; Calhoun & Tedeschi, 2012; Tedeschi & McNally, 2011). This often centers on the use of cognitive processing of the event through self-disclosure (Berger, 2015). From a constructive narrative perspective, this provides the means for trauma survivors to rework their core beliefs and life narrative and to consider alternative perspectives that can assist them in schema change (Berger, 2015; Meichenbaum, 2006; Neimeyer, 2001; Tedeschi & Calhoun, 2004). However, few studies have applied this theoretical discussion to formal development and empirical testing of interventions aimed at increasing PTG. Given the critical roles of schema reconstruction (Janoff-Bulman, 2006) and self-disclosure (Taku et al., 2009) in the growth process, a promising framework upon which to build PTG interventions is verbal and/or written expression. As explored later, such interventions can be developed through experimental studies with both clinical and general populations, as well as in the context of psychotherapeutic treatment.

Expressive writing, a means of mitigating the negative psychological impact of a traumatic event by writing about one's deepest thoughts and concerns surrounding the experience (Pennebaker & Beall, 1986), is a promising strategy for PTG intervention, as it helps survivors form a more coherent trauma narrative, which promotes positive outcomes such as reduced intrusive rumination, depressive symptomatology, and perceived stress (Danoff-Burg, Mosher, Seawell, & Agee, 2010; Lu, Zheng, Young, Kagawa-Singer, & Loh, 2012; Smyth, 1998; Smyth, Hockemeyer, & Tulloch, 2008). For decades, expressive writing interventions have been associated with improved physical and psychological health outcomes in various populations (see Frattaroli, 2006; Smyth, 1998), but only recently have studies implemented this strategy specifically to promote PTG (Danoff-Burg et al., 2010; Groleau, 2015; Knaevelsrud, Liedl, & Maercker, 2010; Slavin-Spenny, Cohen, Oberleitner, & Lumley, 2011; Smyth et al., 2008; Stockton, Joseph, & Hunt, 2014; Ullrich & Lutgendorf, 2002). The format of these interventions is generally an online, short-term (4–8 weeks) program entailing multiple 15-minute writing sessions per week. Overall, these studies have demonstrated the ability of such interventions to significantly increase PTG pre- to post-treatment. Future studies that replicate and refine expressive writing PTG interventions should consider differential effects of the treatment by traumatic event type, dosage (Pennebaker & Chung, 2011), and underlying mechanisms like increased deliberate rumination.

In clinical settings, mental health professionals can foster PTG by serving as expert companions to traumatized clients (see Calhoun & Tedeschi, 2012; Tedeschi, Calhoun, & Groleau, 2015). Beyond this type of relationship for the facilitation of PTG, a few reports suggest that standard trauma treatment may generate PTG. There is some evidence that trauma survivors undergoing prolonged exposure therapy for PTSD experienced significant increases in PTG from pre- to post-treatment, particularly in the domains of relating to others, new possibilities, and personal strength (Hagenaars & van Minnen, 2010). Other cognitive-behavioral interventions have also produced PTG outcomes (Zollner & Maercker, 2006), even though they were not designed specifically to do so. Alternatively,

Senol-Durak and Ayvasik (2010) suggested that interventions should aim to enhance problem-focused coping skills in trauma survivors to enhance PTG. In developing a therapy approach more clearly focused on PTG facilitation, Tedeschi and McNally (2011) and Calhoun and Tedeschi (2013) proposed an integrative therapy utilizing several approaches for promoting PTG. These approaches include psychoeducation about trauma and PTG, teaching strategies for managing autonomic nervous system hyperactivation, encouraging constructive self-disclosure about the event and its aftermath, shaping this story into a trauma narrative that explores each domain of growth, and using a revised life narrative to establish life principles of service and mission (i.e., ways of thinking and acting in the future to solidify and even enhance their growth) that will be robust to future trauma and foster resilience. This integrated approach is anchored in the Tedeschi and Calhoun model of PTG.

Conclusion

In conclusion, it is safe to say that the concept of PTG continues to attract attention at a time when mental health professionals as well as the public are more aware of widespread trauma and there is a need to find ways to help traumatized persons. The PTG concept offers for trauma survivors and those who wish to assist them a possibility for life that is more than mere survival in the aftermath of trauma. Although PTG is not a universal outcome, it is common enough to suggest that with additional understanding of the PTG process, it can be facilitated and become even more common. Hopefully, through this process, trauma survivors will make major contributions to others around them through their hard-earned wisdom.

References

Abu-Raiya, H., Pargament, K. I., & Mahoney, A. (2011). Examining coping methods with stressful interpersonal events experienced by Muslims living in the United States following the 9/11 attacks. *Psychology of Religion and Spirituality, 3*(1), 1–14.

Alisic, E., van der Schoot, om A. W., van Ginkel, J. R., & Kleber, R. J. (2008). Looking beyond posttraumatic stress disorder in children: Posttraumatic stress reactions, posttraumatic growth, and quality of life in a general population sample. *Journal of Clinical Psychiatry, 69*(9), 1455–1461. http://doi.org/10.4088/JCP.v69n0913

Arnold, D., Calhoun, L. G., Tedeschi, R., & Cann, A. (2005). Vicarious posttraumatic growth in psychotherapy. *Journal of Humanistic Psychology, 45*(2), 239–263.

Antoni, M. H., Lehman, J. M., Kilbourn, K M., Boyers, A. E., Culver, J. L., Alferi, S. M., . . . Carver, C. S. (2001). Cognitive-behavioral stress management intervention decreases the prevalence of depression and enhances benefit finding among women under treatment for early-stage breast cancer. *Health Psychology, 20*(1), 20–32.

Antonovsky, A. (1987). *Unraveling the mystery of health: How people manage stress and stay well.* San Francisco: Jossey-Bass.

Antonovsky, A., & Sourani, T. (1988). Family sense of coherence and family adaptation. *Journal of Marriage and the Family, 50*(1), 79–92. doi:10.2307/352429

Baker, J. M., Kelly, C., Calhoun, L. G., Cann, A., & Tedeschi, R. G. (2008). An examination of posttraumatic growth and posttraumatic depreciation: Two exploratory studies. *Journal of Loss and Trauma, 13*, 45–465.

Barton, S., Boals, A., & Knowles, L. (2013). Thinking about trauma: The unique contributions of event centrality and posttraumatic cognitions in predicting PTSD and posttraumatic growth. *Journal of Traumatic Stress, 26*(6), 718–726.

Berger, R. (2015). *Stress, trauma, and posttraumatic growth: Social context, environment, and identities.* New York: Routledge.

Berger, R., & Weiss, T. (2009). The posttraumatic growth model: An expansion to the family system. *Traumatology, 15*(1), 63–74. doi:10.1177/15347656 08323499

Berntsen, D., & Rubin, D. C. (2006). The centrality of event scale: A measure of integrating a trauma into one's identity and its relation to post-traumatic stress disorder symptoms. *Behaviour research and therapy, 44*(2), 219–231.

Blackie, L. E., Jayawickreme, E., Helzer, E. G., Forgeard, M. J., & Roepke, A. M. (2015). Investigating the veracity of self-perceived posttraumatic growth: A profile analysis approach to corroboration. *Social Psychological and Personality Science, 6*(7), 788–796.

Blix, I., Birkeland, M. S., Hansen, M. B., & Heir, T. (2015). Posttraumatic growth and centrality of event: A longitudinal study in the aftermath of the 2011 Oslo bombing. *Psychological Trauma: Theory, Research, Practice, and Policy, 7*(1), 18–23.

Blix, I., Solberg, Ø., & Heir, T. (2014). Centrality of event and symptoms of posttraumatic stress disorder after the 2011 Oslo bombing attack. *Applied Cognitive Psychology, 28*(2), 249–253.

Bloom, S. (1998). By the crowd they have been broken, by the crowd they shall be healed: The social transformation of trauma. In R.G. Tedeschi, C. L. Park, & L. G. Calhoun (Eds.), *Posttraumatic growth: Positive changes in the aftermath of crisis* (pp. 179–213). Mahwah, NY: Lawrence Erlbaum Associates.

Bluvstein, I., Moravchick, L., Sheps, D., Schreiber, S., & Bloch, M. (2013). Posttraumatic growth, posttraumatic stress symptoms and mental health among coronary heart disease survivors. *Journal of Clinical Psychology in Medical Settings, 20*(2), 164–172.

Bodenmann, G., & Randall, A. K. (2012). Common factors in the enhancement of dyadic coping. *Behavior Therapy, 43*(1), 88–98. doi:10.1016/j.beth.2011.04.003

Brown, A. D., Antonius, D., Kramer, M., Root, J. C., & Hirst, W. (2010). Trauma centrality and PTSD in veterans returning from Iraq and Afghanistan. *Journal of Traumatic Stress, 23*(4), 496–499.

Büchi, S. J., Mörgeli, H., Schnyder, U., Jenewein, J., Glaser, A., Fauchère, J.-C., . . . Sensky, T. (2009). Shared or discordant grief in couples 2–6 years after the death of their premature baby: Effects on suffering and posttraumatic growth. *Psychosomatics: Journal of Consultation Liaison Psychiatry, 50*(2), 123–130.Bush, N. E., Skopp, N. A., McCann, R., & Luxton, D. D. (2011). Posttraumatic growth as protection against suicidal ideation after deployment and combat exposure. *Military Medicine, 176*(11), 1215–1222.

Cadell, S., Regehr, C., & Hemsworth, D. (2003). Factors contributing to posttraumatic growth: A proposed structural equation model. *American Journal of Orthopsychiatry, 73*(3), 279–287.

Calhoun, L. G., & Tedeschi, R.G. (1989–1990). Positive aspects of critical life problems: recollections of grief. *Omega, 20,* 265–272.Calhoun, L. G., & Tedeschi, R. G. (Eds.). (1999). *Facilitating posttraumatic growth: A clinician's guide.* New York: Routledge.

Calhoun, L.G., & Tedeschi, R.G. (2006). *Handbook of posttraumatic growth: Research and practice.* Mahwah, NJ: Lawrence Erlbaum Associates.

Calhoun, L. G., & Tedeschi, R. G. (2006). The foundations of posttraumatic growth: An expanded framework. In L. G. Calhoun & R. G. Tedeschi (Eds.), *Handbook of posttraumatic growth: Research & practice.* Mahwah, NJ: Lawrence Erlbaum Associates.

Calhoun, L. G., & Tedeschi, R.G. (2013). *Posttraumatic growth in clinical practice.* New York: Routledge.

Calhoun, L. G., Cann, A., Tedeschi, R. G., & McMillan, J. (2000). A correlational test of the relationship between posttraumatic growth, religion, and cognitive processing. *Journal of Traumatic Stress, 13*(3), 521–527.

Calhoun, L. G., Cann, A., & Tedeschi, R. G. (2010). The posttraumatic growth model: Sociocultural considerations. In T. Weiss & R. Berger, (Eds.), *Posttraumatic growth and culturally competent practice: Lessons learned from around the globe,* (pp. 1–14). Hoboken, NJ: Wiley.

Canevello, A., Michels, V., & Hilaire, N. (in press-a). The consequences of spouses' posttraumatic growth for own relationship quality and psychological distress. *Journal of Loss and Trauma.*

Canevello, A., Michels, V., & Hilaire, N. (in press-b). Supporting close others' growth after trauma: The role of responsiveness in romantic partners' mutual posttraumatic growth. *Psychological Trauma: Theory, Research, Practice, and Policy.*

Cann, A., Calhoun, L. G., Tedeschi, R. G., Kilmer, R. P., Gil-Rivas, V., Vishnevsky, T., & Danhauer, S. C. (2009) The Core Beliefs Inventory: A brief measure of disruption in the assumptive world. *Anxiety, Stress & Coping, 23*, 19–34.

Cann, A., Calhoun, L. G., Tedeschi, R. G., Triplett, K. N., Vishnevsky, T., & Lindstrom, C. M. (2011). Assessing posttraumatic cognitive processes: The event related rumination inventory. *Anxiety, Stress, & Coping, 24*(2), 137–156.

Cann, A., Calhoun, L. G., Tedeschi, R. G., & Solomon, D. T. (2010). Posttraumatic growth and depreciation as independent experiences and predictors of well-being. *Journal of Loss and Trauma, 15*(3), 151–166.

Cann, A., Calhoun, L. G., Tedeschi, R. G., Taku, K., Vishnevsky, T., Triplett, K. N., & Danhauer, S. C. (2010). A short form of the Posttraumatic Growth Inventory. *Anxiety, Stress & Coping: An International Journal, 23*, 127–137.

Caplan, G. (1964). *Principles of preventive psychiatry.* New York: Basic Books.

Carr, A. (2011). *Positive psychology: The science of happiness and human strengths.* New York: Routledge.

Castonguay, A. L., Crocker, P. R., Hadd, V., McDonough, M. H., & Sabiston, C. M. (2015). Linking physical self-worth to posttraumatic growth in a sample of physically active breast cancer survivors. *Journal of Applied Biobehavioral Research, 20*(2), 53–70.

Chopko, B., & Schwartz, R. (2009). The relation between mindfulness and posttraumatic growth: A study of first responders to trauma-inducing incidents. *Journal of Mental Health Counseling, 31*(4), 363–376.

Cieslak, R., Benight, C., Schmidt, N., Luszczynska, A., Curtin, E., Clark, R. A., & Kissinger, P. (2009). Predicting posttraumatic growth among Hurricane Katrina survivors living with HIV: The role of self-efficacy, social support, and PTSD symptoms. *Anxiety, Stress & Coping: An International Journal, 22*(4), 449–463.

Colville, G., & Cream, P. (2009). Post-traumatic growth in parents after a child's admission to intensive care: Maybe Nietzsche was right?. *Intensive Care Medicine, 35*(5), 919–923.

Coroiu, A., Körner, A., Burke, S., Meterissian, S., & Sabiston, C. M. (2016). Stress and posttraumatic growth among survivors of breast cancer: A test of curvilinear effects. *International Journal of Stress Management, 23*, 84–97.

Coyne, J. C., & Tennen, H. (2010). Positive psychology in cancer care: Bad science, exaggerated claims, and unproven medicine. *Annals of Behavioral Medicine, 39*(1), 16–26.

Cryder, C. H., Kilmer, R. P., Calhoun, L. G., & Tedeschi, R. G.(2006). An exploratory study of posttraumatic growth in children following a natural disaster. *American Journal of Orthopsychiatry, 76*, 65–69.

Danhauer, S. C., Russell, G., Case, L. D., Sohl, S. J., Tedeschi, R. G., Addington, E. L., . . . & Avis, N. E. (2015). Trajectories of posttraumatic growth and associated characteristics in women with breast cancer. *Annals of Behavioral Medicine, 49*, 650–659.

Danhauer, S., Russell, G., Tedeschi, R. G., Jesse, M., Vishnevsky, T., Daley, K., . . . Powell, B. (2013). A longitudinal investigation of posttraumatic growth in adult patients undergoing treatment for acute leukemia. *Journal of Clinical*

Psychology in Medical Settings, 20(1), 13–24. http://doi.org/10.1007/s10880 -012-9304-5

Danoff-Burg, S., Mosher, C. E., Seawell, A. H., & Agee, J. D. (2010). Does narrative writing instruction enhance the benefits of expressive writing? *Anxiety, Stress & Coping, 23*(3), 341–352. http://doi.org/10.1080/10615800903 191137

Dekel, S., Ein-Dor, T., & Solomon, Z. (2012). Posttraumatic growth and posttraumatic distress: A longitudinal study. *Psychological Trauma: Theory, Research, Practice, and Policy, 4*(1), 94.

Dekel, R., & Nuttman-Shwartz, O. (2009). Posttraumatic stress and growth: The contribution of cognitive appraisal and sense of belonging to the country. *Health & Social Work, 34*(2), 87–96.

Dirik, G., & Karanci, A. N. (2008). Variables related to posttraumatic growth in Turkish rheumatoid arthritis patients. *Journal of Clinical Psychology in Medical Settings, 15*(3), 193–203.

Epstein, S. (1985). The implications of cognitive-experiential self-theory for research in social psychology and personality. *Journal for the Theory of Social Behavior, 15*, 283–310.

Epstein, S. (1991). The self-concept, the traumatic neurosis, and the structure of personality. In D. Z. Ozer, J. M. Healy, Jr., & A. J. Stewart (Eds.), *Perspectives on personality* (Vol. 3, pp. 63–98). London: Jessica Kingsley Publishers.

Figley, C. R. (1989). *Helping traumatized families.* San Francisco: Jossey-Bass.

Forstmeier, S., Kuwert, P., Spitzer, C., Freyberger, H. J., & Maercker, A. (2009). Posttraumatic growth, social acknowledgment as survivors, and sense of coherence in former German child soldiers of World War II. *The American Journal of Geriatric Psychiatry, 17*(12), 1030–1039.

Frazier, P., Tennen, H., Gavian, M., Park, C., Tomich, P., & Tashiro, T. (2009). Does self-reported posttraumatic growth reflect genuine positive change? *Psychological Science, 20*(7), 912–919.

Frankl, V. E. (1963). *Man's search for meaning: An introduction to logotherapy.* New York: Pocket Books.

Frattaroli, J. (2006). Experimental disclosure and its moderators: A meta-analysis. *Psychological Bulletin, 132*(6), 823–865. http://doi.org/10.1037/0033-2909 .132.6.823

Garmezy, N. (1985). Stress resistant children: The search for protective factors. In J. E. Stevenson (Ed.), *Recent research in developmental psychopathology. Journal of child psychology and psychiatry* (Book Suppl. No. 4). Oxford, England: Pergamon.

Gallaway, M. S., Millikan, A. M., & Bell, M. R. (2011). The association between deployment-related posttraumatic growth among US army soldiers and negative behavioral health conditions. *Journal of Clinical Psychology, 67*(12), 1151–1160.

Garcia, F. E., & Wlodarczyk, A. (2016). Psychometric properties of the Posttraumatic Growth Inventory-Short Form among Chilean adults. *Journal of Loss and Trauma, 21*, 303–314.

Groleau, J. M., Calhoun, L. G., Cann, A., & Tedeschi, R. G. (2013). The role of centrality of events in posttraumatic distress and posttraumatic growth. *Psychological Trauma: Theory, Research, Practice, and Policy, 5*(5), 477.

Haas, M. (2015). *Bouncing forward: Transforming bad breaks into breakthroughs.* New York: Enliven.

Hall, B. J., Hobfoll, S. E., Palmieri, P. A., Canetti-Nisim, D., Shapira, O., Johnson, R. J., & Galea, S. (2008). The psychological impact of impending forced settler disengagement in Gaza: Trauma and posttraumatic growth. *Journal of Traumatic Stress, 21,* 22–29.

Hafstad, G. S., Gil-Rivas, V., Kilmer, R. P., & Raeder, S. (2010). Parental adjustment, family functioning, and posttraumatic growth among Norwegian children and adolescents following a natural disaster. *American Journal of Orthopsychiatry, 80*(2), 248–257.

Hagenaars, M. A., & van Minnen, A. (2010). Posttraumatic growth in exposure therapy for PTSD. *Journal of Traumatic Stress, 23*(4), 504–508.

Harvey, J. H., Barnett, K., & Rupe, S. (2006). Posttraumatic growth and other outcomes of major loss in the context of complex family lives. In L. G. Calhoun & R. G. Tedeschi (Eds.), *Handbook of posttraumatic growth: Research & practice* (pp. 100–117). Mahwah, NJ: Lawrence Erlbaum Associates.

Helgeson, V. S., Reynolds, K. A., & Tomich, P. L. (2006). A meta-analytic review of benefit finding and growth. *Journal of Consulting and Clinical Psychology, 74*(5), 797.

Hobfoll, S. E., Hall, B. J., Canetti-Nisim, D., Galea, S., Johnson, R. J., & Palmieri, P. A. (2007). Refining our understanding of traumatic growth in the face of terrorism: Moving from meaning cognitions to doing what is meaningful. *Applied Psychology: An International Review, 56,* 345–366.

Hussain, D., & Bhushan, B. (2013). Posttraumatic growth experiences among Tibetan refugees: A qualitative investigation. *Qualitative Research in Psychology, 10*(2), 204–216.

Janoff-Bulman, R. (1985). The aftermath of victimization: Rebuilding shattered assumptions. In C.R. Figley (Ed.), *Trauma and its wake* (pp. 15–35). New York: Brunner/Mazel.

Janoff-Bulman, R. (1992). *Shattered assumptions: Towards a new psychology of trauma.* New York: The Free Press.

Janoff-Bulman, R. (2006). Schema-change perspectives on posttraumatic growth. In L. G. Calhoun & R. G. Tedeschi (Eds.), *Handbook of posttraumatic growth: Research & practice* (pp. 81–99). Mahwah, NJ: Lawrence Erlbaum Associates Publishers.

Jayawickreme, E., & Blackie, L. E. (2014). Post-traumatic growth as positive personality change: Evidence, controversies and future directions. *European Journal of Personality, 28*(4), 312–331.

Johnson, S. F., & Boals, A. (2015). Refining our ability to measure posttraumatic growth. *Psychological Trauma: Theory, Research, Practice, And Policy, 7*(5), 422–429. doi:10.1037/tra0000013

Joseph, S., Williams, R., & Yule, W. (1993). Changes in outlook following disaster: The preliminary development of a measure to assess positive and negative responses. *Journal of Traumatic Stress, 6*(2), 271–279. doi:10.1002/jts.2490060209

Kelly, G. (1955). *The psychology of personal constructs.* New York: Norton.

Kılıç, C., Magruder, K. M., & Koryürek, M. M. (2015). Does trauma type relate to posttraumatic growth after war? A pilot study of young Iraqi war survivors living in Turkey. *Transcultural Psychiatry, 53*(1), 110–123.

Kilmer, R. P. (2006). Resilience and posttraumatic growth in children. In L. G. Calhoun & R. G. Tedeschi (Eds.), *Handbook of posttraumatic growth: Research & practice* (pp. 264–288). Mahwah, NJ: Lawrence Erlbaum Associates Publishers.

Kilmer, R. P., & Gil-Rivas, V. (2010). Exploring posttraumatic growth in children impacted by Hurricane Katrina: Correlates of the phenomenon and developmental considerations. *Child Development, 81*(4), 1211–1227.

Kilmer, R., Gil-Rivas, V., Tedeschi, R., Cann, A., Calhoun, L., Buchanan, T., & Taku, K. (2009). Use of the revised Posttraumatic Growth Inventory for Children. *Journal of Traumatic Stress, 22,* 248–253.

Kleim, B., & Ehlers, A. (2009). Evidence for a curvilinear relationship between posttraumatic growth and posttrauma depression and PTSD in assault survivors. *Journal of Traumatic Stress, 22*(1), 45–52.

Knaevelsrud, C., Liedl, A., & Maercker, A. (2010). Posttraumatic growth, optimism and openness as outcomes of a cognitive-behavioural intervention for posttraumatic stress reactions. *Journal of Health Psychology, 15*(7), 1030–1038.

Kobasa, S. C. (1979). Stressful life events, personality, and health: An inquiry into hardiness. *Journal of Personality and Social Psychology, 37,* 1–11.

Kunst, M., Winkel, F. W., & Bogaerts, S. (2010). Prevalence and predictors of posttraumatic stress disorder among victims of violence applying for state compensation. *Journal of Interpersonal Violence, 25*(9), 1631–1654.

Lamela, D., Figueiredo, B., Bastos, A., & Martins, H. (2014). Psychometric properties of the Portuguese version of the Posttraumatic Growth Inventory Short Form among divorced adults. *European Journal of Psychological Assessment, 30,* 3–14.

Larsen, S. E., & Berenbaum, H. (2015). Are specific emotion regulation strategies differentially associated with posttraumatic growth versus stress? *Journal of Aggression, Maltreatment & Trauma, 24*(7), 794–808.

Laufer, A., Solomon, Z., & Levine, S. Z. (2010). Elaboration on posttraumatic growth in youth exposed to terror: The role of religiosity and political ideology. *Social Psychiatry & Psychiatric Epidemiology, 45*(6), 647–653. http://doi.org/10.1007/s00127-009-0106-5

Levine, S. Z., Laufer, A., Stein, E., Hamama-Raz, Y., & Solomon, Z. (2009). Examining the relationship between resilience and posttraumatic growth. *Journal of Traumatic Stress, 22*(4), 282-286.

Lindstrom, C. M., Cann, A., Calhoun, L. G., & Tedeschi, R. G. (2013). The relationship of core belief challenge, rumination, disclosure, and sociocultural elements to posttraumatic growth. *Psychological Trauma: Theory, Research, Practice, and Policy, 5*(1), 50.

Linley, P. A., & Joseph, S. (2004). Positive change following trauma and adversity: A review. *Journal of Traumatic Stress, 17*(1), 11–21.

Linley, P. A., Joseph, S., Cooper, R., Harris, S., & Meyer, C. (2003). Positive and negative changes following vicarious exposure to the September 11 terrorist attacks. *Journal of Traumatic Stress, 16*(5), 481–485.

Liu, J., Wang, H., Hua, L., Chen, J., Wang, M., & Li, Y. (2015). Psychometric evaluation of the Simplified Chinese version of the Posttraumatic Growth Inventory for assessing breast cancer survivors. *European Journal of Oncology Nursing, 19*, 391–396.

Lu, Q., Zheng, D., Young, L., Kagawa-Singer, M., & Loh, A. (2012). A pilot study of expressive writing intervention among Chinese-speaking breast cancer survivors. *Health Psychology, 31*(5), 548–551.

Magruder, K. M., Kılıç, C., & Koryürek, M. M. (2015). Relationship of posttraumatic growth to symptoms of posttraumatic stress disorder and depression: A pilot study of Iraqi students. *International Journal of Psychology, 50*(5), 402–406.

Maguen, S., Vogt, D. S., King, L. A., King, D. W., & Litz, B. T. (2006). Posttraumatic growth among Gulf War I veterans: The predictive role of deployment-related experiences and background characteristics. *Journal of Loss and Trauma, 11*(5), 373–388.

Markus, H., & Nurius, P. (1986). Possible selves. *American Psychologist, 41*, 954–969.

Matsui, T., & Taku, K. (2016). A review of posttraumatic growth and help-seeking behavior in cancer survivors: Effects of distal and proximate culture. *Japanese Psychological Research, 58*(1), 142–162.

McCaslin, S. E., de Zoysa, P., Butler, L. D., Hart, S., Marmar, C. R., Metzler, T. J., & Koopman, C. (2009). The relationship of posttraumatic growth to peritraumatic reactions and posttraumatic stress symptoms among Sri Lankan university students. *Journal of Traumatic Stress, 22*(4), 334–339.

Meichenbaum, D. (2006). Resilience and posttraumatic growth: A constructive narrative perspective. In L. G. Calhoun & R. G. Tedeschi (Eds.), *Handbook of posttraumatic growth: Research & practice* (pp. 355–367). Mahwah, NJ: Lawrence Erlbaum Associates Publishers.

Meyerson, D. A., Grant, K. E., Carter, J. S., & Kilmer, R. P. (2011). Posttraumatic growth among children and adolescents: A systematic review. *Clinical Psychology Review, 31*(6), 949–964. http://doi.org/10.1016/j.cpr.2011.06.003

Moore, A. M., Gamblin, T. C., Geller, D. A., Youssef, M. N., Hoffman, K. E., Gemmell, L., . . . Steel, J. L. (2011). A prospective study of posttraumatic growth as assessed by self report and family caregiver in the context of advanced cancer. *Psycho-Oncology, 20*(5), 479–487. http://doi.org/10.1002/pon.1746

Morris, B. A., & Shakespeare-Finch, J. (2011a). Rumination, post-traumatic growth, and distress: Structural equation modelling with cancer survivors. *Psycho-Oncology, 20*(11), 1176–1183.

Morris, B. A., & Shakespeare-Finch, J. (2011b). Cancer diagnostic group differences in posttraumatic growth: Accounting for age, gender, trauma severity, and distress. *Journal of Loss and Trauma, 16*(3), 229–242.

Morris, B. A., & Shakespeare-Finch, J. (2012). Psychosocial experiences of cancer: Surpassing survival and recognising posttraumatic growth as well as distress. In K. Gow & M. Celinski (Eds.) *Individual trauma: Recovering from deep wounds and exploring the potential for renewal.* (pp. 261–276). Hauppauge, NY: Nova Science Publishers.

Morris, B. A., Shakespeare-Finch, J., & Scott, J. L. (2011). Posttraumatic growth after cancer: The importance of health-related benefits and newfound compassion for others. *Supportive Care in Cancer, 20*(4), 749–756. http://doi.org/10.1007/s00520-011-1143-7

Neimeyer, R. A. (2001). *Meaning reconstruction and the experience of loss.* Washington, DC: American Psychological Association.

O'Leary, V. E., Alday, C. S., & Ickovics, J. R. (1998). Models of life change and posttraumatic growth. In R. G. Tedeschi, C. L. Park, & L. G. Calhoun (Eds.), *Posttraumatic growth: Positive changes in the aftermath of crisis* (pp. 127–151). Mahwah, NJ: Lawrence Erlbaum Associates.

Park, C. L. (2010). Making sense of the meaning literature: An integrative review of meaning making and its effects on adjustment to stressful life events. *Psychological Bulletin, 136*(2), 257.

Park, C. L., Cohen, L. H., & Murch, R. L. (1996). Assessment and prediction of stress-related growth. *Journal of Personality, 64*(1), 71–105.

Parkes, C. M., & Weiss, R. S. (1983). *Recovery from bereavement.* New York: Basic Books.

Pennebaker, J. W., & Beall, S. K. (1986). Confronting a traumatic event: Toward an understanding of inhibition and disease. *Journal of Abnormal Psychology, 95*(3), 274.

Pennebaker, J. W., & Chung, C. K. (2011). Expressive writing and its links to mental and physical health. In H. S. Friedman (Ed.), *Oxford handbook of health psychology.* New York: Oxford University Press.

Pennebaker, J. W., & Stone, L. D. (2003). Words of wisdom: Language use over the life span. *Journal of Personality and Social Psychology, 85*(2), 291–301.

Peterson, C., Park, N., Pole, N., D'Andrea, W., & Seligman, M. E. (2008). Strengths of character and posttraumatic growth. *Journal of Traumatic Stress, 21*(2), 214–217.

Piaget, J. (1954). *The construction of reality in the child.* New York: Basic Books.

Pietrzak, R. H., Johnson, D. C., Goldstein, M. B., Malley, J. C., Rivers, A. J., Morgan, C. A., & Southwick, S. M. (2010). Psychosocial buffers of traumatic stress, depressive symptoms, and psychosocial difficulties in veterans of Operations Enduring Freedom and Iraqi Freedom: The role of resilience, unit support, and postdeployment social support. *Journal of Affective Disorders, 120*(1), 188–192.

Prati, G., & Pietrantoni, L. (2009). Optimism, social support, and coping strategies as factors contributing to posttraumatic growth: A meta-analysis. *Journal of Loss & Trauma, 14*(5), 364–388.

Rendon, J. (2015). *Upside: The new science of posttraumatic growth.* New York: Touchstone.

Robinaugh, D. J., & McNally, R. J. (2011). Trauma centrality and PTSD symptom severity in adult survivors of childhood sexual abuse. *Journal of Traumatic Stress, 24*(4), 483–486.

Roepke, A. M., Jayawickreme, E., & Riffle, O. M. (2014). Meaning and health: A systematic review. *Applied Research in Quality of Life, 9*(4), 1055–1079.

Rogers, C. R. (1957). The necessary and sufficient conditions of therapeutic personality change. *Journal of Consulting Psychology, 21*(2), 95–103. doi:10.1037/h0045357

Roland, A. G., Currier, J. M., Rojas-Flores, L., & Herrera, S. (2014). Event centrality and posttraumatic outcomes in the context of pervasive violence: A study of teachers in El Salvador. *Anxiety, Stress, & Coping, 27*(3), 335–346.

Rosenbach, C., & Renneberg, B. (2008). Positive change after severe burn injuries. *Journal of Burn Care & Research, 29*(4), 638–643.

Rutter, M. (1987). Psychosocial resilience and protective mechanisms. *American Journal of Orthopsychiatry, 57*, 316–331.

Salsman, J. M., Segerstrom, S. C., Brechting, E. H., Carlson, C. R., & Andrykowski, M. A. (2009). Posttraumatic growth and PTSD symptomatology among colorectal cancer survivors: A 3-month longitudinal examination of cognitive processing. *Psycho-Oncology, 18*(1), 30–41.

Salter, E., & Stallard, P. (2004). Posttraumatic growth in child survivors of a road traffic accident. *Journal of Traumatic Stress, 17*(4), 335–340.

Sawyer, A., Ayers, S., & Field, A. P. (2010). Posttraumatic growth and adjustment among individuals with cancer or HIV/AIDS: A meta-analysis. *Clinical Psychology Review, 30*(4), 436–447.

Schroevers, M. J., Helgeson, V. S., Sanderman, R., & Ranchor, A. V. (2010). Type of social support matters for prediction of posttraumatic growth among cancer survivors. *Psycho-Oncology, 19*(1), 46–53.

Seligman, M., & Csikszentmihalyi, M. (2000). Positive psychology: An introduction. *American Psychologist, 55*, 5–14.

Senol-Durak, E., & Ayvasik, H. B. (2010). Factors associated with posttraumatic growth among myocardial infarction patients: Perceived social support, perception of the event and coping. *Journal of Clinical Psychology in Medical Settings, 17*(2), 150–158. http://doi.org/10.1007/s10880-010-9192-5

Shakespeare-Finch, J., & Armstrong, D. (2010). Trauma type and posttrauma outcomes: Differences between survivors of motor vehicle accidents, sexual assault, and bereavement. *Journal of Loss and Trauma, 15*(2), 69–82.

Shakespeare-Finch, J., & Barrington, A. J. (2012). Behavioural changes add validity to the construct of posttraumatic growth. *Journal of Traumatic Stress, 25*(4), 433–439.

Shakespeare-Finch, J., & Enders, T. (2008). Corroborating evidence of posttraumatic growth. *Journal of Traumatic Stress, 21*(4), 421–424.

Shakespeare-Finch, J., Gow, K., & Smith, S. (2005). Personality, coping and posttraumatic growth in emergency ambulance personnel. *Traumatology, 11*(4), 325–334.

Shakespeare-Finch, J., & Lurie-Beck, J. (2014). A meta-analytic clarification of the relationship between posttraumatic growth and symptoms of posttraumatic distress disorder. *Journal of Anxiety Disorders, 28*(2), 223–229.

Shand, L. K., Cowlishaw, S., Brooker, J. E., Burney, S., & Ricciardelli, L. A. (2014). Correlates of post-traumatic stress symptoms and growth in cancer patients: A systematic review and meta-analysis. *Psycho-Oncology, 24*(6), 624–634.

Shigemoto, Y., & Poyrazli, S. (2013). Factors related to posttraumatic growth in US and Japanese college students. *Psychological Trauma: Theory, Research, Practice, and Policy, 5*(2), 128–134.

Shoji, K., Bock, J., Cieslak, R., Zukowska, K., Luszczynska, A., & Benight, C. C. (2014). Cultivating secondary traumatic growth among healthcare workers: The role of social support and self-efficacy. *Journal of Clinical Psychology, 70*(9), 831–846.

Silva, S. M., Crespo, C., & Canavarro, M. C. (2012). Pathways for psychological adjustment in breast cancer: A longitudinal study on coping strategies and posttraumatic growth. *Psychology & Health, 27*(11), 1323–1341.

Silva, S. M., Moreira, H. C., & Canavarro, M. C. (2012). Examining the links between perceived impact of breast cancer and psychosocial adjustment: The buffering role of posttraumatic growth. *Psycho-Oncology, 21*(4), 409–418.

Slavin-Spenny, O. M., Cohen, J. L., Oberleitner, L. M., & Lumley, M. A. (2011). The effects of different methods of emotional disclosure: Differentiating post-traumatic growth from stress symptoms. *Journal of Clinical Psychology, 67*(10), 993–1007.

Smyth, J. M. (1998). Written emotional expression: Effect sizes, outcome types, and moderating variables. *Journal of Consulting and Clinical Psychology, 66*(1), 174.

Smyth, J. M., Hockemeyer, J. R., & Tulloch, H. (2008). Expressive writing and post-traumatic stress disorder: Effects on trauma symptoms, mood states, and cortisol reactivity. *British Journal of Health Psychology, 13*(1), 85–93.

Solomon, Z., & Dekel, R. (2007). Posttraumatic stress disorder and posttraumatic growth among Israeli ex-POWs. *Journal of Traumatic Stress, 20*(3), 303–312.

Stockton, H., Joseph, S., & Hunt, N. (2014). Expressive writing and posttraumatic growth: An Internet-based study. *Traumatology: An International Journal, 20*(2), 75–83. http://doi.org/10.1037/h0099377

Sumalla, E. C., Ochoa, C., & Blanco, I. (2009). Posttraumatic growth in cancer: Reality or illusion?. *Clinical Psychology Review, 29*(1), 24–33.

Taku, K., Calhoun, L. G., Kilmer, R. P., & Tedeschi, R. G. (2008). Posttraumatic growth and non-traumatic growth in Japanese youth. In *54th annual meeting of the Southeastern Psychological Association*. Charlotte, NC.

Taku, K., Cann, A., Calhoun, L. G., & Tedeschi, R. G. (2008). The factor structure of the Posttraumatic Growth Inventory: A comparison of five models using confirmatory factor analysis. *Journal of Traumatic Stress, 21*(2), 158–164. doi:10.1002/jts.20305

Taku, K., Cann, A., Tedeschi, R. G., & Calhoun, L. G. (2009). Intrusive versus deliberate rumination in posttraumatic growth across US and Japanese samples. *Anxiety, Stress, & Coping, 22*(2), 129–136.

Taku, K., Cann, A., Tedeschi, R. G., & Calhoun, L. G. (2015). Core beliefs shaken by an earthquake correlate with posttraumatic growth. *Psychological Trauma: Theory, Research, Practice, and Policy, 7,* 563–569.

Taku, K., Tedeschi, R. G., & Cann, A. (2015). Relationships of posttraumatic growth and stress responses in bereaved young adults. *Journal of Loss and Trauma, 20*(1), 56–71.

Taku, K., Tedeschi, R. G., Cann, A., & Calhoun, L. G. (2009). The culture of disclosure: Effects of perceived reactions to disclosure on posttraumatic growth and distress in Japan. *Journal of Social and Clinical Psychology, 28*(10), 1226–1243.

Taylor, S. E., & Armor, D. A. (1996). Positive illusions and coping with adversity. *Journal of Personality, 64*(4), 873–898. http://doi.org/10.1111/1467-6494.ep9706272190

Taylor, S. E., Kemeny, M. E., Reed, G., Bower, J. E., & Gruenewald, T. L. (2000). Psychological resources, positive illusions, and health. *American Psychologist, 5,* 99–109.

Tedeschi, R.G. (1999). Violence transformed: Posttraumatic growth in survivors and their societies. *Aggression and Violent Behavior, 4,* 319–341.

Tedeschi, R. G. (2011). Posttraumatic growth in combat veterans. *Journal of Clinical Psychology in Medical Settings, 18*(2), 137–144.

Tedeschi, R., Addington, E., Cann, A., & Calhoun, L. G. (2014). Posttraumatic growth: Some needed corrections and reminders. *European Journal of Personality, 28,* 350–351.

Tedeschi, R.G., & Calhoun, L. G. (1995). *Trauma and transformation: Growing in the aftermath of suffering.* Thousand Oaks, CA: Sage.

Tedeschi, R. G., & Calhoun, L. G. (1996). The Posttraumatic Growth Inventory: Measuring the positive legacy of trauma. *Journal of Traumatic Stress, 9*(3), 455–471.

Tedeschi, R. G., & Calhoun, L. G. (2004). Posttraumatic growth: Conceptual foundations and empirical evidence. *Psychological Inquiry, 15*(1), 1–18.

Tedeschi, R. G., & Calhoun. L. G. (2010). A surprise attack, a surprise result: Posttraumatic growth through expert companionship. In G. W. Burns (Ed.).

Happiness, healing, enhancement: Your casebook collection for applying positive psychology in therapy (pp. 226–236). Hoboken, NJ: Wiley.

Tedeschi, R. G., & Calhoun, L. G. (2012). Pathways to personal transformation: Theoretical and empirical developments. In P. Wong (Ed.). *The human quest for meaning: Theories, research and applications* (2nd ed., pp. 559–572). New York: Routledge.

Tedeschi, R.G., Calhoun, L. G., & Cann, A. (2007). Evaluating resource gain: Understanding and *misunderstanding* posttraumatic growth. *Applied Psychology: An International Review, 56,* 396–406.

Tedeschi, R. G., Calhoun, L. G., & Groleau, J. M. (2015). Clinical applications of posttraumatic growth. In S. Joseph (Ed.), *Positive psychology in practice: Promoting human flourishing in work, health, education, and everyday life* (2nd ed., pp. 503–518). Hoboken, NJ: Wiley.

Tedeschi, R. G., & McNally, R. J. (2011). Can we facilitate posttraumatic growth in combat veterans?. *American Psychologist, 66*(1), 19–24.

Tedeschi, R.G., Park, C. L., & Calhoun, L. G. (Eds.) (1998). *Posttraumatic growth: Positive change in the aftermath of crisis.* Mahwah, NJ: Lawrence Erlbaum Associates.

Tennen, H., & Affleck, G. (2002). Benefit-finding and benefit-reminding. In C. R. Snyder & S. J. Lopez (Eds.), *The handbook of positive psychology* (pp. 584–594). New York: Oxford University Press.

Tennen, H., & Affleck, G. (2009). Assessing positive life change: In search of meticulous methods. In Park, C. L., Lechner, S. C., Antoni, M. H., & Stanton, A. L. (Eds.), *Medical illness and positive life change: Can crisis lead to personal transformation?* (pp. 31–49). Washington, DC: American Psychological Association.

Thombre, A., Sherman, A. C., & Simonton, S. (2010). Posttraumatic growth among cancer patients in India. *Journal of Behavioral Medicine, 33,* 15–23.

Thornton, A. A., & Perez, M. A. (2006). Posttraumatic growth in prostate cancer survivors and their partners. *Psycho-Oncology, 15*(4), 285–296. doi:10.1002/pon.953

Triplett, K. N., Tedeschi, R. G., Cann, A., Calhoun, L. G., & Reeve, C. L. (2012). Posttraumatic growth, meaning in life, and life satisfaction in response to trauma. *Psychological Trauma: Theory, Research, Practice, and Policy, 4*(4), 400–410.

Tsai, J., Mota, N. P., Southwick, S. M., & Pietrzak, R. H. (2016). What doesn't kill you makes you stronger: A national study of US military veterans. *Journal of Affective Disorders, 189,* 269–271.

Turner-Sack, A. M., Menna, R., & Setchell, S. R. (2012). Posttraumatic growth, coping strategies, and psychological distress in adolescent survivors of cancer. *Journal of Pediatric Oncology Nursing, 29*(2), 70–79. http://doi.org /10.1177/1043454212439472

Ullrich, P. M., & Lutgendorf, S. K. (2002). Journaling about stressful events: Effects of cognitive processing and emotional expression. *Annals of Behavioral*

Medicine, 24(3), 244–250.Valdez, C. E., & Lilly, M. M. (2015). Posttraumatic growth in survivors of intimate partner violence: An assumptive world process. *Journal of Interpersonal Violence, 30*(2), 215–231. doi:10.1177/0886260514533154

Vazquez, C., Perez-Sales, P., & Ochoa, C. (2015). Posttraumatic growth: Challenges from a cross-cultural viewpoint. In G. A. Fava & C. Ruini (Eds.), *Increasing psychological well-being in clinical and educational settings: Interventions and cultural contexts* (Vol. 8). Dordrecht, Netherlands: Springer.

Vernon, L. L. (2012). Relationships among proactive coping, posttrauma gratitude, and psychopathology in a traumatized college sample. *Journal of Aggression, Maltreatment & Trauma, 21*(1), 114–130. http://doi.org/10.1080/10926771.2012.633298

Vishnevsky, T., Cann, A., Calhoun, L. G., Tedeschi, R. G., & Demakis, G. J. (2010). Gender differences in self-reported posttraumatic growth: A meta-analysis. *Psychology of Women Quarterly, 34*(1), 110–120.

Wang, A. W. T., Chang, C. S., Chen, S. T., Chen, D. R., & Hsu, W. Y. (2014). Identification of posttraumatic growth trajectories in the first year after breast cancer surgery. *Psycho-Oncology, 23*(12), 1399–1405.

Watkins, E. R. (2008). Constructive and unconstructive repetitive thought. *Psychological Bulletin, 134*, 163–206.

Weiss, T. (2004). Correlates of posttraumatic growth in married breast cancer survivors. *Journal of Social and Clinical Psychology, 23*(5), 733–746.

Weiss, T., & Berger, R. (2010). Posttraumatic growth around the globe: Research findings and practice implications. In T. Weiss & R. Berger (Eds.), *Posttraumatic growth and culturally competent practice: Lessons learned from around the globe* (pp. 189–195). Hoboken, NJ: John Wiley & Sons, Inc.

Werner, E. (1984, November). Resilient children. *Young Children, 40*, 68–72.

Wild, N. D., & Paivio, S. C. (2003). Psychological adjustment, coping, and emotion regulation as predictors of posttraumatic growth. *Journal of Aggression, Maltreatment & Trauma, 8*(4), 97–122.

Wilson, J. T., & Boden, J. M. (2008). The effects of personality, social support and religiosity on posttraumatic growth. *Australasian Journal of Disaster and Trauma Studies,* (1).

Wolchik, S. A., Coxe, S., Tein, J. Y., Sandler, I. N., & Ayers, T. S. (2008). Six-year longitudinal predictors of posttraumatic growth in parentally bereaved adolescents and young adults. *Omega: Journal of Death & Dying, 58*(2), 107–128.

Wu, Z., Xu, J., & Sui, Y. (2016). Posttraumatic stress disorder and posttraumatic growth coexistence and the risk factors in Wenchuan earthquake survivors. *Psychiatry Research.* Advance online publication.

Yi, J., Zebrack, B., Kim, M. A., & Cousino, M. (2015). Posttraumatic growth outcomes and their correlates among young adult survivors of childhood cancer. *Journal of Pediatric Psychology, 40*(9), 835–839.

Zhou, X., & Wu, X. (2016). The relationship between rumination, posttraumatic stress disorder, and posttraumatic growth among Chinese adolescents after earthquake: A longitudinal study. *Journal of Affective Disorders, 193,* 242–248.

Zoellner, T. & Maercker, A. (2006). Posttraumatic growth in clinical psychology— A critical review and introduction of a two component model. *Clinical Psychology Review, 26,* 626–653.

Zoellner, T., Rabe, S., Karl, A., & Maercker, A. (2008). Posttraumatic growth in accident survivors: Openness and optimism as predictors of its constructive or illusory sides. *Journal of Clinical Psychology, 64*(3), 245–263. doi:10.1002/jclp.20441

Positive Youth Development: How Intrinsic Motivation Amplifies Adolescents' Social-Emotional Learning

Reed W. Larson, Carolyn Orson, and Jill R. Bowers

Preparation for adulthood has become more difficult in the last 100 years as the distance has lengthened between the world of childhood and the increasingly complex and demanding "real world" of adulthood. Adulthood is challenging. In the fluid global 21st century, adults need to be ready to move between occupations. Basic career, family, and lifestyle decisions are less delimited. Adulthood requires more initiative and adaptability (Larson, 2000). To develop a career, cultivate healthy relationships, sustain positive well-being, and contribute to one's community, contemporary youth need to acquire not just the cognitive skills, but an expanded portfolio of noncognitive, *social-emotional (SE) skills*[1] (Larson, Brown, & Mortimer, 2002; National Research Council [NRC], 2012). These SE skills include those for navigating more complex and varied social worlds and for managing one's emotions in the multifold types of demanding situations and relationships that now make up adult life. Evidence suggests that these SE skills are as important as cognitive skills for adulthood (Heckman, Stixrud, & Urzua, 2006).

How do youth develop these skills? How can young people become prepared to handle the SE challenges of life in the 21st century and become mature, resilient, contributing adults? These are central questions addressed by the field of positive youth development. In this chapter, we give particular attention to how youth can be motivated to learn these social-emotional skills—skills that can be elusive and difficult to learn. To find answers, we focus on the rich developmental settings provided by youth programs, such as arts, technology, and leadership programs. Research indicates that programs are a context in which youth are both highly motivated (Larson, 2011a; Vandell et al., 2006) and learn SE skills (Catalano, Berglund, Ryan, Lonczak, & Hawkins, 2004; Durlak, Weissberg, & Pachan, 2010; Vandell, Larson, Mahoney, & Watts, 2015) more so than in school classes (Larson, Hansen, & Moneta, 2006). The chapter shows how intrinsic motivation (IM) and SE learning can be synergistic. We draw on research in the United States, where youth programs are prevalent. But we believe that many of our conclusions can be adapted to other national and cultural contexts.

Positive Youth Development

Positive Youth Development (PYD) is an emerging field of research and practice concerned with supporting young people's acquisition of SE skills and related positive assets (Larson, 2000; Lerner, Phelps, Forman, & Bowers, 2009). Much research and youth policy in the late 20th century focused on adolescents' problem behaviors and how to prevent them. Pittman (1999, p. 1) articulated a central rationale for the PYD field with the poignant observation: "Problem free is not fully prepared." To help youth prepare for adulthood, we need to attend to their SE development. The PYD field has made two contributions relevant to our topic.

One contribution has been efforts to delineate the *youth outcomes* that define positive development.[2] A frequently used list of positive youth outcomes is the *Six Cs*: competence, connection, character, confidence, caring/compassion, and contribution (Lerner, Almerigi, Theokas, & Lerner, 2005). Benson and colleagues (2006) provided a more nuanced list of 20 internal developmental assets (such as integrity, school engagement, cultural competence, peaceful conflict resolution skills) and 20 external developmental assets (e.g., positive relationships with adults, peers, and community institutions).

The term *social-emotional skills* is a new conceptual rubric for formulating positive youth outcomes (CASEL, 2015; Smith, McGovern, Larson, Hilltaker, & Peck, 2016). This term was imported from developmental psychology, and its focus on "skills" is narrower than the scope of Lerner's and Benson's lists of outcomes, which include other types of valuable developmental assets like positive relationships and social capital. Nonetheless, the focus on "skills" is useful because it identifies outcomes that can be learned in one setting and potentially transferred into future settings in youth's adult lives. In our research we have focused on six domains of SE skills (emotional management, empathy, teamwork, responsibility, strategic problem-solving, and initiative). These six SE domains were chosen because they have frequently been identified by panels charged with identifying needed skills for adulthood in the 21st century (Larson et al., 2002; NRC, 2012; Partnership for 21st Century Skills, 2009).

The other major contribution of PYD research has been findings on the supports and processes that facilitate youth's development. First, research has identified environmental and relationship supports that promote SE learning and development.[3] Eccles and Gootman (2002) conducted a review of research on development in families, schools, and youth programs and identified a list of eight features of settings that facilitate positive development (e.g., safety, supportive relationships, opportunities to belong, support for efficacy and mattering). Vandell and colleagues (2015) provided an updated review that focuses specifically on features of youth programs, and their findings highlight the importance of staff training and youth experiencing supportive relationships with staff and peers. These reviews and other studies provide a useful foundation for this chapter because they describe basic program conditions that contribute to SE learning. They also help define what a *high-quality program* looks like.

Second, research has begun to identify the youth processes that are related to SE learning, particularly in the context of programs. The PYD field shares a strength-based philosophy that focuses on empowering youth to learn through activities and relationships. Practitioners and researchers adhere to the belief that given the right supports, youth have enormous (often underappreciated) capacities to be *producers of their own development* (Larson, 2000; Lerner, Lerner, Bowers & Geldhof, 2015; Smith et al., 2016). Findings from multiple studies (e.g., Halpern, 2009; Kirshner, 2015; Larson, 2011a) are confirming this central role of youth as active learners, and they have begun to describe these processes. Youth in programs learn SE skills through analyzing situations, reasoned trial and error, watching others, actively reflecting on the outcomes of experiences, and other processes of consciously constructing knowledge and skills. We will say more about these processes in the third section of the chapter, after we have discussed the contribution of motivation to youth's learning.

Overview of the Chapter

In this chapter, we describe how youth's experience of *intrinsic motivation* is key to youth playing this active role in SE learning. It unlocks and amplifies their capacities to be producers of their own development. In the first section, we provide a foundation by reviewing scientific knowledge on intrinsic motivation (IM)—its relationship to learning and the conditions that facilitate it. In the second section, we describe how effective youth programs are able to create conditions that activate IM in program activities. In the third section, we examine the processes of SE learning in programs and discuss how IM can amplify these learning processes.

Fundamentals of Intrinsic Motivation

IM is a psychological process that facilitates sustained human engagement in challenging activities, including learning activities (Csikszentmihalyi, 1990; Ryan & Deci, 2008). What is powerful about IM is that, in contrast to other motivational processes that are elicited by external threats or rewards, IM is *self-directed*. It is elicited and controlled by personal interests and goals. A lot is known about how IM functions. Each new generation of psychologists has contributed new research and concepts: theories of flow (Csikszentmihalyi, 1975), mastery motivation (Bloom, 1985), self-determination theory (Ryan & Deci, 2000), interest (Renninger & Hidi, 2016), and engagement (Shernoff & Bempechat, 2014), which have illuminated important facets of intrinsic motivation. The following section first describes how IM enhances learning and then lays out the conditions that facilitate IM. These two parts set the stage for understanding the powerful role of IM in positive adolescent development.

How Intrinsic Motivation Enhances Learning

The Psychological State of Intrinsic Motivation

How does IM help people learn? To begin with, it is important to understand IM as a psychological *state* (like anger or pleasure) that influences attention, subjective feelings, and conditions of physiological arousal. Several elements to this state have been identified by Csikszentmihalyi (1990) and others (e.g., Renninger & Hidi, 2016). First, when a person is intrinsically motivated, they have the subjective feeling of being positively "challenged" by the tasks and problems of the activity. They experience a desire to address the challenges that arise. Second, when intrinsically motivated people experience deep absorption in the activity, their thoughts are fully engaged. Awareness of their outside lives may disappear. Third, they feel empowered and energized by a sense of control over the steps ahead. They experience a sense of confidence in their abilities to address challenges. And fourth, perhaps because of this confidence, people feel more flexible and creative (Csikszentmihalyi, 1996). In sum, the state of IM is one in which a person's mind is mobilized and devoted to the goals of a challenging activity.

Controlled studies have verified that experiencing this psychological state in an activity is related to positive behavioral outcomes, including positive learning outcomes. People who experience IM demonstrate more strategy use in their work, including self-regulatory and problem-solving strategies (Krapp, 1999; Pintrich & DeGroot, 1990; Renninger & Hidi, 2016). Further, they engage in deeper processing of the material. The products of their work demonstrate that they explore a wider range of ideas, employ more effective learning strategies, encode information more deeply, and generate more original solutions to problems (Amabile, 1983; Renninger & Hidi, 2016; Schiefele, 1996). Most importantly, young people who experience the state of intrinsic motivation learn more from the activity and remember it longer (Larson & Rusk, 2011; Ryan & Deci, 2000). This evidence shows that IM can amplify learning processes and outcomes.

From State to Disposition: Developing Sustained Motivation

Another important element of the state of IM is that it can lead to self-sustaining motivation in an activity (Larson & Rusk, 2011). People find the experience of being deeply engaged, feeling in control, and overcoming challenges as enjoyable and rewarding. Indeed, neurological research suggests that IM positively stimulates reward centers of the brain (Renninger & Hidi, 2016). Thus, after the experience of IM, people often want to engage in the activity again; and, if they have repeated positive experiences, people develop favorable affective and cognitive dispositions toward the activity. Renninger and Hidi (2016) provide a theory on how these repeated experiences lead a person to develop stable "individual interest" that makes the activity consistently motivating, even during times when the activity is not immediately rewarding, for example, when it is tedious or stressful. Similarly, Duckworth (2016) describes how continued IM in an activity develops the motivation to struggle and persist with difficult challenges. As a whole, all of these elements of IM can enhance youth's capacities as producers of their own development.

What Conditions Activate Intrinsic Motivation?

Given these powerful effects, there is much to be gained from understanding what creates IM. How can we cultivate it in PYD activities? Extant research identifies a consistent set of conditions that help activate IM—both as a short-term state and a longer-term sustained disposition toward an activity. We highlight five conditions that have been found to consistently activate intrinsic motivation in learning activities.

Meaningful Goals

Research shows that young people are more likely to be intrinsically motivated when the goals of an activity are meaningful to them (Eccles, 2009; Nasir & Hand, 2008; Wortham, 2006). IM can be especially strong when an activity serves a larger purpose, when it contributes to goals that are personally meaningful and have significance beyond the self (Damon, 2008). Students in one study, for example, were more engaged and produced higher-quality work when writing brochures for a local nature center than when writing brochures for a class grade (Purcell-Gates, Duke, & Martineau, 2007).

Manageable Challenges

Another important condition for IM is that a person experiences challenges to reaching the goals and that they are manageable; they are within a person's current skill level—or just above it, so the person is stretched (Csikszentmihalyi, 1990; Eccles, 2009). If you are learning a new piano piece, for example, the challenges may involve new passages requiring difficult hand positions and pedal work. If these challenges are within reach, mastering them can feed IM. However, if they are too far beyond your current ability to master, you are not likely to get these rewards. Frustration and anxiety can mount, and feelings of competence can fade. At the same time, too little challenge can cause boredom. After repeatedly playing piano pieces at one skill level, using the same types of finger positions may not be as rewarding. Thus, to experience deep engagement and mastery, one needs to take on novel challenges. Csikszentmihalyi (1990) suggests that IM is maximized when a person experiences a gradient of gradually increasing new challenges that progressively stretch and expand their skills.

Feedback on Progress

To sustain intrinsic motivation in an activity, people also need good information about whether their actions are making a difference. Are you making progress? What did you do that worked? What didn't? Without this kind of information, it is hard to feel satisfied with what you are doing (Deci & Ryan, 1995). In many instances, a person is able to get this feedback directly from the activity (Priest & Gass, 2005). In learning a new piece on the piano, hearing that you are hitting the right notes helps you know you are making progress. This feeds motivation because it contributes to experiences of positive emotions, mastery, control, and competence, all of which have been identified as core contributors to IM (Deci, Koestner & Ryan, 1999; Renninger & Hidi, 2016). Being able to hear when you hit *wrong* notes is also important because it provides information on strategies that failed—or new challenges ahead.

Knowledgeable Mentoring and Support

In learning activities, having a mentor or teacher can also facilitate IM. Sometimes people are motivated enough to learn on their own. But support from someone who is experienced, trustworthy, and caring can help sustain motivation (Furrer, Skinner, & Pitzer, 2014; Shernoff, 2013). A knowledgeable piano teacher, for example, can help you stay in a zone where you are working at a manageable level of challenges. The teacher also can provide feedback that helps you see your progress or points you to things to work on. A large amount of research establishes that feedback from others can improve learning (Hattie & Timperley, 2007); so for a student who cares about learning, feedback can be a boon to IM. But this depends on how feedback and guidance are provided. Controlling or punitive feedback can undercut motivation. To facilitate IM, a mentor's feedback and guidance need to be provided in ways that support students' sense of competence and control over the activity, for instance, by listening to and supporting students' efforts to learn. This is called "autonomy support," and it has a well-documented relationship to youth's IM (Brown & Ryan, 2015).

Positive Relationships with Collaborators

Much research shows that positive relationships contribute to IM (Ryan & Deci, 2000). Studies in classrooms, for example, have shown that positive relationships among students increase motivation to learn because it "engages students both socially and intellectually in learning together" (Meyer & Smithenry, 2014, p. 142). Newer research suggests that people collaborating on a challenging activity can experience IM not just as individuals, but *collectively—as a group* (Graham & Taylor, 2002; Shernoff, 2013). Positive collaborative relationships lead to collective investment, sharing tasks, and reciprocal scaffolding of learning (Meyer & Smithenry, 2014). Research finds that people in well-functioning groups pool ideas, experiences, and skills in ways that can lead to better work, as compared to individuals working alone (Hinsz, Tindale, & Vollrath, 1997; Magen & Mangiardi, 2005). Therefore, we should recognize that IM is not solely an individual experience; it can also be a collective experience within a collaborating group.

Synthesis: Motivation Is Multidetermined

It is useful to think of these five conditions as a set that as a whole determines whether and how much IM occurs. The likelihood of a person (or collaborating team) being intrinsically motivated in an activity is shaped by their experience of meaningful goals, manageable challenges, useful feedback, supportive mentoring, and positive collaborative relationships.[4] It also is important to ask whether the present conditions *interfere* with IM, such as competing goals (physical needs, extrinsic rewards), strong emotions (anger, fear), and distractions or chaotic conditions in the environment. Ryan and Deci (2000) suggest that IM "can be fairly readily disrupted" (p. 70). In general, the more favorable conditions are present (and the fewer interfering conditions), the more likely people are to experience the absorption, engagement, and self-sustaining properties of IM.

Youth Programs as Rich Contexts for Experiencing IM in Developmental Activities

How can these favorable conditions be created in activities that prepare youth for adulthood? It can be useful to start at the institutional level. Schools and youth programs are institutions whose primary mission is preparing youth for adulthood; however, they differ in how readily they support youth's experiences of IM in learning activities. Several studies have been conducted in which secondary school students were signaled at random times across their waking hours and asked to report on their psychological state at the moment of each signal. When students were in class or doing homework, they frequently reported boredom, and their level of IM was low (Larson, 2011a; Vandell et al., 2006). In contrast, when signaled during youth programs, they reported levels of IM that were higher than in nearly all their other daily activities. Youth programs are more successful in activating the powerful state of IM.

Many explanations have been offered on why schoolwork is rarely intrinsically motivating. Students exercise limited choice over classroom activities, and they are expected to learn about topics that are not meaningful to them. Further, research shows that use of external motivators (e.g., grades) interferes with IM (Ryan & Deci, 2000). Of course, there are exceptions, such as experimental schools that use youth-centered approaches to create conditions for IM and skilled teachers who are able to bring classroom material to life (Shernoff & Bempechat, 2014). These exceptions offer hope that schools may eventually be improved, but inflexible structures and adult control of classrooms are fundamental obstacles for improving IM.

What is it about the youth programs as institutions that create higher rates of IM? In contrast to schools, youth programs have a mandate to adapt learning activities to youth, and program staff have the flexibility to do this (Eccles & Gootman, 2002). Frontline staff typically deal with fewer youth at once, are able to cultivate positive relationships with youth, and, as we discuss later, play vital roles in cultivating all the conditions for IM. An important feature of many programs for high school–aged youth is that they are project based. Their principle activities involve youth working over time toward substantive goals, such as production of a play, creating videos, or planning events (Heath, 1999). As we will see, these activities provide beneficial affordances for creating IM.

In this section, we zero in on the ongoing experiences of youth and examine how programs are able to produce the five conditions for IM. We draw primarily on two large studies we conducted aimed at understanding the developmental processes that occur in higher-quality,[5] project-based arts, leadership, and technology programs for high school–aged youth. In both studies youth were interviewed at multiple times over the course of the program, with the goal of understanding the youth's developmental change processes as they unfolded over time. The first study, *TYDE*, included 113 youth from 12 programs (Larson, Pearce, Sullivan, & Jarrett, 2007); the second study, *The Pathways Project*, included 108 youth from 13 programs (Griffith & Larson, 2016); both focused on youth from low- to middle-income families, and the interview samples contained approximately equal numbers of White Latino, and African American youth. In the interviews we asked youth about their motivation in their projects, and nearly all described high IM. We also asked them to describe their ongoing learning processes within the six SE domains. Grounded theory analyses were used to analyze and identify developmental processes as they were experienced and enacted by large numbers of these youth. Because programs were higher quality, the findings can be seen as representing the IM conditions and SE learning processes that occur in programs with experienced staff and intentional PYD programming.

Meaningful Goals

First, youth programs are able to support IM because they provide rich affordances for youth to experience meaningful goals in their work. Teens exercise choice in selecting programs that fit their interests, which means many enter caring about the activity (Akiva & Horner, 2016). But many also report that meaning increases as they get into the work (Smith et al., 2016). Youth discover and create new personal connections to the activity and its goals, which makes them more invested and intrinsically motivated (Dawes & Larson, 2011).

An example demonstrates how this works. Liliana Villalobos[6] joined Unified Youth because her grandmother urged her to go. Liliana said, "It was a pain to leave the comfort of home and TV." But youth in the program planned events for Latino youth and families in their small, mostly White Midwestern town, and Liliana described how her IM increased as she saw the impact of their work:

> You see that you can make a difference in your community. It makes you feel really good to be able to help and be productive. The more you do, the more you realize that it's really important, not only to us but also to other people.

Liliana found meaning in an altruistic goal. Some youth report that program activities became meaningful and motivating because they started to connect the activities to a potential career choice (Dawes & Larson, 2011). We found that leaders actively supported youth's meaning-making processes. Youth said leaders' enthusiasm and seriousness about the program work directly influenced their motivation (Griffith & Larson, 2016).

Manageable Challenges

Youth programs also have the flexibility to help youth experience challenges matched to their individual skill levels. Many offer roles and projects with different kinds of challenges at multiple skill levels. Experienced youth can step into new roles that provide greater or new challenges (Smith et al., 2016). For example, Ryan at Nutrition Rocks had first been a "Section Leader" at the summer camp they ran, and he became good at that role. But he said his motivation increased the next summer when he moved to the role of "Group Leader," which required him to be in charge of groups of children for a whole week. He explained his increased motivation in terms of the new challenges of learning to better manage his emotions, including "to keep my temper down." The increased demands, then, served as challenges that both raised his IM and were a stimulus for SE learning.

Youths' projects do not always provide the kind of orderly gradient of increasing challenges that Csikszentmihalyi (1990) describes as optimal. Youth can encounter situations where they feel overwhelmed. But in these situations, leaders often step in judiciously to help youth with advice or reframing that helps youth experience the situation as still challenging, but manageable (Larson & Angus, 2011a; Smith et al., 2016). One youth described this kind of assistance in overcoming challenges while making a video: "If it's something difficult, they'll figure out a way for me to over-pass it, or to like, beat it . . . They'll make us go deeper, so like open our eyes." By providing timely assistance, leaders help youth overcome challenges that are too difficult. In other cases, leaders provide support that boosts youth's confidence and helps them see they can address the challenges by employing skills they have (Griffith & Larson, 2016).

Leaders' measured assistance with youth's projects helps youth experience the manageable gradient of challenges that feed self-motivation.

Feedback on Progress

Youth in programs get information directly from program activities, as well as from leaders. Direct feedback is powerful, but it can sometimes be difficult to obtain. Youth in programs making robots get direct information when the bot zips forward for the first time—or keeps falling over. Youth teaching children, we found, get direct feedback from children's faces on how well they are doing. This kind of direct feedback is powerful because it is "authentic"—it is information about the "real-world" success or failure of their actions (Heath, 1999). But in some program activities, like creating a work of art, planning an event, or tending a garden, youth may not be able to assess the quality of their work or may have to wait for weeks to know if their decisions and strategies work as they hoped. This is especially true when youth are novices or trying new things in the activity. They do not have experiences to accurately anticipate a decision's consequences.

In these situations program leaders often provide youth feedback to help sustain youth's motivation and sense of forward motion (Smith et al., 2016). They may reassure youth that they are making sound decisions or steer youth away from a decision that they know from experience is certain to fail (Larson, Izenstark, Rodriguez, & Perry, 2016). For example, a youth in a theater program described how his motivation was raised by "those little looks and helpful hints" he received from the director. But youth in programs also appreciate that leaders give them truthful feedback and that they "never sugar coat" and give "honest assessments, especially at the stuff I'm not good at" (Griffith, Larson & Johnson, 2016). At the same time, effective leaders do not need to micromanage youth or give feedback on everything. Part of their goal is to help youth feel comfortable learning from trying things out (Larson, Walker, Rusk, & Diaz, 2015). In real-world situations, there often is not a clear right and wrong choice, so depending on circumstances, leaders balance giving youth useful feedback with giving them freedom to experiment with their own ideas. This balancing act is autonomy support—it provides a combination of useful feedback and freedom that optimizes youth's IM (Larson & Dawes, 2015).

Knowledgeable Mentoring and Support

Effective program leaders provide this kind of autonomy support across diverse kinds of mentoring situations. It is part of the ethos of youth programs (Larson et al., 2016). We have found that experienced leaders place a high priority on supporting youth's agency in their work. As one leader said, she and her partner "limited their limit setting." In other words, leaders restrict how and when they impose a limit on their youth or provide explicit guidance. Leaders or mentors can provide a structured environment without limiting youths' potential for developing their own ideas, strategies, and boundaries. Experienced leaders use their authority judiciously to ensure safety, steer youth away from pragmatic difficulties that youth would not foresee, and provide coaching that they *increase* opportunities for youth to develop skills for independent action (Larson et al., 2016). Xavier, a youth who was making a video, explained how the leader:

> . . . wouldn't be like, "No you can't do that." But he would try and lead us in a different way so that we could see it from maybe a different way. And then we could make our own decision on whether we still wanted to do our thing or if we wanted to take the advice that he [was] giving us. (Griffith, Larson & Johnson, 2016)

The leader provided input in ways that empowered Xavier.

Part of the reason that leaders are able to provide this kind of nuanced support is that they develop trusting relationships with youth. We found that 104 out of 108 youth in our second study reported having at least one leader in the program that they trusted, a striking rate given the mistrust youth often report toward school teachers and other adults (Griffith & Larson, 2016). This trust, the youth explained, made them more willing to accept leaders' advice, feedback, and encouragement in ways that increased their feelings of competence and motivation in their work (Griffith & Larson, 2016). Effective program leaders contribute to youth's intrinsic motivation in numerous additional ways, including by cultivating a motivating task *and* social environment (Larson & Rusk, 2011; Smith et al., 2016).

Positive Relationships with Collaborators

Youth programs are especially rich contexts for youth to experience the power of collective IM in learning activities. Program leaders make a special effort to cultivate positive relationships among youth, and activities are often collaborative (Smith et al., 2016). The bonds youth form around shared goals create strong collective investment and motivation (Larson, 2007; Salusky et al., 2014). For example, at Sisterhood, a consciousness-raising program, young African American women formulated rules at the beginning of the year that became the basis of high-functioning interactions and highly rewarding, probing discussions about their experiences of race, class, and gender. They were highly motivated to engage in collaborative emotional sharing and analyses of their experiences (Larson, Jensen, Kang, Griffith, & Rompala, 2012).

Youth Programs as Ecosystems for IM

It is important to think about these five different conditions holistically. Together they are more than the sum of the parts. Effective programs create an ecosystem that supports all five. Youth experience IM in projects not only because their goals are aligned with the goals of these projects but because program structures and leaders' practices help keep challenges manageable, ensure that youth obtain useful feedback, and experience knowledgeable and autonomy-supporting assistance. Effective programs also support youth's participation in constructive collaborations. Leaders play vital roles in sustaining these ecosystems. Trained and experienced leaders have the skills and credibility to cultivate these five conditions in response to changing situations and the needs of specific youth (Griffith & Larson, 2016; Larson & Rusk, 2011).

As we see in the next section, youth's high IM in programs has a large payoff for their positive development. Because SE learning typically occurs through youth's projects, youth's high IM in their project work readily contributes to this learning. In some cases, the same challenges that contribute to IM also function as challenges that spur learning.

How IM Amplifies Processes of Social Emotional Learning

High-quality youth programs are effective in facilitating SE learning (Durlak et al., 2010; Vandell et al., 2015), so they are a good context to examine how this learning occurs and how IM contributes to it. In this section, we first report findings on SE learning. As we show, there are diverse SE skills and learning processes, but there are commonalities among them. Then we discuss how IM amplifies these processes, and we provide two case examples that illustrate how IM and SE learning converge over the course of youth's unfolding program experiences.

SE Learning Processes

Six Domains of SE Learning

Our research is concerned with how youth become mature, resilient, and contributing adults, and we have concentrated on six domains of SE learning outcomes—or skill sets—that are critical for adulthood in the 21st century. These six are also domains that were prominent in programs. Table 7.1 lists the six and identifies the empirical articles we have published for each. Column 2 of the table provides concise descriptions of the skill set for each domain, formulated by a team of 24 expert program staff from across the United States (Smith et al., 2016). An important feature of these six domains is that each corresponds to major *SE challenges* of adult life. Each deals with a distinct category of issues, puzzles, and sometimes contradictions that youth need to be prepared for in adulthood. Some of these challenges are elusive, unstated, and quite difficult to grasp prior to adolescence (Larson, 2011a), for example, that emotional states alter how you think (Emotion management); people from different backgrounds can have profoundly different worldviews (Empathy, Teamwork); and trying to achieve a goal in the real world often involves hidden obstacles, setbacks, and adapting to people who have different viewpoints (Strategic problem-solving). The skill sets youth must develop are those for engaging with these different kinds of difficult real-world challenges.

Challenge-Driven Processes

How do youth in programs develop competencies to deal with these SE challenges? Research by multiple scholars shows that youth's projects are

Table 7.1   Six Domains of Social and Emotional Learning in Youth Programs

Domain	Descriptions of the Skill Set (from Smith et al., 2016)	Examples of Challenges (and Opportunities) That Drive Learning	Articles on the Learning Processes
Emotion management	Abilities to be aware of and constructively handle both positive and challenging emotions	• Situations requiring understanding and managing strong emotions (anger, anxiety, pride) in ways that are not disruptive. • Opportunities to use and learn from emotions.	Larson, 2011a; Larson & Brown, 2007; Rusk et al., 2013
Empathy	Relating to others with acceptance, understanding, and sensitivity to their diverse perspectives and experiences	• Peers describe strong emotions. • Differences in culture and power between people that create inequality or exclusion. • Youth are offended by stereotypes, offensive language, or prejudice toward a group.	Gutiérrez et al., in press; Watkins, Larson & Sullivan, 2007
Teamwork	Abilities to collaborate and coordinate action with others	• Encountering peers with different priorities and goals for a shared project. • Dealing with slackers, "bossy-pants," etc. • Collaborations between youth with different skills and skill levels.	Larson, 2007; Larson, Hansen, & Walker, 2005; Perry, 2015

(continued)

Table 7.1 (continued)

Domain	Descriptions of the Skill Set (from Smith et al., 2016)	Examples of Challenges (and Opportunities) That Drive Learning	Articles on the Learning Processes
Responsibility	Dispositions and abilities to reliably meet commitments and fulfill obligations of challenging roles	• Youth take on demanding program roles with obligations toward others. • Demands of roles become bigger than expected. • Situations that require a youth to make sacrifices to meet the needs of others or of the group.	Salusky et al., 2014; Wood, Larson & Brown, 2009
Strategic problem-solving [also called "Strategic thinking"]	Abilities to plan, strategize, and implement complex tasks	• Having to communicate effectively with people from different professional worlds, such as reporters, teachers, and police. • Real-world dynamics: catch-22s, hidden rules, "adults say yes, but mean no." • A strategy fails to achieve its goal or has unintended consequences.	Larson & Angus, 2011a & 2011b; Larson & Hansen, 2005; Larson, Lampkins, uThando, & Armstrong, 2014
Initiative [similar to self-motivation]	Capacities to take action, sustain motivation, and persevere through challenges toward an identified goal	• An activity is overwhelming or boring. • Disappointment or frustration when a project hits a roadblock or fails to achieve its intended goals. • Opportunities to successfully make a difference and see the results.	Dawes & Larson, 2011; Larson & Rusk, 2011; Pearce & Larson, 2006

valuable for SE learning because they provide microcosms of adult real-world situations. Projects typically engage youth in human social worlds (e.g., teams, professional worlds, community worlds) and they present youth with fundamental SE challenges inherent in working toward goals in these complex social worlds (Halpern, 2009; Heath, 1999; Larson, 2011a). In our research with over 200 youth, we asked them to describe their learning processes in each SE domain. Across domains, the processes we identified fit into a *challenge-driven model* of development. This challenge model has a long history. Developmental psychologists, including Erikson (1950), Havighurst (1972), and Masten (2013), have described how growth emerges from a process of dealing with a major life crisis or difficult psychological tasks. The SE learning our youth described emerged not from dealing with such large existential challenges but with practical SE challenges they encountered in their projects (Larson, 2011a & 2011b).

Distinct types of challenges were the impetus for learning in each domain (see Column 3 of Table 7.1). Thus, for example, the most central challenges that stimulated learning for *emotion management* were strong emotions that created a problem they wanted to avoid. For example, they were troubled by how anger or anxiety altered and narrowed how they thought, or they saw how emotions could be disruptive to the group's work (Larson & Brown, 2007). For Ryan at Nutrition Rocks, his prior experiences with disruptive anger, with his temper, were an impetus to practice and learn how to control it. The initial challenge, however, was not always a problem to be controlled. Sometimes, the challenge was learning to *use* emotions for the information and motivation they can provide (Rusk et al, 2013).

The learning processes initiated by these challenges entailed diverse components. Youth in different situations described learning through thinking and talking about the challenges, brainstorming strategies, trying multiple approaches, getting input from staff, and evaluating the effectiveness of approaches they tried, including making comparisons to other trials and the results of other people's actions in similar situations. From these different processes, coupled with coaching from leaders, youth extracted insights, strategies, and new ways of thinking (Heath, 1999; Larson, 2011a; Perry, 2015). Then they applied what they learned to other situations, including those outside the program (Diaz, Larson, Armstrong, & Perry, 2015; Larson & Angus, 2011a; Larson & Brown, 2007).[7] We identified distinctive key experiences for each of the six domains, but there was also much overlap (Smith et al., 2016). The common element is that youth were *active and creative learners*—they were producers, often co-producers (with peers and staff), of their SE development.

How Intrinsic Motivation Amplifies Learning Processes

We are now ready to add IM to this picture: these active and creative processes are the key to understanding the vital role of IM in SE learning. Research in controlled studies shows that without IM, learners' engagement is more superficial, passive, and short lived; people explore fewer ideas, employ fewer strategies, and are less flexible and creative (Larson & Rusk, 2011).[8] Our interviews with youth who were highly motivated showed how IM amplified their active engagement in response to the challenges of their projects. It not only energized them, it appeared to mobilize diverse and deeper cognitive processes in ways that enhanced youth's engagement in the processes of SE learning. We saw that IM helped transform difficult and laborious activities—analyzing challenges, thinking them through, brainstorming, trying out approaches, and evaluating—into personally meaningful and rewarding learning processes. In short, it made them active producers of their own learning.

We provide two case examples, one of a group and another of a single person, showing how this amplification works in two different domains. These examples illustrate how IM and SE learning are experienced and enacted in the complex daily unfolding of program activities.

Case Example: How Youth Learned Strategic Problem-Solving in a Social Justice Program

The central challenges that drive youth's learning in the domain *strategic problem-solving* are the strategic and tactical problems they encounter in navigating human systems to reach a goal (Heath, 1999; Larson & Angus, 2011a). For example, youth planning events or conducting social action campaigns were repeatedly challenged by the real-world difficulties of trying to organize or influence the institutions and target audiences that were central to their plans. Members of the social justice program Youth Action encountered many of these strategic challenges in their campaign to stop Chicago school principals from suspending students for minor offenses (which were not legitimate grounds for suspension in the school system).

Developing IM. Most youth joined Youth Action to fill a high school service requirement. Many were initially bored. But they kept coming back because they formed friendships, which developed into *collaborative relationships* (Pearce & Larson, 2006). As youth started planning their campaign, they began sharing experiences of being suspended. For example, Aisha had been late for class several times due to overcrowded hallways and was given a six-day suspension. From this sharing, youth discovered that many of their peers, especially in schools with Latino and Black students, were having the same experiences. As a result of this discovery, they became invested in their work as a *meaningful goal*. Elena said, "I see freshmen and sophomores, and I don't want them to go through what I went through."

Other conditions contributed to youth's development of IM. The leader, Jason, provided autonomy support for the campaign that the youth developed and carried out. This included keeping them focused on *manageable challenges* and providing *information and feedback* on effective tactics. Youth started describing their work as "exciting" and "enjoyable," indicators of IM. As Donato prepared a talk for a rally, he said, "I'm just really into it, I'm really psyched."

Influence of IM on the youth's work and learning. Because of this motivation youth became deeply engaged in the formidable tactical challenges of social action. Youth described this engagement in a set of activities that were part of their campaign (Larson & Hansen, 2005):

- Standing outside high schools surveying students about their suspensions
- Organizing rallies and trying to get students to show up
- Talking with teachers in the school to identify potential allies
- Rehearsing their presentations to the school board, including responding to aggressive comments by adults playing roles as school board members

These were difficult activities. They were talking to students who did not share their passion and to adults who were sometimes hostile to their goals. But because of their strong motivation, youth persevered. Being effective also required that youth think creatively to anticipate how students, teachers, and school board members might react to different approaches. They had to develop tactical strategies that would surmount opposition. Again, the benefits of deep motivation appeared to contribute. Youth described enjoying brainstorming and role-playing sessions in which they generated many strategic choices and critiqued them. Then they tried them out. Donato was recruiting students for a rally and said that if one strategy didn't work, he would try another. It is *not* likely that unmotivated youth would be as engaged as these youth in months of hard work, brainstorming, trying strategies, and trying to influence adults and students they did not know. The energy provided by IM and the cognitive state of deep and creative thinking appeared to be essential.

Not all of the youth's strategies worked, and youth learned either way. But some strategies did, and their successes contributed markedly to their motivation. They found that 37 percent of the 667 students they surveyed had been suspended at least once during the prior year, nearly all for minor offenses. This hard evidence then helped them get a meeting with the school board, and after many rehearsals to prepare for the meeting, they succeeded in persuading the board to act (Larson & Hansen, 2005). In addition to being energized by their success (contributing to their IM), they gained direct feedback on the strategies they used (contributing to their SE learning).

SE learning outcomes. Youth said it was their experiences with the strategic challenges of their work that helped them learn problem-solving skills. By analyzing the situations they faced and observing the results of their actions, they learned to think strategically about how to solve problems and achieve difficult goals (Larson, 2011a; Larson & Hansen, 2005). Aisha reported learning to expect the unexpected, "Always have a backup plan," and for adversarial situations: "Think ahead of the opponents, just go overboard with it."

It was apparent that youth's IM—their deep engagement, creativity, and perseverance—amplified these learning processes. Further, because IM leads to deeper processing of information, youth were better able to remember and use these skills later. When interviewed three years later, many reported having applied strategic problem-solving skills to other domains of their lives. Elena said the program shaped how she faces problems, "It definitely helped me to be like: 'Okay what steps do I need to take to change that, or address this issue that I have?'" Mateo said, "Life's nothing but choices. It helped me make better decisions." He had used skills from Youth Action to organize workers at his job to successfully lobby for wage increases.

Case Example: Learning Emotion Management in an Arts Program

Similar amplification of cognitive processes was illustrated by Lucia's account of emotional learning at Toltecat Muralists. The learning process for emotion management involves grappling with the challenging dynamics of emotions, including the effects they have on a person when they are denied and not discussed. Lucia reported that her father was very strict, so she could not express emotions in her family; she described feeling on "lockdown" at home. She also had a lot of anxiety, including fear of failing in school and doing art work that was less than perfect. In her words, "I would judge myself harshly and say I wasn't good enough." When Lucia first started the program, she said, "I was really hesitant about my abilities." She said she could not even fill in parts of murals that were a solid color. This emotional paralysis became the challenge that drove her SE learning.

Toltecat Muralists provided Lucia an open learning environment that motivated her to actively address her emotions by approaching her anxiety in a new way. Unlike art teachers at school, the leader, Desiree, "tries to make it about us instead of where you have to be very strict. She lets us do things that most other programs wouldn't really do. She's very open." This autonomy support from Desiree (along with collaborative backing from peers in the program) and the meaningful goal they had of counteracting the neighborhood "gangbangers" by sending a positive message to the community with their murals created strong IM for Lucia. The emotional challenges created by her perfectionism also contribute to her IM. Part of the ethos at Toltecat Muralists was that mistakes were a learning opportunity. Desiree's approach was: "If you make a big mistake, twist it and turn it so it looks like it's supposed to be there." Lucia embraced this approach and she got deeply engaged in this playful way of doing art.

This forgiving and playful environment coupled with Lucia's intrinsic motivation gave her the opportunity to think and talk about her fear of failure with Desiree and her peers. She also practiced taking risks in her art and not worrying: "Sometimes you just go with it and it turns out well." This helped Lucia reduce her fears, not only in the program but elsewhere. She said that because of this experience:

> Now, if I have an A (at school), I'm like that's good and I'm keeping up with my stuff. If I have a C, I wouldn't take it like I would back then, like "Oh, it's going to ruin my career." Now, it is just like "Oh, I just need to work better and not slack off."

Having the opportunity to explore her emotions and grow as an artist, amplified by high IM, helped Lucia learn to manage her fears.

Conclusion: The Synergies of Intrinsic Motivation and Positive Youth Development

We started this chapter with the difficult challenges adolescents face in preparing for adulthood. There is increased urgency that young people gain flexible social-emotional skills that allow them to navigate our increasingly complex and changing world. By extension, there is increased urgency that researchers and educational institutions better understand how youth can best learn these SE skills. The field of PYD is making progress in addressing these tasks, articulating the roles of supportive relationships, developmental environments, and youth's active engagement in SE learning.

Our aim here has been to illuminate the powerful synergies that effective youth programs create between IM and positive development. In Figure 7.1 we have summarized the main points of the chapter. The left box of the chart recognizes the *program supports* that are foundational to effective programs. These include the general supports that are fundamental to SE learning (and to other positive development outcomes). The box also includes the specific conditions that facilitate IM (e.g., meaningful goals, manageable challenges). Youth programs are rich contexts for PYD because, in addition to providing general supports, they have the institutional flexibility to sustain these IM conditions for different youth across varied situations in their work.

IM appears to play a critical role as an amplifier of SE learning: it unlocks and enhances youth's often-underappreciated capacities to be producers of their own development. By providing the conditions for IM in an activity, programs and staff help youth experience a psychological state that is more than motivational. It brings with it greater engagement with challenges, more strategy use, and deeper processing. We have discovered abundant manifestations of these IM elements in youth's accounts of employing diverse components of active SE learning, including analyzing challenges, brainstorming strategies, trying different approaches, and evaluating the results of approaches they tried (Figure 7.1). When intrinsically motivated by an activity, youth become *active and creative* producers of their SE learning. Thus, because Lucia was deeply engaged in a rewarding, playful mode of doing art, she was able to use her artwork at Toltecat Muralists to learn about her emotions and confront her fear of failure.

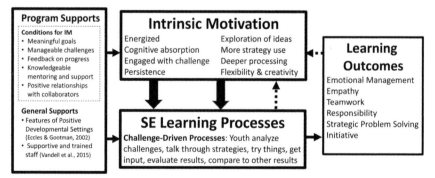

Figure 7.1   Intrinsic Motivation as an Amplifier of Social-Emotional Learning Processes in Youth Programs

We have added to the chart additional pathways, suggested by theory and by our data (dotted arrows). These are pathways through which success in projects and learning from these projects (including learning from mistakes) can provide feedback and reinforce IM because they contribute to youth's confidence and skills in the activity.

The effectiveness of programs in facilitating SE learning, we believe, stems from these and other synergies between IM and this learning. In our observations, the same challenges often drove both motivation and learning. At Youth Action, for example, the leader Jason ensured that youth experienced the challenges of their action campaign as manageable. As a result, members of Youth Action were both highly motivated by the work and by learning skills for strategic problem-solving. Similarly, we have found that positive peer collaborations both create high IM and allow youth to benefit from powerful peer scaffolding processes to learn SE skills (Larson et al., 2012; Salusky et al., 2014). Likewise, adult leaders' skills in providing assistance in autonomy-supportive ways permits them to facilitate youth's IM at the same time they are providing advice and coaching that support youth's SE learning (Larson et al., 2016).

There remains much to understand about how to best facilitate IM in SE learning. We highlight several critical next steps for research:

1. *Quantitative research.* Using methods of grounded theory, we identified a consistent pattern in which IM amplified processes of SE learning. Quantitative research is needed to test IM as a mediator and moderator of this learning. Further, as high-quality performance measures of SE skills become available, it will be important to evaluate the quality and transferability of SE learning obtained from direct experience in projects vs. more didactic approaches.

2. *Practitioner expertise.* In separate articles we analyzed interviews with the experienced adult leaders of these programs and learned that they have deliberate strategies for keeping youth in a sweet spot in which conditions for IM are sustained (e.g., skills are manageable) and youth are learning (Larson & Dawes, 2015; Larson et al., 2016; Smith et al., 2006). There is much more to learn from expert practitioners about these strategies.

3. *Generalizing across cultures.* We have focused on an ethnically diverse U.S. learning context. It is important to understand how motivational and learning processes, as well as effective staff practices, might be distinct in other culture milieus.

4. *Generalizing beyond programs.* Finally, how can knowledge about combing IM with SE learning in programs be applied to other settings, like schools, families, and youth Internet sites?

Acknowledgments

This research was supported by generous grants from the William T. Grant Foundation. We thank the youth and program leaders in our research. We also thank Gina McGovern for valuable comments on the manuscript.

Notes

1. Social and emotional skills have been defined as "the knowledge, attitudes, and skills necessary to understand and manage emotions, set and achieve positive goals, feel and show empathy for others, establish and maintain positive relationships, and make responsible decisions" (CASEL, 2015).

2. Most of these efforts have been carried out in the U.S. or Western contexts, with notable exceptions (e.g., Guerra & Bradshaw, 2008).

3. We use the terms "learning" and "development" interchangeably.

4. It should be noted that motivation scholars have identified additional contributing conditions, especially for development of long-term sustained IM. These include prior experiences in the activity, mind-sets and beliefs, dispositions, and the developing self (Larson & Rusk, 2011; Renninger & Hidi, 2016).

5. We selected programs that had experienced leaders, were youth centered, and had stable youth participation.

6. All names of youth, leaders, and programs are pseudonyms.

7. One might describe these processes as experiential learning: they involved cycles of doing and reflection (Priest & Gass, 2005; Walsh & Golins, 1976). However, that label does not tell us much; it does not capture the ad hoc, creative, and wide-ranging combinations of components youth described.

8. These findings are based on laboratory and classroom studies, not youth programs. Quantitative studies have shown that motivated youth in programs reported greater developmental change compared to unmotivated youth (Hansen & Larson, 2007; Mahoney, Parente, & Lord, 2007), but more rigorous tests of amplification are needed.

References

Akiva, T. & Horner, C. G. (2016). Adolescent motivation to attend youth programs: A mixed-methods investigation. *Applied Developmental Science. 20*(4), 278–293.

Amabile, T. M. (1983). Social psychology of creativity: A componential conceptualization. *Journal of Personality and Social Psychology, 45*, 357–376.

Benson, P. L., Scales, P., Hamilton, S., & Sesma, A. (2006). Positive youth development: Theory, research and applications. In W. Damon & R. M. Lerner (Eds.), *Theoretical models of human development, vol. 1. Handbook of child psychology* (6th ed.), (pp. 894–941) New York Wiley.

Bloom, B. S. (1985). *Developing talent in young people.* New York: Ballantine.

Brown, K. W., & Ryan, R. M. (2015). A self-determination theory perspective on fostering healthy self-regulation from within and without. In S. Joseph (Ed.) *Positive psychology in practice* (pp. 139–157). New York: Wiley.

CASEL (2015). *What is social and emotional learning?* Collaborative for Academic, Social, and Emotional Learning. Retrieved from http://www.casel.org /social-and-emotional-learning

Catalano, R. F., Berglund, M. L., Ryan, J. A., Lonczak, H. S., & Hawkins, J. D. (2004). Positive youth development in the United States: Research findings on evaluations of positive youth development programs. *The Annals of the American Academy of Political and Social Science, 591*, 98–124. doi: 10.1177/0002716203260102

Csikszentmihalyi, M. (1975). *Beyond boredom and anxiety.* San Francisco: Jossey-Bass.

Csikszentmihalyi, M. (1990). *Flow: The psychology of optimal experience.* New York: Harper Perennial.

Csikszentmihalyi, M. (1996). *Creativity: Flow and the psychology of discovery and invention.* New York: HarperCollins.

Damon, W. (2008). *Path to purpose: Helping our children find their calling in life.* New York: Free Press.

Dawes, N. P., & Larson, R. W. (2011). How youth get engaged: Grounded-theory research on motivational development in organized youth programs. *Developmental Psychology, 47*(1), 259–269.

Deci, E. L., Koestner, R., & Ryan, R. M. (1999). A meta-analytic review of experiments examining the effects of extrinsic rewards on intrinsic motivation. *Psychological Bulletin, 125*, 627–668.

Deci, E. & Ryan, R. (1995). Human autonomy: The basis of true self-esteem. In M. Kernis (Ed.) *Efficacy, agency and self-esteem* (pp. 31–49). New York: Plenum

Diaz, L., Larson, R., Armstrong, J., & Perry, S. C. (2015, April). A case study of youth learning to lead: The power of iterative cycles of situated learning. AERA meeting Chicago.

Duckworth, A. (2016). *Grit: The power of passion and perseverance.* New York: Charles Scribner's Sons.

Durlak, J. A., Weissberg, R. P., & Pachan, M. (2010). A meta-analysis of after-school programs that seek to promote personal and social skills in children and adolescents. *American Journal of Community Psychology, 45*(3–4), 294–309.

Eccles, J. S. (2009). Who am I and what am I going to do with my life? Personal and collective identities as motivators of action. *Educational Psychologist, 44*, 78–89.

Eccles, J. & Gootman, J. A. (Eds.). (2002). *Community programs to promote youth development.* Board on Children, Youth, and Families, National Research Council & Institute of Medicine. Washington, DC: National Academies Press.

Erikson, E. (1950). *Childhood and society.* New York: Norton.

Furrer, C., Skinner, E., & Pitzer, J. (2014). The influence of teacher and peer relationships on students' classroom engagement and everyday motivational resilience. *National Society for the Study of Education, 113*(1), 101–123.

Graham, S., & Taylor, A. Z. (2002). Ethnicity, gender, and the development of achievement values. In A. Wigfield & J. Eccles (Eds.), *The development of achievement motivation.* (pp. 123–146). San Diego: Academic Press.

Griffith, A. N., & Larson, R. W. (2016). Why trust matters: How confidence in leaders transforms what adolescents gain from youth programs. *Journal of Research on Adolescence*, in press.

Griffith, A., Larson, R., & Johnson, H. (2016). "Always putting you up. They're never shutting you down": The art of providing critical feedback on work in project-based youth programs. Paper in process.

Guerra, N. G., & Bradshaw, C. P. (2008). Linking the prevention of problem behaviors and positive youth development: Core competencies for positive youth development and risk prevention. *New Directions for Child and Adolescent Development, 2008*(122), 1–17. http://doi.org/10.1002/cd.225

Gutiérrez, V., Larson, R. W., Raffaelli, M., Fernandez, M., & Guzman, S. (in press). How staff of youth programs respond to cultural incidents: Non-engagement vs. 'full-right-in'. *Journal of Adolescent Research.*

Halpern, R. (2009). *The means to grow up: Reinventing apprenticeship as a developmental support in adolescence.* Chicago: Routledge.

Hansen, D. M., & Larson, R. W. (2007). Amplifiers of developmental and negative experiences in organized activities: Dosage, motivation, lead roles, and adult-youth ratios. *Journal of Applied Developmental Psychology, 28,* 360–374.

Hattie, J., & Timperley, H. (2007). The power of feedback. *Review of Educational Research, 77,* 81–112.

Havighurst, R. J. (1972). *Developmental tasks and education.* New York: David McKay.

Heath, S. B. (1999). Dimensions of language development: Lessons from older children. In A. S. Masten (Ed.), *Cultural processes in child development: The Minnesota symposium on child psychology* (Vol. 29, pp. 59–75). Mahwah, NY: Erlbaum.

Heckman, J., Stixrud, J., & Urzua, S. (2006). The effects of cognitive and noncognitive abilities on labor market outcomes and social behavior. *Journal of Labor Economics, 24,* 411–482.

Hinsz, V., Tindale, R., & Vollrath, D. (1997). The emerging conceptualization of groups as information processors. *Psychological Bulletin, 121,* 43–64.

Kirshner, B. (2015). *Youth activism in an era of educational inequality.* New York: NYU Press.

Krapp, A. (1999). Interest, motivation, and learning: An educational-psychological perspective. *Learning and Instruction, 14,* 23–40.

Larson, R. W. (2000). Toward a psychology of positive youth development. *American Psychologist, 55,* 170–183.

Larson, R. (2007). From "I" to "we": Development of the capacity for teamwork in youth programs. In R. Silbereisen & R. Lerner (Eds.), *Approaches to positive youth development* (pp. 277–292) Thousand Oaks, CA: Sage.

Larson, R. W. (2011a). Positive development in a disorderly world: SRA Presidential Address. *Journal of Research on Adolescence, 21*, 317–334.

Larson, R. W. (2011b). Adolescents' conscious processes of developing regulation: Learning to appraise challenges. *Thriving in Childhood and Adolescence: The Role of Self-Regulation Processes: New Directions for Child and Adolescent Development, 133*, 87–97.

Larson, R. W., & Angus, R. M. (2011a). Adolescents' development of skills for agency in youth programs: Learning to think strategically. *Child Development, 82*, 277–294.

Larson, R. W., & Angus, R. (2011b). Pursuing paradox: The role of adults in creating empowering settings for youth. In M. Aber, K. Maton, & E. Seidman (Eds.), *Empowering settings and voices for social change* (pp. 65–93). New York: Oxford.

Larson, R., Brown, B. B., & Mortimer, J. (Eds.). (2002). Adolescents' preparation for the future: Perils and promise [special issue]. *Journal of Research on Adolescence, 12*(1), 1–166.

Larson, R. W., & Brown, J. R. (2007). Emotional development in adolescence: What can be learned from a high school theater program. *Child Development, 78*, 1083–1099.

Larson, R. W., & Dawes, N. P. (2015). How to cultivate adolescents' motivation: Effective strategies employed by the professional staff of American youth programs. In S. Joseph (Ed.), *Positive psychology in practice* (pp. 313–326). New York: Wiley.

Larson, R., & Hansen, D. (2005). The development of strategic thinking: Learning to impact human systems in a youth activism program. *Human Development, 48*, 327–349.

Larson, R., Hansen, D., & Moneta, G. (2006). Differing profiles of developmental experiences across types of organized youth activities. *Developmental Psychology, 42*(5), 849–863.

Larson, R., Hansen, D., & Walker, K. (2005). Everybody's gotta give: Adolescents' development of initiative and teamwork within a youth program. In Mahoney, J., Larson, R., & Eccles, J. (Eds.), *Organized activities as contexts of development: Extracurricular activities, after-school and community programs* (pp. 159–184). Hillsdale, NJ: Erlbaum.

Larson, R. W., Jensen, L., Kang, H., Griffith, A., & Rompala, V. (2012). Peer groups as a crucible of positive value development in a global world. In G. Trommsdorff & X. Chen (Eds.), *Values, religion, and culture in adolescent development*. Cambridge, England: Cambridge Press.

Larson, R. W., Izenstark, D., Rodriguez, G., & Perry, S. C. (2016). The art of restraint: How experienced program leaders use their authority to support youth agency. *Journal of Research on Adolescence*, in press.

Larson, R. W., Lampkins-uThando, S., & Armstrong, J. (2014). Adolescents' development of new skills for prospective cognition: Learning to anticipate, plan and think strategically. *Journal of Cognitive Education and Psychology, 13*(2), 232–244.

Larson, R., Pearce, N., Sullivan, P., & Jarrett, R. L. (2007). Participation in youth programs as a catalyst for negotiation of family autonomy with connection. *Journal of Youth and Adolescence, 36*(1), 31–45.

Larson, R. W., & Rusk, N. (2011). Intrinsic motivation and positive development. In R. M. Lerner, J. V. Lerner, & J. B. Benson (Eds.), *Advances in child development and behavior: Positive youth development,41* (pp. 89–130). Oxford, England: Elsevier.

Larson, R. W., Walker, K. C., Rusk, N., & Diaz, L. B. (2015). Understanding youth development from the practitioner's point of view: A call for research on effective practice. *Applied Developmental Science, 19*(2), 74–86.

Lerner, R. M., Almerigi, J. B., Theokas, C., & Lerner, J. V. (2005). Positive youth development: A view of the issues. *Journal of Early Adolescence, 25*(1), 10–16.

Lerner, J. V., Phelps, E. Forman, Y., & Bowers, E. (2009). Positive youth development. In R. M. Lerner & L. Steinberg (Eds.), *Handbook of adolescent psychology* (3rd ed., Vol. 1, pp. 524–558). Hoboken, NJ: Wiley.

Lerner, R. M., Lerner, J. V., Bowers, E., & Geldhof, J. (2015). Positive youth development and relational-developmental-systems. In *Handbook of child psychology and developmental science*. New York: Wiley Retrieved from http://onlinelibrary.wiley.com/doi/10.1002/9781118963418.childpsy116 /abstract

Magen, R. H., & Mangiardi, E. (2005). Groups and individual change. In S. Wheelan (Ed.), *Handbook of group research and practice* (pp. 351–361). Thousand Oaks, CA: Sage Publications.

Mahoney, J. L., Parente, M. E., & Lord, H. (2007). After-school program engagement: Links to child competence and program quality and content. *Elementary School Journal, 107*(4), 385–404.

Masten, A. S. (2013). Risk and resilience in development. In P. D. Zelazo (Ed.), *Oxford handbook of developmental psychology* (pp. 579–607). New York: Oxford Press.

Meyer, D. K., & Smithenry, D. W. (2014). Scaffolding collective engagement. In D. J. Shernoff & J. Bempechat (Eds.), *Engaging youth in schools: Evidence-based models to guide future innovation. National Society for the Study of Education Yearbook. Teachers College Record, Vol. 113* (Issue 1), pp. 124–145.

Nasir, N. S., & Hand, V. (2008). From the court to the classroom: Opportunities for engagement, learning and identity in basketball and classroom mathematics. *Journal of the Learning Sciences, 17*, 143–180.

National Research Council (2012). *Education for life and work: Developing transferable knowledge and skills in the 21st Century*. Washington, DC: National Academy Press. Partnership for 21st Century Skills. (2009). *Framework definitions.* Retrieved from http://www.p21.org/storage/documents/docs/P21_framework_0816.pdf

Pearce, N., & Larson, R. W. (2006). The process of motivational change in a civic activism organization. *Applied Developmental Science, 10,* 121–131.

Perry, S. C. (2015). How teens learn teamwork: Agentic and constructive peer processes. PhD dissertation. University of Illinois at Urbana-Champaign.

Pintrich, P. R., & DeGroot, E. V. (1990). Motivational and self-regulated learning components of classroom academic performance. *Journal of Educational Psychology, 82,* 33–40.

Pittman, K. (1999, September). *The power of engagement.* Washington, DC: The Forum for Youth Investment. Retrieved from http://forumfyi.org/content/youth-today-power-enga

Priest, S., & Gass, M. A. (2005). *Effective leadership in adventure programming* (2nd ed.). Champaign, IL: Human Kinetics.

Purcell-Gates, V., Duke, N. K., & Martineau, J. A. (2007). Learning to read and write genre-specific text: Roles of authentic experience and explicit teaching. *Reading Research Quarterly, 42,* 8–45.

Renninger, K. A., & Hidi, S. (2016). *The power of interest for motivation and learning.* New York: Routledge.

Rusk, N., Larson, R. W., Raffaelli, M., Walker, K., Washington, L., Gutierrez, V., . . . & Perry, S. C. (2013). Positive youth development in organized programs: How teens learn to manage emotions. In C. Proctor & P. A. Linley (Eds.), *Positive psychology: Research, applications and interventions for children and adolescents* (pp. 247–261). New York: Springer.

Ryan, R. M., & Deci, E. L. (2000). Self-determination theory and the facilitation of intrinsic motivation, social development, and well-being. *American Psychologist, 55,* 68–78.

Ryan, R. M., & Deci, E. L. (2008). Self-determination theory and the role of basic psychological needs in personality and the organization of behavior. In O. P. John, R. W. Robbins, & L. A. Pervin (Eds.), *Handbook of personality: Theory and research* (pp. 654–678). New York: Guilford.

Salusky, I., Larson, R. W., Griffith, A., Wu, J., Raffaelli, M., Sugimura, N., & Guzman, M. (2014). How youth develop responsibility: What can be learned from youth programs. *Journal of Research on Adolescence, 24*(3), 417–430.

Schiefele, U. (1996). Topic interest, text representation, and quality of experience. *Contemporary Educational Psychology, 21,* 3–18.

Shernoff, D. (2013). *Optimal learning environments to promote student engagement.* New York: Springer.

Shernoff, D. J., & Bempechat, J. (Eds.) (2014). *Engaging youth in schools: Evidence-based models to guide future innovations. NSSE Yearbook, Teachers College Record* (Vol. 113).

Smith, C., McGovern, G., Larson, R. W., Hilltaker, B., & Peck, S. C. (2016). *Preparing youth to thrive: Promising practices for social emotional learning.* Washington, DC: Forum for Youth Investment.

Vandell, D. L., Reisner, E. R., Pierce, K. M., Brown, B. B., Lee, D., Bolt, D., Pechman, E. M. (2006, August). *The study of promising after-school programs: Examination of longer term outcomes after two years of program experiences.* Madison, WI: Wisconsin Center for Education Research. Retrieved from http://childcare.wceruw.org/statements.html

Vandell, D. L., Larson, R. W., Mahoney, J. L., & Watts, T. W. (2015). Children's organized activities. In M. H. Bornstein, T. Leventhal, & R. Lerner, (Eds.), *Handbook of child psychology and developmental science* (7th ed., Vol. 4, pp. 305–355). New York: Wiley.

Walsh, V., & Golins, G. L. (1976). *The exploration of the Outward Bound process.* Denver: Colorado Outward Bound School.

Watkins, N., Larson, R., & Sullivan, P. (2007). Learning to bridge difference: Community youth programs as contexts for developing multicultural competencies. *American Behavioral Scientist, 51,* 380–402.

Wood, D., Larson, R. W., & Brown, J. (2009). How adolescents come to see themselves as more responsible through participation in youth programs. *Child Development, 80,* 295–309.

Wortham, S. (2006). *Learning identity: The joint emergence of social identification and academic learning.* New York: Cambridge University Press.

CHAPTER EIGHT

Taking Positive Psychology to the Workplace: Positive Organizational Psychology, Positive Organizational Behavior, and Positive Organizational Scholarship

Meg A. Warren, Stewart I. Donaldson, and Fred Luthans

Theory, research, and application on positive approaches to work and organizations have been gaining considerable popularity in the last 15 years. Although only one chapter in the *Handbooks of Positive Psychology* have been devoted to the workplace (Lopez & Snyder, 2009; Snyder & Lopez, 2002), scholarship aligned with positive approaches to work and organizations has taken off. Positive psychology is now clearly evidenced in various streams of organizational research such as organizational psychology (Bakker, 2013; Donaldson & Ko, 2010), industrial-organizational psychology (Graen & Grace, 2015), occupational health (Bakker & Derks,

2010), management, organizational behavior and development (Cameron, Dutton, & Quinn, 2003; Cameron & Spreitzer, 2012; Luthans, 2002a, 2002b; Roberts, 2006), leadership (Avolio & Luthans, 2006; Luthans & Avolio, 2003; Youssef & Luthans, 2012; Youssef-Morgan & Luthans, 2013a), and human resource management (Luthans, 2012). This positive perspective has also influenced research and practice across all levels of analysis, that is, micro (organizational behavior; Luthans, Avolio, Avey, & Norman, 2007; Avey, Reichard, Luthans, & Mhatre, 2011), meso (teams; Richardson & West, 2010; West, Patera, & Carsten, 2009), and macro (organizational development and change; Cameron & McNaughtan, 2014; Cantore & Cooperrider, 2013; organization science; Baker & Bulkley, 2014).

In this chapter, we first trace the history of positive approaches to work and organizations in order to help determine what inspired this area of inquiry. Next, we review some of the main contributions of the various positive orientations to organizational research and scholarship and some of the innovations that this positive lens helped to germinate. Finally, we offer some suggestions for integrating and unifying the three major approaches of positive organizational psychology (POP), positive organizational behavior (POB), and positive organizational scholarship (POS) and offer some needed future research directions with special emphasis on strengthening marginalized groups.

History of Positive Work and Organizational Research

A positive approach to psychological science grew out of a response to the overwhelming focus on pathology (Seligman & Csikszentmihalyi, 2000). In the case of organizational research, however, despite strong concerns about managing organizational problems, research also investigated organizational opportunities. Although organizational psychologists have been concerned with issues such as employee stress, burnout, counterproductive behavior, conflict, and turnover, beneficial organizational and individual outcomes such as job satisfaction, organizational commitment, creativity, organizational citizenship behavior, and especially effective performance have also been of interest to organizational scholars and practitioners for a long time. It is in this somewhat open perspective that three major streams of positively oriented inquiry gained a foothold in the workplace.

The *positive psychology* movement inspired interest in the well-being of organizations and employees. In their seminal conceptualization of positive psychology, Seligman and Csikszentmihalyi (2000) considered positive institutions as a pillar and the context in which positive states (e.g., flow, hope, and positive emotions) were experienced and positive characteristics (e.g., creativity, meaning, and purpose) were cultivated and practiced. Consequently, they construed positive institutions broadly as including organizations, education, marriage, family, religion, judicial systems, governments, and societies. While in this broad, generalized form it remained a rather underdeveloped area of positive psychology (Hart & Sasso, 2011), the conceptual and philosophical orientation of positive psychology caught the interest of applied organizational researchers and practicing managers. As such, positive psychology constructs (e.g., well-being, flow, meaning, and mindfulness) that were gaining momentum in social, personality, cognitive, and other areas of psychology were introduced and studied in the applied settings of organizations. Some of the growing areas of research in organizational psychology became employee well-being (Page & Vella-Brodrick, 2009; Wright, 2010), meaning (Steger & Dik, 2010), positive leadership (Diener, 2000), coaching (Grant & Spence, 2010), mindfulness at work (Good, et al. 2016), and organizational interventions that enhance positive work experiences, build positive employee traits, and foster positive institutions (Meyers, van Woerkom, & Bakker, 2013).

Inspired by the presentations of Seligman, Diener, Csikszentmihalyi, and Fredrickson at the inaugural Positive Psychology Summit at the Gallup Organization in Lincoln, Nebraska, in 1999, University of Nebraska organizational behavior professor, and at the time a fellow Gallup senior scientist with the presenters, Fred Luthans had a trigger moment to take this newly emerging positive psychology to the workplace (see Luthans, in press and Luthans & Avolio, 2009 for more details). Soon after, Luthans published the first work on what he termed *positive organizational behavior* or simply POB (Luthans, 2002a, 2002b). His intent in general was to take positive psychology to the workplace, but more specifically to construct and build awareness of a rejuvenated, comprehensive positive approach with a new perspective, theory, valid measure, basic research support, and effective application for the management fields of organizational behavior and human resources. He accordingly defined POB as "the study and application of positively oriented human resource strengths and psychological capacities that can be measured, developed, and effectively managed for performance improvement in today's workplace" (Luthans, 2002b, p. 59).

To operationally define exactly what Luthans meant by POB, and subsequently what he called *Psychological Capital* or simply PsyCap (Luthans, Luthans, & Luthans, 2004; Luthans & Youssef, 2004), he established the following objective, scientific inclusion criteria: (1) strong theoretical and research grounding, (2) published valid measurement, (3) be open to development or "state-like" (as opposed to relatively fixed or "trait-like"), and (4) have demonstrated impact on desired employee attitudes, behaviors, and performance (Luthans, 2002a). Drawing from positive psychology (not organizational behavior), hope (the will and the way), efficacy (confidence and belief), resilience (overcoming adversity and going beyond), and optimism (positive attributions of success and failure and positive future expectations) were determined to best meet the inclusion criteria for POB and PsyCap (see Luthans & Youssef-Morgan, 2017; Luthans, Youssef-Morgan, & Avolio, 2015 for in-depth background and the extensive research findings). In sum, POB does recognize the considerable past, present, and future of positive constructs in OB, but concentrates on underrepresented constructs from positive psychology and their relevance to employee and organizational performance and, more recently, employee and team well-being.

Parallel to Luthans taking positive psychology to the workplace with POB and PsyCap, organizational researchers from the University of Michigan began to take a positive perspective with what they termed *positive organizational scholarship (POS)* (Cameron, Dutton, & Quinn, 2003). At Michigan, they founded the Center for Positive Organizational Scholarship (now known as the Center for Positive Organizations). This area of research is primarily concerned with the positive contextual features of organizations that shape individual and team flourishing (Cameron et al., 2003; Cameron & Spreitzer, 2012).

The POS perspective considers how organizational processes and practices nurture or inhibit employee and organizational flourishing. The main premise of POS is that understanding the sources of positive behavior in the workplace (e.g., reflecting on best self) allows organizations to elevate to new levels of accomplishment (i.e., extraordinary performance) (Roberts, Dutton, Spreitzer, Heaphy, & Quinn, 2005). POS analyzes organizations characterized by "appreciation, collaboration, virtuousness, vitality, and meaningfulness where creating abundance and human well-being are key indicators of success" (Bernstein, 2003, p. 267). This perspective attracted the attention of prominent as well as upcoming management/ organizational and organizational psychology scholars, and new ideas, research, and knowledge were cultivated and nurtured at specific POS conferences, POS-led workshops, and sessions at the Academy of Management, and most recently at IPPA (International Positive Psychology Association, well-known POS scholar Kim Cameron was the past program chair of this biannual conference). These efforts have led to theory and research on organizational virtuousness (Cameron, Bright, & Caza, 2004), positive work relationships (Dutton & Ragins, 2007), compassion at work (Lilius et al., 2008), positive identity (Dutton, Roberts, & Bednar, 2010), positive deviance (Spreitzer & Sonenshein, 2004), and other topics, published in management and organization journals.

In an effort to assess the extent to which positively oriented organizational research had gained momentum and spurred organized lines of inquiry, Donaldson and Ko (2010) catalogued peer-reviewed literature that self-identified with a positive orientation (either as positive psychology in work settings, positive organizational scholarship, or positive organizational behavior) and called this extant literature *positive organizational psychology (POP)*. This term was meant to serve as an umbrella that captured all peer-reviewed literature that self-identified with a positive orientation to work and organizational phenomena. They found that through 2010, some of the most popular areas of research that had developed a growing evidence base were positive leadership, positive organizational development and change, psychological capital, organizational virtuousness and ethics, happiness and well-being at work, and work engagement.

Whereas the positive psychology movement (Seligman & Csikszentmihalyi, 2000) emphasized the need for shifting focus from exclusively negative orientations to considering positive phenomena, positive organizational scholars emphasized opportunities for building a broader, grander, and more compassionate vision. Each of the positive organizational streams (POP, POB, and POS) interpreted the positive agenda as a way to set a higher bar for their respective areas: positive organizational psychologists shifted their focus from employee productivity to include employee well-being and flourishing; POB scholars went beyond attracting, retaining, and managing human capital to developing their positive psychological resources; and POS researchers focused on raising the bar from high performance to extraordinary performance, from focusing on competition and productivity to viewing the organization as a space where virtue and compassion lead to organizational thriving. The overall aim of positively oriented scholars was to expand horizons, and through intentional organized inquiry on what was positive and affirmative, they opened up fresh new spaces for dialogue and growth.

Theory and Research in Positive Organizational Psychology

Our review of the empirical literature associated with positive psychology (Ackerman, Warren, & Donaldson, 2017) indicates that employees are the most-studied population in positive psychology. In addition, the numerous specific contributions of POB and POS make POP research an important source of knowledge for positive psychology in general. Taken together, the question becomes to what topics has the positive orientation offered the most generative contributions to the management and organizational literature? A further question is what are the most popular innovations that have emerged due to the positive orientation? In the following sections, we address these questions and review some of the latest contributions.

Some key contributions of positive organizational psychology scholars are those that have led to the expansion of the field's understanding of existing phenomena, employee attributes, and organizational processes. We have selected for special attention some of the most popular topics infused with positively oriented theorizing and research, namely, happiness and well-being at work, positive leadership, positive work relationships, psychological capital, and organizational virtuousness.

Happiness and Well-Being at Work

Since the initial framing of positive psychology by Seligman and Csikszentmihalyi (2000), the most popular area of interest has been well-being and happiness (Donaldson, Dollwet, & Rao,[1] 2015). But why should organizations be concerned with employee well-being and happiness? Page and Vella-Broderick (2008) suggest that in general, employee well-being is an important precursor to organizational well-being. Next, we briefly review the extent to which research supports this observation.

Happiness and Productivity

Although happiness as a predictor of productivity has been debated for a long time (since the Hawthorne studies in the 1920s), positive psychology conceptualization and research reignited this long-standing discussion (Quick & Quick, 2004; Wright & Cropanzano, 2004, 2007). Over the last few years, there is now conceptual (Youssef-Morgan & Luthans, 2015) and a wealth of empirical research that shows that employee well-being predicts intention to stay (Harter, Schmidt, & Keyes, 2003; Sears, Shi, Coberley, & Pope, 2013; Singh, Burke, & Boekhorst, 2016; Wright & Bonett, 2007; Wright & Hobfoll, 2004). Similarly, considerable research has demonstrated that employee psychological well-being predicts job performance (Edgar, Geare, Halhjem, Reese, & Thoresen, 2015; Taris & Schreurs, 2009; see review of 36 quantitative studies: Van De Voorde, Paauwe, & Van Veldhoven, 2012; Wright & Cropanzano, 2004; Wright, Cropanzano, & Bonett, 2007; Wright & Huang, 2012). Furthermore, Wright and Cropanzano (2000) found psychological well-being to be a stronger predictor of job performance than job satisfaction. This considerable evidence base makes a strong case for prioritizing employee well-being in organizations.

Happiness, Organizational Culture, and Relationships

Organizational culture is an important context that facilitates employee well-being. For instance, an ethical organizational culture predicts high levels of well-being, whereas unethical culture predicts cynicism and low levels of well-being (Huhtala, Kaptein, & Feldt, 2016). Recent studies show that poor relationships and incivility negatively predict employee well-being (Lim, Cortina, & Magley, 2008; Paulin & Griffin, 2016). On the other hand, positive work relationships (Santos, Hayward, & Ramos, 2012) and organizational citizenship behaviors directed to other employees (Kumar, Jauhari, & Singh, 2016) are positively associated with employee well-being. Similarly, a recent study of Swedish auditors found that organizational cultures that emphasized relationships predicted higher job satisfaction, life balance, and life satisfaction (Umans, Broberg, Schmidt, Nilsson, & Olsson, 2016). Further, managerial support and supportive work-home culture that facilitates flexible practices and family-friendly initiatives also predict well-being, particularly for women (Beauregard, 2011). Thus, recent research suggests that cultivating positive work relationships is key to fostering employee well-being.

Positive Leadership

Leadership theory and research have received considerable attention in management, organizational behavior, and organizational psychology through the years. Although considerable scholarship has been devoted to leadership traits, skills, styles, approaches, development, and contexts, the POB perspective has offered some additive contributions, especially to authentic leadership, and indirectly to transformational leadership, servant leadership, ethical leadership, and spiritual leadership. Positive leadership is an umbrella term that encompasses these various types of leadership styles and theories that are aligned with positive work and organizations. Youssef-Morgan and Luthans (2013) recently defined positive leadership as "the systematic and integrated manifestation of leadership traits, processes, intentional behaviors and performance outcomes that are elevating, exceptional and affirmative of the strengths, capabilities and developmental potential of leaders, their followers and their organizations over time and across contexts" (p. 201). In doing so, they build on the extant leadership literature of traits, states, and situational factors by focusing on both trait-like strengths and positive state-like psychological resources while taking context into account. As such, this concept of positive leadership serves as a term that encompasses elements of both psychological capital (Luthans et al., 2015) and authentic leadership (Avolio & Luthans, 2006; Luthans & Avolio, 2003), as well as more traditional transformational leadership. Positive leadership approaches have also been theorized to be relevant to a global context and to engage organizational leadership practice across cultures (Youssef & Luthans, 2012; Youssef-Morgan & Luthans, 2013a). A deeper examination of authentic leadership perhaps best represents how positivity can play an important role in leading today's organizations.

There has been a variety of conceptualizations of authentic leadership and authenticity among leaders since the 1960s, including a focus on organizational and personal responsibility (Henderson & Hoy, 1983), good intentions, and meaningful relationships characterized by sensitivity to others' feelings, needs, and aspirations (Bhindi & Duignan, 1997). Luthans and Avolio (2003) brought fresh attention to the discussion of authentic leadership by focusing on the recognition and development of employees' positive psychological resources such as the PsyCap components of hope, efficacy, resilience, and optimism. They also emphasized the importance of well-developed organizational contexts that foster leader and follower self-awareness, self-regulation, and positive self-development.

Authentic leadership affects not only individual followers, but also teams, in terms of voice, cohesion, and performance. For instance, a recent study found authentic leadership can reduce silence in teams among followers who are low on proactiveness (Guenter, Schreurs, van Emmerik, & Sun, 2016). In a couple of Chinese studies, at the individual level it was found that authentic leadership, moderated by PsyCap and mediated by relational processes (Leader Member Exchange [LMX] theory), predicted follower performance (Wang, Sui, Luthans, Wang, & Wu, 2012), and at the group level authentic leadership was positively related to internal whistleblowing, partially mediated by team psychological safety and personal identification (Liu, Liao, & Wei, 2015). In a study involving police and fire department teams in Spain, authentic leadership was positively related to group cohesion and group identification (López, Alonso, Morales, & León, 2015), whereas in another study conducted among 53 teams in the UK and Greece, authentic leadership predicted team reflexivity (i.e., reflection and adaptation), which in turn predicted team performance (operationalized as effectiveness and productivity) (Lyubovnikova, Legood, Turner, & Mamakouka, 2015).

Finally, authentic leadership's link with virtuousness has been linked to positive organizational outcomes. For instance, authentic leadership predicted team virtuousness and team affective commitment, and consequently, team potency (i.e., a team's generalized self-efficacy) (Rego, Vitória, Magalhães, Ribeiro, & Cunha, 2013), and authentic leadership predicted sales achievement in retail stores through the mediating role of perceived virtuousness and perceived potency (Rego, Júnior, & Cunha, 2015).

Positive Work Relationships

Much of the research on relationships in the workplace has been characterized by a focus on the dark side: workplace bullying (Bartlett & Bartlett, 2011), incivility (Schilpzand, De Pater, & Erez, 2016), abusive supervision (Martinko, Harvey, Brees, & Mackey, 2013), social undermining (Duffy, Ganster, & Pagan, 2002), workplace mistreatment (Perrewé, Halbesleben, & Rosen, 2015), and ostracism (Robinson, O'Reilly, & Wei, 2013). In other words, the focus in this literature is often on the negative interpersonal behaviors and their negative outcomes, rather than on the uplifting nature and quality of the relationship (for an exception, see LMX theory; Bauer & Erdogen, 2016; Graen & Scandura, 1987). Over the last few years, the POS perspective has attempted to fill this gap by offering testable theoretical frameworks for the study and research of high-quality, positive coworker relationships and their desirable outcomes.

One of the key theoretical contributions has been the theory of high-quality interpersonal connections by Dutton and Heaphy (2003). Connections were conceptualized as dyadic micro-interactions that were the dynamic, generative, life-giving "connective tissue" between individuals (Dutton, 2003, p. 25). In high-quality connections, the connective tissue is flexible, strong, and resilient; in low-quality connections, the connective tissue between individuals becomes more brittle with every interaction. The research on high-quality connections and relationships has shown considerable promise. For instance, high-quality relationships predicted psychological safety, and consequently, learning from failures (Carmeli & Gittell, 2009), as well as learning behaviors in general (Carmeli, Brueller, & Dutton, 2009).

High-quality relationships have also been found to predict positive outcomes for teams. In a study of intrateam and external relationships, high-quality intrateam relationships were associated with greater psychological safety and learning processes, and high-quality external relationships were associated with better team learning and team performance (Brueller & Carmeli, 2011). Similarly, constructive emotional expression (i.e., emotion-carrying capacity, a marker of high-quality relationships) was related to individual and team resilience and mediated the link between trust and team resilience (Stephens, Heaphy, Carmeli, Spreitzer, & Dutton, 2013). Another interesting stream of research involving four studies demonstrated that respectful engagement (a marker of high-quality relationships) predicted relational information processing, which in turn predicted creative behavior at individual as well as team levels (Carmeli, Dutton, & Hardin, 2015). Thus, high-quality relationships are linked with outcomes that foster individual and team flourishing.

There is evidence suggesting that high-quality connections can also be useful in knowledge creation. A qualitative study of a management consulting company and an oil exploration organization found that high-quality connections played an important role in positively deviant practices for knowledge creation (Aarrestad, Brøndbo, & Carlsen, 2015). Intensified collaboration was witnessed when the stakes were high. Specifically, appreciative questions and joint problem-solving reportedly stimulated help seeking and help giving. By the same token, collaborative space and shared visuals and artifacts reportedly strengthened information processing and knowledge creation.

Finally, a recent study on high-quality relationships and relationship thoughts suggests that although high-quality relationships are beneficial for both women and men, they are especially important for women (Warren & Warren, 2017). Findings indicated that both women and men who had higher-quality work relationships engaged more often in relationship-enhancing positive affect thoughts (such as dwelling on positive memories of shared experiences) and more generative thoughts focused on expanding their networks (such as connecting with colleagues of colleagues). However, for women, those with higher-quality work relationships engaged in fewer distress-maintaining, ruminative, questioning thoughts (e.g., whether they were being treated well; whether others had their best interests in mind). By contrast, for men questioning thoughts were unrelated to the quality of their work relationships. These findings underscore that high-quality relationships may be especially important for women, given the role of rumination in depressive symptoms and the link of depression to lower productivity (McTernan, Dollard, & LaMontagne, 2013).

The topics discussed earlier (well-being at work, leadership, and work relationships) had considerable existing research and literature before being extended by positive organizational psychology. On the other hand, positive organizational psychology also offered unique theoretical innovations, including psychological capital and organizational virtuousness, which stemmed from POB and POS, respectively. We briefly review some of the main contributions on these two innovative, positive approaches to management and organizational behavior.

Psychological Capital (PsyCap)

The major contribution of POB is the theory building, research, and application of PsyCap. PsyCap is a theoretically (Luthans et al., 2015; Youssef-Morgan & Luthans, 2013b) and empirically (Avey et al., 2011; Luthans et al., 2007) supported second-order core construct consisting of the four positive psychological resources of hope, efficacy, resilience, and optimism or "the HERO within." Luthans and colleagues (2015, p. 2) define PsyCap as "an individual's positive psychological state of development that is characterized by (1) having confidence (efficacy) to take on and put in the necessary effort to succeed at challenging tasks; (2) making a positive attribution (optimism) about succeeding now and in the future; (3) persevering toward goals and, when necessary, redirecting paths to goals (hope) in order to succeed; and (4) when beset by problems and adversity, sustaining and bouncing back and even beyond (resiliency) to attain success."

Research has demonstrated that the multidimensional core construct of PsyCap has a stronger relationship with desired outcomes than each of the four psychological resources that make it up (Luthans et al., 2007) and adds value over and above personal demographics and established positive OB traits such as self-evaluations and personality and person-organization and person-job fit in predicting desired attitudes and behaviors (Avey, Luthans, & Youssef, 2010). Moreover, experimental (Luthans, Avey, Avolio, & Peterson, 2010; Luthans, Avey, & Patera, 2008) and longitudinal (Peterson, Luthans, Avolio, Walumbwa, & Zhang, 2011) studies have clearly shown within-person PsyCap is changeable (i.e., is "state-like"), and can be developed and managed to improve performance outcomes. There is even an ideal, but very seldom used, Solomon Four Group–designed study demonstrating the significant development of PsyCap in a short training program (Ertosun, Erdil, Deniz, & Alpkan, 2015).

Hope is a motivational energy operationalized as planning for goals and an agentic pursuit of goals (see Snyder, 2000 and Lopez, 2013, for reviews). Efficacy is the confidence and belief about one's "abilities to mobilize the motivation, cognitive resources or courses of action needed to successfully execute a specific task within a given context" (Stajkovic & Luthans, 1998, p. 66). Resilience refers to the ability to bounce back from setbacks or even positive events such as increased responsibility (Luthans, 2002a). Finally, optimism refers to a positive explanatory style about present and future success (i.e., success is internally driven, global in scope, and permanent; Seligman, 1998).

Beyond the foundational research previously cited, over the past 15 years, PsyCap has accumulated a wealth of empirical evidence of its success in predicting desirable outcomes in the workplace. For example, a meta-analysis of 51 studies showed that PsyCap significantly predicted desired (and negatively with undesired) attitudes (e.g., job satisfaction, organizational commitment, and psychological well-being), behaviors (e.g., organizational citizenship), and performance (self-rated, supervisor rated, and objective) (Avey et al., 2011). A more recent comprehensive review that included 66 PsyCap studies verified these findings (Newman, Ucbasaran, Zhu, & Hirst, 2014). The two outcomes that have received the most interest and attention were initially performance and, more recently, well-being.

To verify the PsyCap psychological resources inclusion criterion of having demonstrated impact on performance outcomes, both the foundational (Luthans et al., 2007) and then research through the years around the world have been devoted to and found a significant relationship between PsyCap and performance (see Avey et al., 2011; Luthans & Youssef-Morgan, 2017; Newman et al., 2014 for comprehensive reviews). For instance, in a study in the quick service restaurant industry, collective PsyCap (*c*PsyCap) was found to predict service quality and customer satisfaction, which in turn predicted unit-level performance (Mathe-Soulek, Scott-Halsell, Kim, & Krawczyk, 2014). Similarly, a study conducted among marketers in Vietnam showed that PsyCap predicted quality of work life, job attractiveness, and job effort, which in turn predicted job performance (Nguyen, Nguyen, & Minh, 2014). In another multilevel study conducted in a telecom company in Taiwan, leaders' PsyCap was related to followers' PsyCap, which in turn predicted job engagement and job performance (Chen, 2015). Through systematic analysis, Kalla (2016) makes the case that PsyCap is the real key to the effectiveness of organizations in India.

Because the relationship between PsyCap and performance is now so well established across the world, attention has recently focused on the role of PsyCap in well-being (Avey, Luthans, Smith, & Palmer, 2010) and non-business domains. For instance, Firestone and Anngela-Cole (2015) found a relationship between PsyCap and non–work-related quality-of-life factors of nonprofit human service workers. Also, a large study of U.S. army soldiers showed that those who had higher levels of work-related PsyCap before they were deployed were less likely to be diagnosed with post-traumatic stress disorder (PTSD), anxiety, depression, and alcohol and drug abuse post-deployment (Krasikova, Lester, & Harms, 2015). Another study by Cassidy, McLaughlin, and McDowell (2014) found PsyCap was positively related to well-being and negatively related to ill-being, and PsyCap and social resources mediated the link between bullying and well-being and ill-being.

Similarly, PsyCap has been found to predict well-being outcomes across cultures and diverse organizational contexts. For instance, studies have found that PsyCap predicted psychological well-being among unemployed youth in India (Rani, 2015); work well-being and lower intention to quit among Chinese police officers in Hong Kong (Siu, Cheung, & Lui, 2015); well-being and work-life balance among Chinese employees (Siu, 2013); lower depression symptoms of a very large sample of Chinese state bank employees (Kan & Yu, 2016); safety perceptions of Australian hospital nurses (Brunetto, Xerri, Farr-Wharton, Shacklock, & Farr-Wharton, 2016) and maritime workers in Norwegian shipping firms (Bergheim, Nielsen, Mearns, & Eid, 2015); mental well-being of New Zealand entrepreneurs and top, middle, and junior managers (Roche, Haar, & Luthans, 2014); healthy coping behaviors and well-being among Israeli employees (Rabenu, Yaniv, & Elizur, 2016); and well-being in an Italian health care setting (Di Sipio, Falco, & De Carlo, 2012). The recent development and validation of a new projective measure of PsyCap in the health domain, that is, the Implicit Psychological Capital Questionnaire–Health (IPCQ-H) promises to boost further research in this area (Harms, Vanhove, & Luthans, 2016).

Organizational Virtuousness

Whereas PsyCap has dominated POB, one of the early and enduring contributions of POS is the concept of organizational virtuousness. The basic premise that inspired research on organizational virtuousness is that although ethics and standards may help avoid harm, in order to do some good there is a need for virtuousness in organizations (Cameron, 2006). Organizational virtuousness goes beyond ethics, corporate social responsibility, and citizenship, and focuses on three virtuous attributes: positive human impact, moral goodness, and social betterment (Cameron, 2003). Further, Cameron (2003) conceptualizes two types of virtuousness: tonic virtuousness, that is, an ambient condition such as integrity that fosters flourishing, and phasic virtuousness, that is, behavior that occurs in response to an event (e.g., forgiveness that can exist only in response to an offense).

Although organizational virtuousness is meant to be pursued for its intrinsic value, it has positive instrumental outcomes for organizations. In particular, organizational virtuousness seems to be useful in times of distress such as during downsizing and financial crises when there is potential for trust to be eroded. For instance, in one study (Bright, Cameron, & Caza, 2006), forgiveness and tonic virtuousness (i.e., hope-optimism, humility, integrity, compassion, virtuous fulfillment) buffered the negative effects of downsizing. Further, taking responsibility was associated with more forgiveness, and both responsibility and forgiveness were associated with more tonic virtuousness. Simply, when top managers expressed responsibility, employees were more likely to forgive layoffs. Thus, they found support for a self-perpetuating virtuous cycle, wherein responsibility fostered forgiveness, which in turn encouraged more responsible behaviors.

In another study involving recently downsized organizations, virtuousness predicted higher organizational performance, innovation, customer retention, quality, profitability, and lower turnover (Cameron, Bright, & Caza, 2004). Similarly, another study (Nikandrou & Tsachouridi, 2015) found that in the context of a financial crisis, perception of organizational virtuousness predicted higher job satisfaction, lower intention to quit, and higher willingness to support the organization. Similarly, in an analysis of crisis management strategies that were employed by U.S. airline companies after the September 11, 2001, terrorist attacks in the United States, the airlines that demonstrated virtuousness by protecting their employees' jobs at a cost to the company (i.e., avoiding layoffs) outperformed others through lower financial losses, faster stock price recovery, and higher passenger miles (Gittell, Cameron, Lim, & Rivas, 2006).

One of the most powerful examples of organizational virtuousness has been the nuclear clean-up of the Rocky Flats Nuclear Arsenal (Lavine & Cameron, 2012). Despite immense technical, political, and cultural obstacles, the site was decontaminated and turned into a wildlife refuge ahead of schedule (by 60 years), under budget (by $30 billion), and with high-quality standards. Among several other positive practices, one key practice that underlay such an extraordinary performance was a focus on integrity and transparency that helped create trust and optimism. Thus, although still in a nascent stage, the research of organizational virtuousness shows much promise for positive organizational outcomes in addition to contributing to social betterment.

Integration of Perspectives

The review earlier highlights representative contributions of taking positive psychology to the workplace through POP, POB, and POS. A few years ago, Youssef and Luthans (2011) called for more integration between the various positive orientations. We briefly review the extent to which we find integration and discussion across the positive approaches and concepts discussed earlier.

Some seminal studies examine happiness and well-being as an outcome of authentic leadership (Rahimnia & Sharifirad, 2015), positive work relationships (Colbert, Bono, & Purvanova, 2016), and organizational virtuousness (Rego, Ribeiro, Cunha, & Jesuino, 2011). As reviewed earlier, the link between PsyCap and well-being is receiving tremendous support across the world. Also, unsurprisingly, PsyCap and authentic leadership, in which there was intended overlap when first formulated (Luthans & Avolio, 2003; Avolio & Luthans, 2006), have both turned out to be major POB contributions both separately and together. For instance, PsyCap mediated the link between authentic leadership and job satisfaction and intention to leave in state-owned enterprises in Namibia (Amunkete & Rothmann, 2015) and PsyCap and work-related flow mediated the link between authentic leadership and employee creativity (Zubair & Kamal, 2015). Other studies have found the link between PsyCap, organizational virtuousness, and happiness at work (Williams, Kern, & Waters, 2016) and PsyCap and the POS construct of thriving at work (Paterson, Luthans, & Jeung, 2014). However, to date, integration of the positive approaches in the workplace is still largely missing, and we hope this chapter takes a step toward helping to fill this gap.

Future Directions

As indicated, there is still a need for more cross-pollination of research among POP, POB, and POS approaches and concepts. Furthermore, there is also a need for collaboration in positively oriented research beyond that which self-identifies with one of the three areas of POP, POB, and POS. As the influence of positive approaches in general continues to grow, we propose a broader umbrella term such as "positive work and organizations" that may serve to encompass all three and an overall positive orientation in the workplace based on the foundation of positive psychology.

Positive Work and Organizations

As the research and scholarship within the three main strands of POP, POB, and POS body of knowledge have grown and developed, their contributions have gained deep roots within specific spaces. Research on POP is found primarily in applied psychology journals and POB and POS research in management, organizational behavior, organizational development, and human resource management journals.

Along the lines of the review of POP published by Donaldson and Ko in 2010, we (first and second authors) have been expanding and updating the archive of the extant research inspired by the positive orientation. Our

current analyses reveal that over the last few years, the positive orientation has stimulated research that goes beyond the original fields in which
POP, POB, and POS originated (i.e., applied, industrial/organizational psychology, management, organizational behavior, human resource management). The positive approach is now witnessed in technology (Botella et al.,
2012; Riva, Baños, Botella, Wiederhold, & Gaggioli, 2012), hospitality and
tourism (Coghlan, 2015), program evaluation (Patton, 2003; Preskill &
Catsambas, 2006), law (Huntington, 2009), financial planning (Asebedo &
Seay, 2015), education (Luthans, Luthans, & Avey, 2014), management
accounting (Venkatesh & Blaskovich, 2012), sales (Friend, Johnson,
Luthans, & Sohi, 2016), and consulting psychology (Foster & Lloyd, 2007),
among others.

Whereas some investigations explicitly draw from one or more of the
three positive streams, others do not. Thus, the positive orientation is influencing research beyond its original boundaries. This creates a need for a
space for cross-pollination of research with the innovations that are ger-
minating beyond the three main streams. Further, as Rusk and Waters
(2013) observed, there is now considerable research that engages a positive orientation but does not identify with positive labels. Thus, there is a
need for creation of a space that facilitates cross-pollination across such
research. Further, this can help avoid the problems of redundancy and
duplication of efforts as witnessed in multiple operationalizations of constructs, and new development of constructs that considerably overlap with
existing constructs elsewhere, both growing issues in positive research
(Ackerman et al., 2017). Finally, cross-pollination of positive research
across organizational subdisciplines can ultimately enrich the entire field
of positive psychology.

Similarly, the positively oriented organizational research is also influencing *practice* in a wide variety of areas. Although scholars in POP, POB,
and POS have focused exclusively on theory building and research, there
is a need for an umbrella term that captures all practice-related scholarship in one place. This centrality will tend to encourage dialogue across
subfields and serve as a reservoir and clearinghouse for best evidence-
based practices. It is to this end that a catchall term such as "positive work
and organizations" may be unifying and useful.

In 2014, the International Positive Psychology Association (IPPA)
launched its first professional division, the Work and Organizations Division. The members included scholars and practitioners interested in applying positive concepts in the workplace. The division leadership team (the
first author served as president of the division) invited and represented
interests of individuals connected to POP, POB, POS, and beyond. The

division publication, *Positive Work and Organizations: Research and Practice (PWORP)*, received and published contributions that spanned each of three areas. The discussions that have emerged from this common home for positive work and organizational literature suggest that as the influence of positive approaches is growing and new uses and applications are discovered, there is a need for collaborative scholarship and practice across and beyond the streams. After two years of success as a division (over 800 members that represent close to half of the entire IPPA member base) and two successful issues of the PWORP newsletter (over 3,500 views), the positive work and organizations term seems to be a useful tool for capturing a broad swath of work in this general area and for attracting researchers and practitioners who may not otherwise interact.

Positive Work and Organizations for Marginalized Groups

A criticism of positive psychology research has been that it is inadequate in examining issues relevant to marginalized groups. In a recent review focused on issues of gender, race, and ethnicity in positive psychology, we (first and second authors) found scarce evidence of extant research that investigated the strengths and assets of marginalized groups, their positive lived experiences, and how they could thrive and flourish (Rao & Donaldson, 2015). Similarly, in a review of positive psychology's contributions to engaging differences in the workplace, we found few investigations considered issues of gender, sexual orientation, race, socioeconomic status, and age (Wilder, Rao, & Donaldson, 2016). Although Pedrotti and Edwards (this volume) offer a deeper and more comprehensive review of positive psychology contributions to issues of marginalized groups in general, we focus on topics relevant to work and organizations.

Happiness and Well-Being at Work

Aside from a few investigations on the well-being of women and marginalized groups in the workplace, the dynamics of their experiences remain largely underexamined. Many of those that do investigate this link find that marginalized groups often suffer from poor employee well-being. For instance, a recent study of college graduates found that relative to White workers, Asian American and Black workers experienced far less job satisfaction after controlling for gender, immigrant status, job fit, and other individual and job characteristics (Hersch & Xiao, 2016). Similarly, a study that used nationally representative linked employer-employee data of over 18,000 employees in Britain showed that women suffered from lower well-being when they were in organizations with high gender diversity (Haile, 2012). Although such empirical investigations reveal some of the issues, there is a need for research that investigates the mechanisms for these (sometimes counterintuitive) outcomes, examines the positive experiences that deviate from these norms, considers how the strengths and assets of these marginalized groups can be harnessed to improve their well-being at work, and how organizational systems and processes can foster happiness and well-being for marginalized groups.

Positive Leadership

As indicated, several studies on authentic leadership have demonstrated its value and relevance cross-culturally. However, there is room for growth in demonstrating its relevance for women and minority groups. Hopkins and O'Neil (2015) argue that given the predominance of gender stereotypes in what it means to be a leader (i.e., think leader, think male), it is challenging for women to be authentic as they are caught between norms of femininity and norms of leadership. Further, they may not be perceived as authentic by their followers when women display leadership characteristics that defy gender norms. Thus, complex dynamics limit the application of authentic leadership for women in its current form. There is a need for more theory and research on what authentic leadership might look like for women.

Similarly, in one recent study of Caucasian and Asian Americans, Caucasian respondents perceived Asian American leaders as less authentic, whereas Asian Americans perceived Caucasian leaders as less authentic (Burris, Ayman, Che, & Min, 2013). Thus, racial dynamics play a role in followers' perceptions of authentic leadership. Future research should explore whether there are common virtues (e.g., integrity, transparency) that, when exhibited, may be interpreted as authentic, regardless of racial biases. Thus, we call for more inclusive theorizing and empirical research so that positive leadership theories can attend to the unique challenges of leading diverse groups.

Positive Work Relationships

Gender and race dynamics can play unique roles in relationships. Socialization and gender norms influence how women and men relate to others, think about relationships, and experience relationships (Acitelli & Young, 1996). For instance, gender differences have been found in relational aspects of work such as response to competition (Lee, Kesebir, & Pillutla, 2016) and in the display, perception, and evaluation of emotion in work relationships (Ragins & Winkel, 2011). A recent study found that the link between quality of relationships with coworkers and life satisfaction was stronger for women than men (Jiang & Hu, 2016). In another interesting set of studies, high-quality mentoring relationships helped buffer negative effects of racial discrimination in the workplace (Ragins, Ehrhardt, Lyness, Murphy, & Capman, 2016). Specifically, employees who were aware of racial discrimination had lower organizational commitment, but this effect was buffered by the presence of mentors. Thus, seminal research suggests that positive work relationships may be capable of improving work outcomes for marginalized groups. Future research should examine the positive emotional and cognitive benefits of positive interpersonal work relationships that can accrue for individuals who identify with marginalized groups. Similarly, future research on dyads across races, ethnicities, and genders who exemplify positive relationships can help identify characteristics of such positive relationships; if and how they might overcome surface-level differences through deep-level similarities (Harrison, Price, & Bell, 1998); and impact on individual, interpersonal, and organizational outcomes.

Psychological Capital

As shown earlier, there is considerable research on the relevance of PsyCap across cultures. PsyCap has been clearly found to improve well-being and performance outcomes across a range of contexts and industries around the world. A few seminal articles have also examined PsyCap in the context of diversity and marginalized groups. For instance, in one study, strong ethnic identity (an asset) predicted higher PsyCap, which in turn predicted a preference for intrinsically motivating job attributes such as competence and growth, rather than status or independence (Combs, Milosevic, Jeung, & Griffith, 2012).

In an in-depth case analysis of Robben Island (a notorious South African prison that during apartheid held political prisoners such as Nelson Mandela), mostly using direct recall from the prisoners themselves, PsyCap was clearly exhibited by the majority of the prisoners. Led by Mandela and others, these prisoners, through their positivity and hope, efficacy, resilience, and optimism (i.e., their PsyCap and HERO within), literally transformed their very abusive, closed-minded correctional officers, and ultimately through a contagion effect, disrupted and changed the extremely oppressive institution to a new paradigm of learning and growth (Cascio & Luthans, 2014). This interesting historical case study demonstrated how PsyCap has the potential to change not only relatively normal organizational climates (Luthans, Norman, Avolio, & Avey, 2008), but also hostile and oppressive institutional contexts. This leads to our call for future research that examines how PsyCap can be developed in marginalized groups and its role in amplifying strengths and assets of marginalized groups and buffering deleterious consequences of discrimination and prejudice faced by them.

Organizational Virtuousness

Organizational virtuousness has the potential to make important contributions to managing diversity and attending to the unique needs and concerns of marginalized groups. Conversely, effective management of diversity is also found to predict better ethical and organizational virtuousness outcomes. For instance, findings from business ethics research suggest that gender diversity can improve ethical outcomes in the workplace. In one study, gender diversity on the board of directors was related to lower frequency and severity of fraud and less pronounced stock market response in the event of fraud (Cumming, Leung, & Rui, 2015). Similarly, high gender diversity on corporate boards is positively related to corporate social performance (Boulouta, 2013). Future empirical examinations should examine the role of gender in other forms of organizational virtuousness. Research that explores whether and how virtues (e.g., integrity, transparency, and responsibility) can repair and foster trust across individuals of different races and genders, improve work relationships, and amplify the benefits of diversity can further the agenda of social betterment for all.

Conclusion

This chapter aimed to summarize some of the most promising recent scientific findings in taking positive psychology to the workplace through the lens of positive organizational psychology, positive organizational behavior, and positive organizational scholarship. These findings spanned the topics of happiness and productivity, organizational culture, positive leadership, positive work relationships, psychological capital, and organizational virtuousness.

After examining and finding a general lack of integration among the three major positive approaches (POP, POB, POS) to the workplace, we suggested they may better come together under an expanded umbrella term such as positive work and organizations. Finally, we offer some future research directions, giving specific focus on improving the lives of marginalized groups through the topics reviewed in the chapter. It is our hope that the growing impressive scientific advances and possible new directions discussed will inspire the next generation of positive work and organization scholars and practitioners to make important contributions to personal development, teams, organizations, and eventually society.

Acknowledgments

Special thanks to Joo Young Lee, Vitoria De Valentim Meira, Russell Donaldson, and Michael Warren for assistance and feedback.

Note

1. Rao, in all citations in this chapter, refers to the first author, Warren, who was previously Rao.

References

Aarrestad, M., Brøndbo, M. T., & Carlsen, A. (2015). When stakes are high and guards are low: High-quality connections in knowledge creation. *Knowledge and Process Management, 22*, 88–98. doi:10.1002/kpm.1469

Acitelli, L. K., & Young, A. M. (1996). Gender and thought in relationships. In G. O. Fletcher & J. Fitness (Eds.), *Knowledge structures in close relationships: A social psychological approach* (pp. 147–168). Hillsdale, NJ: Lawrence Erlbaum Associates, Inc.

Ackerman, C. E., Warren, M. A., & Donaldson, S. I. (2017). *Scaling the heights of positive psychology: A review of trends and opportunities in measurement scales.* Manuscript under review.

Amunkete, S., & Rothmann, S. (2015). Authentic leadership, psychological capital, job satisfaction and intention to leave in state-owned enterprises. *Journal of Psychology in Africa, 25*(4), 271–281.

Asebedo, S. D., & Seay, M. C. (2015). From functioning to flourishing: Applying positive psychology to financial planning. *Journal of Financial Planning, 28*(11), 50–58.

Avey, J. B., Luthans, F., & Jensen, S. M. (2009). Psychological capital: A positive resource for combating employee stress and turnover. *Human Resource Management, 48*(5), 677–693.

Avey, J. B., Luthans, F., Smith, R. M., & Palmer, N. F. (2010). Impact ˙ ˑositive psychological capital on employee well-being over time. *Jou⸍ pational Health Psychology, 15*, 17–28.

Avey, J. B., Luthans, F., & Youssef, C. M. (2010). The additive vɐ psychological capital in predicting work attitudes and bɾ *of Management, 36*(2), 430–452. doi:10.1177/014920630ˑ

Avey, J. B., Reichard, R. J., Luthans, F., & Mhatre, K. H. (2011). Meta-analysis of the impact of positive psychological capital on employee attitudes, behaviors, and performance. *Human Resource Development Quarterly, 22*(2), 127–152. doi:10.1002/hrdq.20070

Avolio, B. J., & Luthans, F. (2006). *The high impact leader: Moments matter in accelerating authentic leadership development.* New York: McGraw-Hill.

Baker, W. E., & Bulkley, N. (2014). Paying it forward vs. rewarding reputation: Mechanisms of generalized reciprocity. *Organization Science, 25*(5), 1493–1510. doi:10.1287/orsc.2014.0920

Bakker, A. B. (Ed.). (2013). *Advances in positive organizational psychology.* Bingley, England: Emerald Group Publishing Limited.

Bakker, A. B., & Derks, D. (2010). Positive occupational health psychology. In S. Leka & J. Houdmont (Eds.), *Occupational health psychology* (pp. 194–224). New York: Wiley-Blackwell.

Bartlett, J. E., & Bartlett, M. E. (2011). Workplace bullying: An integrative literature review. *Advances in Developing Human Resources, 13*(1), 69–84. doi:10.1177/1523422311410651

Bass, B. M., & Avolio, B. J. (1993). Transformational leadership and organizational culture. *Public Administration Quarterly, 17*(1), 112–121.

Bauer, T. N., & Erdogan, B. (2016). Leader-member exchange (LMX) theory: An introduction and overview. In T. N. Bauer & B. Erdogan (Eds.), *The Oxford handbook of leader-member exchange* (pp. 3–8). New York: Oxford University Press.

Beauregard, T. A. (2011). Direct and indirect links between organizational work-home culture and employee well-being. *British Journal of Management, 22*(2), 218–237. doi:10.1111/j.1467-8551.2010.00723.x

Bergheim, K., Nielsen, M., Mearns, K., & Eid, J. (2015). The relationship between psychological capital, job satisfaction, and safety perceptions in the maritime industry. *Safety Science, 74,* 27–36.

Bernstein, S. D. (2003). Positive organizational scholarship: Meet the movement. *Journal of Management Inquiry, 12*(3), 266–271.

Bhindi, N., & Duignan, P. (1997). Leadership for a new century: Authenticity, intentionality, spirituality, and sensibility. *Educational Management and Administration, 25*(2), 117–132.

Botella, C., Riva, G., Gaggioli, A., Wiederhold, B. K., Alcaniz, M., & Baños, R. M. (2012). The present and future of positive technologies. *Cyberpsychology, Behavior & Social Networking, 15*(2), 78–84. doi:10.1089/cyber.2011.0140

Boulouta, I. (2013). Hidden connections: The link between board gender diversity and corporate social performance. *Journal of Business Ethics, 113*(2), 185–197. doi: 10.1007/s10551-012-1293-7

Bright, D. S., Cameron, K. S., & Caza, A. (2006). The amplifying and buffering effects of virtuousness in downsized organizations. *Journal of Business Ethics, 64*(3), 249–269. doi: 10.1007/s10551-005-5904-4

Brueller, D., & Carmeli, A. (2011). Linking capacities of high-quality relationships to team learning and performance in service organizations. *Human Resource Management, 50*(4), 455–477.

Brunetto, Y., Xerri, M., Farr-Wharton, B., Shacklock, K., Farr-Wharton, R., & Trinchero, E. (2016). Nurse safety outcomes: Old problem, new solution: The differentiating roles of nurses' psychological capital and managerial support. *Journal of Advanced Nursing, 72*(11), 2794–2805. doi: 10.1111/jan.13036

Burris, K., Ayman, R., Che, Y., & Min, H. (2013). Asian Americans' and Caucasians' implicit leadership theories: Asian stereotypes, transformational, and authentic leadership. *Asian- American Journal of Psychology, 4*(4), 258–266. doi:10.1037/a0035229

Cameron, K. S. (2003). Organizational virtuousness and performance. In K. S. Cameron, J. E. Dutton, & R. E. Quinn (Eds.), *Positive organizational scholarship: Foundations of a new discipline* (pp. 48–65). San Francisco: Berrett-Koehler.

Cameron, K. S. (2006). Good or not bad: Standards and ethics in managing change. *Academy of Management Learning & Education, 5*(3), 317–323. doi: 10.5465/AMLE.2006.22697020

Cameron, K. S., Bright, D., & Caza, A. (2004). Exploring the relationships between organizational virtuousness and performance. *American Behavioral Scientist, 47*(6), 766–790. doi: 10.1177/0002764203260209

Cameron, K. S., Dutton, J. E., & Quinn, R. E. (2003). Foundations of positive organizational scholarship. In K .S. Cameron, J. E. Dutton, & R. E. Quinn (Eds.), *Positive organizational scholarship: Foundations of a new discipline* (pp. 3–13). San Francisco: Berrett-Koehler.

Cameron, K. S., & McNaughtan, J. (2014). Positive organizational change. *Journal of Applied Behavioral Science, 50*(4), 445–462.

Cameron, K. S., & Spreitzer, G. M. (2012). *The Oxford handbook of positive organizational scholarship.* New York: Oxford University Press.

Cantore, S. P., & Cooperrider, D. L. (2013). Positive psychology and appreciative inquiry: The contribution of the literature to an understanding of the nature and process of change in organizations. In H. S. Leonard, R. Lewis, A. M. Freedman, & J. Passmore (Eds.), *The Wiley-Blackwell handbook of the psychology of leadership, change, and organizational development* (pp. 267–287). New York: Wiley-Blackwell. doi:10.1002/9781118326404.ch13

Carmeli, A., Brueller, D., & Dutton, J. E. (2009). Learning behaviours in the workplace: The role of high-quality interpersonal relationships and psychological safety. *Systems Research and Behavioral Science, 26*(1), 81–98.

Carmeli, A., Dutton, J. E., & Hardin, A. E. (2015). Respect as an engine for new ideas: Linking respectful engagement, relational information processing, and creativity among employees and teams. *Human Relations,68*(6), 1021–1047. doi: 10.1177/0018726714550256

Carmeli, A., & Gittell, J. H. (2009). High-quality relationships, psychological safety, and learning from failures in work organizations. *Journal of Organizational Behavior, 30,* 709–729. doi:10.1002/job.v30:610.1002/job.565

Cascio, W. F., & Luthans, F. (2014). Reflections on the metamorphosis at Robben Island: The role of institutional work and positive psychological capital. *Journal of Management Inquiry, 23*(1), 51–67. doi: 10.1177/1056492612474348

Cassidy, T., McLaughlin, M., & McDowell, E. (2014). Bullying and health at work: The mediating roles of psychological capital and social support. *Work & Stress, 28*(3), 255–269. doi:10.1080/02678373.2014.927020

Chen, S. (2015). The relationship of leader psychological capital and follower psychological capital, job engagement and job performance: A multilevel mediating perspective. *International Journal of Human Resource Management, 26*(18), 2349–2365. doi:10.1080/09585192.2015.1020443

Coghlan, A. (2015). Tourism and health: Using positive psychology principles to maximise participants' wellbeing outcomes—a design concept for charity challenge tourism. *Journal of Sustainable Tourism, 23*(3), 382–400. doi: 10.1080/09669582.2014.986489

Colbert, A. E., Bono, J. E., & Purvanova, R. K. (2016). Flourishing via workplace relationships: Moving beyond instrumental support. *Academy of Management Journal, 59*(4), 1199–1223. doi:10.5465/amj.2014.0506

Combs, G. M., Milosevic, I., Jeung, W., & Griffith, J. (2012). Ethnic identity and job attribute preferences: The role of collectivism and psychological capital. *Journal of Leadership & Organizational Studies, 19*(1), 5–16. doi: 10.1177/1548051811433359

Cumming, D., Leung, T. Y., & Rui, O. 2015. Gender diversity and securities fraud. *Academy of Management Journal, 58,* 1572–1593.

Diener, E. (2000). Positive leadership: Moving into the future. *The Psychologist-Manager Journal, 4*(2), 233–236. doi: 10.1037/h0095895

Di Sipio, A., Falco, A., & De Carlo, N. A. (2012). Positive personal resources and organizational well-being: Resilience, hope, optimism, and self-efficacy in an Italian health care setting. *TPM—Testing, Psychometrics, Methodology in Applied Psychology, 19*(2), 81–95.

Donaldson, S. I., & Ko, I. (2010). Positive organizational psychology, behavior, and scholarship: A review of the emerging literature and evidence base. *The Journal of Positive Psychology, 5*(3), 177–191. doi: 10.1080/17439761003790930

Donaldson, S. I., Dollwet, M., & Rao, M. A. (2015). Happiness, excellence, and optimal human functioning revisited: Examining the peer-reviewed literature linked to positive psychology. *Journal of Positive Psychology, 10,* 185–195. http://dx.doi.org/10.1080/17439760.2014.943801

Duffy, M. K., Ganster, D. C., & Pagon, M. (2002). Social undermining in the workplace. *Academy of Management Journal, 45*(2), 331–351. doi: 10.2307/3069350

Dutton, J. E. (2003). *Energize your workplace: How to build and sustain high-quality connections at work.* San Francisco: Jossey-Bass Publishers.

Dutton, J. E., & Heaphy, E. D. (2003). The power of high-quality connections. In K. S. Cameron, J. E. Dutton, & R. E. Quinn (Eds.), *Positive organizational scholarship* (pp. 263–278). San Francisco: Berrett-Koehler.

Dutton, J. E., & Ragins, B. R. (2007). *Exploring positive relationships at work: Building a theoretical and research foundation.* Mahwah, NJ: Lawrence Erlbaum Associates Publishers.

Dutton, J. E., Roberts, L. M., & Bednar, J. (2010). Pathways for positive identity construction at work: Four types of positive identity and the building of social resources. *Academy of Management Review, 35*(2), 265–293. doi: 10.5465/AMR.2010.48463334

Edgar, F., Geare, A., Halhjem, M., Reese, K., & Thoresen, C. (2015). Well-being and performance: Measurement issues for HRM research. *International Journal of Human Resource Management, 26*(15), 1983–1994. doi:10.1080/09585192.2015.1041760

Ertosun, O. Z., Erdil, O., Deniz, N., & Alpkan, L. (2015). Positive psychological capital development: A field study by the Solomon four group design. *International Business Research, 8*(10), 102–111.

Firestone, J., & Anngela-Cole, L. (2015). Exploring positive psychological capital in nonprofit human service organizations. *Human Service Organizations: Management, Leadership & Governance, 40*(2), 118–130. doi: 10.1080/23303131.2015.1120249

Foster, S. L., & Lloyd, P. J. (2007). Positive psychology principles applied to consulting psychology at the individual and group level. *Consulting Psychology Journal: Practice & Research, 59*(1), 30–40. doi:10.1037/1065-9293.59.1.30

Friend, S. B., Johnson, J. S., Luthans, F., & Sohi, R. S. (2016). Positive psychology in sales: Integrating psychological capital. *Journal of Marketing Theory & Practice, 24*(3), 306–327. doi:10.1080/10696679.2016.1170525

Gittell, J. H., Cameron, K., Lim, S., & Rivas, V. (2006). Relationships, layoffs, and organizational resilience: Airline industry responses to September 11. *Journal of Applied Behavioral Science, 42*(3), 300–329. doi: 10.1177/0021886306286466

Good, D. J., Lyddy, C. J., Glomb, T. M., Bono, J. E., Brown, K. W., Duffy, M. K., & . . . Lazar, S. W. (2016). Contemplating mindfulness at work: An integrative review. *Journal of Management, 42*(1), 114–142. doi: 10.1177/0149206315617003

Graen, G., & Grace, M. (2015). Positive industrial and organizational psychology: Designing for tech-savvy, optimistic, and purposeful millennial professionals' company cultures. *Industrial and Organizational Psychology: Perspectives on Science and Practice, 8*(3), 395–408. doi: 10.1017/iop.2015.57

Graen, G. B., & Scandura, T. A. (1987). Toward a psychology of dyadic organizing. *Research in Organizational Behavior, 9*, 175.

Grant, A. M., & Spence, G. B. (2010). Using coaching and positive psychology to promote a flourishing workforce: A model of goal-striving and mental health. In P. A. Linley, S. Harrington, & N. Garcea (Eds.), *Oxford handbook of positive psychology and work* (pp. 175–188). New York: Oxford University Press.

Guenter, H., Schreurs, B., van Emmerik, H. I., & Sun, S. (2016). What does it take to break the silence in teams: Authentic leadership and/or proactive followership?. *Applied Psychology: An International Review, 66*(1), 49–77. doi:10.1111/apps.12076

Haile, G. A. (2012). Unhappy working with men? Workplace gender diversity and job-related well-being in Britain. *Labour Economics, 19*(3), 329–350. doi:10.1016/j.labeco.2012.02.002

Harms, P., Vanhove, A., & Luthans, F. (2016). Positive projections and health: An initial validation of the implicit psychological capital health measure. *Applied Psychology: An International Review, 66*(1), 78–102. doi:10.1111/apps.12077

Harrison, D. A., Price, K. H., & Bell, M. P. (1998). Beyond relational demography: Time and the effects of surface- and deep-level diversity on work group cohesion. *Academy of Management Journal, 41*, 96–107.

Hart, K. E., & Sasso, T. (2011). Mapping the contours of contemporary positive psychology. *Canadian Psychology/Psychologie Canadienne, 52*(2), 82–92. doi:10.1037/a0023118

Harter, J. K., Schmidt, F. L., & Keyes, C. L. (2002). Well-being in the workplace and its relationship to business outcomes: A review of the Gallup studies. In C. L. Keyes & J. Haidt (Eds.), *Flourishing: The positive person and the good life* (pp. 205–224). Washington, DC: American Psychological Association.

Henderson, J. E., & Hoy, W. K. (1983) Leader authenticity: The development and test of an operational measure. *Educational and Psychological Research, 3*(2), 63–75.

Hersch, J., & Xiao, J. (2016). Sex, race, and job satisfaction among highly educated workers. *Southern Economic Journal, 83*(1), 1–24. doi: 10.1002/soej.12133

Hopkins, M. M., & O'Neil, D. A. (2015). Authentic leadership: Application to women leaders. *Frontiers in Psychology, 6*, 959.

Huhtala, M., Kaptein, M., & Feldt, T. (2016). How perceived changes in the ethical culture of organizations influence the well-being of managers: A two-year longitudinal study. *European Journal of Work & Organizational Psychology, 25*(3), 335–352. doi:10.1080/1359432X.2015.1068761

Huntington, C. (2009). Happy families? Translating positive psychology into family law. *Virginia Journal of Social Policy & the Law, 16*(2), 385–424.

Jiang, Z., & Hu, X. (2016). Knowledge sharing and life satisfaction: The roles of colleague relationships and gender. *Social Indicators Research, 126*, 379–394. doi: 10.1007/s11205-015-0886-9

Johnson, R. E., Venus, M., Lanaj, K., Mao, C., & Chang, C. H. (2012). Leader identity as an antecedent of the frequency and consistency of transformational, consideration, and abusive leadership behaviors. *Journal of Applied Psychology, 97*(6), 1262.

Kalla, N. (2016). Psychological capital: Key to organizational effectiveness. *International Journal of Business, Management and Allied Sciences, 3*, 3013–3018.

Kan, D., & Yu, X. (2016). Occupational stress, work-family conflict and depressive symptoms among Chinese bank employees: The role of psychological capital. *International Journal of Environmental Research and Public Health, 13*, 134–145. doi: 10.3390/ijerph13010134

Krasikova, D. V., Lester, P. B., & Harms, P. D. (2015). Effects of psychological capital on mental health and substance abuse. *Journal of Leadership & Organizational Studies, 22*(3), 280–291. doi: 10.1177/1548051815585853

Kumar, M., Jauhari, H., & Singh, S. (2016). Organizational citizenship behavior & employee well-being. *Indian Journal of Industrial Relations, 51*(4), 594–608.

Lavine, M., & Cameron, K. (2012). From weapons to wildlife: Positive organizing in practice. *Organizational Dynamics, 41*(2), 135–145. doi: 10.1016/j.orgdyn.2012.01.007

Lee, S. Y., Kesebir, S., & Pillutla, M. M. (2016). Gender differences in response to competition with same-gender coworkers: A relational perspective. *Journal of Personality and Social Psychology, 110*(6), 869–886. doi: 10.1037/pspi0000051

Lilius, J. M., Worline, M. C., Maitlis, S., Kanov, J., Dutton, J. E., & Frost, P. (2008). The contours and consequences of compassion at work. *Journal of Organizational Behavior, 29*(2), 193–218. doi: 10.1002/job.508

Lim, S., Cortina, L. M., & Magley, V. J. (2008). Personal and workgroup incivility: Impact on work and health outcomes. *Journal of Applied Psychology, 93*(1), 95–107.

Liu, S., Liao, J., & Wei, H. (2015). Authentic leadership and whistleblowing: Mediating roles of psychological safety and personal identification. *Journal of Business Ethics, 131*(1), 107–119. doi: 10.1007/s10551-014-2271-z

López, C. G., Alonso, F. M., Morales, M. M., & León, J. M. (2015). Authentic leadership, group cohesion and group identification in security and emergency teams. *Psicothema, 27*(1), 59–64.

Lopez, S. (2013). *Making hope happen: Create the future you want for yourself and others*. New York: Atria.

Lopez, S., & Snyder, C. R. (Eds.). (2009). *Oxford handbook of positive psychology* (2nd ed.). New York: Oxford University Press.

Luthans, B. C., Luthans, K. W., & Avey, J. B. (2014). Building the leaders of tomorrow: The development of academic psychological capital. *Journal of Leadership and Organizational Studies, 21*, 191–200.

Luthans, F. (2002a). The need for and meaning of positive organizational behavior. *Journal of Organizational Behavior, 23*(6), 695–706. doi:10.1002/job.165

Luthans, F. (2002b). Positive organizational behavior: Developing and managing psychological strengths. *Academy of Management Executive, 16*(1), 57–72.

Luthans, F. (2012). Psychological capital: Implications for HRD, retrospective analysis, and future directions. *Human Resource Development Quarterly, 23*(1), 1–8. doi: 10.1002/hrdq.21119

Luthans, F. (in press). Positive organizational behavior and psychological capital. In F. Bietry & J. Creusier (Eds.). *The backstage of major discoveries in organizational behavior.* London: Routledge.

Luthans, F., Avey, J. B., Avolio, B. J., & Peterson, S. (2010). The development and resulting performance impact of positive psychological capital. *Human Resource Development Quarterly, 21,* 41–66.

Luthans, F., Avey, J. B., & Patera, J. L. (2008). Experimental analysis of a web-based training intervention to develop positive psychological capital. *Academy of Management Learning and Education, 7,* 209–221.

Luthans, F., & Avolio, B. J. (2003). Authentic leadership development. In K. S. Cameron, J. E. Dutton, & R. E. Quinn (Eds.), *Positive organizational scholarship: Foundations of a new discipline* (pp.241–261). San Francisco: Barrett-Koehler.

Luthans, F., & Avolio, B. J. (2009). The "point" of positive organizational behavior. *Journal of Organizational Behavior, 30,* 291–307.

Luthans, F., & Avolio, B. J. (2014). Brief summary of psychological capital and introduction to the special issue. *Journal of Leadership & Organizational Studies, 21*(2), 125–129. doi: 10.1177/1548051813518073

Luthans, F., Avolio, B. J., Avey, J. B., & Norman, S. M. (2007). Positive psychological capital: Measurement and relationship with performance and satisfaction. *Personnel Psychology, 60,* 541–572.

Luthans, F., Luthans, K. W., & Luthans, B. C. (2004). Positive psychological capital: Beyond human and social capital. *Business Horizons, 47,* 45–50.

Luthans, F., Norman, S. M., Avolio, B. J., & Avey, J. B. (2008). The mediating role of psychological capital in the supportive organizational climate—employee performance relationship. *Journal of Organizational Behavior, 29*(2), 219–238.

Luthans, F., & Youssef, C. M. (2004). Human, social, and now positive psychological capital management: Investing in people for competitive advantage. *Organizational Dynamics, 33*(2), 143–160.

Luthans, F., & Youssef-Morgan, C. M. (2017). Psychological capital: An evidence-based positive approach. In F. Morgeson (Ed.). *Annual review of organizational psychology and organizational behavior* (Vol. 4.). New York: Wiley.

Luthans, F., Youssef-Morgan, C. M., & Avolio, B. (2015). *Psychological capital and beyond.* New York: Oxford University Press.

Lyubovnikova, J., Legood, A., Turner, N., & Mamakouka, A. (2015). How authentic leadership influences team performance: The mediating role of team reflexivity. *Journal of Business Ethics,* Advance online publication. doi: 10.1007/s10551-015-2692-3

Martinko, M. J., Harvey, P., Brees, J. R., & Mackey, J. (2013). A review of abusive supervision research. *Journal of Organizational Behavior, 34,* S120–S137. doi:10.1002/job.1888

Mathe-Soulek, K., Scott-Halsell, S., Kim, S., & Krawczyk, M. (2014). Psychological capital in the quick service restaurant industry: A study of unit-level performance. *Journal of Hospitality & Tourism Research,* Advance online publication. doi:10.1177/1096348014550923

McTernan, W. P., Dollard, M. F., & LaMontagne, A. D. (2013). Depression in the workplace: An economic cost analysis of depression-related productivity loss attributable to job strain and bullying. *Work & Stress, 27*(4), 321–338. doi: 10.1080/02678373.2013.846948

Meyers, M. C., van Woerkom, M., & Bakker, A. B. (2013). The added value of the positive: A literature review of positive psychology interventions in organizations. *European Journal of Work and Organizational Psychology, 22,* 618–632. doi: 10.1080/1359432X.2012.694689

Newman, A., Ucbasaran, D., Zhu, F., & Hirst, G. (2014). Psychological capital: A review and synthesis. *Journal of Organizational Behavior, 35,* 120–138.

Nguyen, D. T., Nguyen, D. P., & Minh, T. H. (2014). Marketers' psychological capital and performance. *Asia-Pacific Journal of Business Administration, 6*(1), 36–48.

Nikandrou, I., & Tsachouridi, I. (2015). Towards a better understanding of the "buffering effects" of organizational virtuousness' perceptions on employee outcomes. *Management Decision, 53*(8), 1823–1842. doi: 10.1108/MD-06-2015-0251

Page, K., & Vella-Brodrick, D. (2009). The 'what', 'why' and 'how' of employee well-being: A new model. *Social Indicators Research, 90*(3), 441–458. doi: 10.1007/s11205-008-9270-3

Paterson, T. A., Luthans, F., & Jeung, W. (2014). Thriving at work: Impact of psychological capital and supervisor support. *Journal of Organizational Behavior, 35,* 434–446.

Patton, M. Q. (2003), Inquiry into appreciative evaluation. *New Directions for Evaluation, 100,* Winter, 85–98. doi: 10.1002/ev.102

Paulin, D., & Griffin, B. (2016). The relationships between incivility, team climate for incivility and job-related employee well-being: A multilevel analysis. *Work & Stress, 30*(2), 132–151. doi: 10.1080/02678373.2016.1173124

Perrewé, P. L., Halbesleben, J. B., & Rosen, C. C. (2015). *Mistreatment in organizations.* Bingley, United Kingdom: Emerald Group Publishing. doi: 10.1108/S1479-3555201513

Peterson, S. J., Luthans, F., Avolio, B. J., Walumbwa, F. O., & Zhang, Z. (2011). Psychological capital and employee performance: A latent growth modeling approach. *Personnel Psychology, 64,* 427–450.

Preskill, H., & Catsambas, T. T. (2006). *Reframing evaluation through appreciative inquiry.* Thousand Oaks, CA: Sage Publications, Inc.

Quick, J. C., & Quick, J. D. (2004). Healthy, happy, productive work: A leadership challenge. *Organizational Dynamics, 33*(4), 329–337. doi: 10.1016/j.orgdyn.2004.09.001

Rabenu, E., Yaniv, E., & Elizur, D. (2016). The relationship between psychological capital, coping with stress, well-being, and performance. *Current*

Psychology: A Journal for Diverse Perspectives on Diverse Psychological Issues, Advance online publication. doi: 10.1007/s12144-016-9477-4

Ragins, B. R., Ehrhardt, K., Lyness, K. S., Murphy, D. D., & Capman, J. F. (2016). Anchoring relationships at work: High-quality mentors and other supportive work relationships as buffers to ambient racial discrimination. *Personnel Psychology,* Advance online publication. doi:10.1111/peps.12144

Ragins, B. R., & Winkel, D. E. (2011). Gender, emotion and power in work relationships. *Human Resource Management Review, 21,* 377–393. doi: 10.1016/j.hrmr.2011.05.001

Rahimnia, F. R., & Sharifirad, M. I. (2015). Authentic leadership and employee well-being: The mediating role of attachment insecurity. *Journal of Business Ethics, 132*(2), 363–377.

Rani, E. K. (2015). The role of psychological capital (PsyCap) in psychological well-being of unemployed Indian youth. *Journal of Psychosocial Research, 10*(1), 149–157.

Rao, M. A., & Donaldson, S. I. (2015). Expanding opportunities for diversity in positive psychology: An examination of gender, race, and ethnicity. *Canadian Psychology/Psychologie Canadienne, 56*(3), 271–282. doi: 10.1037/cap0000036

Rego, A., Júnior, D. R., & Cunha, M. P. (2015). Authentic leaders promoting store performance: The mediating roles of virtuousness and potency. *Journal of Business Ethics, 128*(3), 617–634.

Rego, A., Ribeiro, N., Cunha, M. E., & Jesuino, J. C. (2011). How happiness mediates the organizational virtuousness and affective commitment relationship. *Journal of Business Research, 64*(5), 524–532.Rego, A., Vitória, A., Magalhães, A., Ribeiro, N., & Cunha, M. P. (2013). Are authentic leaders associated with more virtuous, committed and potent teams?. *The Leadership Quarterly, 24*(1), 61–79.

Richardson, J., & West, M. A. (2010). Dream teams: A positive psychology of team working. In P. A. Linley, S. Harrington, & N. Garcea (Eds.), *Oxford handbook of positive psychology and work* (pp. 235–249). New York: Oxford University Press.

Riva, G., Baños, R. M., Botella, C., Wiederhold, B. K., & Gaggioli, A. (2012). Positive technology: Using interactive technologies to promote positive functioning. *Cyberpsychology, Behavior & Social Networking, 15*(2), 69–77. doi: 10.1089/cyber.2011.0139

Roberts, L. M. (2006). Shifting the lens on organizational life: The added value of positive scholarship. *Academy of Management Review, 31*(2), 292–305. doi: 10.5465/AMR.2006.20208681

Roberts, L. M., Dutton, J. E., Spreitzer, G. M., Heaphy, E. D., & Quinn, R. E. (2005). Composing the reflected best-self portrait: Building pathways for becoming extraordinary in work organizations. *Academy of Management Review, 30*(4), 712–736. doi: 10.5465/AMR.2005.18378874

Robinson, S. L., O'Reilly, J., & Wei, W. (2013). Invisible at work: An integrated model of workplace ostracism. *Journal of Management, 39*(1), 203–231. doi: 10.1177/0149206312466141

Roche, M. A., Harr, J. M., & Luthans, F. (2014). The role of mindfulness and psychological capital on the well-being of leaders. *Journal of Occupational Health Psychology, 19*, 476–489.

Rusk, R. D., & Waters, L. E. (2013). Tracing the size, reach, impact, and breadth of positive psychology. *The Journal of Positive Psychology, 8*(3), 207–221. doi: 10.1080/17439760.2013.777766

Santos, A., Hayward, T., & Ramos, H. M. (2012). Organizational culture, work and personal goals as predictors of employee well-being. *Journal of Organizational Culture, Communications & Conflict, 16*(1), 25–48.

Schilpzand, P., De Pater, I. E., & Erez, A. (2016). Workplace incivility: A review of the literature and agenda for future research. *Journal of Organizational Behavior, 37*(Suppl 1), S57–S88. doi: 10.1002/job.1976

Sears, L. E., Shi, Y., Coberley, C. R., & Pope, J. E. (2013). Overall well-being as a predictor of health care, productivity, and retention outcomes in a large employer. *Population Health Management, 16*(6), 397–405. doi: 10.1089/pop.2012.0114

Seligman, M. E. P. (1998). *Learned optimism.* New York: Pocket Books.

Seligman, M. E. P., & Csikszentmihalyi, M. (2000). Positive psychology: An introduction. *American Psychologist, 55*, 5–14. doi: 10.1037/0003-066X.55.1.5

Singh, P., Burke, R. J., & Boekhorst, J. (2016). Recovery after work experiences, employee well-being and intent to quit. *Personnel Review, 45*(2), 232–254. doi: 10.1108/PR-07-2014-0154

Siu, O. L. (2013). Psychological capital, work well-being, and work-life balance among Chinese employees: A cross-lagged analysis. *Journal of Personnel Psychology, 12*(4), 170–181. doi: 10.1027/1866-5888/a000092

Siu, O. L., Cheung, F., & Lui, S. (2015). Linking positive emotions to work well-being and turnover intention among Hong Kong police officers: The role of psychological capital. *Journal of Happiness Studies, 16*(2), 367–380. doi: 10.1007/s10902-014-9513-8

Snyder, C. R. (2000). *Handbook of hope.* San Diego: Academic Press.

Snyder, C. R., & Lopez, S. J. (Eds.). (2002). *Handbook of positive psychology.* New York: Oxford University Press.

Spreitzer, G. M., & Sonenshein, S. (2004). Toward the construct definition of positive deviance. *American Behavioral Scientist, 47*(6), 828–847. doi: 10.1177/0002764203260212

Stajkovic, A. D., & Luthans, F. (1998). Social cognitive theory and self-efficacy: Going beyond traditional motivational and behavioral approaches. *Organizational Dynamics, 26*, 62–74.

Steger, M. F., & Dik, B. J. (2010). Work as meaning: Individual and organizational benefits of engaging in meaningful work. In P. A. Linley, S. Harrington,

& N. Garcea (Eds.), *Oxford handbook of positive psychology and work* (pp. 131–142). New York: Oxford University Press.

Stephens, J., Heaphy, E. D., Carmeli, A., Spreitzer, G. M., & Dutton, J. E. (2013). Relationship quality and virtuousness: Emotional carrying capacity as a source of individual and team resilience. *Journal of Applied Behavioral Science, 49*(1), 13–41. doi: 10.1177/0021886312471193

Taris, T. W., & Schreurs, P. G. (2009). Well-being and organizational performance: An organizational-level test of the happy-productive worker hypothesis. *Work & Stress, 23*(2), 120–136. doi: 10.1080/02678370903072555

Umans, T., Broberg, P., Schmidt, M., Nilsson, S., & Olsson, E. (2016). Feeling well by being together: Study of Swedish auditors. *Work, 54*(1), 79–86. doi: 10.3233/WOR-162270

Van De Voorde, K., Paauwe, J., & Van Veldhoven, M. (2012). Employee well-being and the HRM-organizational performance relationship: A review of quantitative studies. *International Journal of Management Reviews, 14*(4), 391–407. doi: 10.1111/j.1468-2370.2011.00322.x

Venkatesh, R., & Blaskovich, J. (2012). The mediating effect of psychological capital on the budget participation-job performance relationship. *Journal of Management Accounting Research, 24*(1), 159–175. doi: 10.2308/jmar-50202

Wang, H., Sui, Y., Luthans, F., Wang, D., & Wu, Y. (2012). Impact of authentic leadership on performance: Role of follower's positive psychological capital and relational processes. *Journal of Organizational Behavior, 35*, 5–21. doi: 10.1002/job.1850

Warren, M. A., & Warren, M. T. (2017). *Examining high-quality work relationships and relationship thoughts: Does gender matter?.* Manuscript under review.

West, B. J., Patera, J. L., & Carsten, M. K. (2009). Team level positivity: Investigating positive psychological capacities and team level outcomes. *Journal of Organizational Behavior, 30*(2), 249–267. doi: 10.1002/job.593

Wilder, N. N., Rao, M. A., & Donaldson, S. I. (2016). Positive psychology's contributions and prospects for engaging differences at work. In L. M. Roberts, L. P. Wooten, & M. N. Davidson (Eds.), *Positive organizing in a global society: Understanding and engaging differences for capacity building and inclusion* (pp. 17–23). New York: Routledge/Taylor & Francis Group.

Williams, P., Kern, M. L., & Waters, L. (2016). Exploring selective exposure and confirmation bias as processes underlying employee work happiness: An intervention study. *Frontiers in Psychology, 7*.

Wright, T. A. (2010). More than meets the eye: The role of employee well-being in organizational research. In P. A. Linley, S. Harrington, & N. Garcea (Eds.), *Oxford handbook of positive psychology and work* (pp. 143–154). New York: Oxford University Press.

Wright, T. A., & Bonett, D. G. (2007). Job satisfaction and psychological well-being as nonadditive predictors of workplace turnover. *Journal of Management, 33*(2), 141–160. doi: 10.1177/0149206306297582

Wright, T. A., & Cropanzano, R. (2000). Psychological well-being and job satisfaction as predictors of job performance. *Journal of Occupational Health Psychology, 5*(1), 84–94. doi: 10.1037/1076-8998.5.1.84

Wright, T. A., & Cropanzano, R. (2004). The role of psychological well-being in job performance: A fresh look at an age-old quest. *Organizational Dynamics, 33*(4), 338–351. doi: 10.1016/j.orgdyn.2004.09.002

Wright, T. A., & Cropanzano, R. (2007). The happy/productive worker thesis revisited. In J. J. Martocchio (Ed.), *Research in personnel and human resources management* (Vol. 26, pp. 269–307). San Diego Elsevier Science/JAI Press.

Wright, T. A., Cropanzano, R., & Bonett, D. G. (2007). The moderating role of employee positive well-being on the relation between job satisfaction and job performance. *Journal of Occupational Health Psychology, 12*(2), 93–104. doi: 10.1037/1076-8998.2293

Wright, T. A., & Hobfoll, S. E. (2004). Commitment, psychological well-being and job performance: An examination of conservation of resources (COR) theory and job burnout. *Journal of Business & Management, 9*(4), 389–406.

Wright, T. A., & Huang, C. (2012). The many benefits of employee well-being in organizational research. *Journal of Organizational Behavior, 33*(8), 1188–1192. doi: 10.1002/job.1828

Youssef, C. M., & Luthans F. (2011). Positive psychological capital in the workplace: Where we are and where we need to go. In Kennon T. B. K., Sheldon M., & Steger M. F. (Eds.), *Designing positive psychology: Taking stock and moving forward* (pp. 351–364). New York: Oxford University Press.

Youssef, C. M., & Luthans, F. (2012). Positive global leadership. *Journal of World Business, 47,* 539–547.

Youssef-Morgan, C. M., & Luthans, F. (2013a). Positive leadership: Meaning and application across cultures. *Organizational Dynamics, 42,* 198–208.

Youssef-Morgan, C. M., & Luthans, F. (2013b). Psychological capital theory: Toward a positive holistic model. In A. B. Bakker (Ed.), *Advances in positive organizational psychology* (Vol. 19, pp. 145–166). Bingley, England: Emerald.

Youssef-Morgan, C. M., & Luthans, F. (2015). Psychological capital and well-being. *Stress and Health, 31,*180–188.

Zubair, A., & Kamal, A. (2015). Authentic leadership and creativity: Mediating role of work-related flow and psychological capital. *Journal of Behavioural Sciences, 25*(1), 150–171.

CHAPTER NINE

Progressing Positive Education and Promoting Visible Well-Being in Schools

Lea Waters

Introduction

Positive psychologists have emphasized the importance of cultivating positive subjective experiences and traits in young people since the inception of the field (Seligman, 1999; Csikszentmihalyi & Seligman, 2000; Figure 9.1). Over the past decade, there have been especially prominent efforts to explore whether we can harness the wide reach of schools[1] in service of this goal (Chafouleas & Bray, 2004; Huebner & Hills, 2011; Seligman, Ernst, Gillham, Reveich, & Linkins, 2009; Shankland & Rosset, 2016). The incorporation of well-being into national curriculum frameworks (OECD, 2015b), the development of associations such as the International Positive Education Network,[2] and the development of school-based programs such as the Penn Resiliency Program are examples of such efforts (Brunwasser, Gillham, & Kim, 2009). The alliance between positive psychology and education has been given the name *positive education* (Seligman et al., 2009), defined as education that develops academic skills *and* well-being skills.

In line with the view that a full state of well-being involves more than the absence of illness (Keyes & Lopez, 2002), positive education aims to

"The bit in the middle is my
     mind when it is really
     full.
The bits falling down the
     page are the bad things
     that happen to make me
     angry.
The bottom bit is that 'thing'
     (amygdala) that tries to
     take over.
All the rays coming from the
     sun are the happy
     thoughts I think.
They come into my brain
     and 'pop' the bad
     thoughts go away and I
     feel good."

Figure 9.1   Picture and description of the link between thoughts and emotions by a first grade boy in Australia who receives positive education

both *prevent mental illness* and *promote wellness*. The approach has been applied in a targeted way to harness and build strengths—and not just reduce deficits—in troubled and at-risk students (Huebner & Gilman, 2003; Terjesen, Jacofsky, Froh, & DiGiuseppe, 2004; Alford & White, 2015). An equally exciting prospect is the potential for positive psychology to improve the mental health of *all* students through universal interventions, which are defined as proactive programs delivered to an entire population for the purpose of building well-being and preventing illness. Universal programs are distinguished from the targeted programs mentioned earlier that are delivered to specific subgroups for remediation purposes (Clonan, Chafouleas, McDougal, & Riley-Tillman, 2004; Seligman et al., 2009; Waters, 2011).

By employing universal programs to prevent illness and promote wellness in large numbers of young people, positive education, if widely diffused in schools, could improve flourishing at a population level (Seligman, 2011). Indeed, Seligman and his colleagues argue that "positive education will form the basis of a 'new prosperity,' a politics that values both wealth *and* wellbeing" (Seligman et al., 2009, p. 293, my emphasis).

To date, however, the potential of positive education has not been fully realized (Huebner & Hills, 2011; Waters, 2015). Although two large-scale reviews suggest that there has been a substantial amount of educational research done within the field of positive psychology (Donaldson, Doll-wet, & Rao, 2015; Rusk & Waters, 2013), Froh, Huebner, Youssef and Con-te's (2011) analysis of school psychology journals found no increase in research on positive topics over the past 50 years. Similarly, Kristjánsson (2012) reviewed articles in the last decade of the *Educational Psychologist*, the top-ranked journal for the field of educational psychology, and con-cluded that "[p]ositive psychology has so far mostly eluded discussion" (p. 87).

The seemingly contradictory nature of these findings may be a func-tion of the different data sets used by the researchers. When positive psy-chology publications are used as the database in Donaldson et al. (2015) and Rusk and Waters (2013), the results show that education is a promi-nent topic. But when the database consists of education/school psychol-ogy publications, positive psychology is not a dominant topic compared to the many other topics studied in this older and more established field (Froh et al., 2011; Kristjánsson, 2012). It appears that whereas education is a big fish in the relatively new and small pond of positive psychology, positive psychology is a small fish in the older and bigger pond of educa-tional psychology.

According to Huebner and Hills (2011), "At best, the legs of positive psy-chology in schools are moving slowly" (p. 89). Waters (2015) asserts that not all schools take up positive education programs, and even within those schools that do, the programs are only delivered to certain students—resulting in limited reach. In White's (2016) critique he argues that "[e] ven after 15 years of evidence gathered by researchers in the movement, it seems positive psychology, positive education, and wellbeing won't stick" (p. 4).

According to White (2016), a major barrier for the diffusion of positive education is that it is still viewed by many educators as a marginal topic to the core business of academic learning. He also suggests that either-or thinking ("It is either math or making them feel good," p. 5) has contrib-uted to the limited dissemination of positive education in schools. Other barriers listed by White (2016) include insufficient finances, maverick pro-viders who do not deliver adequate teacher training, and the "silver bullet" claim by some that well-being interventions will fix all student problems.

How can we foster the wide adoption of universal positive psychology approaches in our education systems to more fully realize their broader social impact? The current chapter addresses this question in two main ways. First, I begin by outlining areas of evidence that can be used to support the diffusion of positive education: (1) evidence that well-being is becoming more important in global policy, (2) evidence that positive education enhances student well-being, and (3) evidence that student well-being is related to academic outcomes. Second, after reflecting on the limitations of the current approaches to positive education, I propose a new approach—*visible well-being*—as a future direction that can be used to more successfully diffuse positive psychology into schools across society.

The Rise of Well-Being in Global Policy

Well-being is not a niche concern for a small scholarly community in positive psychology; to the contrary, it is now featured in policy conversations at international (e.g., World Health Organization, 2013) and national levels (e.g., for the UK see UK Office for National Statistics, 2015; for Bhutan see Ura, Alkire, Zangmo, & Wangdi, 2012). Prominent international organizations such as the Organisation for Economic Co-operation and Development (OECD) (OECD, 2013, 2015a), World Bank (World Bank 2016), and the United Nations (Helliwell, Layard, & Sachs, 2013) are now measuring well-being and assisting relevant policy makers to create policies and interventions that promote global well-being (Bok, 2010; Self, 2014).[3]

Not surprisingly, education is a key topic in the global well-being conversation given its ability to raise societal prosperity, health, and stability (United Nations Educational, Scientific and Cultural Organization [UNESCO], 2015; Stiglitz, Sen, & Fitoussi, 2009). Consistent with Seligman et al.'s (2009) call for positive education, various international humanitarian and economic organizations have argued that education should be extended beyond academic learning to also include well-being outcomes over the last 25 years (variously referred to as noncognitive skills, social-emotional skills, soft skills, or character skills). For example, the document put forward by the United Nations Children's Fund (UNICEF, 1989) proposes that education should seek to develop each child's personality and character as much as it develops numeracy and literacy. The Learning Metrics Task Force (2013), a joint initiative between UNESCO and the Center for Universal Education, proposed that children across the world should universally learn about (and learn in ways that develop) well-being, social values, and community values. Their report specifically highlights that education can help students develop self-regulation, efficacy, empathy, emotional awareness, social awareness, creativity, curiosity, engagement, persistence, resilience, and grit. Finally, the OECD's Centre for Educational Research and Innovation (2015b) states that "[p]erhaps the ultimate goal of education policy makers, teachers, and parents is to help children achieve the highest level of wellbeing possible" (p. 32).

Calls from these high-profile international bodies have had an impact on governments who are now using National Curriculum Frameworks as a means to promote youth well-being through schools. The OECD Centre for Educational Research and Innovation's (OECD, 2015b) recent analysis of the National Curriculum Frameworks across 37 OECD countries[4] showed that student well-being is an explicit aim in 72 percent of these national frameworks.[5] Beyond this broad aim, the frameworks also included three subgoals, and the analysis revealed that 70 percent of countries included the goal of "working with others" (sociability, respect, and caring), 67.5 percent included "teaching students to achieve their goals" (perseverance, self-control, and passion for goals), and 62 percent covered the goal of "emotional management skills" (self-esteem, optimism, and confidence). These statistics show that many OECD countries are now aiming to systematically foster both academic outcomes *and* well-being outcomes in school students.

Thus, in looking at the bigger context within which the field of positive education sits, what can be clearly seen is that the aim of positive education to teach both traditional academic skills and well-being skills in schools is clearly aligned with a general global push for population-level flourishing. Moreover, the trend for OECD countries to formalize and codify the teaching of well-being through National Curriculum Frameworks delivers a ripe environment for using schools as a "diffusion institution" for positive psychology.

In addition to showing how disseminating positive psychology through schools supports the aims of increasing our global well-being, there is an economic argument for bringing positive psychology into schools. Researchers at Columbia University's Center for Benefit-Cost Studies in Education (Belfield et al., 2015) conducted an analysis to see if the educational benefits justify the costs of well-being programs to schools. Specifically, they studied the monetary costs of investing in well-being programs for schools (e.g., teacher time, materials, program costs) against the monetary value of benefits (e.g., decreased conduct problems, reduced substance abuse, decreased aggression, increased positive social behaviors and future earning potential). This cost-benefit analysis revealed an average economic return to the school of $11 for every dollar invested in teaching well-being.

The economic benefits were also calculated at the individual level and results showed that each standard deviation increase in a student's social-emotional skills predicted a 4–15 percent increase, or at least $23,000 (as a conservative estimate) in their potential future earnings. Belfield et al. (2015) posit two causal mechanisms for the link between a student's social-emotional skills and their potential future earnings. First, students with a greater ability to regulate their emotions and adapt to the social-behavioral expectation of a classroom are better able to concentrate and learn in class and, thus, are more likely to stay in school, get good grades, and get a college education—resulting in higher-paid jobs. Second, students who develop high-quality social-emotional skills are more attractive as employees who are concerned with both the technical knowledge and the "soft skills" of a potential hire.

Do Positive Education Interventions Enhance Student Well-Being?

The global context undoubtedly provides the right conditions for the diffusion of positive education in schools. However, given that school curriculums and timetables are already overcrowded (Seldon, 2011), educational policy makers, school leaders, teachers, and other stakeholders understandably want to see evidence that positive education interventions actually work.

Over the past 18 years, positive education researchers have striven to build an evidence base using the science of positive psychology interventions (PPIs) to help school leaders and teachers make decisions about what to teach in schools. Collectively the field has studied the effects of a range of PPIs on student well-being with focuses on gratitude (Froh, Sefick, & Emmons, 2008), hope (Marques, Lopez, & Pais-Ribeiro, 2011), character strengths (Madden, Green, & Grant, 2011), mindfulness (Huppert & Johnson, 2010), socially responsible behavior (Bear & Manning, 2004), and resilience (Gillham, Brunwasser, & Freres, 2008). To date, five major reviews have summarized the evidence across 315 interventions involving over 300,000 students. These reviews have considered the impact of two types of programs: PPIs that have a single focus (e.g. enhancing gratitude) and multicomponent interventions that teach students a range of well-being skills. The overarching finding is that the PPIs are successful in boosting student well-being. However, as will be explored later a number of factors moderate the relationship between a PPI and student well-being, including the length of program, the quality of implementation, who delivers the program, and the outcome measured used.

Single-Focus Positive Education Interventions

Waters (2011) reviewed the impact of 12 universal positive education interventions from Australia, Canada, Europe, the UK, and the United States ($N = 3,400$ students). The programs were implemented in junior, middle, or senior schools across different school systems (e.g., public schools and private schools). Students completed programs that focused on developing one specific positive state (e.g., hope, gratitude, mindfulness, resilience, character strengths). These studies found significant post-intervention improvements in well-being outcomes (e.g., life satisfaction, self-esteem, self-acceptance, relationship satisfaction, optimism) among students who completed these interventions relative to control group students. The review by Waters shows that students who completed positive education interventions also reported that they found school more interesting, felt better at school, were learning more, and were more eager to go to school.

In another review of universal interventions, Waters, Barsky, Ridd, and Allen (2015) examined the impact of mindfulness and meditation programs on student well-being. Programs included mindfulness-based stress reduction, mindfulness, transcendental meditation, guided visualization, tai chi, yoga, mantra, and prayer. The programs were variously administered across junior, middle, and senior schools in countries such as Australia, Canada, Taiwan, and the United States ($N = 1,797$). The meta-analysis revealed that 61 percent of the effects on well-being were statistically significant and included increases in optimism, calmness, positive affect, self-acceptance, and prosocial behavior, as well as decreases in anxiety, stress, and negative affect. Program elements such as duration, frequency of practice, and type of instructor also influenced student well-being. Namely, longer programs, programs where students practiced daily, and teacher-delivered (vs. externally delivered) interventions were more effective. Transcendental meditation (TM) programs had more consistent significant effects on well-being (83 percent of effects in TM programs were significant) in comparison to mindfulness (44 percent) and other meditation techniques (42 percent).

Multicomponent Positive Education Interventions

Durlak, Weissberg, Dymnicki, Taylor, and Schellinger (2011) conducted a meta-analysis of 213 universal social and emotional learning (SEL) programs designed to foster positive adjustment in students from kindergarten through to high school students ($N=270,034$). The interventions were delivered predominately by teachers and were designed to assist students in acquiring the core competencies that allow them to recognize and manage emotions, set and achieve positive goals, appreciate the perspectives of others, establish and maintain positive relationships, make responsible decisions, and handle interpersonal situations constructively (Elias et al., 1997).

Durlak et al.'s (2011) results show that students who went through the programs demonstrated significantly improved social skills and emotional skills. Specifically, students became better at identifying their emotions, reading social cues, solving interpersonal problems, and perspective taking. The results also showed increased levels of positive social behaviors such as getting along with others and working cooperatively in team assignments. In addition, attitudes toward self and others were significantly improved with students reporting higher levels of self-esteem and self-efficacy as well as higher prosocial beliefs (e.g., helping others, social justice, and antiviolence beliefs).

As with Waters et al. (2015), Durlak and his colleagues found a number of moderators that affected student outcomes. First, consistent with the Waters et al.'s meta-analysis, teacher-delivered programs were more effective than programs delivered by other people. Second, programs that had high-quality implementation as assessed by the SAFE framework (an acronym that stands for programs that are sequenced, active, focused, and explicit) achieved better well-being outcomes for students than programs that did not meet the SAFE criteria.

In an earlier meta-analysis, Durlak, Weissberg, and Pachan (2010) explored the effect of after-school SEL programs on student well-being. The authors analyzed 68 after-school programs ($N=34,989$ students) on four broad well-being–related categories: 1) self-perceptions (e.g., self-esteem, self-concept, self-efficacy); 2) school bonding (e.g., liking school or reports that the school/classroom environment or teachers are supportive); 3) positive social behaviors (e.g., effective expression of feelings, positive interactions with others, cooperation, and leadership); and 4) problem behaviors (e.g., noncompliance, aggression, delinquent acts, and disciplinary referrals). They found that students who participated in SEL after-school programs reported significant increases in self-perceptions, school bonding, and positive social behaviors, as well as significant reductions in problem behaviors relative to students in control groups. As with the SEL programs run during class time (Durlak et al., 2011), programs that had high-quality implementation, as assessed by the SAFE framework, achieved the best well-being outcomes for students.

Turning to another multicomponent intervention, the Penn Resiliency Program (PRP) is a curriculum-based program that is designed to boost student resilience by teaching cognitive reframing, assertiveness, decision-making, coping skills, creative brainstorming, and relaxation and has been used with students from ages 8 to 15. The PRP has been implemented in schools in Australia, China, Portugal, the United States, and the UK. In a meta-analytic review of the findings from 17 controlled evaluations with a mix of targeted and universal samples ($N = 2,498$), Brunwasser et al. (2009) reported that the PRP resiliency intervention reduced symptoms of depression, hopelessness, and anxiety as compared to students in control groups. Encouragingly, the positive benefits of the PRP appear to be long lasting with significant continued reductions in depression found at 6-, 8- and 12-month follow-ups.

Challen, Machin, and Gillham's (2014) large-scale dissemination of PRP in 16 schools across the United Kingdom ($N = 2,498$) found that depression was reduced immediately post-intervention. However, in contrast to the meta-analytic findings earlier, the benefits of PRP in UK schools were not sustained at the one- and two-year follow-ups. A key difference in this study compared to the meta-analysis of PRP earlier was that the 16 UK schools implemented PRP as a universal program (provided to all students for proactive reasons) compared to the meta-analysis paper where 10 schools (58 percent) used PRP with targeted high-risk student samples. Given that students in universal programs already have good mental health, the focus of PRP on alleviating depression is not likely to be as impactful as it is for at-risk students. As speculated by Challen et al. (2014) a "floor effect" for this sample may have existed whereby depression scores were already so low that they did not need to drop further over time.

These findings can be used to motivate future researchers to be more strategic when choosing outcome measures in order to ensure that the measures fit the purpose of the program and sample used. If the research is to be done on universal programs with mentally healthy students, the outcome measures need to move beyond illness indicators (e.g., depression and anxiety) to also include positive indicators of well-being. A good example of this comes from Rivet-Duval, Heriot, and Hunt (2011) who implemented a universal program, measured both illness and wellness indicators, and found significant improvements in self-esteem and coping skills but no change in depressive symptoms.

In summary, the reviews and research suggest that positive education interventions can enhance student well-being, especially when certain conditions are in place such as teacher-delivered interventions and high-quality implementation. More research is needed to explore the outcomes of positive education programs in non-Western settings—a glaring gap in the current literature—to better understand the factors that moderate the effectiveness of these programs and, more importantly, to study the long-term effects of these interventions. However, the existing evidence can be presented to policy makers, school leaders, and teachers to encourage the adoption of such interventions in schools.

Is Well-Being Related to Academic Outcomes?

For those stakeholders in the education sector who want to know whether investing in student well-being improves academic performance, there is now correlational, longitudinal, intervention, and meta-analytic studies providing evidence for a link between the two.

Several correlational studies have found a significant relationship between various indicators of well-being and academic performance in high school students. These well-being resources include happiness (Chen & Lu, 2009), subjective well-being (Ye, Mei, & Liu, 2012), self-concept (Marsh, Trautwein, Lüdtke, Küller, & Baumert, 2006), and grit (Duckworth, Peterson, Matthews, & Kelly, 2007). At the national level, one study also found that levels of happiness were consistently related to the Programme for International Student Assessment (PISA) scores on reading literacy, mathematical literacy, and scientific literacy across 30 countries[6] (Kirkcaldy, Furnham, & Siefen, 2004). However, these correlational studies cannot establish causality; for example, high academic grades may lead to high well-being rather than the other way around, or a third variable (e.g., socioeconomic status) could explain the association between well-being and academic performance. Further, associations at the level of nations may not hold at the individual level, as there will always be considerable variation across the individuals who exist within the population trends.

Prospective longitudinal studies provide slightly stronger evidence for the potential influences of well-being on academic outcomes across time. Studies have found that subjective well-being predicts grade point average (GPA) in middle school students over the course of one year (Suldo, Thalji, & Ferron, 2011). In addition, a sense of hope at the start of the academic year for first-year high school students was found to predict their end-of-year school grades (Ciarrochi, Heaven, & Davies, 2007). Three studies have also found that self-discipline robustly predicts higher academic performance among middle school students one year later (Duckworth, Quinn, & Tsukayama, 2012; Duckworth & Seligman, 2005).

The strongest evidence comes from intervention studies. Two individual intervention studies found that positive effects of school-based meditation programs improved academic performance. Nidich and Nidich (1989) examined the impact of meditation interventions on achievement on standardized tests and found that third- to seventh-graders demonstrated an increase in reading, vocabulary, language, and study skills. Ninth- to eleventh-graders who participated in the intervention showed improvement in social studies, literary materials, reading, and quantitative thinking skills on the Iowa Tests of Basic Skills and Iowa Tests of Educational Development. In another study, Nidich et al. (2011) reported significant improvements in English and math scores on the California Standards Test for 125 sixth- and seventh-grade students who underwent three months of twice-daily (i.e., before and after school) 12-minute meditation practice, relative to a randomly assigned control group.

Finally, meta-analytic summaries of individual intervention studies show that overall, well-being interventions have positive effects on academic achievement. The two meta-analytic studies by Durlak and colleagues (2010, 2011), outlined in the previous section, examined the impact of SEL interventions on academic outcomes such as standardized achievement test scores, performance on standardized reading or math achievement tests, GPA, and grades in specific subjects (usually reading or math). The meta-analysis of school-based programs found that students who completed SEL programs (relative to students in control groups) demonstrated an 11 percentile point increase in academic achievement (Durlak et al., 2011), whereas the meta-analysis of after-school programs found an eight percentile point increase in standardized achievement test scores (Durlak et al., 2010). Similarly, Dix, Slee, Lawson, and Keeves (2012) examined the effect of a universal school-wide mental health program over two years in 96 elementary schools and found positive effects on academic performance on national numeracy and literacy test scores.

All three meta-analyses, however, found that there were greater academic gains when implementation quality was high. Specifically, Dix and colleagues (2012) found that students who completed the intervention in high-quality implementing schools[7] showed a difference in academic gains equivalent to six months of schooling, compared to students who completed the intervention in low-quality implementing schools.

In summary, there is increasing evidence for a significant positive association between well-being and academic performance. This link has been demonstrated across 294 studies that range from relatively weak cross-sectional evidence to stronger evidence from intervention studies and meta-analytic summaries. Although more research is needed, the evidence to date supports Broderick and Metz's (2009) assertion that student well-being "seeps into the fabric of their academic pursuits" (p. 35) and can be used by proponents of positive education to harness the wide reach of schools as a way of diffusing positive psychology to young people.

Moving Beyond Positive Education Programs

So far, I have highlighted three key enablers that can make the case for diffusion of positive psychology into schools: 1) capitalizing on the global push for population flourishing, 2) evidence that such interventions improve student well-being, and 3) evidence that student well-being is related to academic performance. Advocates for positive education, therefore, have a strong foundation from which to spread their mission. However, as argued earlier in this chapter, positive education is not yet meeting its potential for wide impact. In order to make the most of the supportive contexts for positive education and the evidence regarding its impact on well-being and learning, we need to more clearly understand the strengths and limitations of the programmatic approach we have adopted to diffuse positive psychology into schools.

To date, the prevailing approach for disseminating positive psychology into schools is through the delivery of dedicated positive education programs. Indeed, there are a plethora of such programs now available to schools (see Appendix 9.1 for examples of positive education programs). These programs are typically implemented as units within an existing academic course (e.g., physical and health education, civic and citizenship education, moral education, and/or religious education; see OECD, 2015b), through tutorial/house/pastoral groups (e.g., see Green, Grant, & Rynsaardt, 2007; Proctor et al., 2011), or in after-school programs (e.g., see Durlak et al., 2010).

Most programs are delivered within the time frame of one or two school terms (e.g., Flook et al., 2010; Huppert & Johnson, 2010; Madden et al., 2011; Marques et al., 2011; Nidich et al., 2011; Seligman et al., 2009; Suldo, Savage, & Mercer, 2014; Proctor et al., 2011), with some shorter (e.g., two weeks; Froh, Sefick, & Emmons, 2008) or longer interventions (e.g., year-long; see Norrish, 2015; White & Murray, 2015).

Although positive education programs have been shown to improve the well-being and learning of students, they also create many of the barriers identified by White (2016) that limit the widespread diffusion of positive psychology into schools. For example, because many positive education programs are stand-alone curriculums that are not integrated into other academic curriculums, they run the risk of confirming the perception that well-being is a marginal topic that is separate from the core business of academic learning. Additionally, the reality of having to find extra room in the timetable to fit in the positive education program (and, thus, squeeze out another subject from the timetable) adds fuel to the barrier of either-or thinking. As White (2016) says, schools who have the mentality of "Well, you can't have your cake and eat it. It is either math or making them feel good" (p. 5) are unlikely to bring in positive psychology programs. The way to get around the barriers of binary thinking and seeing well-being as marginal requires us to find an approach that does not implement well-being lessons separately from academic classes, and we will turn to that in the next section.

Another barrier listed by White (2016) includes insufficient finances, and this is certainly a barrier in the programmatic approach. Programs pose additional costs to schools, both for the program itself and for the additional budget commitment required to pay for substitute staff while teachers attend program training. This cost barrier creates equity issues in diffusing positive education. Indeed Shankland and Rosset (2016) express their concern that "the schools in which the students are already better off are those that can afford to implement PPIs" (online article, paragraph 4).

Beyond White's (2016) list, two further barriers to programs may prevent the successful and sustained diffusion of positive psychology to all young people. First, programs have limited reach to the full population of students in schools. Unless the school adopts a whole-staff training approach and the program is then administered throughout all year levels, the programs only reach a limited proportion of students within each school. Second, given the relative short time frames of these programs and the lack of long-term evaluations (see Waters, 2011), it is unclear to what extent these programs create *sustainable* increases in well-being. Just as learning academic skill requires repeated practice and experience, it is likely that students need to be exposed to the principles of positive psychology over a substantial duration of their schooling years to reap the full benefits of these skills (Waters, Barsky, & McQuaid, 2012).

This is not an argument against programs that are highly effective and have been shown by research to boost the well-being of students. Rather the argument is that when schools *only* implement positive education through programs—which has been the common approach so far—they are not having as wide reach as they can. Hence, although we should continue to implement programs (see Appendix 9.1 for a list of successful, high-quality, evidence-based programs), we also need to find additional approaches that allow positive education to be more widely delivered throughout the entire school.

Creating Visible Well-Being in All Schools: Positive Education Teacher Practice

So how does the field of positive education evolve so that we can make the most of well-being programs but also get around the barriers that come with these programs? One possibility is to imbue positive education into teacher practice, defined as the beliefs, goals, and actions displayed by a teacher in class (Aguirre & Speer, 1999; Stipek, Givvin, Salmon, & Mac-Gyvers, 2001; van der Schaaf, Stokking, & Verloop, 2008). Infusing positive education into the practice of all teachers would enable the very act of teaching itself to be a PPI in all classrooms, thus, allowing positive education to spread beyond the clearly demarcated boundaries of dedicated well-being programs.

Speaking anecdotally, most of you will have had the experience at school of certain teachers who fostered your well-being, made you feel confident and optimistic, encouraged you to be a good person, and did this while they also imparted the academic content of their discipline. These teachers embodied the very essence of positive education—educating you for both academic and well-being outcomes. On the flip side, you're likely to also have had teachers who may (or may not) have been skilled in getting across the academic content but did so in a way that drained your well-being and zapped you of confidence. It seems reasonable to hypothesize that you would have learned the academic content more effectively with your teachers who created a well-being–promoting learning environment in class.

This hypothesis is supported by empirical research (Cornelius-White, 2007; Rowe, Hirsh, & Anderson, 2007; Wadlinger & Isaacowitz, 2006), underpinned by Fredrickson's broaden and build theory (1998; 2001). Fredrickson's theory outlines how positive emotions support many of the key cognitive processes a student needs to learn by broadening their cognitive and behavioral repertoire to encourage greater creativity in the learning process (Rathunde, 2000). Research has established a strong link between cognition (e.g., attention, memory, and decision-making) and emotion (Damasio et al., 2000; Goswami, 2006) at the neural level. This neural connectivity may underpin findings like those of Estrada, Isen, and Young (1997), where participants in a positive mood found more creative solutions to a problem and took less time to solve the problem. As Immordino-Yang and Damasio (2007) so eloquently state: "We feel, therefore we learn" (p. 3).

If teachers taught students about the academic content in ways that also build well-being, the classroom then becomes a dynamic and continuous

PPI. For example, consider the math teacher who strategically uses a challenging math problem to help students understand their emotions (e.g. fear, uncertainty, excitement, curiosity), to help build their resilience by bouncing back if they make a mistake, to encourage them to develop a (growth) mind-set where they believe that they can work through the problem if they continue to try rather than give up, to eventually find moments of flow as their skills develop enough to meet the challenge, and to experience the satisfaction of mastering a difficult problem. Hence, an unassuming math problem holds the potential to impart a wealth of lessons about well-being. In this way, teachers can consciously turn everyday classroom activities into micro-PPIs that allow them to improve both academic learning and well-being.

Positive education teacher practice is therefore a promising route for system-wide dissemination of positive education. It opens the door to an exciting new line of cross-disciplinary research that seeks to integrate positive psychology principles together with pedagogical practices.

The question is: How might such a practice be organized and what would the intervention look like? I have recently put forward an organized approach to positive education teacher practice called Visible Well-Being (VWB) (Waters, 2015, Waters, Sun, Rusk, Aarch, & Cotton, 2016) that integrates the three separate fields of positive education (Seligman et al., 2009), visible thinking (Ritchhart, Church, & Morrison, 2011), and visible learning (Hattie, 2008; Hattie, Masters, & Birch, 2015). VWB moves beyond the current boundaries of the field of positive education by including the science of teacher practice, stemming from the visible thinking literature, and teacher effectiveness, stemming from the visible learning literature. It also adds a new lens to the fields of visible thinking and visible learning by examining these areas not only for student learning outcomes but also for student well-being outcomes.

VWB is not a program or a set curriculum about well-being. Rather, it is a flexible approach for integrating student well-being into the learning process at all year levels (early learning, elementary, middle, and secondary) and in any subject matter.

The aim of the VWB approach is to teach in a way that shifts well-being from a subjective, internal experience occurring *within* the student to a tangible, observable phenomenon that is visible in class for students and teachers alike. When well-being becomes visible in class, it means that students are learning about (understanding and seeking to improve) their own well-being throughout the entire school day. They learn how they feel in certain subjects, with certain teachers, during different learning activities and assignments. They start to see patterns in their well-being and what triggers it to go up or down. When teachers see well-being in class (like the example of the math teacher earlier) they are better able to determine the effectiveness of their teaching in terms of the impact it is having both on the learning and well-being of their students. Teachers can more systematically capitalize on high levels of well-being to boost learning or can better see when stress and other ill-being aspects are getting in the way of learning.

The capacity of VWB to assist teachers to more systematically see the link between well-being and learning removes the barrier identified by White (2016) of teachers seeing well-being as a marginal topic. The fact that VWB is integrated into all classrooms through teacher practice and spread through all academic curriculums, rather than being implemented as a separate positive education program, also removes the barrier of binary thinking. Finally, because VWB is a practice that teachers integrate into their classroom rather than a program that the school has to purchase, there are no associated program costs. The removal of these three barriers means that VWB stands a much higher chance of wider diffusion into schools than the current programmatic approach.

So what does VWB look like? VWB is a three-part framework that gives teachers a language and process for enhancing their efforts to teach in ways that foster well-being. Positive education brings in the teacher *knowledge* of well-being, visible thinking brings in teacher *practice*, and visible learning brings in teacher *effectiveness*. As shown in Figure 9.2, the three elements of well-being, teacher practice, and teacher effectiveness are mutually reinforcing. The first requirement of fostering a VWB approach in class is to instill in teachers a well-defined body of positive education knowledge. This would require teacher training, and if we are to achieve the goal of diffusing positive psychology in all schools, VWB would need to be incorporated into teacher training programs and continuing education at a nationwide level.

Once the teachers have knowledge of well-being, they are then encouraged to use various evidence-informed teacher practices that have been shown to have a positive impact on student well-being. These practices include activities that have come from the field of positive education such as studying the strengths of the main character of a novel in English class (White & Waters, 2014) or starting class with a brief mindfulness exercise (Huppert & Johnson, 2010) (see Shankland & Rosset, 2016, for a list of brief PPIs that teachers can use in class). Student-centered teaching practices that emphasize a student's interests and provide autonomous and team-based learning opportunities can also be used by teachers across a range of disciplines to build student well-being (Jones, 2007).

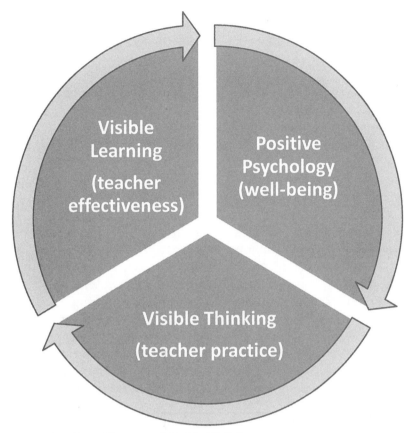

Figure 9.2   Three Elements of Visible Well-Being

In the third phase of VWB, teachers use data and evidence to routinely evaluate the effectiveness of their practice on student well-being. In fact, the only way for teachers to confidently see if well-being moves forward (or backwards) based on their teaching practices is by examining data. Teachers can gain valuable data from self-report well-being surveys completed by students, such as the Well-being Profiler for schools developed by the Centre for Positive Psychology at the University of Melbourne (http://www.wbprofiler.com.au). Teachers can also run regular focus groups with their classes as ways to assess shifts in student well-being.

I have developed a VWB rubric that is currently under trial with Kambrya Secondary College, a large public high school in Australia. A pilot group of teachers is using the rubric after each class to rate the degree to which students are displaying six key elements of well-being in class:

attentional skills, emotional awareness, coping skills, goal-driven behavior, virtuous behavior, and relationship skills. The rubric is being used in math classes, science classes, and English classes and in an alternative education stream. The rubric is providing important data to the teachers with respect to how their academic teaching practices and curricula are building well-being (or not) in their students. The rubric is also being used by students to assess and track their own well-being and examine links between their well-being and learning.

Using data to assess teacher effectiveness when it comes to well-being then feeds into the cycle again where teachers observe student well-being (based on their positive education knowledge), change their teacher practice, and re-evaluate their effectiveness. This becomes a self-sustaining process that teachers can cycle through in all of their classes over the year.

So far I have shown you what the three-pronged VWB intervention looks like, suggested where it can be implemented (i.e., in all classes), discussed the training needs, and presented options for measuring success. However, zooming out to the bigger picture, we also need to consider whether the VWB approach can truly assist in the goal to diffuse well-being into schools on a large scale. As already discussed, VWB is likely to sidestep the barriers of cost, binary thinking, and viewing well-being as a marginal topic. Zooming out even wider, VWB, if used in teacher training, aligns with national and international education policies that place student well-being as a clear and important goal that schools should be seeking to achieve. The reduction of barriers created by a teacher practice approach (rather than a program approach) and the supportive national and international context for well-being suggest that VWB could be a successful intervention that allows schools to be used as a societal institution via which to disperse positive psychology to young people.

The approach of diffusing positive psychology into schools in order to boost collective, wide-scale wellbeing in young people is a big task and much is still to be studied. Although VWB holds promise, many questions still need to be answered such as how much of the success of a VWB approach is based on students' receptivity to this approach. What are the moderators and mediators in the classroom that influence the success of VWB? What are the cultural differences that might influence the way VWB is integrated into different schools? Are there certain personality types in teachers that are more amenable to integrating positive psychology into their pedagogical practices? Can we train teachers to use their strengths to create VWB classrooms? What might the implications be for teachers' well-being, and not just student well-being, when using a VWB approach?

Final Thoughts

Csikszentmihalyi and Seligman's (2000) foundational paper on positive psychology called for the promotion of "positive institutions" (p. 5): institutions that foster citizenship, virtue, and well-being. If we are to create a flourishing society, it is critical that our schools become positive institutions that foster well-being in today's students. Such an approach is necessary for the students themselves in order to prevent mental illness, promote flourishing, and enhance academic performance. Importantly, given that schools have access to wide numbers of young people, over time, the individual benefits that schools provide to students translate to aggregate increases in societal well-being.

In this chapter, I recommend that proponents of positive education capitalize on the global push for population flourishing, align with the global emphasis on educating for well-being from international and national education bodies, cite the evidence that positive education interventions improve student well-being and academic performance, and complement programs with positive education teacher practice. As flourishing students graduate to be the adults and leaders of our society, a collective upward spiral can be triggered and the dream of global well-being can come closer to becoming a reality.

Appendix 9.1   Examples of Positive Education Programs

*   *Positive Detective*

    http://www.positivedetective.com
*   *Strath Haven Positive Psychology Curriculum*

    https://www.authentichappiness.sas.upenn.edu/learn/educatorresilience
*   *Penn Resiliency Program*

    https://www.authentichappiness.sas.upenn.edu/learn/educatorresilience
*   *Celebrating Strengths*

    http://www.amazon.com/Celebrating-Strengths-Building-Strengths-Based
    -Strengthening/dp/1906366020
*   *Making Hope Happen*

    http://www.amazon.com.au/Making-Hope-Happen-Create-Yourself-ebook
    /dp/B008J2AEN4
*   *Self-Science*

    http://www.amazon.com/Self-Science-The-Emotional-Intelligence
    -Curriculum/dp/0962912344

- *Bounce Back*

  http://www.bounceback.com.au/

- *The Positive Living Early Skills Wellbeing Program*

  https://www.kidsmatter.edu.au/early-childhood/programs/positive-living
  -skills-early-childhood-wellbeing-program

- *Mind Up*

  http://thehawnfoundation.org/mindup/

- *DotB (Mindfulness)*

  https://mindfulnessinschools.org/what-is-b/

- *School-wide Positive Behavior Support*

  https://nt.gov.au/learning/primary-and-secondary-students/health-and
  -wellbeing-of-students

- *Bonniwell Program*

  http://positivepsychology.org.uk/pp-directory/people/44-ilona-boniwell
  .html

- *Learning to Breathe*

  http://learning2breathe.org/

- *Lessons by Ian Morris*

  http://www.amazon.com/Teaching-Happiness-Wellbeing-Schools
  -elephants/dp/0826443036

- *RULER (Emotional Intelligence)*

  http://ei.yale.edu/ruler/

- *Think Positively: Adolescent Coping (Erica Frydenberg)*

  http://ericafrydenberg.com.au/resources

- *Building Happiness and Resilience (Ruth McConville)*

  http://www.jkp.com/uk/building-happiness-resilience-and-motivation-in
  -adolescents.html

- *Going for the Goal*

  https://dornsife.usc.edu/labs/scrap/the-goal/

- *You Can Do It!*

  http://www.asg.com.au/you-can-do-it-education/you-can-do-it-home

Notes

1. Although positive education is starting to make its way into early education (Eggum et al., 2011) and tertiary settings (Oades, Robinson, Green, & Spence, 2011), this chapter focuses on K–12 education.

2. Other associations and networks include the Positive Education Schools Association; the Collaboration for Academic, Social, and Emotional Learning (CASEL); and Social, Academic, and Emotional Learning (SEAL).

3. A number of private research institutions and charity-based organizations also conduct international well-being assessments across developed and developing nations, such as the Boston Consulting Group's "SEDA Report" (Sustainable, Economic, Development Assessment), the Gallup Institute's "State of Global Wellbeing Report," and the New Economic Foundation's "Happy Planet Index."

4. Australia, Austria, Belgium (Flanders), Canada, Cyprus, the Czech Republic, Denmark, Estonia, Finland, France, Germany, Ireland, Italy, Japan, Korea, the Netherlands, Norway, Poland, the Russian Federation, the Slovak Republic, Spain, Sweden, the United Kingdom (England and Northern Ireland), and the United States.

5. The well-being curriculums are typically taught in subjects such as physical and health education, civic and citizenship education, moral education, and/ or religious education.

6. Australia, Austria, Belgium, Brazil, Canada, Czech Republic, Denmark, Finland, France, Germany, Greece, Hungary, Iceland, Ireland, Italy, Japan, Korea, Latvia, Luxembourg, Mexico, New Zealand, Norway, Poland, Portugal, Russian Federation, Spain, Sweden, Switzerland, United Kingdom, and the United States

7. Quality of implementation as assessed along three domains: fidelity of implementation, extent of dosage delivered, and quality of the delivery process.

References

Aguirre, J., & Speer, N. M. (1999). Examining the relationship between beliefs and goals in teacher practice. *The Journal of Mathematical Behavior, 18*, 327–356. doi: 10.1016/S0732-3123(99)00034-6

Alford, Z., & White, M. A. (2015). Positive school psychology. In E. White & S. Murray (Eds.), *Evidence-based approaches in positive education* (pp. 93–109). Dordrecht: Netherlands: Springer.

Bear, G., & Manning, M. (2014). Positive psychology and school discipline. In R. Gilman, S. Huebner, & M. Furlong (Eds.), *Handbook of positive psychology in schools* (pp. 347–364). New York: Routledge.

Belfield, C., Bowden, B., Klapp, A., Levin, H., Shand, R., & Zander, S. (2015). *The economic value of social and emotional learning.* Retrieved from http://cbcse.org/wordpress/wp-content/uploads/2015/02/SEL-Revised.pdf

Bok, D. (2010). *The politics of happiness: What government can learn from the new research on wellbeing.* Princeton, NJ: Princeton University Press.

Broderick, P. C., & Metz, S. (2009). Learning to BREATHE: A pilot trial of a mindfulness curriculum for adolescents. *Advances in School Mental Health Promotion, 2*(1), 35–46.

Brunwasser, S. M., Gillham, J. E., & Kim, E. S. (2009). A meta-analytic review of the Penn Resiliency Program's effect on depressive symptoms. *Journal of Consulting and Clinical Psychology, 77*, 1042. doi: 10.1037/a0017671

Chafouleas, S. M., & Bray, M. A. (2004). Introducing positive psychology: Finding a place within school psychology. *Psychology in the Schools, 41*(1), 1–5. doi: 10.1002/pits.10133

Challen, A. R., Machin, S. J., & Gillham, J. E. (2014). The UK Resilience Programme: A school-based universal nonrandomized pragmatic controlled trial. *Journal of Consulting and Clinical Psychology, 82*, 75–89. doi: 10.1037/a0034854

Chen, S-Y., & Lu, L. (2009). Academic correlates of Taiwanese senior high school students' happiness. *Adolescence, 44*, 979–992.

Ciarrochi, J., Heaven, P. C. L., & Davies, F. (2007). The impact of hope, self-esteem, and attributional style on adolescents' school grades and emotional wellbeing: A longitudinal study. *Journal of Research in Personality, 41*, 1161–1178. doi: 10.1016/j.jrp.2007.02.001

Clonan, S. M., Chafouleas, S. M., McDougal, J. L., & Riley-Tillman, T. C. (2004). Positive psychology goes to school: Are we there yet? *Psychology in the Schools, 41*(1), 101–110. doi: 10.1002/pits.10142

Cornelius-White, J. (2007). Learner-centered teacher-student relationships are effective: A meta-analysis. *Review of Educational Research, 77*, 113–143. doi: 10.3102/003465430298563

Csikszentmihalyi, M., & Seligman, M. E. (2000). Positive psychology: An introduction. *American Psychologist, 55*(1), 5–14.

Damasio, A. R., Grabowski, T. J., Bechara, A., Damasio, H., Ponto, L. L., Parvizi, J., & Hichwa, R. D. (2000). Subcortical and cortical brain activity during the feeling of self-generated emotions. *Nature Neuroscience, 3*, 1049–1056. doi: 10.1038/79871

Dix, K. L., Slee, P. T., Lawson, M. J., & Keeves, J. P. (2012). Implementation quality of whole-school mental health promotion and students' academic performance. *Child and Adolescent Mental Health, 17*(1), 45–51.

Donaldson, S. I., Dollwet, M., & Rao, M. A. (2015). Happiness, excellence, and optimal human functioning revisited: Examining the peer-reviewed literature linked to positive psychology. *The Journal of Positive Psychology, 10*, 185–195. doi: 10.1080/17439760.2014.943801

Duckworth, A. L., & Seligman, M. E. (2005). Self-discipline outdoes IQ in predicting academic performance of adolescents. *Psychological Science, 16*, 939–944. doi: 10.1111/j.1467-9280.2005.01641

Duckworth, A. L., Peterson, C., Matthews, M. D., & Kelly, D. R. (2007). Grit: Perseverance and passion for long-term goals. *Journal of Personality and Social Psychology, 92*, 1087–1101. doi: 10.1037/0022-3514.92.6.1087

Duckworth, A. L., Quinn, P. D., & Tsukayama, E. (2012). What No Child Left Behind leaves behind: The roles of IQ and self-control in predicting standardized achievement test scores and report card grades. *Journal of Educational Psychology, 104*, 439–451. doi: 10.1037/a0026280

Durlak, J. A., Weissberg, R. P., & Pachan, M. (2010). A meta-analysis of after-school programs that seek to promote personal and social skills in children and adolescents. *American Journal of Community Psychology, 45*(3–4), 294–309. doi: 10.1007/s10464-010-9300-6

Durlak, J. A., Weissberg, R. P., Dymnicki, A. B., Taylor, R. D., & Schellinger, K. B. (2011). The impact of enhancing students' social and emotional learning: A meta-analysis of school-based universal interventions. *Child Development, 82*(1), 405–432. doi: 10.1111/j.1467-8624.2010.01564.x

Eggum, N. D., Eisenberg, N., Kao, K., Spinrad, T. L., Bolnick, R., Hofer, C., . . . & Fabricius, W. V. (2011). Emotion understanding, theory of mind, and prosocial orientation: Relations over time in early childhood. *The Journal of Positive Psychology, 6*, 4–16. doi: 10.1080/17439760.2010.536776

Elias, M. J., Zins, J. E., Weissberg, R. P., Frey, K. S., Greenberg, M. T., Haynes, N. M., & . . . Shriver, T. P. (1997). *Promoting social and emotional learning: Guidelines for educators.* Alexandria, VA: Association for Supervision and Curriculum Development.

Estrada, C. A., Isen, A. M., & Young, M. J. (1997). Positive affect facilitates integration of information and decreases anchoring in reasoning among physicians. *Organizational Behavior and Human Decision Processes, 72*, 117–135. doi: 10.1006/obhd.1997.2734

Flook, L., Smalley, S. L., Kitil, M. J., Galla, B. M., Kaiser-Greenland, S., Locke, J., . . . & Kasari, C. (2010). Effects of mindful awareness practices on executive functions in elementary school children. *Journal of Applied School Psychology, 26*(1), 70–95.

Fredrickson, B. L. (1998). What good are positive emotions? *Review of General Psychology, 2*(3), 300–319. doi: 10.1037/1089-2680.2.3.300

Fredrickson, B. L. (2001). The role of positive emotions in positive psychology: The broaden-and-build theory of positive emotions. *American Psychologist, 56*, 218–226. doi: 10.1037/0003-066X.56.3.218

Froh, J. J., Huebner, E. S., Youssef, A. J., & Conte, V. (2011). Acknowledging and appreciating the full spectrum of the human condition: School psychology's (limited) focus on positive psychological functioning. *Psychology in the Schools, 48*, 110–123. doi: 10.1002/pits.20530

Froh, J. J., Sefick, W. J., & Emmons, R. A. (2008). Counting blessings in early adolescents: An experimental study of gratitude and subjective wellbeing. *Journal of School Psychology, 46*, 213–233. doi: 10.1016/j.jsp.2007.03.005

Gillham, J., Brunwasser, S. M., & Freres, D. R. (2008). *Preventing depression in early adolescence* (pp. 309–322). New York: Guilford Press.

Goswami, U. (2006). Neuroscience and education: from research to practice? *Nature Reviews Neuroscience, 7*, 406–413. doi: 10.1038/nrn1907

Green, S., Grant, A., & Rynsaardt, J. (2007). Evidence-based life coaching for senior high school students: Building hardiness and hope. *International Coaching Psychology Review, 2*, 24–32.

Hattie, J. (2008). *Visible learning: A synthesis of over 800 meta-analyses relating to achievement.* New York: Routledge.

Hattie, J., Masters, D., & Birch, K. (2015). *Visible learning into action: International case studies of impact.* New York: Routledge.

Helliwell, J. F., Layard, R., & Sachs, J. (2013). *World happiness report [2012].* doi: 10.14288/1.0053622

Huebner, E. S., & Gilman, R. (2003). Toward a focus on positive psychology in school psychology. *School Psychology Quarterly, 18,* 99–102. doi: 10.1521/scpq.18.2.99.21862

Huebner, E. S., & Hills, K. J. (2011). Does the positive psychology movement have legs for children in schools? *Journal of Positive Psychology, 6,* 88–94. doi: 10.1080/17439760.2010.536778

Huppert, F. A., & Johnson, D. M. (2010). A controlled trial of mindfulness training in schools: The importance of practice for an impact on well-being. *The Journal of Positive Psychology, 5*(4), 264–274. doi: 10.1080/17439761003794148

Immordino-Yang, M. H., & Damasio, A. (2007). We feel, therefore we learn: The relevance of affective and social neuroscience to education. *Mind, Brain, and Education, 1,* 3–10. doi: 10.1111/j.1751-228X.2007.00004.x

Jones, L. (2007). *The student-centered classroom.* New York: Cambridge University Press.

Keyes, C. L. M., & Lopez, S. J. (2002). Towards a science of mental health: Positive directions in diagnosis and intervention. In C. R. Snyder & S. J. Lopez (Eds.), *Handbook of positive psychology* (pp. 45–62). Oxford, England: Oxford University Press.

Kirkcaldy, B., Furnham, A., & Siefen, G. (2004). The relationship between health efficacy, educational attainment, and wellbeing among 30 nations. *European Psychologist, 9,* 107–119. doi: 10.1027/1016-9040.9.2.107

Kristjánsson, K. (2012). Positive psychology and positive education: Old wine in new bottles? *Educational Psychologist, 47,* 86–105. doi: 10.1080/00461520.2011.610678

Learning Metrics Task Force. (2013). *Toward universal learning: What every child should learn. Report 1.* Retrieved from http://www.brookings.edu/research/reports/2013/02/learning-metrics

Madden, W., Green, S., & Grant, A. M. (2011). A pilot study evaluating strengths-based coaching for primary school students: Enhancing engagement and hope. *International Coaching Psychology Review, 6*(1), 71–83.

Marques, S. C., Lopez, S. J., & Pais-Ribeiro, J. L. (2011). "Building hope for the future": A program to foster strengths in middle-school students. *Journal of Happiness Studies, 12,* 139–152. doi: 10.1007/s10902-009-9180-3

Marsh, H. W., Trautwein, U., Lüdtke, O., Köller, O., & Baumert, J. (2006). Integration of multidimensional self-concept and core personality constructs: Construct validation and relations to well-being and achievement. *Journal of Personality, 74,* 403–456. doi: 10.1111/j.1467-6494.2005.00380

Nidich, S. I., & Nidich, R. J. (1989). Increased academic achievement at Maharishi School of the Age of Enlightenment: A replication study. *Education, 109*(3), 302–304.

Nidich, S., Mjasiri, S., Nidich, R., Rainforth, M., Grant, J., Valosek, L., . . . & Zigler, R. L. (2011). Academic achievement and transcendental meditation: A study with at-risk urban middle school students. *Education, 131*(3), 556.

Norrish, J. M. (2015). *Positive education: The Geelong Grammar School journey.* Oxford, England: Oxford University Press.

Oades, L. G., Robinson, P., Green, S., & Spence, G. B. (2011). Towards a positive university. *The Journal of Positive Psychology, 6*, 432–439. doi: 10.1080/17 439760.2011.634828

OECD. (2013). *How's life? 2013: Measuring well-being.* Paris, France: OECD Publishing. doi: http://dx.doi.org/10.1787/9789264201392-en

OECD. (2015a). *Measuring well-being and progress: Well-being research.* Retrieved from http://www.oecd.org/statistics/measuring-well-being-and-progress .htm

OECD. (2015b). *Skills for social progress: The power of social and emotional skills.* Paris, France: OECD Publishing. doi: http://dx.doi.org/10.1787/9789264226159 -en

Proctor, C., Tsukayama, E., Wood, A. M., Maltby, J., Eades, J. F., & Linley, P. A. (2011). Strengths gym: The impact of a character strengths-based intervention on the life satisfaction and wellbeing of adolescents. *Journal of Positive Psychology, 6*, 377–388. doi: 10.1080/17439760.2011.594079

Rathunde, K. (2000). Broadening and narrowing in the creative process: A commentary on Fredrickson's "broaden-and-build" model. *Prevention & Treatment, 3*(1), article 6c. doi: 10.1037/1522-3736.3.1.36c

Rivet-Duval, E., Heriot, S., & Hunt, C. (2011). Preventing adolescent depression in Mauritius: A universal school-based program. *Child and Adolescent Mental Health, 16*, 86–91. doi: 10.1111/j.1475-3588.2010 .00584.x

Ritchhart, R., Church, M., & Morrison, K. (2011). *Making thinking visible: How to promote engagement, understanding, and independence for all learners.* San Francisco: John Wiley & Sons.

Rowe, G., Hirsh, J. B., & Anderson, A. K. (2007). Positive affect increases the breadth of attentional selection. *Proceedings of the National Academy of Sciences, 104*(1), 383–388. doi: 10.1073/pnas.0605198104

Rusk, R. D., & Waters, L. E. (2013). Tracing the size, reach, impact, and breadth of positive psychology. *Journal of Positive Psychology, 8*, 207–221. doi: 10.1080/17439760.2013.777766

Seldon, A. (2011). Stillness in schools. *Resurgence & Ecologist, 269.* Retrieved from http://www.resurgence.org/magazine/article3503.html

Self, A. (2014). *Measuring national wellbeing: Insights across society, the economy and the environment.* Retrieved from http://webarchive.nationalarchives.gov.uk /20160105160709/http://www.ons.gov.uk/ons/dcp171766_371427.pdf

Seligman, M. E. (1999). The president's address. *American Psychologist, 54*(8), 559–562.

Seligman, M. E. (2011). Building resilience. *Harvard Business Review, 89*(4), 100–6.

Seligman, M. E., Ernst, R. M., Gillham, J., Reivich, K., & Linkins, M. (2009). Positive education: Positive psychology and classroom interventions. *Oxford Review of Education, 35*(3), 293–311. doi: 10.1080/03054980902934563

Shankland, R., & Rosset, E. (2016). Review of brief school-based positive psychological interventions: A taster for teachers and educators. *Educational Psychology Review,* 1–30. doi: 10.1007/s10648-016-9357-3

Stiglitz, J. E., Sen, A., & Fitoussi, J. P. (2009). *Report of the commission on the measurement of economic performance and social progress.* Retrieved from http://www.insee.fr/fr/publications-et-services/dossiers_web/stiglitz/doc-commission/RAPPORT_anglais.pdf

Stipek, D. J., Givvin, K. B., Salmon, J. M., & MacGyvers, V. L. (2001). Teachers' beliefs and practices related to mathematics instruction. *Teaching and Teacher Education, 17,* 213–226. doi: 10.1016/s0742-051x(00)00052-4

Suldo, S. M., Savage, J. A., & Mercer, S. H. (2014). Increasing middle school students' life satisfaction: Efficacy of a positive psychology group intervention. *Journal of Happiness Studies, 15,* 19–42. doi: 10.1007/s10902-013-9414-2

Suldo, S., Thalji, A., & Ferron, J. (2011). Longitudinal academic outcomes predicted by early adolescents' subjective wellbeing, psychopathology, and mental health status yielded from a dual factor model. *Journal of Positive Psychology, 6,* 17–30. doi: 10.1080/17439760.2010.536774

Terjesen, M. D., Jacofsky, M., Froh, J., &, DiGiuseppe, R. (2004). Integrating positive psychology into schools: Implications for practice. *Psychology in the Schools, 41*(1), 163–172. doi: 10.1002/pits.10148

UK Office for National Statistics (2015). *Measuring national well-being: Personal well-being in the UK, 2014 to 2015.* Retrieved from http://www.ons.gov.uk/peoplepopulationandcommunity/wellbeing/bulletins/measuringnationalwellbeing/2015-09-23

United Nations Educational, Scientific and Cultural Organization. (2015). *Four pillars of education.* Retrieved from http://www.unesco.org/new/en/education/networks/global-networks/aspnet/about-us/strategy/the-four-pillars-of-learning/

United Nations Convention on the Rights of the Child. (1989). *Convention on the rights of the child.* Retrieved from http://www.unicef.org/crc/

Ura, K., Alkire, S., Zangmo, T., & Wangdi, K. (2012). *An extensive analysis of GNH index.* Retrieved from http://www.grossnationalhappiness.com/wp-content/uploads/2012/10/An%20Extensive%20Analysis%20of%20GNH%20Index.pdf

van der Schaaf, M. F., Stokking, K. M., & Verloop, N. (2008). Teacher beliefs and teacher behavior in portfolio assessment. *Teaching and Teacher Education, 24,* 1691–1704. doi: 10.1016/j.tate.2008.02.021

Wadlinger, H. A., & Isaacowitz, D. M. (2006). Positive mood broadens visual attention to positive stimuli. *Motivation and Emotion, 30,* 87–99. doi: 10.1007/s11031-006-9021-1

Waters, L. (2011). A review of school-based positive psychology interventions. *The Australian Educational and Developmental Psychologist, 28*, 75–90. doi: 10.1375/aedp.28.2.75

Waters, L. (2015). Why positive education? *TLN Journal, 22*(3), 16.

Waters, L., Barsky, A., & McQuaid, M. (2012). Positive education: A whole-school approach. *International Positive Psychology Association Newsletter, 5*(2).

Waters, L., Barsky, A., Ridd, A., & Allen, K. (2015). Contemplative education: A systematic, evidence-based review of the effect of meditation interventions in schools. *Educational Psychology Review, 27*, 103–134. doi:10.1007/s10648-014-9258-2

Waters, L., Sun, J., Rusk, R., Aarch, A., & Cotton, A. (2016). Positive education: Visible wellbeing and the five domains of positive functioning. In M Slade., L Oades., & A Jarden (Eds.), *Wellbeing, recovery and mental health.*(pp. 235–260). London: Cambridge University Press.

White, M., & Murray, S. (2015). *Evidence-based approaches in positive education in schools: Implementing a strategic framework for wellbeing in schools.* Dordrecht: Netherlands: Springer.

White, M. A. (2016). Why won't it stick? Positive psychology and positive education. *Psychology of Well-Being, 6*(2), published first online

White, M., & Waters, L. (2014). The good school: A case study of the use of Christopher Peterson's work to adopt a strengths-based approach in the classroom, chapel and sporting fields. *Journal of Positive Psychology, 10*, 69–76.

World Bank (2016). *World development indicators: Bhutan.* Retrieved from: http://data.worldbank.org/country/bhutan

World Health Organization (2013). *Mental health action plan 2013-2020.* Retrieved from http://www.who.int/mental_health/publications/action_plan/en

Ye, Y., Mei, W., Liu, Y., & Li, X. (2012). Effect of academic comparisons on the subjective wellbeing of Chinese secondary school students. *Social Behavior and Personality: An International Journal, 40*, 1233–1238. doi: 10.2224/sbp.2012.40.8.1233

Cultural Context in Positive Psychology: History, Research, and Opportunities for Growth

Jennifer Teramoto Pedrotti and Lisa M. Edwards

When Martin Seligman reintroduced the concepts of positive psychology in the beginning of his presidency of the American Psychological Association in the year 2000, many were curious about this "new" field of study, whereas others were dismissive of the "newness" of the idea that research might apply a more balanced focus on strengths and weaknesses (Seligman & Csikszentmihalyi, 2000). Though some in the field had an almost immediate attraction to the idea of studying such "new" characteristics as happiness, hope, and courage, others reacted with criticism that positive psychology was not only not "new," but seemed to forget to give credit to past research in resilience, motivation, and other constructs derived from humanistic psychology (Christopher & Howe, 2014). This heated debate dominated discussions of positive psychology at the time; however, some groups also noted that regardless of the newness of these constructs, positive psychology was still a psychology that tended to promote Western and majority culture ideals as positive, while ignoring or pathologizing traits in non-Western populations (Christopher & Howe, 2014; Sue & Constantine, 2003).

At first, discussions focused more on the potential universalism of particular constructs such as happiness or gratitude, however newer and more current research has delved into these topics in a more nuanced way (Pedrotti, Edwards, & Lopez, in press). Today, it is well accepted that culture is a determinant in the human experience, regardless of the application of scientific principles, and as such, cultural context affects all of our experiences, including our understandings of what "the good life" truly means (Pedrotti, 2014). Though culture is often described by the layperson as merely encompassing race or country of origin, in the current state of the field of psychology, most psychologists and researchers recognize *culture* as a broad and multifaceted concept that includes such social identity facets as race, ethnicity, gender, sexual orientation, disability, and social class, among others (Hays, 2016). Cultural values that stem from these identities serve as lenses for interacting with the social world and can refer to religious and spiritual values, the role of the family and relationships, and gender roles, among others (Edwards & Cardemil, 2015). If culture is ignored or pushed to the side, the field again runs the risk of setting up deficit models that both exclude and pathologize underrepresented and disenfranchised groups. This is a history that the field of psychology as a whole carries with it from as far back as Freud's gender-specific descriptions of hysteria, to more modern (though now defunct) diagnoses of "homosexuality" and "gender identity disorder" that pathologize same-sex–oriented and transgender populations (Horne, Puckett, Apter, & Levitt, 2014). As positive psychology calls for more focus on strengths to counterbalance the tendency in the field to focus on weaknesses, we must remind ourselves that there is also a need to establish thinking about different cultural groups so as to avoid creating new inequalities (Pedrotti & Edwards, 2014).

In addition to considering individual facets about social identity, it is important to think about how multiple facets may overlap within one individual, that is, someone may identify as African American, female, and heterosexual and thus experience life differently from someone who identifies as White, male, and gay. Many researchers note that impact of multiple cultural facets, or *intersectionality*, must be attended to in discussing any individual (Levant & Silverstein, 2005). Thus, the discussion of culture is complex; each identity facet cannot be siloed within a person. A chapter on culture cannot hope to do justice to every area in any kind of comprehensive way, but must still acknowledge the complexity that is a part of our cultural experience.

These facets of identity and their intersections shape the worldview of different individuals and groups and help to define what is normal, beneficial, or problematic. These definitions, in turn, influence our understanding of which constructs can be considered "positive." When considering certain traits and characteristics as useful, helpful, or beneficial, one must look to the individual, groups to which they belong and the situation for full understanding. Further, simply noting that a particular construct exists within different cultural groups does not mean that the construct functions in the same way or has the same definitions in these groups. Indeed, these are all questions of measurement and context, both of which are critical to understanding the intersection of positive psychology and multiculturalism. This chapter provides a brief overview of measurement with regard to cultural issues and then continues to describe research and theory in several cultural facet areas. Rather than be comprehensive, our intention is to present several ideas and studies relevant to cultural facets such that the reader may be able to use them as a starting point for additional research and understanding of how the field is progressing.

Measurement and Culture in Positive Psychology

Given that all constructs can vary depending on the cultural group or facet (Sue & Constantine, 2003), the measurement of strengths can also be complicated. For example, what is the meaning or relevance of a construct such as optimism within different cultural groups? Precision regarding measurement is critical in order to accurately understand the nature of positive psychological constructs, and using measures that have been normed primarily on mainstream populations (e.g., White, middle class, male) may create problems with cross-cultural equivalence or the comparability of test scores across cultures (Ægisdóttir, Gerstein, & Çinarbaş, 2008).

Although authors have proposed different terms for various types of equivalence, the most commonly described forms are conceptual, functional, metric, and linguistic (Ægisdóttir et al., 2008; Lonner, 1985). *Conceptual equivalence* refers to a notion or construct having the same meaning across cultures. *Functional equivalence* denotes the equivalence of meaning that a certain behavior has in different cultures. For example, if behaviors among individuals of different groups (e.g., different forms of coping such as social support and venting) achieve the same goal (e.g., well-being), these behaviors can be considered functionally equivalent. *Metric equivalence* refers to identifying whether there are similar psychometric properties across groups for a scale developed to measure the same concept. Finally, *linguistic equivalence* looks at equality in the phrasing of items in different language versions of an instrument (Lonner, 1985; Ægisdóttir et al., 2008).

In addition to the complexity of establishing equivalence, bias is another issue that can affect the generalizability of measures or constructs across cultures (Ægisdóttir et al., 2008). *Construct bias*, which leads to nonequivalence, occurs when the construct (e.g., happiness) being measured is not the same across cultures. For example, in some countries happiness may be derived from interpersonal connectedness and balanced affect, whereas in others it may come from personal achievement through positive affect (He & van de Vijver, 2012). Another form of bias, *method bias*, occurs when characteristics of administration create differences in scores across cultural groups, which can happen as a result of differences in response styles, communication problems between researchers and participants, and variations in physical conditions during the administration of the instrument (Ægisdóttir et al., 2008). Finally, *item bias* may produce a threat to cross-cultural comparison as a result of inadequate translation, unsatisfactory item construction, or differential relevance of item content for the cultural groups being compared (Ægisdóttir et al., 2008).

Researchers investigating strengths among individuals who speak different languages commonly seek to establish linguistic equivalence of translated measures. Rather than relying on one simple translation, Brislin (1986) suggested a procedure that increases linguistic equivalence. The first step in this method is to have two bilingual individuals who speak both the original and target language translate the instrument. Next, different individuals conduct a *back translation*, where the translated version of a measure is independently translated back to the original language. Finally, the two versions are compared to refine and ensure equivalence (Brislin, Lonner, & Thorndike, 1973). It is important to note that this method is meant to ensure that phrasing in one language has the same meaning in the second language but does not necessarily address other types of equivalence. A construct, as defined in a Western context, for example, has the same conceptual meaning in both the original language and translated language versions if correctly translated, and thus does not necessarily capture culturally specific definitions of the construct in the second population (Stolk, Kaplan, & Szwarc, 2014). In addition, researchers in this area state that making efforts to obtain more than one type of equivalence is ideal prior to using a scale with a new population (van de Vijever & Leung, 2011).

The challenge of accurately assessing positive psychological constructs across and within different cultural groups is clear and an issue with which researchers will have to contend as the field progresses. Different aspects of diversity may bring unique measurement challenges that may or may not be relevant to other facets. For example, Wehmeyer and Shogren (2014) note that within the assessment of quality of life in individuals with disabilities, measurement "remains a relatively contentious issue in the field, in part because of difficulties experienced by some people with disabilities in reliably completing self-report measures" (p. 180). In cases in which parents, caretakers, or partners have to decipher or translate various responses from a disabled individual, an extra element of interpretation comes into play, which may affect psychometric properties of validity and reliability in some cases. Taking care to both increase equivalence and decrease bias is essential to accurate study in any part of the field.

Positive Psychology and Specific Populations: An Overview of the Current Research

For the purposes of this chapter, we have decided to give brief overviews of research conducted in positive psychology that highlight race and ethnicity, gender, sexual orientation, social class, or disability. McNulty and Fincham (2012) speak broadly about the need to incorporate context when evaluating the utility and benefits of particular strengths for various individuals. In this section, several examples are presented highlighting ways in which various cultural facets may make a difference in defining, observing, and cataloging traits and characteristics within the field of positive psychology.

Race and Ethnicity

As positive psychology was brought back into the forefront of the field in the late 1990s, Seligman and Csikszentmihalyi wrote the lead article for the January 2000 issue of the *American Psychologist*, which included articles by Diener and several other psychologists on a variety of positive constructs. Some multicultural psychologists (e.g., Sue & Constantine, 2006) began to question why no researchers of color were included in this issue and why no issues of cultural context were discussed. Thus began the call that inclusion of experiences from different racial groups be taken into consideration in talking about strengths.

Psychology as a field in general has a history of pathologicalization with regard to nonwhite races in many areas (Sue & Sue, 2013). From deeming groups with facial features that did not conform to European standards as less intelligent (Gould, 1996), to deficit models that favor European American ideals in parenting, relationships, and family style (Sue & Constantine, 2006), the field has often represented experiences of people of color as "less than." In a field that has traditionally focused more on weakness as opposed to strength, and with the added layer of pathologizing any non-White experience, people of color have often been forced to "deal with a sort of double-jeopardy; they are branded as pathological in comparison to the majority group, and within a system that only acknowledges weakness" (Pedrotti & Edwards, 2014, p. xv). Thus, positive psychology provides a particular benefit to people of color as it allows the field to recognize strengths in all groups, but only if equal attention is given toward researching minority and majority groups. Differences have been shown in terms of definitions, value, and links between constructs in different racial groups (Pedrotti, Edwards, & Lopez, in press). Several exemplars will be discussed in this section.

Definitional differences have been found between members of differing racial and ethnic groups with regard to a number of different constructs. In particular, the construct of happiness has been shown to have "substantial cultural variations" in definitions given by participants from Eastern cultures and those from Western ones (Uchida, Norasakkunkit, & Kitayama, 2004, p. 223). In a study by Uchida and colleagues (2004), White participants were more likely to define happiness by measures that included personal achievement and success, whereas Asian participants more often used definitions that emphasized harmony and success in social relationships. As a second example, the construct of wisdom has differed definitionally across different cultural groups. Though majority-culture college students in the United States tend to focus on cognitive aspects when defining the construct, Slovak college students in the same study focused almost solely on affective aspects of wisdom (Benedikovičová & Ardelt, 2008). In another study, Yang (2008) found that Taiwanese college students focused more equally on both cognitive and affective aspects of wisdom. Thus, cultural context influenced different definitions of the same construct in these different groups.

In addition, culture seems to determine the value of particular characteristics that differ across racial and ethnic groups as well. In a study comparing European American and Asian American participants, Tsai, Knutson, and Fung (2006) found that Asian American participants in their study valued low-arousal positive emotions, such as states of calm, relaxation, and serenity, more than their European American counterparts. Conversely, European American participants valued high-arousal positive emotions such as excitement, elation, and enthusiasm more than the Asian American participants (Tsai et al., 2006). In other studies, traits such as interdependence and reliance on the group have been found to be viewed as more positive by collectivist groups than traits such as independence or reliance on self, which are often given higher value in White American, individualist samples (Ahluwalia, Flores Locke, & Hylton, 2014; Markus & Kitayama, 1991). These traits can be denoted as *culturally relevant strengths* and differ from group to group.

Manifestation of various constructs may also vary according to differences in cultural background. In cross-cultural studies comparing individuals from Asian groups to those who identify as European American, differences have been found in levels of life satisfaction and happiness such that Asian participants report lower levels (Diener, Suh, Smith, & Shao, 1995). Differences also exist, however, in terms of the frequency of experience of life satisfaction related to positive events. In a study by Oishi, Diener, Choi, Kim-Prieto, & Choi (2007) Asian Americans (and Korean and Japanese respondents) experienced daily satisfaction at higher rates as a result of positive events than their European American counterparts. In addition, other behaviors and emotions have differing relationships to happiness and life satisfaction within Asian and European American cultural groups (e.g., type of self-construal [Markus & Kitayama, 1991] and engaging vs. disengaging emotions and behaviors [Kitayama, Markus, & Kurokawa, 2000]). Thus, it appears that different relationships among a variety of constructs may exist within the overall manifestation of happiness in these different cultural groups and may only be understood by unpacking these experiences using a lens of cultural context (see Shin & Lyubomirsky, this volume).

Chang and Banks (2007) depict the importance of paying attention to race and ethnicity in discussing the construct of hope, as described by Snyder and colleagues (1991). Snyder's definition of hope is composed of pathways (finding avenues around obstacles) and agentic (motivational) thinking toward goals. In their study, Chang and Banks (2007) looked at African American, White American, Asian American, and Latino/a participants and found that although hope can be beneficial to individuals of all races, different factors predicted agentic thinking and pathways thinking in different racial groups. In African American participants, for example, the highest predictor of agentic thinking was a negative association with negative problem-solving orientation; that is, when these participants were low in fear of problem-solving, they were highest in agentic thinking. However, this was not the highest predictor of agentic thinking for any other group. Further, differences were also found between the other racial groups, with life satisfaction best predicting agentic thinking in White American participants, rational problem-solving best predicting Latino agentic thinking, and positive affect best predicting agentic thinking in Asian Americans (Chang & Banks, 2007). Additionally, some of these "best predictors" in the various groups were not significantly correlated with agentic thinking at all in other groups. For example, though negative problem orientation was the highest significant predictor for agentic thinking for African Americans, as mentioned previously, and strongly and negatively correlated with agency, this factor was not significantly related to agency in Latino participants at all. Rational problem-solving, the best predictor of agentic thinking in Latino participants, was not significantly correlated with agency in the White participants (Chang & Banks, 2007). These differences indicate that hope (and potentially other positive constructs) may function and be cultivated differently in different racial and ethnic groups.

Finally, Chang (2001) has studied optimism, pessimism, and depression in both Chinese American and White American college students and found distinct differences in the correlations between these factors and others. Specifically, whereas optimism significantly predicts better problem-solving behaviors in White American samples, Chang found the opposite to be true in Chinese Americans, with higher pessimism being positively correlated with better problem-solving in this group. Results here point to pessimism as functioning as a strength in the Chinese American sample, though it is often touted as a weakness in White American culture.

Thus, it is clear that what are traditionally denoted as "strengths" may function differently based on racial and ethnic differences. Even in cases where two racial or ethnic groups may find a particular construct or trait to be positive in both cultures, differences may exist within the manifestation of these strengths (e.g., the way wisdom is valued but displayed differently by different cultural groups; Benedikovičová & Ardelt, 2008; Yang, 2008), the level of value (e.g., the type of arousal that is most valuable; Tsai et al., 2006), or importance in terms of function within the cultural group (e.g., optimism functioning differently in Asian American and White American cultural groups; Chang, 2001).

Gender

When looking at the different, but linked, histories of the psychology of women and the psychology of men, overlap is discovered between the paths these areas of psychology have pursued and positive psychology as a whole. In early work devoted to the psychology of women, deliberate efforts were made to depathologize traits often assigned to women in traditional psychology literature. As an example, Worell and Johnson (2001) in their creation of feminist therapy modalities, discuss the "revaluing" of traits such as nurturing as beneficial for parenting and/or relationship development. These researchers make it clear that many traits viewed as traditionally feminine should be treated as strengths. A second example exists within the change of language that exists around intimate partner violence in pioneer Lenore Walker's (1994) work, specifically the change from "victim" to "survivor" when discussing violence against women. The connotations surrounding the revised terminology are purposefully positive and reflect a desire to highlight strengths of women who have experienced violence (Englar-Carlson & Smart, 2014).

In looking at the much later origins of the psychology of men, scholars have noted that although men have been the emphasized group in the study of psychology, historically research has not included an analysis focused within gender per se, instead treating the male experience as "normal" (O'Neil, 2012). In addition, Englar-Carlson (2009) and others note that what has typically been viewed as "manly" behavior has accentuated traits that are not inherently positive (e.g., aggressiveness, lack of emotionality, detached fathering). Thus, attention to the psychology of men within their gendered context provided an opportunity to reframe ideas of positive masculinity (e.g., self-reliance, generative fathering, worker/provider traditions; Kiselica & Englar-Carlson, 2010). Though feminist beliefs refute the idea that masculinity can ever be viewed as pathologized in the literature due to the reality of the benefits that men receive in society as a function of being male (i.e., power and privilege), it has also been noted that framing masculinity in such a narrow way harms men (as well as women) in that it does not provide opportunities for men to develop more healthy traits and still be seen as masculine (Kiselica & Woodford, 2007). Regardless, the origins of both of these two gendered accounts support a strengths-based perspective (Englar-Carlson & Smart, 2014).

Though discussions of gender have most often been binary until recently (i.e., discussing men or women and no other gender options), it might also be argued that research today surfacing on transgender individuals attempts to ground this gender experience in positive traits. Whereas past diagnoses of "gender identity disorder" pathologized the experience of many individuals who would identify themselves today as transgender, the decision to remove and change the diagnosis in the current edition of the *Diagnostic and Statistical Manual* (DSM) shows a move toward a more balanced view of this identity. The current diagnosis of "gender dysphoria" in transgender individuals instead frames pathology as only existing if the transgender individual is experiencing distress over their transition (American Psychiatric Association, 2013). Thus the experience of being transgender is not necessarily a negative experience via the DSM-5, though it was discussed this way in the past. Providing a healthy gender experience for this group on a gender continuum, as opposed to a polar system, better reflects the diversity that exists within this group (de Cuypere, Knudson, & Bockting, 2011; Fraser, Karasic, Meyer, & Wylie, 2010).

Some research in the field of positive psychology has shown that gender is an important factor to consider when discussing strengths and what traits may have that classification. Rao and Donaldson (2015) note that research addressing gender does not always focus on various identities equally. Specifically, these authors note that where research is focused on gender, there tends to be an overrepresentation of female-identified participants, but also a scarcity of articles devoted specifically to female identity. In addition, most articles addressing gender in their analysis (a little over half) had male-identified first authors, and as such the lens used in research may or may not be consistent with how female-identified or transgender individuals may interpret the same findings (Rao & Donaldson, 2015). Nevertheless, some studies have been conducted looking specifically at gender and with interesting results.

As has been shown with other social identity facets, various constructs may have different impacts in different gender groups. Some research suggests that the change in amount of societal opportunities for women in the United States has also affected well-being differentially across genders (Stevenson & Wolfers, 2009). Whereas well-being in this research showed an apparent decrease in today's women's well-being levels as compared to times when women were primarily home based, well-being has increased for men during this time. Although many interpretations of this finding are offered, Stevenson and Wolfers (2009) state that the difference in well-being is likely a function of the "second shift" (i.e., the higher amount of home responsibility that women seem to maintain even when they work outside the home) that affects women more often than men. As such, the same factor (more women in the workplace) affects well-being for male- and female-identified individuals differently, with men experiencing more well-being and women experiencing a decrease.

In addition, some aspects of positive processes may be differentially effective for different gender groups. It is commonly known that men and women may use problem-focused, emotion-focused, and avoidance-focused coping strategies to different extents; specifically, women have been found to use emotion-focused coping styles more frequently than their male counterparts (Brems & Johnson, 1989). Likely due to the common devaluing of feminine strategies in favor of masculine strategies in the mainstream U.S. cultural context, emotion-focused strategies have been denigrated as unhelpful in the past (Stanton, Danoff-Burg, Cameron, & Ellis, 1994). However, current research shows that not only were emotion-focused strategies not harmful for women in relation to depressed mood, but some emotion-focused strategies (e.g., expression of feelings) actually reduced depressive mood for women, though these results were not found in men (Howerton & Van Gundy, 2009). Thus, emotion-focused strategies may be viewed as a strength for women, but not necessarily for men.

With the field's move toward less pathologicalization of transgender individuals, new positive research is beginning to amass with this gender identity as well. Riggle, Rostosky, McCants, and Pascule-Hague (2011) asked 61 transgender individuals to detail positive aspects of their self-identification. Eight themes were found in the data regarding the nature of these positive aspects, with the top four being unique perspectives/insight ("Being 'both and' is a place of privilege that allows me insights into the complexity of gender identities . . ." p. 152; the most common answer), congruency ("You can live the life that you know should be yours, [not] being stuck in a foreign body," p. 150), personal growth and resiliency ("I am stronger and wiser because of my struggles as a transgender individual," p. 151), and living beyond the binary ("To be bound as a 'woman' or a 'man' is stifling," p. 152). Riggle and colleagues (2011) call for more research in this area to see if links between these positive aspects and well-being exist and, if so, how they might "promote individual well-being and flourishing" (p. 147) in transgender populations. This type of research sheds light on the complexity of experience that exists within any gender group, including transgender, and further validates the changes reflected in the DSM-5 (American Psychiatric Association, 2013).

Finally, some research on gender and positive constructs shows that there may be particular contexts in which usually positive constructs lose their positive quality, and many of these contexts may be those more frequently occupied by women. For example, McNulty and Fincham (2012) report a series of studies showing that for women who are in domestically violent living situations, the construct of forgiveness loses many of its benefits. Specifically, these researchers note that a tendency to forgive was linked to a higher likelihood to return to a violent partner (Gordon, Burton, & Porter, 2004). In addition, more forgiving women tended to experience increasing levels of psychological and physical abuse and aggression at the hands of their partners (McNulty, 2010). Though these results are not necessarily focused on gender, they are situations that women more often experience, and as such, the utility of forgiveness for this group is called into question as a strength in this context.

Social Class

Social class and socioeconomic status have also oft been ignored as mediating factors in psychological health. Early work in the study of intelligence—for example, Goddard's work in this area—paired lack of intelligence with poverty and attempted to draw causal links between these factors such that intelligence predicted socioeconomic status (Gould, 1996). Though these links have been widely discredited today, stereotypes still exist that depict people in poverty as at fault for their own position in society due to lack of psychological strengths (Bullock, 1995). In a study showing that these stereotypes may exist even within young children, fourth-graders were more likely to attribute high skills in academics (including "smartness"), music, and sports to individuals in higher social class groups (Woods, Kurtz-Costes, & Rowley, 2005). Even as later adolescence and adulthood allow for more complex understandings of social class and its relation to various abilities and traits (Woods et al., 2005), some negative stereotypes remain about poorer groups (e.g., substance abuse being more likely in poor social classes; Gilmore & Harris, 2008). Thus, the field of positive psychology becomes an apt vehicle for gaining more accurate information about the strengths of individuals from all backgrounds, including individuals in poverty who have been unfairly stigmatized by ethnocentric or social class-centric theories of the past (Pedrotti, 2013; Pedrotti & Edwards, 2009).

What is viewed as a strength or weakness also may differ depending on the group from which one comes. Liu, Soleck, Hopps, Dunston, and Pickett's (2004) Social Class Worldview Model (SCWM) discusses the effect of worldview on which behaviors and ideas are considered "normal" within a group, "outstanding" (a potential strength), or "detrimental" (a potential weakness). One from a higher social class, for instance, might view a trait like having boundless hope for the future as a strength and a desirable and reasonable characteristic that would help one to achieve full potential. An individual from a lower social class and for whom all dreams may not be financially viable (e.g., attending a prestigious college, attaining a large home, etc.) may consider the boundless nature of this as detrimental to one's ability to maintain personal well-being if the likelihood of achieving these goals is perceived to be low. Thus, an understanding of this great diversity within groups and the influence of this on perception of strengths and weaknesses must first be obtained before investigating links between social class and various positive psychological characteristics (Pedrotti, 2013).

With regard to research in the area of social class and positive psychology, several areas are commonly investigated. Diener and colleagues have conducted a number of international studies involving links between wealth of particular nations and their overall reports of subjective well-being (SWB). In general, four findings have emerged, according to Diener and Biswas-Diener (2009):

(a) There are large correlations between the wealth of nations and the mean reports of SWB in them; (b) There are mostly small correlations between income and SWB within nations, although these correlations appear to be larger in poor nations, and the risk of unhappiness is much higher for poor people; (c) Economic growth in the last few decades in most economically developed societies have been accompanied by little rise in SWB, and increases in individual income lead to variable outcomes; and (d) People who prize material goals more than other values tend to be substantially less happy, unless they are rich. (p. 119)

In summary, this collective research shows that though some links exist between social class, amount of income, and well-being experiences, this is nuanced depending on context and the particular social class one is from.

Other research has focused on certain strengths being particularly prominent in certain social class groups. The constructs of creativity, resilience, and optimism have been studied frequently in this area (Pedrotti, 2013). Some researchers posit that creativity may be higher in lower social class groups, giving support to the old adage "Poverty breeds creativity" (e.g., Simonton, 2009), but many other studies find that socioeconomic status and social class in general appear to advantage higher groups with regard to creativity (Zhang & Postiglione, 2001). In terms of resilience, similar results are found, with more strengths in this construct in higher social class groups (e.g., Liu & Allmon, 2014; Starfield, Riley, Witt, & Robertson, 2002). It is important to note, however, that another large portion of the literature in the field of resilience is devoted to looking at the incredible resilience of some children despite their lower-class social class status (Yates & Masten, 2004). Yates and Masten state, "Repeated observations of such youth [i.e., youth who succeed despite the odds] inspired a generation of research on resilience" (p. 521). Optimism is linked in similar ways to social class, with lower levels of optimism and higher levels of pessimism found in individuals with fewer economic resources (Heinonen et al., 2006). These findings seem to prevail despite changes in socioeconomic class as one ages, with higher social class adults from lower social class childhoods also showing the same trend of lower optimism (Mossakowski, 2008).

These findings raise questions about how accessible "the good life" or strengths may be if so many of them are not found in certain socioeconomic groups. In the previous discussions of strengths in different racial groups or gender groups, the focus is more on the social norms and value of these groups in society, as opposed to an environmental impact that affects the entire group singularly. Research in the area of social class and strengths appears to suggest that some base needs must be met in almost all cases to allow one to develop particular positive traits (Masten, Cutuli, Herbers, & Reed, 2009; Yates & Masten, 2004). Developing a trait such as secure attachment, for example, requires the presence of a safe relationship with an adult figure, which is not under the control of a child per se. This said, it is noted that some specific internal traits (such as a temperament that encourages resilience despite environment) may be developed despite circumstances that do not allow base needs to be met (Yates & Masten, 2004). As such, in the field of positive psychology, research must investigate how the development of various traits and characteristics can be more accessible despite lack of resources. In addition, much of the research in this area uses methods that search for strengths through the lens of the researcher, as opposed to asking individuals to self-identify their own positive traits or those of their families. In a unique study by Israel and Jozefowicz-Simbeni (2009), researchers asked mothers whose families were dealing with homelessness to report strengths in their children. Mothers in this study identified numerous strengths in their children, including intelligence, positive personality, and other factors. Thus, individuals in these lower socioeconomic groups may view their own traits differently than researchers or outside observers (Liu & Allmon, 2014).

Masten and colleagues (Masten et al., 2009; Yates & Masten, 2004) give examples of assets and protective factors that can assist children in developing positive qualities and strengths in the various domains of community (e.g., low community violence), policy (e.g., preventative health care), education (e.g., trained, competent, and appropriately compensated teachers), family (e.g., close relationships to parents or other stable adult caregiver), and individual (e.g., a positive self-concept). These types of protective factors may, of course, be more accessible to children from higher socioeconomic backgrounds, disadvantaging lower socioeconomic children and their families. It is important to note that lower social class is not necessarily synonymous with a troubled childhood or possession of fewer overall strengths. It may be, however, that individual positive traits (e.g., resilience or courage) must transcend the environment such that additional useful strengths (e.g., positive self-concept or self-efficacy) can be developed.

Yates and Masten (2004) argue that a positive psychological framework is ideal for investigating issues that may be related to lower social class status. For example, traditional models follow a pathology-based paradigm that looks for disease instead of health and commonly locates the source of the problem within the individual as opposed to the environment. This is particularly problematic when dealing with a variable such as social class, as this variable is often defined, at least in part, by environment (Pedrotti, 2013). If changes are to be made to assist lower-class children (and their families) with development of various strengths, focus must be shifted to the environment to make positive changes in areas such as poor housing, poor education, and lack of safety that often affect the development of resilience, creativity, optimism, and other strengths (Pedrotti, 2013).

Disability

Similar to research in lower social classes, the focus in the field of psychology at large has been damaging for individuals dealing with both mental and/or physical disabilities because of the extreme focus on *internal* features, as opposed to external (Wehmeyer et al., 2008; Wehmeyer & Shogren, 2014). Specifically, many issues within the diverse disabled community have been attributed to internal features of the disabled individual, as opposed to factors caused by how these features are viewed or affected by the environment. Accessibility, for example, is sometimes discussed as a "disability issue" (e.g., "S/he can't walk up the stairs") when it can also be viewed as an issue within the environment (e.g., "Not enough ramps exist on the entry of the building").

Though currently most people accept both developmental disability and acquired disability as potential social identity facets (Hays, 2016), there is a dearth of information on the topic of disability within the positive psychological literature. In fact, in an analysis of articles published in the *Journal of Positive Psychology* from its inception to the time of study, Shogren (2012) found that only 4 percent of articles in this major journal were focused on the topic of disability. Additionally, Shogren, Wehmeyer, Buchanan, and Lopez (2006) investigated the prevalence of literature focused on the strengths of individuals dealing with an intellectual disability via a content analysis spanning 30 years of literature (1975–2004). Shogren and colleagues separated this literature by decade and found that between 1975 and 1985, a mere 20 percent of articles that focused on intellectual disability included any mention of the strengths of this population. This percentage continued to rise by decade, but peaked in the span between 1995 and 2004 with approximately 50 percent focusing on some aspect of strengths in intellectually disabled populations. Though this increase is a positive move toward thinking of individuals dealing with disabilities as capable of having a variety of strengths, Wehmeyer and Shogren (2014) note that this also implies that the other 50 percent of research articles focused on disability devote more attention to deficits, thus drawing attention to the fact that "research in positive psychology and disability is still emerging" (p. 177).

Today more research is focused on contextual pieces such as the environment of the individual dealing with a disability and how this affects their internal traits and/or how internal traits can be used to deal with various issues related to a disability (Wehmeyer & Shogren, 2014). In addition, many researchers have found that the way in which various positive traits such as optimism or resilience function in disabled populations is very similar to how they function in nondisabled populations. Rand and Shea (2012), for example, found that the utility of optimism in the life of an individual dealing with disability is consistent with research showing that it helps any individual deal with adversity and strife. Thus, differing from previously discussed research with regard to different racial and gender groups, research on disability and positive psychological characteristics may not show major differences in the positive nature of these traits. Instead, the literature shows a propensity to discuss certain traits and characteristics that may be beneficial to develop in people dealing with disability on a day-to-day basis (Wehmeyer & Shogren, 2014). Of these, quality of life, self-efficacy, and self-determination will be discussed here.

Much strengths-based literature on disability is focused on the construct of quality of life with aims to improve the lives of individuals dealing with disabilities (Wehmeyer & Shogren, 2014). Literature in this area mainly compares groups of people with different disabilities—for example, those dealing with paraplegia versus those dealing with a traumatic brain injury, and as such, there are often few comparisons between individuals with a disability and those without (Wehmeyer & Shogren, 2014). This can be problematic in terms of understanding how a particular construct differs (or is similar) in the two populations. It may be helpful, for example, to understand similarities and differences of levels of psychological well-being in the lives of individuals dealing with spinal cord damage in comparison to those who lose a limb, but this type of comparison does not show if these levels differ from (or are similar to) levels found in populations without disabilities. If levels are similar between individuals with spinal cord damage and those who have lost a limb but both are lower than in populations without disabilities, for example, this additional information could assist in resource development, treatment, and better overall understanding of various groups who deal with disabilities.

Some research has been focused on particular characteristics within populations dealing with disability that seem to be related to quality of life. For example, hope and sense of humor were related to positive quality of life in a study looking at coping styles in individuals with spinal cord injuries (Smedema, Catalano, & Ebener, 2010). In addition, life satisfaction in this population has been found to be related to access to proper supports within a work environment and the ability to engage in work that holds meaning (Moore, Konrad, Yang, Ng, & Doherty, 2011). Other research focuses on the age at which a disability occurred with regard to life satisfaction, and this affected a variety of facets related to well-being as well (Moore et al., 2011).

Studies on self-efficacy and self-determination within samples of individuals dealing with disability show results that are similar to nondisabled populations. There is some evidence to show that individuals with disabilities may have lower levels of self-efficacy, but that these levels can be increased with appropriate support and intervention (e.g., Hall & Webster, 2008). One difference found in the literature between disabled and nondisabled peers was that individuals with intellectual disabilities became less sure of their abilities in certain areas as they aged, whereas the opposite is found in nondisabled populations (Wehmeyer, 1994). Finally, self-determination, although an effective strength with utility in both disabled and nondisabled individuals, may show particular benefit for those dealing with disabilities, in that it appears to predict other positive outcomes, including academic success (Lee, Wehmeyer, Soukup, & Palmer, 2010) and life satisfaction (Lachapelle et al., 2005).

Future directions in this area might focus specifically on the investigation of self-identified strengths within contexts important to individuals dealing with disability. In addition, the research would benefit from more positive depictions of life with a disability in general. This population is particularly understudied within the realm of positive psychology.

Sexual Orientation

Another topic that has received very little attention within the field of positive psychology is sexual orientation. It is only in recent years that psychology has begun to explore the strengths relevant to individuals and communities who identify as lesbian, gay, bisexual, or queer (LGBQ; Horne et al., 2014; Riggle, Olson, Whitman, Rostosky, & Strong, 2008). Since the American Psychiatric Association removed homosexuality from the DSM in 1973, the field has slowly shifted from emphasizing the pathology related to being LGBQ to a better understanding of sexual identity, heterosexism, and sexual minority stress. This shift has allowed current explorations that acknowledge resilience and strengths more specifically. In the following sections, we briefly review these areas, focusing on strengths that have been identified related to LGBTQ[1] identity, families, and community.

Being of a minority sexual orientation may allow lesbian, gay, and bisexual individuals to develop more complex understandings of identity

(Horne et al., 2014; Parker, Adams & Phillips, 2007). In one of the first studies that explicitly explored strengths among lesbian and gay adults, participants considered one of their strengths to be freedom from the dichotomies of sexual orientation (Riggle et al., 2008), as well as leading a creative and authentic life. In addition, one study found that sexual minority men and women engaged in more altruistic behavior than their heterosexual counterparts, suggesting that the process of identifying as being of minority sexual orientation might have benefits in the form of being attuned to others, appreciating differences, making strong connections to others, and perspective-taking (Riggle et al., 2008: Rostosky, Riggle, Pascale-Hague, & McCants, 2010).

Within LGBTQ relationships and families, a few studies have shown that same-sex couples have low rates of separation in relationships (Kurdek, 1995) and more equal division of household labor than heterosexual couples (Patterson, 2000). Additionally, Gottman et al. (2003) found that same-sex couples were more positive in their approach toward conflict interactions as compared to heterosexual couples. Authors have also noted that LGBTQ parents may be particularly adept at exposing their children to differences and providing them with coping strategies to navigate discrimination and heterosexism (Ausbrooks & Russell, 2011).

Finally, from the perspective of community engagement, resilience may develop from social connection and activism. For example, in their study (Russell & Richards, 2003), strengths emerged from the social ties that developed among LGBTQ community members who took part in movements to halt anti-LGBTQ amendments, such as a bill passed in Colorado that sought to ban LGB individuals from claiming discrimination based on sexual orientation (Horne et al., 2014; Russell, 2000) or a state marriage amendment preparing for passage in Tennessee (Levitt et al., 2009). Additionally, Ramirez-Valles, Fergus, Reisen, Poppen, and Zea (2005) found that Latino LGBTQ individuals reported decreased maladaptive coping strategies after working with HIV+/AIDS outreach organizations. Finally, Omoto and Snyder (2002) reviewed longitudinal studies of AIDS volunteers and found that LGBTQ volunteers demonstrated a stronger association between their volunteer work and the promotion of community concerns than that of their non-LGBTQ counterparts (Horne et al., 2014).

Taken together, the research within the area of positive psychology and LGBQ identity suggests that many strengths emerge from experiences such as the coming-out process, engaging in relationships, and creating families that do not conform to traditional same-sex models, as well as activism and community engagement. With the research in this area only beginning, there is a great deal that remains to be explored about this identity facet, particularly with regard to a more balanced focus between positive and negative traits (Horne et al., 2014).

Final Thoughts Regarding Specific Populations

It is evident that more research is needed in the area of positive psychology that focuses on culture as an influential factor with regard to a multitude of positive psychological constructs. This is necessary in order for positive psychology to be made fully accessible to individuals from all walks of life. In addition, it is important to note that the experience of any individual person cannot be solely catalogued as a "Latino experience," a "transgender experience," or a "middle-class experience," but instead incorporates status on all identity facets. Various constructs may be defined differently or be seen as more positive or more negative within different intersections. In addition, privilege and power change from person to person depending on the majority/minority nature of any of these cultural pieces. As such, more research must be focused on both unique and shared experiences of individuals within these various groups.

Therapeutic Applications of a More Culturally Competent Positive Psychology

The intersection of multiculturalism and positive psychology has the potential to influence many different life domains, and it is through these applications that the field can better reach the goals of improving well-being among individuals, families, and communities from all groups. Applications of multicultural positive psychology have emerged within school (Holtz & Martinez, 2014) and college campus settings (Pedrotti, 2015), as well as work domains (Youssef-Morgan & Hardy, 2014). In the following section, we briefly discuss how the intersection of multiculturalism and positive psychology can influence counseling and psychotherapy.

The fields of professional psychology and counseling have taken a clear stance on the importance of attending to culture within practice, as evidenced by numerous ethical and practice guidelines and standards (e.g., AERA, APA & NCME, 2014; AMCD, 2015; APA, 2003, 2010). Suggestions from these guidelines include conducting assessments and developing treatments that are culturally informed and address the entire person, which would naturally include a person's strengths and assets. Additionally, these guidelines have highlighted the need for practitioners to develop self-awareness regarding their own cultural backgrounds and biases, as well as knowledge about the worldviews of others (AMCD, 2015). To this

end, authors have proposed frameworks that can help practitioners cultivate an approach to working with culturally diverse individuals.

One framework for working with culturally diverse individuals, *cultural humility* (Tervalon & Murray-Garcia, 1998), takes a positive approach to the concept of cultural competency, such that it is defined as a process rather than an end product. Deriving from medicine but with applications in mental health, cultural humility can be conceptualized as the "ability to maintain an interpersonal stance that is other-oriented (or open to the other) in relation to aspects of cultural identity that are most important to the [person]" (Hook, Davis, Owen, Worthington, & Utsey, 2013; p. 2). Invoking the concept of humility suggests that practitioners who are attend-ing to culture attempt to be oriented to the other, acknowledging that they cannot possibly fully understand someone else, and being modest and open to learning more (Worthington et al., in press).

Downey and Chang (2012) proposed the concept of *multidimensional clinical competence* to describe a framework for practitioners who attend to multiculturalism, positive psychology, and lifespan perspectives in their clients. This framework is unique in its integration of strengths, develop-ment, and multiculturalism. Practitioners who exhibit this form of com-petence are working

> collaboratively and constructively with clients of diverse groups, cultures,
> developmental stages, and levels of functioning, to recognize, utilize, and
> develop their existing and potential strengths in the service of reducing
> existing or potential dysfunction in themselves or within their social sys-
> tems. (Downey & Chang, 2012, p. 373)

Taken together, cultural humility and multidimensional clinical com-petence provide lenses for positive psychological multicultural practice that may be critical for accurate assessment, conceptualization (e.g., forming a model of what might be occurring with a client), and intervention.

Although positive psychological interventions within clinical and coun-seling psychology have increased a great deal in the past years (Wood, in press), to date only a few interventions explicitly integrate multicultural-ism and positive psychology. One of the only examples, Smith's (2006) Strengths-Based Counseling (SBC), attempts to provide a model for con-ducting therapy based on the fields of positive psychology, social work, counseling psychology, prevention, positive youth development, solution-focused therapy, and narrative therapy. SBC takes place across 10 stages, from developing a therapeutic alliance and identifying and utilizing strengths, to termination and evaluation of which strengths were most important in growth. Most relevant to the intersection of positive psychology and multiculturalism, Smith's SBC is based on 12 propositions, 5 of which are related to multiculturalism (e.g., " Strength development is a lifelong process that is influenced by the interaction of [an] individual's heredity and the cultural, social, economic, and political environments in which they find themselves" (p. 38). Although authors have noted that SBC is lacking in terms of specific strengths-enhancing techniques, it does provide one of the only frameworks for strengths therapy that directly attends to culture (Magyar-Moe, 2014).

Conclusions and Future Directions

In this chapter we have tried to highlight the logical, yet imperative, connection between positive psychology and multiculturalism. We argue that neither one of these notions should exist without the other, as it is impossible to understand positive psychology without understanding cultural context, and it is detrimental to only focus on the negative in multicultural populations (Pedrotti & Edwards, 2014). This field has grown a great deal in recent years; however, there is still much more to be explored. In the following section, we discuss specific areas and ways in which the intersection of multiculturalism and positive psychology can move forward.

First, there are increasing opportunities to explore integrative research about biological and genetic underpinnings of positive psychology within a cultural context. For example, within the study of empathy, Chiao (2011) challenges researchers to consider the cultural and genetic influences of this construct and what these influences might reveal regarding the evolutionary role of empathy (Duan & Sager, in press). Chiao suggests that although individuals might possess specific genes associated with empathy, contextual influences such as racism and prejudice can affect how much empathy a person experiences toward targets of other races. Integrative research that considers cultural and genetic factors, or *cultural neuroscience*, may open the door to understanding certain positive psychological constructs.

Another area for future work lies in considering how research about positive psychology and cultural context can be used as a vehicle to address societal concerns. Scholars have noted that with the implementation of new methods, assessments, and interventions, positive psychology is poised to be a "force for societal change" (Biswas-Diener, Linley, Govindji, & Woolston, 2011), and indeed there are examples of ways in which it has already been used in this manner. More specifically, Duan and Sager (in press) note that "socially responsible psychological research must continue to help members of society understand race-related psychological phenomena" (p. 31). We extend this idea to encourage research beyond just race to those who are underserved and those who experience inequities in our society as a result of poverty, oppression, diminished opportunities, and other barriers.

In addition, conducting future positive psychological research from a perspective that involves self-awareness as a researcher, specifically with regard to internal biases, is a way in which we can further accurate understandings of individuals who have often been left out of the literature in the field of psychology at large. As positive psychology researchers who already attend to the balance between strengths and deficits, we are uniquely positioned to understand that balance and equity are important in describing any human experience. As such, we must utilize cultural humility in research as well to develop a positive psychology that is relevant to all.

In closing, Csikszentmihalyi (2014) has discussed the idea that positive psychology has for too long been treated as a "niche field" or "subfield" such that we have separated it from the field of psychology at large. He argues that all psychology research should attend to a more balanced approach between strength and weakness, regardless of our own specific areas of study. Csikszentmihalyi states that we should think about ways that we can now "fold" positive psychology back into the field at large. We offer that this same "folding" must occur with attention to cultural context. For too long, multicultural and cross-cultural psychology have been treated as "special topics" within the field at large, as well as within the study of positive psychology (Sue & Constantine, 2004). This is a false separation, as culture must always be a backdrop to the study of people, and therefore lies at the heart of understanding any cognitive, affective, and behavioral process or state, whether the focus is on strength, weakness, or both. Therefore, it is important to the future of positive psychology to think about how we can blend it with cultural context in a more seamless way in order for this field to remain viable. This may be the greatest accomplishment of positive psychology if it can occur, and as our society becomes more and more diverse, perhaps its greatest salvation. If positive psychology can be used as a vehicle to show that strengths and weakness exist in any context and in any person, disenfranchised or not, we may truly be able to move toward equity across different groups in society.

Notes

1. The acronym "LGBTQ" has often been used in literature prior to better understandings of transgender identity. Today, we recognize that transgender identification (T) is actually a gender category as opposed to one within the facet

of sexual orientation, and thus "LGBQ" may be a better acronym when discussing this facet. Regardless, much research has included transgender individuals in discussion of sexual orientation until very recently, and as such we include the "T" when researchers describe their samples with this acronym.

References

Ægisdóttir, S., Gerstein, L. H., & Çinarbaş, D. C. (2008). Methodological issues in cross-cultural counseling research equivalence, bias, and translations. *The Counseling Psychologist, 36*, 188–219.

AERA, APA, & NCME. (2014). *Standards for educational and psychological testing.* Washington, DC: AERA.

Ahluwalia, M. K., Flores Locke, A., & Hylton, S. (2014). Cross-cultural advancements in positive psychology. In C. Kim-Prieto (Ed.), *Religion and spirituality across cultures* (pp. 125–136). New York: Springer Science+Business Media.

American Psychiatric Association. (2013). *Diagnostic and statistical manual of mental disorders* (5th ed.). Arlington, VA: Author.

American Psychological Association (APA). (2003). Guidelines on multicultural education, training, research, practice and organizational change for psychologists. *American Psychologist, 58*, 377–402.

American Psychological Association (APA). (2010). *Ethical principles of psychologists and code of conduct.* Retrieved from https://www.apa.org/ethics/code/principles.pdf

Association of Multicultural Counseling and Development (AMCD). (2015). *Multicultural counseling competencies.* Retrieved from http://www.counseling.org/docs/default-source/competencies/multicultural-and-social-justice-counseling-competencies.pdf?sfvrsn=20

Ausbrooks, A. R., & Russell, A. (2011). Gay and lesbian family building: A strengths perspective of transracial adoption. *Journal of GLBT Family Studies, 7*, 201–216.

Benedikovičová, J., & Ardelt, M. (2008). The three dimensional wisdom scale in cross-cultural context: A comparison between American and Slovak college students. *Studia Psychologica, 50*, 179–190.

Biswas-Diener, R., Linley, P. A., Govindji, R., & Woolston, L. (2011). Positive psychology as a force for social change. In K. M. Sheldon, T. B. Kashdan, & M. F. Steger (Eds.), *Designing positive psychology: Taking stock and moving forward* (pp. 410–418). Oxford, England: Oxford Press.

Brems, C., & Johnson, M. E. (1989). Problem solving appraisal coping style: The influence of sex-role orientation and gender. *Journal of Psychology, 123*, 187–194.

Brislin, R. N. (1986). *The wording and translation of research instruments. Field methods in cross cultural research* (pp. 159–163). Beverly Hills, CA: Sage Publications.

Brislin, R. W., Lonner, W. J., & Thorndike, R. M. (1973). *Cross-cultural research methods*. New York: John Wiley & Sons.

Bullock, H. E. (1995). Class acts: Middle-class responses to the poor. In B. Lott & D. Maluso (Eds.), *The social psychology of interpersonal discrimination* (pp. 118–159). New York: Guilford Press.

Chang, E. C. (2001). Cultural influences on optimism and pessimism: Differences in Westerners and Eastern construals of the self. In E. C. Chang (Ed.), *Optimism & pessimism: Implications for theory, research, and practice* (pp. 257–280). Washington, DC: American Psychological Association.

Chang, E. C., & Banks, K. H. (2007). The color and texture of hope: Some preliminary findings and implications for hope theory and counseling among diverse racial/ethnic groups. *Cultural Diversity and Ethnic Minority Psychology, 13*, 94–103.

Chiao, J. Y. (2011). Towards a cultural neuroscience of empathy and prosociality. *Emotion Review, 3*, 111–112.

Christopher, J. C., & Howe, K. (2014). Future directions for a more multiculturally competent (and humble) positive psychology. In J. T. Pedrotti & L. M. Edwards (Eds.), *Perspectives on the intersection of multiculturalism and positive psychology* (pp. 253–266). New York: Springer Science + Business Media.

Csikszentmihalyi, M. (September, 2014). *Closing remarks*. Presentation at the first annual Western Positive Psychological Association Conference. Claremont, CA.

De Cuypere, G., Knudson, G., & Bockting, W. (2011). Response of the world professional association for transgender health to the proposed revision of the diagnosis of gender dysphoria for *DSM 5*. *International Journal of Transgenderism, 13*, 51–53.

Diener, E., & Biswas-Diener, R. (2009). Will money increase subjective well-being?: A literature review and guide to needed research. In E. Diener (Ed.), *The science of well-being: The collected works of Ed Diener* (pp. 119–154). New York: Springer.

Diener, E., Suh, E. M., Smith, H., & Shao, L. (1995). National differences in reported subjective well-being: Why do they occur? *Social Indicators Research, 34*, 7–32.

Downey, C. A., & Chang, E. C. (2012). Multidimensional clinical competence: Considering racial group, development, and the positive psychology movement in clinical practice. In E. C. Chang, & C. A. Downey (Eds.) *Handbook of race and development in mental health* (pp. 335–382). New York: Springer.

Duan, C. & Sager, K. (in press). Understanding empathy: Current trends and future research challenges. In S. J. Lopez, L. M. Edwards, & S. Marques (Eds.), *Handbook of positive psychology* (3rd ed.). Oxford, England: Oxford University Press.

Edwards, L. M., & Cardemil, E. V. (2015). Clinical approaches to assessing cultural values among Latinos. In K. F. Geisinger (Ed.), *Psychological testing of*

Hispanics: Clinical, cultural, and intellectual issues (2nd ed., pp. 215–236). Washington, DC: American Psychological Association.

Englar-Carlson, M. (2009). Men and masculinity: Cultural, contextual, and clinical considerations. In C. Ellis & J. Carlson (Eds.), *Cross cultural awareness and social justice in counseling* (pp. 89–120). New York: Routledge.

Englar-Carlson, M., & Smart, R. (2014). Positive psychology and gender. In J. T. Pedrotti, & L. M. Edwards (Eds.), *Perspectives on the intersection of multiculturalism and positive psychology* (pp. 125–141). New York: Springer Science + Business Media.

Fraser, L., Karasic, D. H., Meyer III, W. J., & Wylie, K. (2010). Recommendations for revision of the *DSM* diagnosis of gender identity disorder in adults. *International Journal of Transgenderism, 12*, 80–85.

Gilmore, A. K., & Harris, P. B. (2008). Socioeconomic stereotypes among undergraduate college students. *Psychological Reports, 103*, 882–892.

Goetz, J. L., Keltner, D., & Simon-Thomas, E. (2010). Compassion: An evolutionary analysis and empirical review. *Psychological Bulletin, 136*, 351–374.

Gordon, K. C., Burton, S., & Porter, L. (2004). Predicting the intentions of women in domestic violence shelters to return to partners: Does forgiveness play a role? *Journal of Family Psychology, 18*, 331–338.

Gottman, J. M., Leveson, R. W., Gross, J., Fredrickson, B. L., McCoy, K., Rosenthal, L., . . . Yoshimoto, D. (2003). Correlates of gay and lesbian couples' relationship satisfaction and relationship dissolution. *Journal of Homosexuality, 45*, 1, 23–43.

Gould, S. J. (1996). *The mismeasure of man: The definitive refutation to the argument of The bell curve.* New York: Norton & Co.

Hall, C. W., & Webster, R. E. (2008). Metacognitive and affective factors of college students with and without learning disabilities. *Journal of Postsecondary Education and Disability, 2*, 32–41.

Hays, P. A. (2016). *Addressing cultural competencies in practice, second edition: Assessment, diagnosis, and therapy.* Washington, DC: American Psychological Association.

He, J., & van de Vijver, F. (2012). Bias and equivalence in cross-cultural research. *Online Readings in Psychology and Culture, 2*(2). Retrieved from http://dx .doi.org/10.9707/2307-0919.1111

Heinonen, K., Räikkönen, K., Matthews, K. A., Scheier, M. F., Raitakari, O. T., Pulkki, L., & Keltikangas-Järvinen, L. (2006). Socioeconomic status in childhood and adulthood: Associations with dispositional optimism and pessimism over a 21-year follow-up. *Journal of Personality, 74*, 1111–1126.

Holtz, C. A., & Martinez, M. J. (2014). Positive psychology practices in multicultural school settings. In J. T. Pedrotti & L. M. Edwards (Eds.), *Perspectives on the intersection of multiculturalism and positive psychology* (pp. 205–218). New York: Springer Science + Business Media.

Hook, J. N., Davis, D. E., Owen, J., Worthington Jr., E. L., & Utsey, S. O. (2013). Cultural humility: Measuring openness to culturally diverse clients. *Journal of Counseling Psychology, 60*, 353–366.

Horne, S. G., Puckett, J. A., Apter, R., & Levitt, H. M. (2014). Positive psychology and LGBTQ populations. In J. T. Pedrotti & L. M. Edwards (Eds.), *Perspectives on the intersection of multiculturalism and positive psychology* (pp. 189–202). New York: Springer Science+Business Media.

Howerton, A., & Van Gundy, K. (2009). Sex differences in coping styles and implications for depressed mood. *International Journal of Stress Management, 16*, 333–350.

Israel, N., & Jozefowicz-Simbeni, D. M. H. (2009). Perceived strengths of urban girls and boys experiencing homelessness. *Journal of Community & Applied Social Psychology, 19*, 156–164.

Kiselica, M. S., & Englar-Carlson, M. (2010). Identifying, affirming, and building upon male strengths: The positive psychology/positive masculinity model of psychotherapy with boys and men. *Psychotherapy: Theory, Research, Practice, Training, 47*, 276–287.

Kiselica, M. S., & Woodford, M. S. (2007). Promoting healthy male development: A social justice perspective. In C. Lee (Ed.), *Counseling for social justice* (pp. 111–135). Alexandria, VA: American Counseling Association.

Kitayama, S., Markus, H. R., & Kurokawa, M. (2000). Culture, emotion, and well-being: Good feelings in Japan and the United States. *Cognition and Emotion, 14*, 93–124.

Kurdek, L. A. (1995). Lesbian and gay couples. In A. R. D'Augelli & C. J. Patterson (Eds.), *Lesbian, gay, and bisexual identities over the lifespan: Psychological perspectives* (pp. 243–261). New York: Oxford University Press.

Lachapelle, Y., Wehmeyer, M. L., Haelewyck, M. C., Courbois, Y., Keith, K. D., Schalock, R., . . . Walsh, P.N. (2005). The relationship between quality of life and self-determination: An international study. *Journal of Intellectual Disability Research, 49*, 740–744.

Layous, K., Lee, H., Choi, I., & Lyubomirsky, S. (2013) Culture matters when designing a successful happiness-increasing activity: Comparison of the United States and South Korea. *Journal of Cross-Cultural Psychology, 44*, 1294–1303.

Lee, S. H., Wehmeyer, M. L., Soukup, J. H., & Palmer, S. B. (2010). Impact of curriculum modifications on access to the general education curriculum for students with disabilities. *Exceptional Children, 76*, 213–233.

Levant, R. F., & Silverstein, L. S. (2005). Gender is neglected in both evidence based practices and "treatment as usual." In J. C. Norcross, L. E. Beutler, & R. F. Levant (Eds.), *Evidence-based practice in mental health: Debate and dialogue on the fundamental questions* (pp. 338–345). Washington, DC: American Psychological Association.

Levitt, H. M., Ovrebo, E., Anderson-Cleveland, M. B., Leone, C., Jeong, J. Y., Arm, J. R., . . . Horne, S. G. (2009). Balancing dangers: GLBT experience in a time of anti-GLBT legislation. *Journal of Counseling Psychology, 56*, 67–81.

Liu, W. M., & Allmon, A. (2014). Social class mobility and positive psychology. In J. T. Pedrotti & L. M. Edwards (Eds.), *Perspectives on the intersection of multiculturalism and positive psychology* (pp. 159–173). New York: Springer Science+Business Media.

Liu, W. M., Soleck, G., Hopps, J., Dunston, K., & Pickett, T. (2004). A new framework to understand social class in counseling: The social class worldview model and modern classism theory. *Journal of Multicultural Counseling and Development, 32,* 95–122.

Lonner, W. J. (1985). Issues in testing and assessment in cross-cultural counseling. *The Counseling Psychologist, 13*(4), 599–614.

Lyubomirsky, S., King, L., & Diener E., (2005). The benefits of frequent positive affect: Does happiness lead to success? *Psychological Bulletin, 131,* 803–855.

Magyar-Moe, J. L. (2014). Infusing multiculturalism and positive psychology in psychotherapy. In J. T. Pedrotti & L. M. Edwards (Eds.), *Perspectives on the intersection of multiculturalism and positive psychology* (pp. 235–249). New York: Springer Science+Business Media.

Markus, H. R., & Kitayama, S. (1991). Culture and self: Implications for cognition, emotion and motivation. *Psychological Review, 98,* 224–253.

Masten, A. S., Cutuli, J. J., Herbers, J. E., & Reed, M. J. (2009). Resilience in development. In S. J. Lopez (Ed.), *The Oxford handbook of positive psychology* (pp. 117–131). New York: Oxford University Press.

McNulty, J. K. (2010). When positive processes hurt relationships. *Current Directions in Psychological Science, 19,* 167–171.

McNulty, J. K., & Fincham, F. D. (2012). Beyond positive psychology? Toward a contextual view of psychological process and well-being. *American Psychologist, 67,* 101–110.

Moore, M. E., Konrad, A. M., Yang, Y., Ng, E. S. W., & Doherty, A. J. (2011). The vocational well-being of workers with childhood onset of disability: Life satisfaction and perceived workplace discrimination. *Journal of Vocational Behavior, 79,* 681–698.

Mossakowski, K. N. (2008). Dissecting the influence of race, ethnicity, and socioeconomic status on mental healthy in young adulthood. *Research on Aging, 30,* 649–671.

Oishi, S., Diener, E. F., Choi, D.–W., Kim-Pieto, C., & Choi, I. (2007). The dynamics of daily events and well-being across culture: When less is more. *Journal of Personality and Social Psychology, 93,* 685–698.

Omoto, A. M., & Synder, M. (2002). Considerations of community: The context and process of volunteerism. *American Behavioral Scientist, 45,* 5, 846–867.

O'Neil, J. M. (2012). The psychology of men and boys in the year 2010: Theory, research, clinical knowledge, and future directions. In E. Altmaier & J. Hansen (Eds.), *The Oxford handbook of counseling psychology* (pp. 375–408). New York: Oxford University Press.

Parker, B. A., Adams, H. L., & Phillips, L. D. (2007). Decentering gender: Bisexual identity as an expression of a non-dichotomous worldview. *Identity: An International Journal of Theory and Research, 7,* 205–224.

Patterson, C. J. (2000). Family relationships of lesbians and gay men. *Journal of Marriage and the Family, 62*(4), 1052–1069.

Pedrotti, J. T. (2013). Positive psychology, social class, and counseling. In W. M. Liu (Ed.), *Handbook of social class in counseling* (pp. 131–143). New York: Oxford University Press.

Pedrotti, J. T. (2014, January). Shifting the lens: Including culture in discussions of positive psychology. Keynote address presented at the meeting of the Asian Pacific Conference on Applied Positive Psychology, Hong Kong.

Pedrotti, J. T. (2015). Cultural competence in positive psychology: History, research, and practice. In R. Hetzel, L. Marks, & J. Wade (Eds.), *Positive psychology on the college campus* (pp. 81–98). New York: Oxford University Press.

Pedrotti, J. T., & Edwards, L. M. (2009). The intersection of positive psychology and multiculturalism in counseling. In J. G. Ponterotto, J. M. Casas, L. A. Suzuki, & C. M. Alexander (Eds.), *Handbook of multicultural counseling* (3rd ed., pp. 165–174). Thousand Oaks, CA: Sage.

Pedrotti, J. T., & Edwards, L. M. (Eds.). (2014). *Perspectives on the intersection of multiculturalism and positive psychology.* New York: Springer Science+Business Media.

Pedrotti, J. T., Edwards, L. M., & Lopez, S. J. (in press). Putting positive psychology into a multicultural context. In S. J. Lopez, L. M. Edwards, & S. Marques (Eds.), *Oxford handbook of positive psychology.* New York: Oxford University Press.

Ramirez-Valles, J., Fergus, S., Reisen, C. A., Poppen, P. J., & Zea, M. (2005). Confronting stigma: Community involvement and psychological well-being among HIV-positive Latino gay men. *Hispanic Journal of Behavioral Sciences, 27*, 101–119.

Rand, K. L., & Shea, A. M. (2012). Optimism within the context of disability. In M. Wehmeyer (Ed.), *Handbook of positive psychology and disability* (pp. 48–59). Oxford, England: Oxford University Press.

Rao, M. A., & Donaldson, S. I. (2015). Expanding opportunities for diversity in positive psychology: An examination of gender, race, and ethnicity. *Canadian Psychology, 56*, 271–282.

Riggle, E., Rostosky, S., McCants, L., & Pascule-Hague, D. (2011). The positive aspects of a transgendered self-identification. *Psychology and Sexuality, 2*, 147–158.

Riggle, E. D. B., Whitman, J. S., Olson, A., Rostosky, S. S., & Strong, S. (2008). The positive aspects of being a lesbian or gay man. *Professional Psychology: Research and Practice, 39*, 210–217.

Rostosky, S. S., Riggle, E. D. B., Pascale-Hague, D., & McCants, L. E. (2010). The positive aspects of a bisexual self-identification. *Psychology & Sexuality, 1*, 131–144.

Russell, G. M. (2000). *Voted out: The psychological consequences of anti-gay politics.* New York: New York University Press.

Russell, G. M., & Richards, J. A. (2003). Stressor and resilience factors for lesbians, gay men, and bisexuals confronting antigay politics. *American Journal of Community Psychology, 31*, 313–328.

Seligman, M. E. P., & Csikszentmihalyi, M. (2000). Positive psychology: An introduction. *American Psychologist, 55*, 5–14.

Shin, L., & Lyubomirsky, S. (in press). Increasing well-being in independent and dependent cultures. In M. A. Warren & S. I. Donaldson (Eds.,) *Scientific advances in positive psychology*. Santa Barbara, CA: Praeger Publishers.

Shogren, K. (2012). Positive psychology and disability: A historical analysis. In M. Wehmeyer (Ed.), *Handbook of positive psychology and disability* (pp. 19–33). Oxford, England: Oxford University Press.

Shogren, K. A., Wehmeyer, M. L., Buchanan, C. L., & Lopez, S. J. (2006). The application of positive psychology and self-determination to research in intellectual disability: A content analysis of 30 years of literature. *Research and Practice for Persons with Severe Disabilities, 31*, 338–345.

Simonton, D. K. (2009). Creativity. In S. J. Lopez (Ed.), *The Oxford handbook of positive psychology* (pp. 261–269). New York: Oxford University Press.

Smedema, S. M., Catalano, D., & Ebener, D. J. (2010). The relationship of coping, self-worth, and subjective well-being: A structural equation model. *Rehabilitation Counseling Bulletin, 53*, 131–142.

Smith, E. (2006). The strengths-based counseling model. *The Counseling Psychologist, 34*, 13–79.

Snyder, C. R., Harris, C., Anderson, J. R., Holleran, S. A., Irving, L. M., Sigmon, S. T., . . . Wu, W. Y. (1991). The will and the ways: Development and validation of an individual-differences measure of hope. *Journal of Personality and Social Psychology, 60*, 570–585.

Stanton, A. L., Danoff-Burg, S., Cameron, C. L., & Ellis, A. P. (1994). Coping through emotional approach: Problems of conceptualization and confounding. *Journal of Personality and Social Psychology, 66*, 350–362.

Starfield, B., Riley, A. W., Witt, W. P., & Robertson, J. (2002). Social class gradients in health during adolescence. *Journal of Epidemiology and Community Health, 56*, 354–361.

Stevenson, B., & Wolfers, J. (2009). *Paradox of declining female happiness (Working Paper No. 14969)*. Retrieved from http//www.mber.org/papers/w14969

Stolk, Y., Kaplan, I., & Szwarc, J. (2014) Clinical use of the Kessler distress scales with culturally diverse groups. *International Journal of Methods in Psychiatric Research, 23*, 161–183.

Sue, D. W., & Constantine, M. G. (2003). Optimal human functioning in people of color in the United States. In W. B. Walsh (Ed.), *Counseling psychology and optimal human functioning* (pp. 151–169). Mahwah, NJ: Erlbaum.

Sue, D. W., & Sue, D. (2013). *Counseling the culturally diverse: Theory and practice* (6th ed.). New York: Wiley.

Tervalon, M., & Murray-Garcia, J. (1998). Cultural humility versus cultural competence: A critical distinction in defining physician training outcomes in multicultural education. *Journal of Health Care for the Poor and Undeserved, 9,* 117–125.

Toussaint, L. L., Williams, D. R., Musick, M. A., & Everson, S. A. (2001). Forgiveness and health: Age differences in a U.S. probability sample. *Journal of Adult Development, 8,* 249–257.

Tsai, J. L., Knutson, B., & Fung, H. H. (2006). Cultural variations in affect valuation. *Journal of Personality and Social Psychology, 90,* 288–307.

Uchida, Y., Norasakkunkit, V., & Kitayama, S. (2004). Cultural considerations of happiness: Theory and empirical evidence. *Journal of Happiness Studies, 5,* 223–239.

van de Vijver, F. J. R., & Leung, K. (2011). Equivalence and bias: A review of concepts, models, and data analytic procedures. In D. Matsumoto & F. J. R. van de Vijver (Eds.), *Cross-cultural research methods in psychology* (pp. 17–45). Cambridge, England: Cambridge University Press.

Walker, L. E. A. (1994). *Abused women and survivor therapy: A practical guide for the psychotherapist.* Washington, DC: American Psychological Association.

Wehmeyer, M. L. (1994). Perceptions of self-determination and psychological empowerment of adolescents with mental retardation. *Education and Training in Mental Retardation and Developmental Disabilities, 29,* 9–21.

Wehmeyer, M. L., & Shogren, K. A. (2014). Disability and positive psychology. In J. T. Pedrotti & L. M. Edwards (Eds.), *Perspectives on the intersection of multiculturalism and positive psychology* (pp. 175–188). New York: Springer Science+Business Media.

Wehmeyer, M. L. Buntinx, W. E., Lachapelle, Y., Luckasson, R., Schalock, R., Verdugo-Alonzo, M., . . . Yeager, M. (2008). The intellectual disability construct and its relationship to human functioning. *Intellectual and Developmental Disabilities, 46,* 311–318.

Witvliet, C. V., Ludwig, T., & Vander Laan, K. (2001). Granting forgiveness or harboring grudges: Implications for emotion, physiology, and health. *Psychological Science, 12,* 117–123.

Wood, A. (in press). Applications of positive psychology. In S. J. Lopez, L. M. Edwards, & S. Marques (Eds.), *Handbook of positive psychology* (3rd ed.). Oxford, England: Oxford University Press.

Woods, T. A., Kurtz-Costes, B., & Rowley, S. J. (2005). The development of stereotypes about the rich and poor: Age, race, and family income differences in beliefs. *Journal of Youth and Adolescence, 34,* 437–445.

Worell, J., & Johnson, D. (2001). Therapy with women: Feminist frameworks. In R. K. Unger (Ed.), *Handbook of the psychology of women and gender* (pp. 317–329). New York: Wiley.

Worthington, E. L., Goldstein, L., Cork, B., Griffin, B. J., Garthe, R., Lavelock, C.R., . . . , & Van Tongeren, D. R. (in press). In S. J. Lopez, L. M. Edwards, & S. Marques (Eds.), *Handbook of positive psychology* (3rd ed.). Oxford, England: Oxford University Press.

Yang, S. (2008). Real-life contextual manifestations of wisdom. *International Journal of Aging and Human Development, 67,* 273–303.

Yates, T., & Masten, A. S. (2004). Fostering the future: Resilience theory and the practice of positive psychology. In P. A. Linley & S. Joseph (Eds.), *Positive psychology in practice* (pp. 521–539). Hoboken, NJ: Wiley.

Youssef-Morgan, C. M., & Hardy, J. (2014). A positive approach to multiculturalism and diversity management in the workplace. In J. T. Pedrotti & L. M. Edwards (Eds.), *Perspectives on the intersection of multiculturalism and positive psychology* (pp. 219–233). New York: Springer Science + Business Media.

Zhang, L. F., & Postiglione, G. A. (2001). Thinking styles, self-esteem, and socioeconomic status. *Personality and Individual Differences, 31*, 1333–1346.

About the Editors and Contributors

Editors

Meg A. Warren, MA, MBA, PhD candidate is Past President of the Work and Organizations Division of the International Positive Psychology Association (IPPA); Editor-in-Chief of the Division publication, *Positive Work and Organizations: Research and Practice*; Associate Director and Co-Founder of the Western Positive Psychology Association (WPPA); Chair of the 1st and 2nd WPPA Conferences and is on the editorial board of the *Journal of Leadership and Organizational Studies*. As former Program Director and Assistant Professor of Practice at Claremont Graduate University, she developed the first graduate program in Positive Human Resource Development. Her research focuses on positive work relationships and diversity in organizations. She has presented at numerous national and international conferences, and recent publications on positive psychology include *Expanding Opportunities for Gender, Race, and Ethnicity Research in Positive Psychology* (2015), *Positive Psychology's Contributions for Engaging Differences at Work* (2016), *Positive Psychology Research in the Middle East and North Africa* (2015), and *Positive Institutional Approaches to Professionalizing the Field of Psychology in the Middle East* (2016). To learn more, please visit www.megwarren.com.

Stewart I. Donaldson, PhD, is Professor of Psychology and Community & Global Health; Dean of the School of Social Science, Policy & Evaluation and the School of Community & Global Health; and Director of the Claremont Evaluation Center at Claremont Graduate University. He is on the board of the International Positive Psychology Association (IPPA), Director and Co-Founder of the Western Positive Psychology Association, was Congress Chair of IPPA's Third World Congress on Positive Psychology

(2013), and is on the editorial board of the *International Journal of Applied Positive Psychology*. His recent publications on positive psychology include *Happiness, Excellence, and Optimal Human Functioning Revisited* (2015), *Applied Positive Psychology: Improving Everyday Life, Health, Schools, Work, and Society* (2011), and *Positive Organizational Psychology, Behavior, and Scholarship* (2010).

Contributors

Michael Barton is an undergraduate student majoring in human well-being at the University of Michigan. He is highly passionate about promoting the health and well-being of all people. His areas of interest include positive psychology and wellness. He is currently conducting research in the fields of positive psychology and cognitive neuroscience.

Joshua Bell recently received his MS from Eastern Washington University. He pursued several lines of research during his education, the most fruitful being that which investigates the factors responsible for inhibiting the experience of gratitude, and his thesis examined the roles of narcissism and cynicism in that process. He is currently earning his PhD in pursuit of a career as a university professor.

Jill R. Bowers holds a PhD in human development and family studies and is an Adjunct Assistant Professor in Educational Psychology at the University of Illinois at Urbana-Champaign. Her research focuses on program development and evaluation, specifically positive youth development programs designed to empower adolescents and emerging adults. Most recently, she has been working on developing programs that facilitate healthy relationships and careers among college students while reducing risky decision-making, such as those involving alcohol and drugs.

Cara L. Blevins is a PhD student of the Clinical Health Psychology Program at the University of North Carolina at Charlotte. Her research interests include experiences of posttraumatic growth in military populations, biological antecedents and outcomes of meaning-making and posttraumatic growth, and the application of contemplative science to suffering and the development of compassion.

Alexander F. Danvers is a doctoral student in Social Psychology at Arizona State University. His research emphasizes the dynamics of emotional communication, including the effects of emotion on perception of social narratives, nonverbal behavior, affiliative outcomes, and personality judgments.

Scott I. Donaldson is a doctoral student in Evaluation and Applied Research Methods with a co-concentration in Positive Organizational Psychology at Claremont Graduate University. He received his BA in psychology from the University of California, Los Angeles and his MS in Organizational Psychology from the University of Southern California. His research interests include positive approaches to evaluation, theory-driven evaluation approaches to positive psychological interventions, and the professionalization of evaluation.

Lisa M. Edwards, PhD, is an Associate Professor in the Department of Counselor Education and Counseling Psychology at Marquette University in Milwaukee, Wisconsin. She is co-director of the Marquette University Latina/o Well-Being Research Initiative. Her research and professional interests include Latina/o psychology, maternal mental health, and the intersection of multiculturalism and positive psychology.

Reed W. Larson is a Professor of Human Development and Family Studies, Psychology, and Educational Psychology at the University of Illinois, Urbana-Champaign. His research is aimed at understanding the developmental experiences youth have in afterschool programs and how staff facilitate these experiences. Larson has served as the President of the Society for Research on Adolescence and as Editor-in-Chief of *New Directions for Child and Adolescent Development*.

Fred Luthans received his BA, MBA, and PhD from the University of Iowa and has spent his long academic career at the University of Nebraska, where he is University and George Holmes Distinguished Professor of Management, Emeritus. A former President of the National Academy of Management, Luthans has over 200 articles and numerous books, including *Psychological Capital* (Oxford, 2015). For further information see his entry in Wikipedia, interviews on YouTube, publication profile in Google Scholar, and his Nebraska Web page with downloadable articles.

Sonja Lyubomirsky (AB Harvard, PhD Stanford) is Professor of Psychology at the University of California, Riverside and author of *The How of Happiness* and *The Myths of Happiness*. Lyubomirsky's research focuses on the benefits of happiness, why some people are happier than others, and how happiness can be durably increased. Her works have received many honors, including the Templeton Positive Psychology Prize and a Character Lab grant.

Makenzie J. O'Neil is a doctoral student in Social Psychology at Arizona State University. Her research emphasizes the roles positive emotions and prosocial actions can play in promoting positive intergroup perception and social interaction.

Carolyn Orson is a graduate student at the University of Illinois at Urbana-Champaign in the Department of Human Development and Family Studies. Her research focuses on how adolescents learn to sustain motivation through difficult challenges. Specifically, she is studying how youth learn to translate the challenges they face in out-of-school programs into learning experiences and how adult program leaders facilitate this process

Nansook Park is a Professor of Psychology, Director of the Michigan Positive Psychology Center at the University of Michigan, and a Distinguished Visiting Professor at the University of Johannesburg in South Africa. Her research focuses around the psychology of human strengths and virtues. Her work has had impacts on research and practices in various settings, including education, health care, business, and military worldwide. She is a recipient of the Christopher Peterson Gold Medal Award, the International Positive Psychology Association's highest honor.

Jennifer Teramoto Pedrotti is currently a Professor in the Department of Psychology and Child Development at Cal Poly, San Luis Obispo, where she teaches Multicultural Psychology, Positive Psychology, and Intergroup Dialogues. She earned master's and doctorate degrees in Counseling Psychology from the University of Kansas. Teramoto Pedrotti's research focuses on the intersection of multiculturalism and positive psychological constructs such as hope and well-being, multiracial identity development, and the effects of teaching about multicultural issues.

Jace Pillay is a South African Research Chair in Education and Care in Childhood at the University of Johannesburg, South Africa. His research interests are in the field of educational, community, and positive psychology with particular emphasis on the risk and resilience factors facing orphans and vulnerable children. He has presented and published numerous papers based on his research internationally.

Olivia M. Riffle is a doctoral student in Clinical Health Psychology at the University of North Carolina at Charlotte. She earned her BS in

Neuroscience from Washington & Lee University in 2012. Her research focuses on the role of posttraumatic growth in helping emerging adults identify and pursue meaningful careers. Her clinical interests include mindfulness- and acceptance-based therapies and narrative-constructivist approaches.

Lilian J. Shin, MA, is a doctoral student in the Social/Personality Psychology program at the University of California, Riverside. She completed her BA in psychology at Northwestern University, her MAT in social studies education at Georgia State University, and her MA in psychology at the University of California, Riverside. Lilian's research focuses on how to durably enhance well-being in interdependent cultures and on applications of positive activities to mental health conditions.

Michelle N. Shiota is an Associate Professor of Psychology at Arizona State University. Her research investigates processes in positive emotions, emotion regulation, and emotion in close relationships. She is an Associate Editor of *Emotion*, co-editor of the *Handbook of Positive Emotions* (2014; Guilford), and co-author of the textbook *Emotion* (2012; Wadsworth/Cengage). She is an elected fellow of the Association for Psychological Science and an elected member of the Society for Experimental Social Psychology.

Richard G. Tedeschi, PhD, is Professor of Psychology at the University of North Carolina at Charlotte and core faculty for the Health Psychology PhD program. He has published several books on posttraumatic growth, an area of research that he developed that examines personal transformations in the aftermath of traumatic life events. Tedeschi serves as a consultant to the American Psychological Association on trauma and resilience, and is Past President of the North Carolina Psychological Association.

Lea Waters, PhD, holds the Gerry Higgins Chair in Positive Psychology at the University of Melbourne and has affiliate positions with Cambridge University and University of Michigan. She is the first Australian to be appointed as a Professor in Positive Psychology and was the founding Director of the Centre for Positive Psychology, University of Melbourne (2009–2016). Waters is the president elect of the International Positive Psychology Association.

Philip C. Watkins received his PhD at Louisiana State University and now is Professor of Psychology at Eastern Washington University. Gratitude has been his research focus since 2000. Watkins is the author of two books

(*Gratitude and the Good Life* [Springer, 2014] and *Positive Psychology 101* [Springer, 2016]), and has authored a number of empirical papers on gratitude. His research now investigates questions related to how gratitude enhances well-being and the factors that enhance or inhibit gratitude.

Claire I. Yee is a doctoral student in Social Psychology at Arizona State University. Her research addresses the roles positive emotions, adult attachment styles, and associated biological mechanisms can play in close relationship formation and maintenance.

Index